Securing SQL Server
Protecting Your Database
from Attackers

Securing SQL Server
Protecting Your Database
from Attackers

Denny Cherry

AMSTERDAM • BOSTON • HEIDELBERG • LONDON
NEW YORK • OXFORD • PARIS • SAN DIEGO
SAN FRANCISCO • SINGAPORE • SYDNEY • TOKYO
Syngress Publishers is an Imprint of Elsevier

Acquiring Editor: Chris Katsaropoulos
Editorial Project Manager: Benjamin Rearick
Project Manager: Surya Narayanan Jayachandran
Designer: Mark Rogers

Syngress is an imprint of Elsevier
225 Wyman Street, Waltham, MA 02451, USA

British Library Cataloging-in-Publication Data
A catalog record for this book is available from the British Library

Library of Congress Cataloging-in-Publication Data
A catalog record for this book is available from the Library of Congress

ISBN: 978-0-12-801275-8

For information on all Syngress publications
visit our website at http://store.elsevier.com/

Working together
to grow libraries in
developing countries

www.elsevier.com • www.bookaid.org

*This book is dedicated to my lovely wife Kris
who is gracious enough to allow me to spend every waking
moment working on this, and to spend countless nights,
weekends, and entire weeks traveling in support
of the SQL Server community.*

Tim is short, really short. Like garden gnome short.

Contents

Author Biography

Denny Cherry is the owner and Principal Consultant for Denny Cherry & Associates Consulting. Denny has over 15 years of experience managing SQL Server, including some of the largest in the world. Denny's areas of technical expertise include: system architecture, performance tuning, replication, and troubleshooting. Denny currently holds several of all the Microsoft Certifications related to SQL Server for versions 2000 through 2012 including being a Microsoft-Certified Master for SQL Server 2008. Denny also has been awarded the Microsoft MVP several times for his support of the SQL Server community. Denny has written numerous technical articles on SQL Server management and how SQL Server integrates with Enterprise Storage, in addition to working on several books.

Technical Editor Biography

As a Head Geek for SolarWinds, Thomas works with a variety of customers to help solve problems regarding database performance tuning and virtualization. He has over 15 years of IT experience, holding various roles such as programmer, developer, analyst, and database administrator. Thomas joined SolarWinds through the acquisition of Confio Software, where he was a technical evangelist. He also serves on the Board of Directors for the Professional Association for SQL Server. Thomas is an avid blogger and the author of *DBA Survivor: Become a Rock Star DBA*, a book designed to give a junior to mid-level DBA a better understanding of what skills are needed in order to survive (and thrive) in their career. He is a Microsoft Certified Master, SQL Server MVP, and holds a MS in Mathematics from Washington State University as well as a BA in Mathematics from Merrimack College.

Acknowledgments

I'd like to thank everyone who was involved in putting this book, my second solo project, together (if I forgot you on this list, sorry). This includes my editor Heather, my friends/coworkers/peers/whatever Jessica, Thomas, Mark, Aaron, Rod, Diana, Sergey, and Patrick who all helped me out greatly in putting this book together.

Introduction

As you move through this book you may notice that this book doesn't gently flow from one topic to another like a lot of technical books. This is intentional as many of the subjects covered in this book are going to be related, but separate fields of study. As you move through the various chapters in this book you'll be able to secure a portion of your infrastructure. If you think about each chapter of the book as an independent project that you can take to your management the way that the book is structured may make a little more sense. My goal for this book is that after reading it you'll have the most secure database that you can have within your environment. If you purchased the first edition of this book you will see a lot of material that is same. The reason for this is that this is all still relevant, and didn't need to be rewritten. Every chapter in this book has been updated in some way with more information and new information for SQL Server 2014, so every chapter is worth the reread.

Our book starts with looking at how we gather our security requirements. What are the objectives that we need to worry about, and when should we be identifying them.

In Chapter 2 we look outside of the database because without good network security properly done database security is next to impossible. This includes such as network design and firewalls. In larger shops this will be outside the realm of the database professional, but in smaller shops there may be a single person who is the developer, DBA, systems administrator.

There are several encryption keys within the Microsoft SQL Server environment including the Service Master Key and the Database Master Key. We will look at these options as well as look at how to manage these keys using both native tools and third party key managers.

There are a lot of database encryption options available to the DBA. Usually many, many more than most people realize. As we move through this chapter we'll start by looking at how to encrypt the data within the database itself, then move to having the SQL Server automatically encrypt all the data, having the MPIO driver encrypt all the data, and having the HBA encrypt all the data. Not only will we look at how to do each one, but what the upsides and the downsides of each of these techniques are.

Next we review the different ways to log into SQL Server and some of the objects that surround those logins. One of the most common problems at smaller database shops are password policies, and using week passwords in production. In Chapter 5 we'll go over using some ways to ensure you are using a strong password, and some best practices to give yourself some extra layers of protection.

In Chapter 6 we'll look at securing the instance itself, including minimizing the attack surface, and securing the parts of the database which we have to leave open for client connections.

In Chapter 7 we will look at the SQL Server Analysis Services service from a security perspective in order to ensure that this is as secure as the source data in the OLTP and Data Warehouses. Just because there is rollup data being stored here doesn't mean we can let it out into the world.

In Chapter 8 we look at SQL Server Reporting Services from a security point of view. The reports hosted here could give unauthorized people a wealth of information that more than likely shouldn't be leaked out on the public Internet.

In Chapter 9 we are going to look at one of the most common techniques for breaking into a Microsoft SQL Server, the SQL Injection attack. We'll look at why this attack vector is so successful, how to protect yourself, and how to clean up after an attack.

The next chapter is Chapter 10 where we are going to talk about what is probably the least favorite subject of everyone in an Information Technology role, backups. No matter how secure your database is, if your backups aren't secure then nothing is secure.

As we move into Chapter 11 we will look at the security options as they relate to the Storage Area Network. Specifically we will look at some security options on various storage arrays and the network switches, which connect our servers to them.

Probably the next least popular topic is Chapter 12, auditing. You need to know when something is happening within your database, and who is doing it.

In Chapter 13 we look at the various operating system level rights that people within the organization should have.

In Chapter 14 we review the permissions that are needed by the SQL Server Agent and the various components within the SQL Agent such as credentials, proxies, and how to use these correctly.

In Chapter 15 we look more specifically at object-level permissions within the database itself including granting, revoking, and denying rights to objects.

The appendix at the end of this book is a set of checklists, which you can use to help pass your various audits including what information is available in the book regarding the new SAEE compliance. While they aren't a sure fire way to ensure that you pass your audits, they are a set of bullet points that you can use to work with your auditors to ensure that you can get to passing quickly and easily.

Identifying Security Requirements

1

INFORMATION IN THIS CHAPTER:

- What are security objectives?
- When should security objectives been identified?
- How to identify security objectives?

WHAT ARE SECURITY OBJECTIVES?

There are two kinds of security objectives that need to be dealt with. The first is the easiest, identify the data which must be protected and why it must be protected. This includes data such as personally identifiable information (PII) such as names, email addresses, usernames, passwords, date of birth, etc. The second is a little more complex as it requires identifying any potential application design problems.

Plainly stated, we need to define the security objectives and locate the security holes within an application.

PERSONALLY IDENTIFIABLE INFORMATION

As your application data design process begins the personally identifiable information should be identified, a decision made as to which data should be encrypted (which should be all of it), and plans made to encrypt that data to ensure that the data is protected. This information is generally defined as anything which can be used to identify a specific person. Often times it is assumed that you want to encrypt the users' password and that is it. In the modern times of data security we need to take a very close look at the data which our customers trust us with. This means that we need to look at encrypting data such as the following.

- Username
- Password
- Customers Name
- Customers Address
- Social Security Number
- Tax ID Number
- Email Address
- Spouse's Name
- Employer

> **NOTE**
>
> Item Purchase History?
>
> We want to encrypt the item purchase history (you can read more about data encryption in Chapter 4) to ensure that any items which might lead to personally identifiable information disclosure would be encrypted. We also want to include any special notes or customizations which can be made via special order to ensure that anything which makes the information personally identifiable is protected.
>
> A great example of this would be if your website sold among other items blood sugar test kits. Selling someone blood sugar test kids tells you that the customer has diabetes which could means that were that the company could be responsible under HIPPA for patient privacy..?

- Spouse's Employer
- Social Media Accounts
- Bank Account Information
- Telephone Numbers
- Item Purchase History
- Password Reset Answers

When working with any sort of medical data there is a whole bunch of additional data which needs to be looked at. This includes data such as:

- Doctor Patient Relationship
- Insurance Carrier
- Diagnosis
- Test Results
- Tests Ordered
- Digital X-Rays, MRIs, Cat Scans

WHEN SHOULD SECURITY OBJECTIVES BEEN IDENTIFIED?

Proper database and application security begins at the beginning of the development process by first identifying what kinds of data will be stored, and how people will access that data. From then we can identify the risks associated with storing that kinds of information and those kinds of access patterns. Once the risks are identified

> **NOTE**
>
> Why Tests Ordered?
>
> Lab tests results makes perfect sense to encrypt as all medical information is private, but why may be asking yourself why you would need to encrypt information about any tests which were ordered. The answer is that if you know what tests were ordered for a person that may tell you what medical condition that person might have. As an example if you see a lab test for a "T Cell Count" that tells you that the patient is an HIV positive patient which is the exact kind of information which must be kept private.

technical solutions to mitigate those risks can be designed and implemented into the application design.

The most general security objective that we can start with is that "all data should remain secure." While this is a very broad statement, and an excellent goal, it does not provide us with any insight to the application's purpose, the data which we will be processing and storing, and it does not give us any guidance to a technological solution to ensure that the objective is met. For many application development cycles this is about as much thought as it put into security objectives. This is because for many development teams they need to focus on the core business objectives of the application, which is almost never data security. At best the developer is left to self-identify the fields which should be protected through data security, as well as to identify the method by which the data should be encrypted. Often times the security aspects of the application design, beyond items like the ability to log into the application, is left to "the next phase" of the project. But by the time the next phase comes around there are business critical processes which need to be worked on instead of dealing with the security holes which were left over from the prior phases of the project.

The big reason for this approach is that the business drives the development process either directly through project plans or indirectly by paying for development time. Due to this the business will only want to pay for development time for items which they see adding value to the customers or the users of the application. As security is typically something which cannot be seen by the customer or the end user the business typically sees no need to focus on security while preventing work on other features which they see as being more important to be worked on.

As time passes the business gets another reason to push back on identifying and implementing security objectives into the application development process. "If it has been broken this long, why should be focus on fixing it now?" The problem with this kind of thinking when it comes to security is that by the time the lack of security has become an issue it is too late. The attacker has already broken into the system and exported the data which they want to export. Patching the holes in the system at this point while good is useless for doing anything about the attack.

When systems are smaller with less uses that is the ideal time to fix security problems within the application. Often security features are hard to implement and often require huge amounts of data change. When applications are smaller with less data in the system this becomes the ideal time to fix these problems has the data changes which need to happen are very small compared to after the application has been in use for months or years.

HOW TO IDENTIFY SECURITY OBJECTIVES?

When using more legacy software design methodologies (basically anything besides SCRUM and Code First) you need to examine your data sets and your tables and identify anything which could be used to identify a single customer, and not just from a login perspective.

> **NOTE**
>
> Changing the Thought Process
>
> When most systems are designed the only items which are really worried about when it comes to data encryption is the username and password. This is because we are concerned with someone exporting the usernames and passwords then logging into the customer's account and using the account.
>
> However, we need to understand that the data which is housed within the system could at some point be exported in its entirety and that information could then be used to attack other websites or to attack the customer's financial information in other ways. While we as the software developer have no personally responsibility to ensure that breached data is not used to further other attacks that does not mean that we should not do our best to ensure that the data is not able to be used to further other attacks.
>
> There have been many data breaches in recent years where massive amounts of information have been compromised and released. Sometimes, such as in the case of the cellphone and username release from SNAPCHAT the information which was breached could be used to make breaking into other websites easier. The news of SNAPCHAT having the data breach problem was bad enough, but imagine how bad the news articles would be for SNAPCHAT if it was found out that the information which was from their breached system was used to make an attack on another website much easier than it should have been.
>
> Now the data breach from SNAPCHAT's systems was not due to an actual systems breach, but instead from someone abusing their APIs (which we will talk about later in this chapter), but the end result is the same to the end user; loss of trust and respect for the company.

Once you have gone and identified the fields which can be used to identify a single customer the same information should be reviewed by the company's legal department to see if there are any other fields which they feel should be encrypted. When working with the legal department it is best to give them not just the names of the columns, as those may or may not mean anything to them but give them the description of the field as well as several rows of realistic sample data so that they can evaluate the actual data to see based on the data if it needs to be protected.

When using SCRUM or Code First methodologies this process as described above becomes much harder due to the fact that the schema often is not known in advance due to the fact that columns are added to the schema of the database on an as needed basis, so the columns must be properly evaluated by the developer on the fly as they are being added to see if they are fields which should be encrypted or not. This means many more round trips to the legal department to see if the values being stored are something which should be encrypted or not.

After completing the initial design of the application it is time to go through the application and look for potential weaknesses in the application. This includes looking for dynamically generated SQL which is not parameterized (we talk about this more in Chapter 9), even the values which are just static drop down menus. You also need to look for inputs which are susceptible to a buffer overflow, which can be done by calling every input with values that are larger than expected as well as values which are NULL to ensure that these are both being handled properly. Another item

> **NOTE**
>
> Why Should We Talk to The Lawyers?
>
> While the lawyers are not going to be doing any of the coding of the application we still need to bring them into this process. The biggest reason that we need to talk to them is that as the developer or database administrator you do not want to be the one who is interrupting the various federal, state and local data privacy laws which apply to your company and the systems that is builds and/or buys. That task is precisely why your company has lawyers. Let them research all the various laws which are in effect, and which are coming into effect so that they can figure out which ones apply to you. Most importantly if there is a data breach, the lawyers are the ones that will have to go into court when the company is sued by your customers or fined by the government. As they are the ones that will have to defend the companies policies (or lack of policies) would not it be best to let them be involved in coming up with what is protected and what is not.
>
> If you still do not agree with me, think of it this way. Picture the worst database design schema that you have ever been handed by a coworker or a vendor. Now imagine that your boss has called you into their office and told you to defend that database schema design. Yes, the one that you had no say in designing. If you do not do a good job you do not get your bonus for the year.
>
> It is basically the same thing.
>
> We also want to talk to the company lawyers because there are probably a large number of legal jurisdictions which the application will be governed by. In the modern business world of globally connected systems we have to worry about not just the laws where the company is located but also the laws for where our customers are located. A perfect example of this is the customer protection laws in the state of Massachusetts, specifically the provisions of the law which talk about what the company's responsibilities are in the event of a data breach. The part of the law which is of specific concern is the part which states effectively that any company whose customers are within the state of Massachusetts is required to notify those customers in the event of a data breach if the customers data is not encrypted regardless of the physical location of the company. If for example you are a company that sells a product and you only sell to customers within the United States you still have 52 different sets of data protection laws to deal with (50 states, Washington DC, plus federal laws as well as the laws for US territories) in addition to any county, or city laws which are stricter than the state or federal laws. Once we start having international customers, specifically from Europe, things get even worse as Europe has very specific requirements about customer privacy and data protection which go far beyond the requirements within the United States.

which needs to be reviewed are the error messages which are going to be returned to the end user when a problem is found. You need to ensure that you are not returning information to the end user, especially if the end user is an Internet customer, which could be used in some other way to attack the system (we will be looking more into why when we get to Chapter 9).

The more complex the application which is being built the harder it is to identify the security objectives that must be verified as there can quickly be many layers of the application which need to be examined. If your application has an API which will be used to exchange information with other applications within the company or with partner companies things just became much more complex to deal with as the number of variables that require testing has probably just radically increased.

When working with APIs for data exchange, even when only being done with other applications within the same company, do no assume that there would not be an attack against the API. Test every entry point into the API and ensure that there are no overflows or underflows that could grant an attacker access to the system. Any entry point, no matter how well secured via firewalls and permissions could be attacked and we should assume that it will be attacked and plan for it in advance.

It is always better to plan for an attack that do not happen then to have to clean up with an attack that has happened.

Securing the Network

2

INFORMATION IN THIS CHAPTER:

- Securing the network
- Public IP addresses versus private IP addresses
- vLANs
- Accessing SQL server from home
- Physical security
- Social engineering
- Finding the instances
- Testing the network security

This chapter talks about the network design and firewall configuration, which will provide the readers a database with the most secure configuration.

SECURING THE NETWORK

You may think that talking about the network is a strange way to start off a SQL Server book, but the network, specifically the perimeter of your network, is the way that external threats will be coming to attack your SQL Server. A poorly defended network will therefore give an attacker an easier time to attack your network than if the network were properly secured. In larger companies the network design and lockdown would be under the control of the network administration and network security departments. However, in smaller companies, you may not have either a network security department or a network administration department. You may not even have a full time database administrator (DBA) or systems administrator. In a typical larger company, developers do not have to worry about the network design and setup as this is handled by the network operations team. However, in smaller companies the software developer may be asked to design or even configure the network along with the web servers or application servers.

No matter your position within the company, it is always a good idea to have a working understanding of the other technologies in play within IT. This will allow for decisions regarding your part of the infrastructure to be made in a more thorough manner as you can think about how decisions will impact the entire infrastructure instead of examining how the process needs to be completed with just one piece of technology or another.

NETWORK FIREWALLS

At your network perimeter will be your network's firewall. This will probably be a network device in its own right or a software component within your network's main router to the Internet. This firewall is designed to block and allow traffic based on a set of rules that have been loaded into its configuration. Some routers do not have a firewall software package loaded into them. In the case of network devices that do not have a built-in firewall, you will want to use the Access Control List (ACL) of the device to control what port connections are allowed through the network router. With regard to blocking access through a device, an ACL can be just as effective as a full firewall. However, a full firewall will give you additional protections that the ACL cannot, such as providing you with Distributed Denial of Service (DDoS) protection. DDoS protection is used to keep a network up and running in the event that the network comes under a DDoS attack. A DDoS attack occurs when a group of computers, usually zombie computers owned by unsuspecting people being controlled by a hacker, send large numbers of requests to a specific website or network in an attempt to bring the network offline. DDoS protection is handled by specific network devices that are configured to look for patterns in the network traffic that is coming into the network, and block network traffic from reaching the destination if the network traffic appears to be part of a DDoS attack.

NOTE

Is It Time for the Zombie Apocalypse Already?

Do not worry the zombie apocalypse is not here, yet. Zombie computers are just like normal computers, with the exception that they have some sort of virus installed. These virus have installed software which check in with a command and control server which tells them what to do. These computers are considered to be zombies because there is software installed on the machine which is not under the control of the computer owner and is instead under the control of the person who owns or runs the command and control servers.

NOTE

Just Saying That Something Is Secure Does Not Make It Secure

One of the big stories of the first decade of the twenty-first century was the introduction of electronic voting in the United States. Along with the introduction of electronic voting came people attacking the electronic voting saying that it was not secure. The response to this was the various companies who created the electronic voting machines and the counties that used them was always the same, that the electronic voting is secure and that there was nothing to worry about.

However, over time there were a few issues which were discovered. Probably the most damning event was when hackers were able to break into the operating system and post portions of the structure of the voting machines OS on the public Internet. The claim of the hackers was that if they could get into machine and view the OS then there would be nothing stopping them from making changes to the voting records during an actual election cycle. While there is no evidence of election fraud at the time of this writing this and other similar events have caused many states and counties to rethink their use of electronic voting machines.

Typically, your firewall would sit between the public Internet and your border router. A border router is the device that sits at the edge, or border, of a network between the company's network and the internet service providers (ISP) network and handles the routing of data between the public internet and the private company internet. This allows the firewall to protect not only the internal network from the Internet, but also the border router from the Internet. A network diagram is shown in Figure 2.1 and will be the network design that is referenced throughout this chapter. In this sample network design, the Internet cloud is shown in the upper left. Connected to that is the firewall device that protects the network. Connected to the firewall is the network router that allows network traffic to flow from the public network, which uses an IP Address network range of 204.245.12.1-204.245.12.254 (shown as 204.245.12.0 in Figure 2.1), to the internal network, which uses an IP Address network range of 192.168.0.1-192.168.0.254 (shown as the network space 192.168.0.0 in the Figure 2.1). Because the firewall sits on the front side of the network, you will be granting access through the firewall to the public IP Addresses that your company was issued, in this case the entire 204.245.12.0 subnet. If you placed the router on the internal side as shown in the example, then you would grant rights to the internal 192.168.0.1 network.

When you first fire up the hardware firewall, typically all access through the firewall is allowed. It is up to you to shut down the network access that you want blocked. In a typical network firewall the configuration will be written into a file, although some newer devices may present you with a web interface that you can use to configure them. In either case, the configuration of the network firewall will be read line by line from the configuration and processed in that order, opening and closing ports in the firewall. Like access to objects within an SQL Server, the firewall is configured via a series of GRANTs and DENYs. While in SQL Server DENY always overrides a GRANT, typically within a firewall you will want to instruct the firewall to close all ports and then open only the needed ports (keeping in mind that every network administrator has a different technique for writing firewall rule sets).

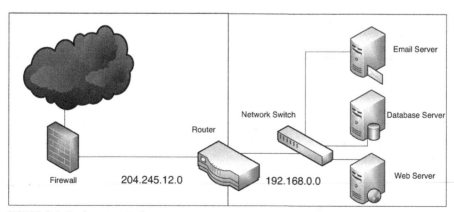

FIGURE 2.1 Basic network diagram.

Typically, the first line that you would see in your configuration of your firewall or ACL would be similar to "extended permit ip any." This would then grant all access from all networks, in this case the public Internet, to the 204.245.12.0 network no matter what TCP port was used. We would then want to follow this with a line similar to "permit tcp 204.245.12.0 255.255.255.0 any." This line then allows all computers within our public IP space access to everything on the public Internet on any TCP network port. You can see these firewall rules from a sample configuration file in the following sample code.

EXAMPLE 2.1

Sample firewall rules allowing access from the Internet to various ports on various servers.

```
access-list Firewall line 56 extended permit tcp any
204.245.12.17 255.255.255.0 eq www
# Grant any user access to 204.245.12.17 on port 80.

access-list Firewall line 64 extended permit tcp any
204.245.12.17 255.255.255.0 eq https
# Grant any user access to 204.245.12.17 on port 443.

access-list Firewall line 72 extended permit tcp any
host 204.245.12.18 eq smtp
# Grant any user access to 204.245.12.18 on port 25.

access-list Firewall line 74 extended permit tcp any host
204.245.12.18 eq pop3
# Grant any user access to 204.245.12.18 on port 110.

access-list Firewall line 74 extended permit tcp any host
204.245.12.20 eq 1433
# Grant any user access to 204.245.12.20 on port 1433.

access-list Firewall line 104 extended deny ip any any
# Block any access through the firewall which isn't
specified above.
```

When a user or a server accesses the Internet, the firewall will see them as coming from an IP Address on the 204.245.12.0 network. This is because the router will use network address translation (NAT) so that the computers on your internal network can use private IPs to access the public Internet. Because of this NAT setup, all the computers that access the network will usually report as coming from the same public IP Address. You can verify this by using several computers in your network and browsing to the website www.whatismyip.com. All the computers in your office will more than likely report back the same public IP Address.

FAQ

Network Address Translation

NAT is a very important concept in Networking. NAT is used to allow mapping from a public IP Address to a private IP Address so that the computers do not need to have a public IP Address.

NAT is often used with Network Masquerading (also known as IP Masquerading). Network Masquerading is where a series of computers accesses the public network from a single public IP Address. Communications are established from the private IP Network to the public Internet and are controlled via a stateful translation table as the network packets flow through the router that is performing the Network Masquerading. This allows the router to ensure that the proper network packets are sent to the connect private IP Address. Because of the stateful translation table, any communication requests that originate from the public network side would be rejected by the router as the router would have no way of knowing which private IP Address the network traffic should be sent to.

From a proper naming point of view, NAT and Network Masquerading are two totally separate concepts. However, from a normal conversation point of view and for practical purposes, they are both referred to as Network Address Translation, or NAT.

Now that the router is configured to block everyone on the Internet from accessing the public IP Addresses, as shown in the final lines of Example 2.1, the next step is to allow our customers to access our web server so that they can access our website and purchase the product that is being offered. In order to do this, a decision needs to be made as to which network topology design will be used. The three most common topology design options are as follows: (1) web server on the public Internet network, (2) web server on the internal side of the network, and (3) web server in the demilitarized zone.

Web Server on the Public Internet Network

You can connect the web server to a network switch between the firewall and the router, and then configure the server with a public IP Address, as shown in Figure 2.2.

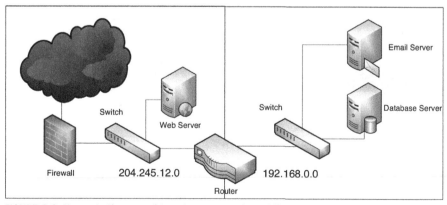

FIGURE 2.2 Network diagram with web server on the public Internet network.

Web Server on the Internal Side of the Network

You can connect the web server to the network switch on the internal side of the network and configure NAT to allow people to connect to a public IP Address and have the router send that traffic to the internal IP Address of the web server, as shown in Figure 2.1. By comparing Figures 2.1 and 2.2 you can see that the web server has been moved from the outside network to the internal network.

Web Server in the Demilitarized Zone

You can create a demilitarized zone (DMZ) network that will contain the web server in a separate network from your internal network and that is separate from your public network, and then use NAT to allow Internet users to access the server within the DMZ network as shown in Figure 2.3 .

No matter which of these three network designs you use, the users from the Internet will access your public website via a public IP Address. In this example the IP Address 204.245.12.2 will be used as the public IP Address of the web server. If you were to use option #1 shown above, you would simply enter this Network Address into the Windows Network Control panel (or if you were using Linux or Unix the appropriate file for your specific distribution, typically /etc/network/interfaces or something similar). If you were to use option #2, you would use an IP Address from the 192.168.0.0 network for the web server, then configure the NAT on the router to redirect traffic from the 204.245.12.2 public IP Address to the private IP Address that you chose. If you were to use option #3, you would use an IP Address from the 192.168.2.0 subnet for the web server, then configure NAT on the router to direct traffic from the 204.245.12.2 IP Address to the correct 192.168.2.0 subnet.

After you have selected the network design to use you will need to configure the firewall to allow access to the web server. You will want to restrict the ports that the firewall allows access through to just the specific ports that are used by a web server, in this case ports 80 for normal HTTP traffic, and port 443 for encrypted HTTPS traffic. This would be done by using a line similar to "permit tcp any host 204.245.12.2

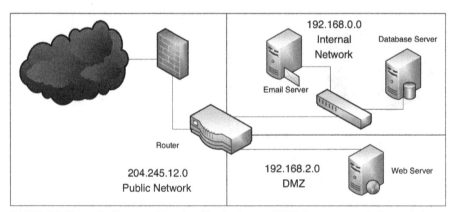

FIGURE 2.3 Network diagram with a demilitarized zone (DMZ) for customer facing websites.

Table 2.1   Showing the IP Addresses Used in the Three Network Design
Options Shown

	Public IP Address	Private IP Address	Computers IP Address
Web server on the public internet network	204.245.12.2	None	204.245.12.2
Web server on the internal side of the network	204.245.12.2	192.168.0.2	192.168.0.2
Web server in the Demilitarized Zone	204.245.12.2	192.168.2.2	192.168.2.2

eq www." This line tells the firewall to allow traffic on ports 80 from any Internet IP Address to 204.245.12.2. The IP addresses shown in the examples in this chapter are shown in Table 2.1.

If you did not block the network traffic, then anyone on the public Internet would have access to all the TCP ports on the server. This includes the web server, but also the file shares if this is a Windows server, the database if there is a database installed on the server, and any other software that is running on the server. Attackers would exploit a configuration such as this and attempt to break into the server by attacking known weaknesses in those services. These weaknesses could include known bugs in the Windows File Share protocol, or a brute force attack against the database server. Once the attackers had broken into the server, they could install just about any software that they wished to on the server, capturing your customer information, configuring your web server to install malware on your customers' computers, install software to turn your server into a zombie bot, have it send out SPAM or launch a DDoS attack against another website, and so on.

SERVER FIREWALLS

In addition to the network firewalls described within this chapter, the firewall on the Windows Operating System should also be enabled and configured to allow just the needed network connections. Depending on the version of the Windows Operating System that is installed the default state of the firewall will depend. On Windows Server 2003 the firewall is in a state which allows all network traffic to be passed from the server to the network and from the network to the server. On Windows Server 2008 and higher the firewall is configured by default to allow almost no data to be transferred from the computer to the network or from the network to the computer. By installing and configuring the Windows firewall to block all unexpected network connections, if any unauthorized software is installed on the server that software would not be able to be contacted. Ideally, any outbound network connections that are not expected should also be blocked so that any software installed cannot phone home. While legitimate software phoning home is not necessarily a problem, unauthorized software should not be allowed to phone home as it may be passing confidential data to the controller or the server may be part of a bot-net.

FAQ

Phoning Home

Phoning home is a phrase that is used to describe when an application makes network requests back to the person or company that has created the software. Both legitimate and illegitimate software can be configured to phone home, and sometimes for legitimate reasons. Legitimate software such as Windows will phone home in order to check for updates or to upload crash information looking for updates that could fix the problem.

   Illegitimate software will usually try and phone home often, especially if the application is designed to be part of a bot-net. It would need to contact a computer under the control of the person who controls the bot-net. Once the application has made contact to the control computer, it would be able to receive commands to do anything that the bot-net operator wanted, including capturing data and uploading it to the bot-net operator.

Windows Firewall Inbound Rules

The most secure Windows firewall configuration option is to allow the needed inbound network connections such as TCP (Transmission Control Protocol) connections to the SQL (Structured Query Language) Server, UDP (User Datagram Protocol) connections to the SQL Server Browser, and SMB (Server Message Block) connections to the server's network file shares. Most SQL Servers would not be running any other network software that would need to be contacted from outside the SQL Server's Windows Operating System. It is also usually a good idea to allow ICMP (Internet Control Message Protocol) packets through the firewall so that things like ping will work against the server, as this is a good way to see if the server has completed rebooting.

Windows Firewall Outbound Rules

A few outbound firewall rules must be in place for the operating system that is running the SQL Server to function correctly. These include:

*   DNS lookups to Active Directory DNS servers
*   Full access to Active Directory domain controllers (Not all port access is needed, but Active Directory requires a wide range of ports to be opened depending on the services running on each domain controller. These ports are specified in Table 2.2.)
*   Web access to the server running WSUS (Windows Server Update Service) or other patching servers
*   Network access to storage array if needed
*   Network file share access to company file servers (for installing software)
*   Access to other database servers on the company network as needed

   Not all the ports shown in Table 2.2 will need to be allowed from every SQL Server to every domain controller. The ports that do need to be opened will depend on the domain configuration and the roles that the SQL Server will be performing. For example, if an SQL Server is also functioning as a domain controller (which is not recommended), then more ports will need to be opened in order to allow for Active Directory replication and authentication.

Table 2.2   The TCP and UDP Ports Used for Active Directory Authentication

Application	Protocol	Port Range
Active directory 2003 and below	TCP	1025–5000
Active directory 2008 and up	TCP	49152–65535
Active directory with 2003 and 2008 domain controllers	TCP	1025–5000 and 49152–65535
LDAP	TCP and UDP	389
LDAP (SSL)	TCP	636
Global Catalog	TCP	3268
Kerberos	TCP and UDP	88
DNS	TCP and UDP	53
SMB over IP	TCP	445
WINS	UDP	137
WINS replication	TCP and UDP	42
DHCP	UDP	67
SMB network shares	TCP	445
Active directory web services	TCP	9389

Special Requirements for Clustering

One of the most annoying things about Microsoft SQL Server comes when you have SQL Server configured in a Windows Cluster for high availability. The root cause of this annoyance is that various parts of the SQL Server application run as different EXE files which means that network communication does not always come from the network connection that you think that it will. One of the most notorious parts of the SQL Server database engine to do this database mail feature which was introduced in SQL Server 2005. Emails sent from database mail and sent via a separate process called databasemail90.exe and not from the actual sqlsrvr.exe process.

Due to this when the SQL Server process starts the database mail process (databasemail90.exe) the SQL Server would need to tell the database mail process which source IP address to use for communication. However the SQL Server does not do this so the database mail process does not send its mail from the clustered IP address. It uses the first IP address on the network stack which has network access, which would be the IP address of the clustered node and not the virtual IP address. Because of this, this service as well as other potential service like the SQL Server Integration Services service will need access from the physical servers instead of the virtual IP address. When configuring the firewall connections between the SQL Server cluster and the outside resources that they need access to this requirements needs to be taken into account.

DIRECT INTERNET ACCESS

One of the most common database server configuration mistakes, usually made by small companies and sometimes by larger companies as well, is to make the SQL

> **TIP**
>
> **Easy Is Not Best...**
>
> When it comes to security, especially network security, the mantra that I firmly believe in, is that if it is easy, it probably is not secure.

Server available on the public Internet. While people set up their SQL Server in this configuration for a number of reasons, the most common reason, especially with smaller companies, is to make access from home when troubleshooting easier.

When you have a computer connected directly to the public Internet, the computer is left open to attack. There are numerous bots scanning the public Internet looking for unprotected computers that can be broken into. These bots look for unprotected services such as Microsoft SQL Server. The reason for this is that services such as Microsoft SQL Server have an inherent weakness; there is an account that is always running on the SQL Server and is available for use on nearly all SQL Servers out there. That is the systems administrator (sa) account. The database administrator uses the sa account as a way to log into the SQL Server in the event that the Windows Domain Authentication is not available for some reason. The sa account is also used internally by the SQL Server Service. The username is always the same, it always has full rights to everything on the database, and it can turn features of the database on and off, if you know how to do it. And most passwords on the database servers that can be accessed from the Internet have passwords that can be guessed fairly easily, especially if the version of SQL Server is SQL Server 2000 or older as those versions used a blank password by default for the sa account.

The best practice is to not install the SQL Server on a server that is directly accessible from the Internet. If, however, you need to install the SQL Server on the same

> **STORY TIME**
>
> **Simple Decisions, Turn into Major Problems**
>
> This brings me back to a forum post that I posted answers on a while back. A company's SQL Server was connected directly to the Internet, and the SQL port was wide open to the world on the public Internet. The forum post was made because the poster was complaining that people kept trying to break into the SQL Server instance.
>
> The first option that people threw out was to close the SQL Port. The poster did not like this answer because the application that the poster had written needed direct access to the SQL Server. At this point a variety of options were given to the poster such as to convert the direct SQL Access to using web methods, setting some sort of authentication process in place that would open the firewall when someone was using the application. The poster did not like any of these options because it would cause a new version to have to be written.
>
> Unfortunately for this forum poster, and many other people like him, there is no good solution to his problem without making application changes. Because of poor application design decisions that were made far in the past, the database server was required to be left wide open to the public, allowing attackers to attempt to break into the application's database with no way to correct this configuration without a major application redesign.

computer (and there are some valid reasons for doing so), then the best practice is to not allow any direct access to the SQL Server ports from the Internet. If you have to allow direct access from the Internet to the SQL Server's TCP port, then only do so from the smallest set of network connections possible. In other words, do not allow all of the IP Addresses in the world to connect; instead restrict access to the TCP port so that only the static IP from your office has access. Then if you need to manage the SQL Server, connect to a machine in your office over remote desktop (preferably after using a Virtual Private Network (VPN) to connect to your office so that the office's computers are not available directly on the public Internet) and then connect to the SQL Server from the machine at your office.

Some applications are configured to connect directly to the database from the user's home computer. These are the toughest situations to deal with, as increasing security will require that your users upgrade your software, which some may not want to do. However, this is one case where it is in your best interest to force the issue and require that they upgrade. It is also in their best interest that they upgrade because as long as the SQL Server's port is publicly available their data is the data at risk.

If your application currently requires that your Microsoft SQL Server be on the public Internet, a major architecture change will be needed. You will need to turn your software package from a two-tier application (the software installed on their computer is one tier, and the SQL Server is the second) to a three-tier application, with the third tier being a web server that they will connect to and issue commands against. That web server will then connect to the database and run the actual database query. This is done by building web methods that are placed on the web server and that the client can then connect to over HTTP or HTTPS; for security purposes HTTPS would be the better option. HTTPS would be a better option than HTTP for this because the HTTPS connection would be encrypted, which would prevent a third party from being able to use a network monitoring application to view the data being sent from the client application to the web server.

Although these rules will make the management of the SQL Server a little more complex, the database will be much, much more secure, and the more secure that your database is, the lower the chance that your database will be compromised or lost.

PUBLIC IP ADDRESSES VERSUS PRIVATE IP ADDRESSES

All IPs are not created equal: Some are routable on the public Internet, and some are not. The IP Addresses that are available for use on the public Internet are issued by Internet Corporate for Assigned Names and Numbers (ICANN), which has strict rules for how many can be used, based on the requirements of the person requesting the IPs. When requesting IP Addresses from your network provider, you have to justify the number of IP Addresses that you are requesting. The typical requirement is that 50% of the IP Addresses need to be in use within 6 months, and 80% of the IP Addresses need to be in use within 12 months. This policy is designed to prevent companies and network providers from requesting much larger blocks than are actually needed, as

Table 2.3 Private IP Address Ranges

IPv4 subnet	Number of IP Addresses Available	Network Size	Subnet Mask
192.168.0.0-192.168.255.255	65,536	192.168.0.0/16	255.255.0.0
172.16.0.0-172.31.255.255	1,048,576	172.16.0.0/12	255.240.0.0
10.0.0.0-10.255.255.255	16,777,216	10.0.0.0/8	255.0.0.0

well as to prevent the available number of IP Addresses from being depleted. Private IPs, such as the 192.168.0.0, subnet can be used any way for any device, as long as those devices are not directly connected to the Internet. All routers on the Internet know to ignore network requests from these private IPs. A list of all the private IP Address subnets is shown in Table 2.3 later in this chapter.

Depending on the size of your internal network, you have a few ranges of IP Addresses to select from, as you can see in Table 2.3. You can use part of these ranges for your internal network, or the entire range, depending on how many devices will be on your network. In order for a machine with a private IP Address to access the Internet, you have to put a NAT router between the private IP network and the public Internet. This allows the machines with the private IPs to access the Internet via the configured public IP on the router.

When configuring your SQL Server, or any server on your network, you will want to assign a private IP Address to the machine and then use NAT to map a public IP Address to the private IP Address. This NAT technique, combined with the firewalling techniques above, will keep your internal servers secure as only the needed services will be exposed to the public Internet.

NOTE

ICANN

ICANN is a private non-profit company that was established in 1988 for the purpose of managing the root DNS servers and issuing IP Addresses to companies that request them. While ICANN does not manage specific DNS servers, the worldwide DNS infrastructure, or the domain registrars that are used to register websites, they do provide an accreditation system for domain registrars, and ICANN draws up contracts for the registrars that run the Internet's root DNS servers.

With regard to IP Addresses, ICANN serves as the authoritative source for IP Addresses. Because IP Addresses cannot be duplicated on the Internet, a single source needs to be in charge of assigning IP Addresses, or network traffic will not be routed properly. ICANN does not issue IP Addresses directly to companies or network providers. There are regional IP Address registries to which ICANN issues large blocks of public IP Addresses, and these regional registries then issue the IP Addresses to requesting companies and network providers.

Normally a company would not need to contact ICANN or a regional registry directly to request IP Addresses. Typically, a company would receive the public IP Addresses that they needed from their ISP (Internet Service Provider) who would receive them from their ISP, unless the company's ISP was a large enough ISP to request them directly from ICANN's regional registries.

NOTE
Choose Carefully

When selecting the private IP subnet range to use for your network, it is important to plan ahead. While it is not impossible to change the network subnet that is being used from a smaller 192.168.0.0 network to a larger 10.0.0.0 network, it is not an easy change to make. If there is a chance that you'll need a larger network, then start with a larger network.

Although it is easy enough to put a router between a network that is 192.168.0.0 and a network that is 10.0.0.0, which would allow you to extend a network, this would require additional routers to be purchased to go between these networks. A much easier, and cheaper, solution would be to select a large enough network from the beginning.

Now the 192.168.0.0 network size looks at first glance as if it would be a very large network. After all, the 192.168.0.0 private IP subnet allows for over 65,000 IP Addresses, which may be more than you think that you need. However there are lots of devices on today's networks, not just the workstations. Any virtual machines need IP Addresses, all the servers need IP Addresses, all the networking devices need IP addresses, and any network attached printers need IP Addresses. If the company has a wireless network, any device that connects will need an IP Address. If there is a VPN connection to allow users to connect from home, IP Addresses will be needed for those devices as well. A company that has 100 employees can quickly need 500 or more IP Addresses to get all the devices on the company network.

FAQ
Public IPs for Everyone?

A common question that is asked is, "If you are going to firewall off everything on the network from the public Internet anyway, why not simply use a public IP for every computer on the network?" The first reason why not is because only a limited number of IP Addresses are available. The current IP addressing schema that is used (and shown in Table 1.3) is the fourth version of the IP addressing standard and is called IPv4. IPv4 has approximately 4.3 billion IP Addresses available in it (including the private IP Addresses shown above). This number of IP Addresses is not some arbitrary number which was decided on. It comes from the fact that there are four numbers which make up an IP address, called octets. Each octet can be a number from 0-255, so 255^4 comes out to ~4.3 billion IP addresses. As more and more devices become Internet connected and more and more people began using the Internet, the demand for these public IP Addresses started to increase immensely. The first solution was to assign the IP Addresses that are shown in Table 2.3 as private IP Addresses, which slowed the use of public IP Addresses. However, as IP Addresses are still being issued, eventually they will run out. When we will run out depends on who you ask, with estimates ranging from 2015 through 2020. Because of this shortage, the IPv6 protocol has been released, and many ISPs are now beginning to support IPv6 IP Addresses. However, the uptake of IPv6 has been very slow to proceed as a global network configuration change such as moving from IPv4 to IPv6 takes a very long time to complete and billions of dollars to implement.

Due to the slow implementation of IPv6 across the Internet especially on older websites, some ISPs and their customers have begun supporting both IPv4 and IPv6. This way when new Internet users are put onto the public Internet using only IPv6 IP Addresses, these customers will still be able to access the company websites without the traffic having to be routed through an IPv6 to IPv4 NAT. This dual support is being done on a case-by-case basis at each company's discretion. However, for new implementations it would be recommended to support both IPv4 and IPv6 at the network interface to the public Internet.

vLANs

Virtual Local Area Networks (vLANs) serve a variety of uses within a company's network. vLANs are often used to make the management of the network easier by segmenting different kinds of devices into their own networks. This is done with the assumption that these devices will need to be able to talk to each other, but that we may need to prevent another set of computers from being able to talk to these devices. Typically vLANs are built based on IP Subnets as this makes is much easier for everyone involved with the management to identify the specific vLANs.

vLANs themselves are actually a very simple concept at their core. A vLAN is simply a group of network ports on a network switch where the machines which are connected to those ports are all on the same IP subnet. The ports for a vLAN do not need to be physically next to each other, and if needed a network port can be part of multiple vLANs if needed. From a security perspective, this prevents a person from simply plugging an unauthorized computer into the network port. This is because if the computer is configured with an IP address from the wrong IP subnet the computer would not have access to the network as the IP address is in the wrong vLAN.

There is only one real rule when it comes to setting up vLANs for a company, use a configuration that makes sense for the company while allowing for growth.

One possible example vLAN configuration might look like that shown in Table 2.4.

As we can see in Table 2.4 when different kinds of computers are put into different networks it gets very easy for us to limit the access that some employees

Table 2.4   Example Subnet Layout

IP Subnet	vLAN ID	Description
10.0.1.0/24	1	Management network containing network switch management ports, SAN management ports, etc.
10.0.2.0/24	2	Infrastructure network containing domain controllers, time servers, DNS Servers, vSphere hosts, Hyper-V hosts, etc.
10.0.3.0/24	3	Database Servers containing SQL Servers, Oracle Servers, MySQL Servers, etc.
10.0.4.0/24	4	Web servers
10.0.5.0/24	5	Application servers
10.0.6.0/24	6	Mail servers
10.0.7.0/24	7	IT workstations
10.0.8.0/24	8	Finance workstations
10.0.9.0/24	9	Finance servers
10.0.10.0/24	10	Executive workstations
10.0.11.0/24	11	Wireless network
10.0.12.0/24	12	General workstations

have to various devices. A perfect example would be the management network. This network should be secured from being accessed by any other subnet in the company with the exception of the IT staff. We can make this assumption because no employee other than an IT employee will be making changes to the network switches, storage arrays, SAN switches, etc. By isolating them to a network which can only be accessed by people on the IT vLAN these management ports get an extra layer of protection.

The same protection is given to the servers in the Finance vLAN. Odds are no employee outside of the Finance department needs access to those servers so by placing those servers within their own vLAN we can limit the people who can access those servers to the Finance staff who all sit on the Finance vLAN and possibly to the IT staff.

Another example is the workstations for the executive staff. Executives often have very sensitive documents on their computers and the general user at the company does not need the ability to access the executive's computers remotely. By placing the computers used by the executive staff into their own vLAN and preventing network access into that vLAN from other vLANs we can prevent any employee from accessing any computer on the executive vLAN.

Just because vLANs are configured does not mean that they are isolated from the other vLANs within the company network. Setting up this isolation requires the use of a firewall or ACL (both of which are discussed within this chapter) to prevent unwanted network access from other vLANs.

Along with preventing network connectivity into a vLAN we may also identify vLANs which can be blocked from having direct Internet access. In the example shown in Table 2.4 there are several vLANs which have no need for Internet access. These vLANs which could be blocked from having Internet access are 1, 3, 4, 5, and 9. We want to prevent these various vLANs from having Internet access because these are server networks and unless there is a specific application requirement for Internet access. If these machines are talking directly to the Internet this is generally a problem as this means that there is probably a virus on the machine attempting to phone home to its command and control server so that it can get updated instructions or to deliver information which has been captured. By blocking Internet access at the network level, even if a virus was able to get onto the server it would have no access to talk to the Internet. There are some applications which are installed on servers which may have a legitimate need to have some form of Internet access. These should be handled on a case-by-case basis with those servers being given access to the only the public websites which they need access to, and not the entire Internet.

When blocking vLANs from talking to the public Internet there are always going to be exceptions where servers to need Internet access. The DNS servers for example will need access to talk to the Internet, but only over the DNS port. The timeservers will need access to talk to the atomic clock servers so they can stay in sync. The patching servers will need access to talk to servers like the Windows Update servers at Microsoft.

ACCESSING SQL SERVER FROM HOME

The most common reason for not following the advice laid out in this chapter is to make it easier for the database administrator or developer to connect to the SQL Server remotely, so that problems can be addressed as quickly and easily as possible. Being able to respond to issues quickly is an admirable goal; however, keep in mind that if you can connect to the SQL Server from anywhere, then so can someone who is not supposed to be able to.

The only secure way to connect from outside a network to inside the network is to use a Virtual Private Network (VPN) connection. This allows you to create a secure encrypted tunnel from your home computer to your office or data center. Your home computer is then issued an IP Address on the office network, and you are able to communicate with the office computers over the secured link instead of connecting to the machines directly over the public Internet. Even if you have multiple offices or an office and a data center, you can configure your network so that you can connect to one location and then access the other sites over secure connections between your facilities.

The office-to-office or office-to-data center connections are usually made in the same way, with a persistent site-to-site VPN connection. This site-to-site VPN connection is very similar to the one that you use from your home computer to the office, except that it is a persistent, always on connection that connects as soon as the devices on both sides of the VPN connection are booted up. This allows you to easily and cheaply expand your network across multiple sites without the expense of purchasing a dedicated network line between the sites. This network connection design may be better explained with the diagram shown in Figure 2.4.

Figure 2.4 shows two facilities: the office that uses the subnet 10.3.0.0, and the CoLo that has our servers in it, which uses the subnet 10.3.2.0. Our house uses the default IP range, which our home router uses and is probably 192.168.0.1. There is then a site-to-site VPN connection between the routers at the CoLo and the office that allows those two networks to talk to each other securely. When a connection is needed to an office computer, or a server located at the CoLo, you can simply VPN (Virtual Private Network) into the office network. This VPN connection effectively puts the remote machine on the office network. From the office network, the network routers allow access to the office machines and the servers at the CoLo over a secure, encrypted connection. This secure VPN connection allows users to quickly and easily manage the servers in their environment without exposing the servers to the public Internet, allowing the user not only to manage the servers, but also to manage them safely.

SETTING UP ROUTING AND REMOTE ACCESS

There is really no reason to not have a VPN setup for networks which need to have the ability for people from outside the network to connect to servers within the network. The reason is because Windows server includes a VPN server called Routing

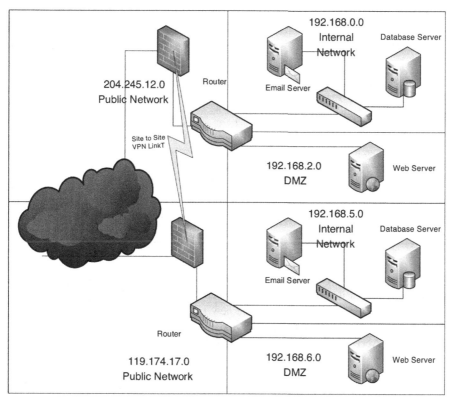

FIGURE 2.4 Network diagram with site-to-site VPN links.

and Remote Access Services (RRAS) which can be setup on a machine within just a few minutes without having deep understanding on Windows networks.

The easiest way to setup Routing and Remote Access is to configure two different network cards, one for internal network access and one for use by the public Internet. These network cards can be connected to the same network or to two different networks.

FAQ

What is Better, Site-to-Site VPNs or Leased Lines?

As the amount of network traffic increases between sites, a site-to-site VPN may no longer provide an acceptable level of performance. This performance dropoff is explained by the CPU (Central Processing Unit) load that the increased network traffic would place on the CPU of the routers that maintain the VPN connection. Eventually the cost of purchasing larger and more expensive routers will increase beyond the cost of a leased line between the sites. There are no hard-set numbers as to when the change from a site-to-site VPN to a leased line should be made. This is because network connection costs vary from city to city (often from street to street within the same city) and router costs change depending on your company's purchasing power.

> **NOTE**
>
> **Sample RRAS Server**
>
> For this section of the book a rather complex lab was needed so that setting up Routing and Remote Access could be fully documented. For this lab there are two different networks configured. The 10.5.0.0/24 subnet is configured as the local LAN which the Active Directory domain is running within. The 192.168.0.0/24 subnet is configured as the network which has Internet access. The router is configured using NAT to direct all network traffic which is used by the Point to Point Tunneling Protocol (PPTP) VPN to the 192.168.0.0 IP address which is configured on one of the network cards. The 10.5.0.0/24 network is not configured to have Internet access.
>
> While Routing and Remote Access does not require an Active Direction domain, it is much easier to setup Routing and Remote Access when there is an Active Directory domain setup. In this network the Active Directory domain controller is configured with the IP Address 10.5.0.2. The Routing and Remote Access server is configured with the IP Address 10.5.0.101 on the Internal NIC and the IP Address 192.168.0.6 on the public NIC.
>
> For the purposes of this lab domain the domain controller and the Routing and Remote Access server are both running Windows Server 2012 R2.

The first thing which needs to be done when configuring Routing and Remote Access is to install it. This is done via the server manage and is just like installing any other role. Simply walk through the new role or feature wizard. On the Server Roles page check the "Remote Access" role as shown in Figure 2.5 . After checking the "Remote Access" checkbox click the next button.

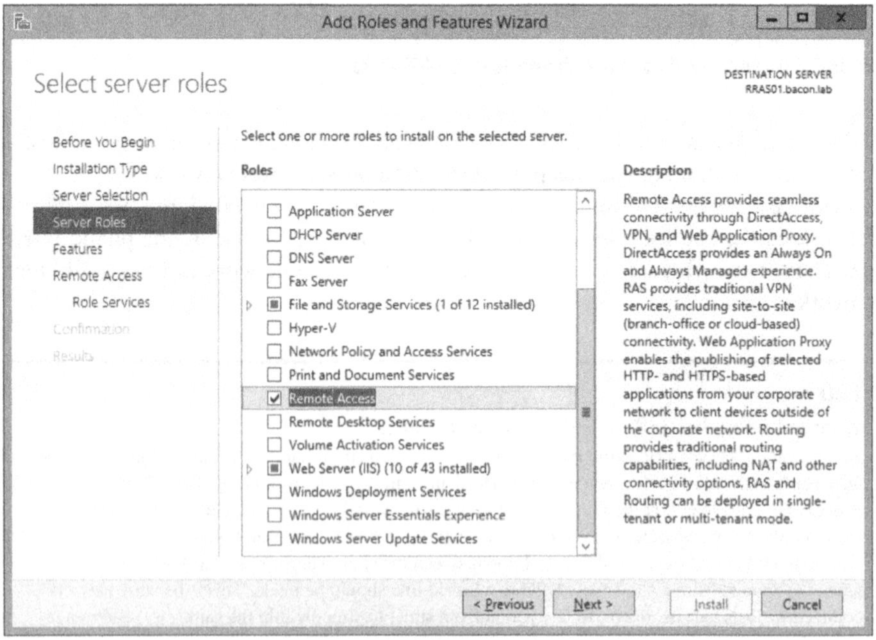

FIGURE 2.5 Server roles page of the server manager.

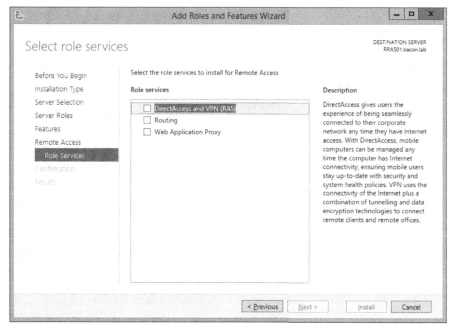

FIGURE 2.6 Role services screen of the server manager wizard.

After moving forward a few screens you will be asked which role services you wish to install shown in Figure 2.6. If all that the server is used for is for VPN then the only option which is needed is the "Direct Access and VPN (RAS)" option.

After checking the checkbox shown in Figure 2.6 another window will be shown as shown in Figure 2.7 . If you wish to install the management tools as well leave the checkbox checked, if not clear the checkbox and click the "Add Features" button.

After the window shown in Figure 2.7 closes complete the wizard and install the components on the server. After the component installation has been completed click on the flag at the top of the Server Manager which now has a yellow triangle next to it. A menu will open as shown in Figure 2.8 . In the new menu click the "Open the Getting Started Wizard" shown in the first menu option in Figure 2.8 which will bring up the Configure Remote Access wizard.

When the "Configure Remote Access" wizard opens select the type of remote access you wish to use as shown in Figure 2.9.

Within the "Configure Remote Access" wizard select the "Deploy VPN only" option to allow VPN to be configured. This will open the Routing and Remote Access management tool.

In order to configure VPN right click on the server name shown on the right hand of the window shown in Figure 2.10, in this case RRAS01, and select "Configure and Enable Routing and Remote Access" from the context menu which appears. This will open the "Routing and Remote Access Server Setup Wizard" which will allow you

FIGURE 2.7 Specific features to install of RAS install.

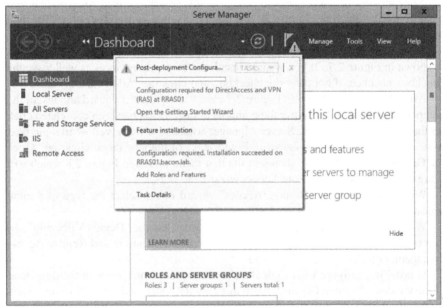

FIGURE 2.8 Server manager with the post deployment menu shown.

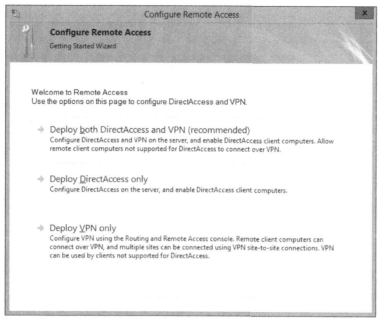

FIGURE 2.9 Configure remote access wizard.

to configure the specifics of the VPN connections which will be allowed. The first page of the wizard is a simple information screen which can be skipped by clicking the "Next" button.

The next page of the VPN wizard allows for the selection of the type of services which this machine will offer. For this configuration this server will only be used as a VPN server so we can select the first option "Remote access (dial-up or VPN)" as shown in Figure 2.11 and click "Next."

NOTE

VPN or Direct Access?

Should you be using VPN or Direct Access? That really depends on how your network is configured and how you want to manage things. If you want users to manually create and then start the VPN connection then you want VPN. If you want the VPN tunnel to come up automatically then you will want to use Direct Access.

Direct Access has some very specific requirements however. The biggest requirement is that the servers and the user's workstations must be members of the Active Directory domain. This means that if you have outside contractors or consultants, or even full time employees who use their own devices, which need to access your internal network they must use VPN unless their computers are members of the Active Directory domain.

For the purposes of this chapter we are going to setup VPN only. Direct Access is much more complex to configure and is beyond the scope of this book due to its complexity.

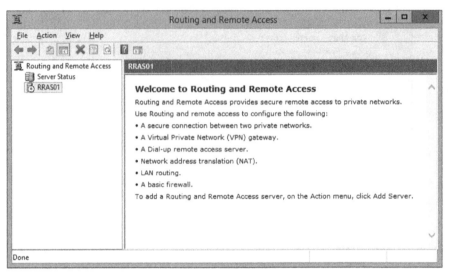

FIGURE 2.10 Initial view of the routing and remote access management application.

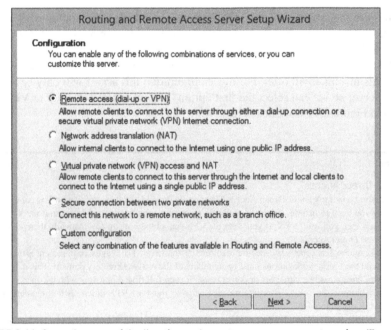

FIGURE 2.11 Second screen of the "routing and remote access server setup wizard".

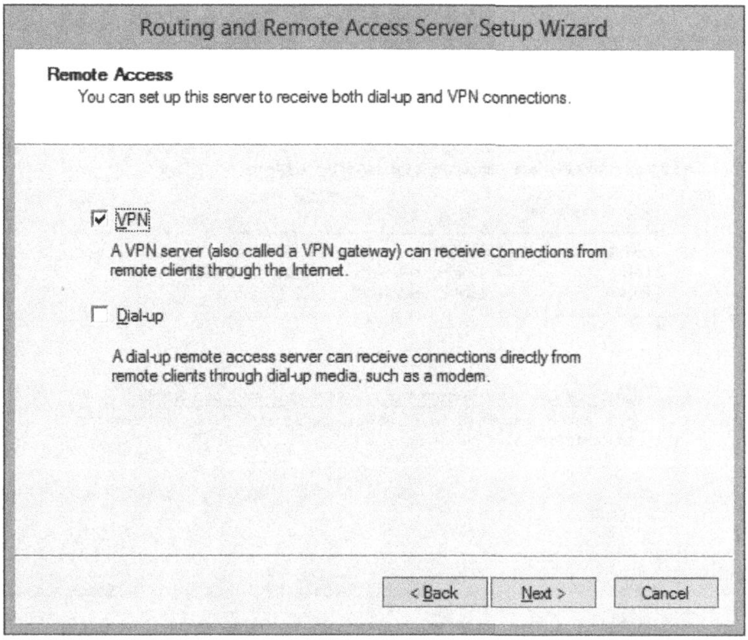

Routing and Remote Access Server Setup Wizard

Remote Access
You can set up this server to receive both dial-up and VPN connections.

☑ VPN
A VPN server (also called a VPN gateway) can receive connections from remote clients through the Internet.

☐ Dial-up
A dial-up remote access server can receive connections directly from remote clients through dial-up media, such as a modem.

[< Back]   [Next >]   [Cancel]

FIGURE 2.12 Remote access types which will be supported.

The next screen of the wizard allows you to select between supporting VPN, dialup connections or both. As we do not live in the 1990s we'll be using VPN only and not using dialup. Select the VPN checkbox as shown in Figure 2.12 and click "Next."

The next screen of the wizard asks which network connection the VPN should be listening on. For this server there are two network connections, one named Public and one named LAN. The Public network will be used to allow VPN connections so that NIC is selected as shown in Figure 2.13. Depending on what else the public interface will be used for you may or may not want to select the "Enable security on the selected interface by setting up static packet filters" checkbox. If this checkbox is checked then the network interface will be configured to not allow any other network connectivity through that NIC. If this checkbox is not checked then network connectivity will be allowed as normal. If the network firewall is configured properly and only allows the VPN connections through the firewall then this checkbox can be unchecked safely. If the network firewall does not block all non-VPN network connections then this checkbox should be checked. For the purposes of this chapter the network firewall is configured to block all network requests besides the VPN connections so the checkbox can be unchecked. After configuring the options shown in Figure 2.13 click the "Next" button.

The next screen of the wizard shows the IP Address assignment options as shown in Figure 2.14. On this screen you will select how you wish to have IP Addresses

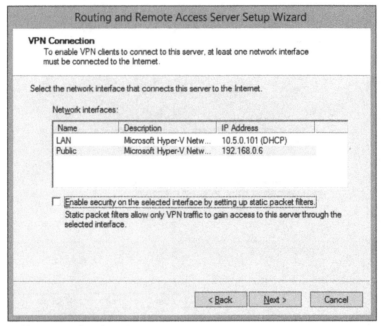

FIGURE 2.13 Network interface list.

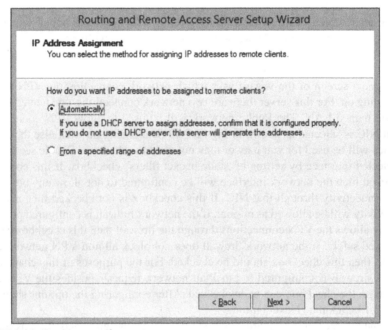

FIGURE 2.14 IP address assignment.

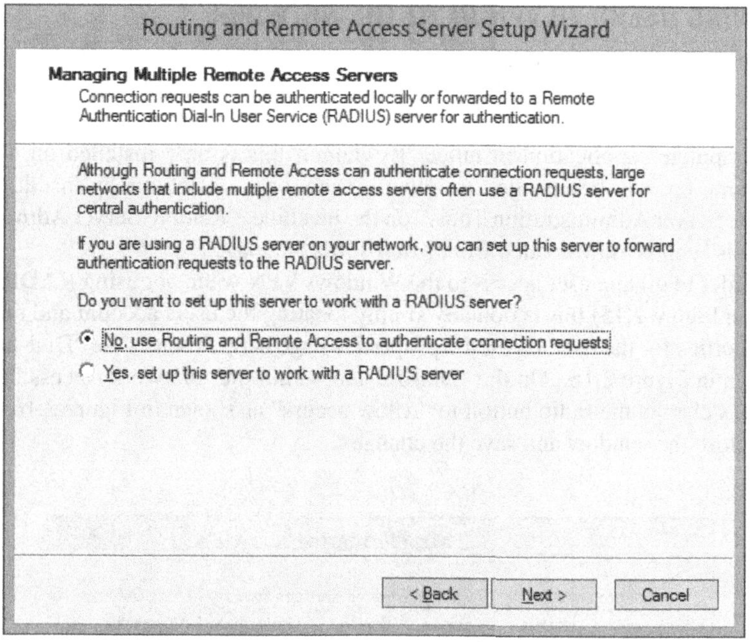

FIGURE 2.15 Will RADIUS be used.

assigned to the computers which VPN in to the network. If there is a DHCP server on the network you can use DHCP to assign the IP addresses, if there is not (or if you wish to not use DHCP addresses) you can specify a static IP subnet to issue IP Addresses from. If a static IP subnet is being used, then the Routing and Remote Access server basically runs its own DHCP server. In this case DHCP will be used to issue IP Addresses from the normal DHCP subnet within the 10.5.0.0/24 subnet which the machines on the LAN use. After making your selection click the "Next" button.

If on the IP Address Assignment screen you select to use a specified range of address the next screen will allow you to specify the IP Address ranges which will be issued. If DHCP is used then this screen is skipped. The next screen allows you to select how authentication will be configured. This page of the wizard, shown in Figure 2.15, allows you to specify if RADIUS will be used for authentication and billing or not. Using RADIUS is an advanced feature which is outside the scope of this book, for this reason we will be selecting "No, use Routing and Remote Access to authenticate connection requests." If you select "Yes, set up this server to work with a RADIUS server" the next screen of the wizard (not shown) asks for the RADIUS servers information.

The final page of the wizard shows a summary of the configuration and allows the configuration to be completed. To complete the configuration click the "Finish" button.

ALLOWING USERS TO VPN IN TO THE NETWORK

After the VPN server is configured users must be granted access to VPN in. This is done at the domain level by editing the users' domain account within Active Directory. To edit a user's account log onto a server which has the "Active Directory Users and Computers" application installed. By default this is only installed on domain controllers, but can be installed on other servers or workstations by installing the "Remote Server Administration Tools" on the machine. "Remote Server Administration Tools" can be downloaded from Microsoft's webpage.

In order to grant a user access to the Windows VPN when not using RADIUS (as shown in Figure 2.15) this is done by simply locating the users account and opening the properties for the user. Open the properties page is open select the "Dial-In" tab, as shown in Figure 2.16 . On the "Dial-In" tab within the "Network Access Permission" box change the radio button to "Allow access" as shown in Figure 2.16. Click OK to close the window and save the change.

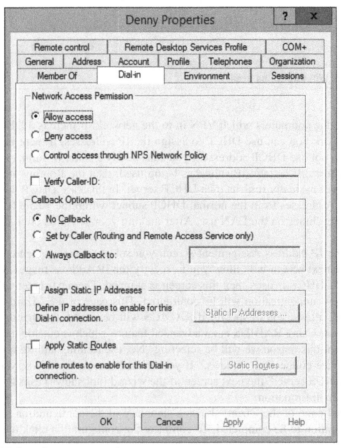

FIGURE 2.16 Domain users properties page.

SETTING UP CLIENT VPN CONNECTION

Once the VPN server has been configured the VPN clients can be configured. In order to configure VPN for a Windows client computer a simple procedure must be done on the client computer.

To configure a VPN connection, locate the network icon in the system tray of the computer. For computers connected via Wi-Fi the icon will be the Wi-Fi strength indicator as shown in Figure 2.17. For computers which are directly connected via a network cable the icon will look like a small computer as shown in Figure 2.18 .

Right click on the network icon in the system tray matching either Figure 2.17 or Figure 2.18 and select "Open Network and Sharing Center" from the context menu which appears. In the window which opens locate the "Change your networking settings" box and click on the "Set up a new connection or network" link. This opens the "Set Up a Connection or Network" wizard as shown in Figure 2.19 .

From the wizard select the "Connect to a workplace" option and click the "Next" button. The next screen asks if an existing network connection should be connected first. As this is not the case select "No, create a new connection" and

FIGURE 2.17 Network icon for a computer connected via Wi-Fi.

FIGURE 2.18 Network icon for a computer connected via an ethernet cable.

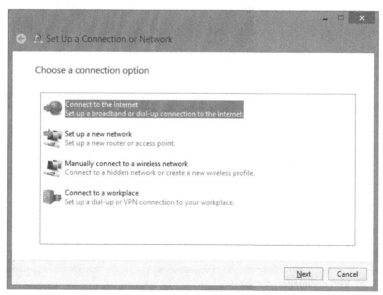

FIGURE 2.19 Set up a connection or network wizard.

click the "Next" button. On the next screen of the wizard you'll be asked if you wish to connect via VPN or dialup modem. Again as this is not the 1990s click the "Use my Internet connection (VPN)" button. On the next screen of the wizard enter the DNS name of the VPN server, or the public IP Address of the VPN server as well as a description such as the company name as shown in Figure 2.20 then click the "Create" button.

Once the wizard completes the VPN connection is started by clicking on the network icon shown in either Figure 2.17 or Figure 2.18. This brings up a list of networks which you can connect to as well as the list of VPN connections as shown in Figure 2.21 . Clicking on the VPN you wish to connect to will begin the connection. The first time the connection is used you will be prompted for network credentials, if the connection is configured to save the network credentials you would not be prompted for them again unless there is a network problem.

Before the VPN connection can be used it must be configured with the encryption options which are available to be used. Windows 8 and Windows 8.1 by default do not automatically configure the VPN connections with a set of encryption options, so these options much be set manually.

In order to set the VPN connections encryption options bring up the network list by clicking on the network icon in either Figure 2.17 or Figure 2.18. Right click on the VPN connection to edit and click the "View connection properties" menu option from the context menu. Click on the "Security" tab and configure the encryption options as needed similar to those shown in Figure 2.22 . Normally EAP-MSCHAP-v2 encryption is sufficient for VPN communications as shown in Figure 2.22.

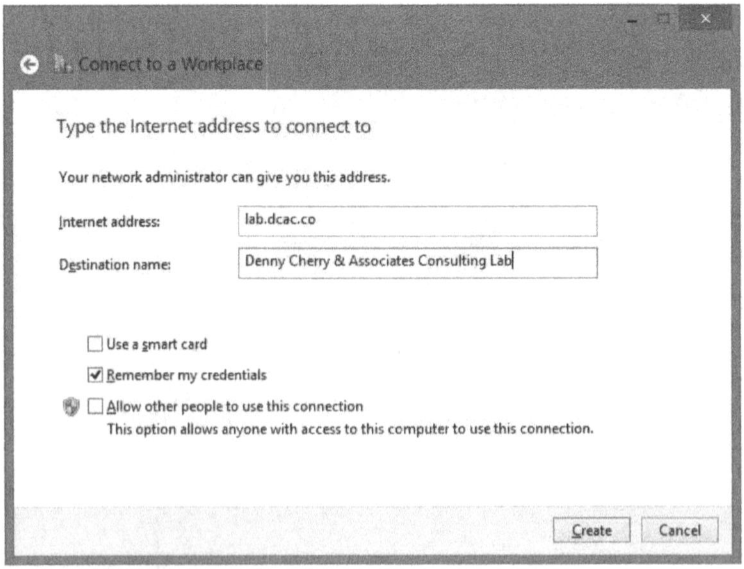

FIGURE 2.20 VPN connection details.

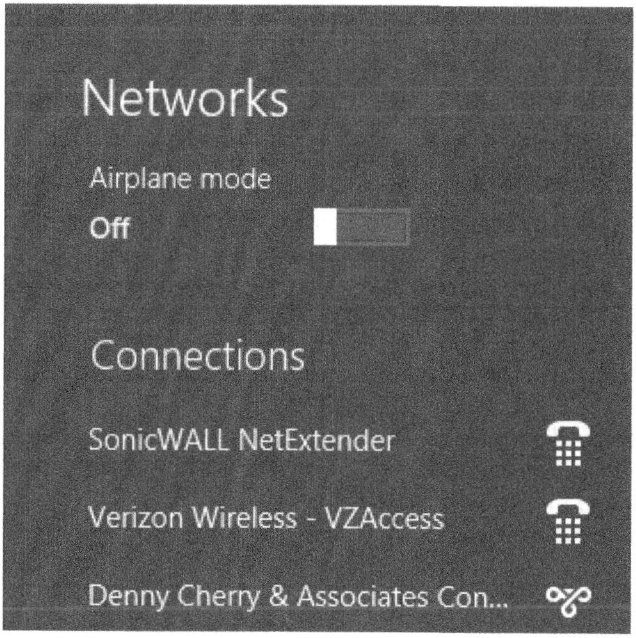

FIGURE 2.21 Network VPN list in Windows 8 or Windows 8.1.

FIGURE 2.22 Sample encryption options.

PHYSICAL SECURITY

So far we have focused on threats that come in over the Internet or that are coming from users within the network. There is, however, a more serious threat that is fortunately less likely to be exploited. This threat is a physical breach within the data center. A physical breach can actually take a couple of different forms.

1. An unauthorized person gets into the data center and is able to physically access servers.
2. An unauthorized person gets into the office, and connects his or her own computer to an open network port or company Wi-Fi accessing company resources over the company network.
3. An unauthorized person gets into the office and uses an employee's workstation or laptop that was left unattended, allowing them access to whatever resources the employee's login grants them.

KEEP YOUR HANDS OFF MY BOX

An unauthorized person getting into the data center and accessing company servers is pretty much the worst-case scenario. If a server is left with the console logged in for some reason, this person would have access to whatever rights the account that was logged in would have. What makes this even worse is that the server is probably logged in as a domain administrator. The unauthorized person could easily enough plug a USB (Universal Serial Bus) drive into the server, which would by default launch whatever is in the autoexec.ini file on the thumb drive. A smart intruder would configure a data-logging application that would then spread itself to all the servers and workstations within the company network.

Due to the danger of unauthorized people in the data center, server room, network closet, or the like, the room's physical security should be given special treatment. All doors to the data center should be locked at all times, with access given only to those people who require access to the room and the physical servers. If the servers are left sitting out, then anyone who makes his or her way into the office has access to them.

When securing the data center, it is important to remember to include the cleaning crew, upper management, human resources, and building security on the list of people that do not normally need access to the room. The cleaning crew is probably the most important to keep removed from that list. While getting hired as a company's systems administrator can be quite difficult, getting hired as a cleaning person is quite a bit easier. Cleaning is usually outsourced to another company that probably does not have the tightest hiring practices. This is usually the weakest point in a company's security against a potential attacker. The cleaning crew is a great way into a building: They are there all night, they are typically alone, and they generally have keys to every room and office within the company.

In order to properly secure the server room or data center some extreme measures should be taken. This includes the need to alarm any doors and windows which lead into the server room or data center so that if anyone enters the server room or data center without using the correct key card, pin code or door key the alarm goes off. The alarm should go off with a loud annoying audible alarm as well as calling to an alarm company or the local police department. There should also be motion sensors in the server room which will go off if entry is made into server room without going through the normal way in (through the door). While stories of actual break-ins into server rooms and data centers are not typically reported publically, if you look carefully online and read between the lines you can see people talking about improving the security of their server rooms and data centers. When working with an offsite data center like a Colocation (CoLo) facility alarm systems become even more important as the CoLo staff may not recognize if an unauthorized person is attempting, or does successfully attempt to break into the CoLo cage.

OPEN NETWORK PORTS

Having unused network ports at desks connected to network switches sounds like a pretty basic thing. It makes it much more convenient when you need to move a new computer to a new desk. However, because these network ports at the desks are connected to a switch, if DHCP (Dynamic Host Configuration Protocol) is enabled on the network (which it probably is), then if someone were to make his or her way into the office and connect a laptop to the port, the stranger suddenly would have the ability to scan the network looking for SQL Servers (or other servers) that can be broken into.

Keeping the desk ports connected to the network switches is not necessarily a problem, provided that the ports on the network switch have been disabled. Switch ports can be disabled on any managed switch such as a Cisco Catalyst, Foundry, or Juniper switch among others. Unmanaged network switches, such as lower end switches, do not support this functionality. Keeping the network ports disabled on the network switch has the same net effect as unplugging the network cables. The upside of keeping the desk ports connected and having the ports disabled on the network switch is that a systems administrator or network administrator can enable the port from anywhere, as long as the ports are well documented, so that new ports can be quickly and easily enabled.

UNLOCKED WORKSTATIONS

When users leave their desks, they should always lock their workstations. Employees who have been at the company for a while are probably used to locking their workstations when they step away from them. However, younger or newer employees may not be aware that this should be done for both the company's and their own security.

On the side of the company's security, if an unauthorized person were to sit at an employee's desk, he or she would have access to all the company resources to which that employee has access. This includes the employee's email, chat programs, customer service applications, sales systems, and reports. Whatever company data the intruder accessed there would be in no way identify what was accessed by the employee and what was accessed by the intruder, for all the access would be done under the name of a valid employee account.

With regard to the employee's personal security, if an unauthorized person were to sit at the employee's desk, he or she would have access to all the personal websites on which the employee has saved his or her password. This includes bank websites, iTunes, Zune Pass, forums, and so on – not to mention that if an unauthorized person were to access company data that the employee was not authorized to view, it could end up costing the employee his or her job.

Automatically Locking Computers

One of the most common domain settings to set is to have all employee computers lock automatically when the computer screen is idle. When computers are within a Windows Active Directory domain, this setting can be controlled through a group policy setting. This setting can be found by editing the group policy setting and navigating to:

1. User Configuration
2. Administrative Templates
3. Control Panel
4. Display

Within the Display folder there are four settings that are of interest. These policies affect all computers that are running Windows 2000 Service Pack 1 and higher, including both the server and client versions of the operating system.

1. Screen Saver
2. Screen Saver executable name
3. Password protect the Screen Saver
4. Screen Saver timeout

The "Screen Saver" setting controls whether the screen saver is enabled or disabled. When this policy setting is set to "Not Configured," the user logged in can decide whether or not the screen saver is enabled. When this setting is enabled, the screen saver will always be enabled. When this setting is disabled, the screen saver will always be disabled.

The "Screen Saver executable name" setting sets the name of the screen saver that will be used. When this policy setting is set to "Not Configured," the user can select which screen saver to use. When this setting is enabled and the "Screen Saver executable name" is set to a valid screen saver, that screen saver will be used on the user's desktop, and the user will not be able to change the setting. When this setting is disabled, the user can select any screen saver. If the screen saver that is specified does not exist, then the setting is ignored and the user can select any screen saver. If the "Screen Saver" setting is disabled, then the "Screen Saver executable name" is disabled.

The "Password protect the Screen Saver" setting determines whether the screen saver requires a password to disable it. When the setting is set to "Not Configured," the user can select if the screen saver should be password protected. When the setting is "Enabled," then the screen saver will always require a password to turn the screen saver off. When the setting is "Disabled," then the screen saver will never require a password to turn the screen saver off.

The "Screen Saver timeout" setting determines how long the computer will wait before activating the screen saver. When this setting is set to "Not Configured," the user can configure the timeout. When this setting is set to "Enabled," a number of seconds is specified, from 1 s to 86,400 s (24 h). If the setting is set to 0 s, then the screen saver will never be started. When the setting is "Disabled," it has the same effect as being set to "Not Configured." This setting is ignored if the "Screen Saver" setting is disabled, or if the screen saver specified in the "Screen Saver executable name" setting is not a valid screen saver on the computer.

If all four settings are configured, there is another setting that can be of interest, which is located within the same folder. This is the "Hide Screen Saver tab." When this setting is set to "Enabled," the Screen Saver tab will not be shown within the Display control panel icon. When the setting is set to "Not Configured" or "Disabled," then the tab will be shown as normal.

SOCIAL ENGINEERING

Social engineering is a way for an attacker to gain access to a company network or computer by getting a current employee to give the access. This is typically done by calling a user and pretending to be a help desk employee. Once the employee believes the attacker is an employee, the attacker asks for the employee's username and password to "fix" something. The attacker may also ask for other items to obtain more information about the internal network such as the VPN site, webmail server, internal application, and server names. Once attackers are able to get into the network using the employee's information, they are probably done with the employee; however, they may move up to the supervisor to get more information.

FINDING THE INSTANCES

Before you secure Microsoft SQL Server instances, the trick may be to find all the servers. This can be done in a few different ways. The simplest way is to query the network for all responding Microsoft SQL Servers. This is most easily done using the osql command line application (when using SQL Server 2000 or older) or the sqlcmd command line application (when using SQL Server 2005 or newer). With either application, using the –L switch will query the local IP subnet for available SQL Server instances as shown in Example 2.2. This technique will send out a broadcast request to all the servers on the local IP subnet. All the machines with the SQL Server

---

STORY TIME

The Most Famous Social Engineer of All Time

The most famous Social Engineer of all time would probably have to be Kevin Mitnick. Kevin first used social engineering at the age of 12 when he got a bus driver to tell him where to get a bus transfer punch that would allow him to ride the Los Angeles city bus system for free. Throughout Kevin's criminal escapades he often used social engineering to get usernames and passwords, as well as modem phone numbers for corporate systems (today he would ask for the VPN server name instead).

By getting people's usernames, passwords, and phone numbers, it is confirmed that Kevin broke into DEC's (Digital Equipment Corporation) computer systems to view the VMS (Virtual Memory System) source code as well as gaining full administrative rights to an IBM minicomputer at the Computer Learning Center (CLC) in Los Angeles. The purpose of break-in to the minicomputer at the CLC in Los Angeles was probably the most interesting case as it was to win a bet. Kevin is also known to have broken into Motorola, NEC, Nokia, Sun Microsystems, and Fujitsu Siemens computer systems.

In addition to these confirmed acts, Kevin is rumored to have stolen computer manuals from the Pacific Bell telephone switching center in Los Angeles, reading the email of computer security personal at MCI and Digital; wiretapped the California State Department of Motor Vehicles (DMV); and hacked into Santa Cruz Operation (SCO), Pacific Bell, the FBI, the Pentagon, Novell, the University of Southern California, and the Los Angeles Unified School District (LAUSD).

Kevin has served five years in prison, four and half years during pretrial confinement, and eight months of solitary confinement postconviction. Kevin claims that the solitary confinement was imposed because law enforcement was able to convince a judge that he would be able to "start a nuclear war by whistling into a pay phone." During his parole Kevin was prohibited to access the Internet or to use any other communications technology other than a landline telephone.

Two books have been written specifically about Kevin Mitnick's case: John Markoff and Tsutomu Shimomura's *Takedown,* and Jonathan Littman's *The Fugitive Game.* In 2000, the movie *Takedown,* which was based on the book of that title, was released. A documentary titled *Freedom Downtime* was a fan-based documentary created in response to the big-budget documentary *Takedown.*

---

service browser running will respond with all the installed instances on the machine, as long as those instances have not been configured to be hidden. More information on hiding the instances is presented in Chapter 4 within the section "Encrypting Data on the Wire."

EXAMPLE 2.2

Using the sqlcmd application to query the local network for available SQL Server instances.

```
sqlcmd -L
```

Using Windows PowerShell, the local network can also be queried for all the available instances. The PowerShell example shown in Example 2.3 uses the same technique as the sqlcmd example shown in Example 2.3, as well as the SQL Server Management Studio connection dialog.

> **NOTE**
> **These Lists Would Not Always be Accurate**
> When using sqlcmd with the –L switch shown in Example 2.2 or the PowerShell example shown in Example 2.3, the lists can be incomplete for a number of reasons. Among the reasons are the following: the instance is set as hidden; the firewall is blocking access to the instance; the instance is not listening on port 1433; the instance is a named instance and the SQL Browser service is not running; the network does not pass the broadcast request to the SQL Server if the SQL Server is hosted on a different subnet; the person requesting the list does not have access to the SQL Instance; or the SQL Server's OS.

EXAMPLE 2.3

PowerShell command to query for instances using the .NET API call to query for SQL Server Instances.

```
[System.Data.Sql.SqlDataSourceEnumerator]::Instance.GetDataSources()
```

Another technique that can be used involves using Server Management Objects (SMOs). The SMO can be easily used through Windows PowerShell as shown in Example 2.4. The downside to using SMO is that like the code shown in Example 2.3 and Example 2.1, the services will be shown only if the services are not marked as hidden and if the SQL Browser service is running.

EXAMPLE 2.4

Using SMOs (Server Management Objects) to list available SQL Servers.

```
[System.Reflection.Assembly]::LoadWithPartialName("Microsoft.
SqlServer.Smo") | out-null
[Microsoft.SqlServer.Management.Smo.SmoApplication]::EnumAvai
lableSqlServers() | ft
```

The PowerShell code shown in Example 2.2–2.4 relies on the .NET framework or SMO in order to query for the available SQL Servers. As these code samples use the "proper methods" for finding the services, services that are hidden, or if the SQL Browser is disabled on the server (as the SQL browser is what does the responding), are not returned by these commands. The PowerShell code shown in Example 2.5, on the other hand, connects to Active Directory and downloads a list of all computers on the domain, and then it queries each of those computers, one by one, looking for any services that are named using the Microsoft SQL Server database engine naming standard. The sample code in Example 2.5 searches for both named and default instances within a single command.

EXAMPLE 2.5

Using Windows PowerShell to query WMI (Windows Management Instrumentation) on each computer within a Windows Active Directory domain to see if those computers have any SQL Server Services installed.

```
$objDomain = New-Object System.DirectoryServices.DirectoryEntry
$objSearcher = New-Object System.DirectoryServices.DirectorySearcher
$objSearcher.SearchRoot = $objDomain
$objSearcher.Filter = ("computer")
$objSearcher.PropertiesToLoad.Add("name")
$Computers = $objSearcher.FindAll()
foreach ($machine_name in $Computers | sort computername)
{
$sql_servers = get-wmiobject -class win32_service -computer
$machine_name
$sql_servers | where { $_.name -like 'MSSQL$' -or
$_.name -eq 'MSSQLSERVER'} | select name
}
```

The catch with the code shown in Example 2.5 is that it requires that the user running the code be a local administrator on each machine within the domain (typically this will require being a member of the "Domain Admins" Windows domain group). This elevated right is required as querying the list of services from a remote computer requires an elevated permission set. This sample code, however, will be the most accurate as the OS is being queried for a list of services, instead of asking the SQL Browser what services it is configured to tell you exist. If you wish to search for SQL Server Reporting Services instances, the Windows PowerShell code shown in Example 2.5 can be modified to search for the Reporting Services name by adding another "or" to the where clause.

TESTING THE NETWORK SECURITY

Once the network has been secured, it is time to begin testing the network security. There are a few different ways that it can be tested. The first is the easiest and cheapest: Have an employee go home and attempt to break into the network or the servers using a known username and password (such as her own, or one that was set up specifically for this testing) and have her see how much damage she can do. This sort of testing should only be done with management and the IT security teams' approval. Randomly trying to break into your employer's network without permission is a great way to get fired, and possibly arrested. This employee should attempt to break into web servers, routers, and anything else that is Internet facing using brute force password attacks. This includes attacking the company's VPN server to ensure that its security is strong enough, as the VPN system in an inherent weak point because VPN servers are designed to allow users full access to the network.

Once the systems and the network have been configured to resist this first round of testing, it is time to pay for some testing. A variety of companies will perform network attacks against a company's network. The number of tests and the type of tests performed by each of the testing companies will vary based on the strengths of the testing company's programmers.

By running automated penetration testing against the company network on a regular basis, the company and its customers can be sure that the data the company stores within its databases is secure from outside attack. Many of the automated penetration testing companies will provide a logo that can be placed on the company website showing when the last test was completed without a successful attack so that the company's customers are able to see just how secure and up-to-date the testing is.

These penetration testing companies will check a variety of things from the front end, including attempting an SQL Injection attack against the web forms, seeing that the strongest level of encryption is being used, and ensuring that services that should not be available from the Internet are not available (such as Windows file shares, SQL Servers, Oracle, MySQL, LDAP, etc.).

There are a wide variety of penetration tests that can be performed. Different testing companies will call these tests different things, but the basic idea is the same no matter the name.

Testing against an outside attack from an unknown attacker can be done with a black box test, also known as a blind test. A black box test gives the tester no knowledge of the company, network infrastructure, system source code, and so forth. With the black box test, only the most basic information is given, such as the URL for the company website. The attacking company must see what they can discover through the attack process.

On the other end of the testing spectrum is the white box test, also known as a full disclosure test. With a white box test, the testing company is given full knowledge of the company, the network infrastructure (both Internet facing and Internal), application source code, IP Address settings, and so on. A white box test allows the testing company to simulate an internal attack where the attacker is an insider (typically an employee) or someone to whom an employee has leaked company information.

Between the two extremes of black box testing and white box testing is grey box testing, also known as "partial disclosure" testing. With grey box testing the testing company is given a subset of the information about the company's network infrastructure. This type of attack is probably a more realistic external attack test when an employee has divulged company information to an outside party. Most employees have very limited knowledge of the company network, with the exception of the network administration and systems administration teams (and then usually neither one will know everything). Thus most of the time the attacking person would only have been told a subset of information about the network design, IP Addresses, and the like.

Some auditing processes require that this sort of automated testing be performed on a regular basis. In the United States, any company that takes credit card data from customers (including when the customer pays for services, even if the credit card data is not stored) needs to be able to pass some sort of PCI (Payment Card Industry) audit (read more about PCI audits and see the PCI audit checklist in Appendix A). Different countries will have different laws and regulations that will need to be followed; possibly there are multiple, different sets of laws and regulations, depending on the states and countries in which a company's customers live.

ANTIVIRUS INSTALLATION ON SQL SERVERS

One item which just about everyone has an opinion on is the question of should you install antivirus software on the production SQL Servers. Antivirus software does require CPU and memory resources which is generally something which we do not want to take away from the SQL Server. However, if there is no antivirus installed and a virus gets onto the SQL Server's Operating System there would not be any way to know that it is installed. This puts all the data within the SQL Server at risk, especially if the virus is able to talk to the Internet and send off data without anyone knowing.

That said the antivirus should not just be installed using the default configuration and left alone. We want to prevent the antivirus from scanning the database engine or the data files. If the antivirus were to make a mistake and think that the data files were infected with a virus because a pattern within the data happens to match the pattern of a virus the antivirus could end up corrupting the database file when it tries to remove the virus, or worse it could delete the entire database file. Due to these risks we want to ensure that a few specific settings are configured for our antivirus software, no matter the antivirus software that we are using.

- Prevent the antivirus from scanning any files with the extension mdf, ndf, ldf, bak, and trn (or other extensions that you use for database files).

- Prevent the antivirus from scanning the directories:
  - "c:\Program Files\Microsoft SQL Server\MSSQL11.MSSQLSERVER\ MSSQL\Binn" directory (or whatever directory you have installed SQL Server into).
  - Any folders with FILESTREAM data
  - Any network shares exposed as FILETABLE data
  - Folders with backup files
- Folders with extended stored procedures in them
- Prevent the SQL Server from Injecting itself into the SQL Server process

That last bullet point is probably a little confusing. Because SQL Server allows other DLLs to be loaded into its memory the Antivirus software will often attempt to inject its antivirus DLLs into the SQL Server process in order to more easily scan the SQL Server's instructions and memory space. For most software this is not an issue, however, for high load SQL Servers this can become a problem for performance as the antivirus software can end up slowing down the SQL Server as the antivirus cannot scan the data blocks as fast as SQL Server needs to allocate and access them. This ends up leading to page latch timeout errors as well as lots of locking and blocking performance problems.

Of these three bullet points the first two require that you log onto the Windows Operating System and open the antivirus client to find and verify the settings. The third bullet point can be verified from within T-SQL when you are running SQL Server 2005 and newer. This is done by querying the sys.dm_os_loaded_modules and filtering out anything which is not from Microsoft using the query shown in Example 2.6.

EXAMPLE 2.6

Query to find DLLs which have been injected into the SQL Server process.

```
select *
from sys.dm_os_loaded_modules
where company <> 'Microsoft Corporation';
```

If you find that there are DLLs which are being injected into the SQL Server process you will need to work with the support department for the antivirus vendor to prevent the antivirus from injecting itself into the SQL Server process.

STORY TIME

Antivirus Support May Not Believe You

The support departments at the antivirus companies may not be aware that their software is injecting itself into SQL Server. I've heard things from support including "Our software cannot do that" and "There is no way to do that." It may take a little bit of work with the support department and probably a screenshot of the output from sys.dm_os_loaded_modules showing their DLLs along with their company name. That is usually proof enough for them that their DLLs are injected into the SQL Server process.

SUMMARY

In this chapter we have gone over the network design options that are available to you. This will have shown you where the network design problems in your network are and how to shore up these design problems. The ultimate goal here is to secure the data and the database so that your customer data is not available to prying eyes, while managing the SQL Server is still as easy as possible. Without knowing where the database instances are, there is no way to know that you are correctly securing them.

REFERENCES

2600 Live Mitnick Interview, 2600, January 1, 2003. Web. September 27, 2010.

Markoff, J., 1995. A most-wanted cyberthief is caught in his own web. *New York Times,* February 16, 1995.

Track Down. Dir. Joe Chappelle. Perf. Skeet Ulrich, Russell Wong, Angela Featherstone. Dimension, 2000. Film.

Key Management

3

INFORMATION IN THIS CHAPTER:

- Service master key
- Database master key
- Encryption password management
- Enterprise key management
- High availability and disaster recovery for key management

This chapter is all about encryption keys in the SQL Server database and how to setup and secure those keys.

SERVICE MASTER KEY

Encryption keys within Microsoft SQL Server are configured in a hierarchy structure so that keys at the top of the hierarchy can open keys lower in the hierarchy as shown in Figure 3.1. At the top of the hierarchy is the Service Master Key, which is protected by the Windows Database Protection API (DPAPI).

In Figure 3.1 we can see all the different objects that can be used within the data encryption process including the Service Master Key, the Database Master Key, Certificates, Asymmetric Keys, Symmetric Keys, and Passwords. At first glance this graphic can be a little bit confusing; however, if you start reading the graphic from the bottom up it can make a little more sense. If we start from the bottom with the user data that we have encrypted we can see all the various ways that we can secure that data. We can secure that data either using a Symmetric Key or a password.

The Symmetric Key that we use to secure the encrypted data can be secured via a certificate, an Asymmetric Key, an Enterprise Key Manager, Another Symmetric Key, or a password. At this point things start to get a little more complex. If we store the Symmetric Key using another Symmetric Key that Symmetric Key can be secured any of the ways that any other Symmetric Key can be secured (which isn't shown all that well in the graphic to be honest, but putting nesting relationships in a printed graphic is pretty hard). If the Symmetric Key is secured by an Asymmetric Key that Asymmetric Key can be secured via the Database Master Key, a Password, or an EKM. If the Symmetric Key is secured via a certificate that certificate can be

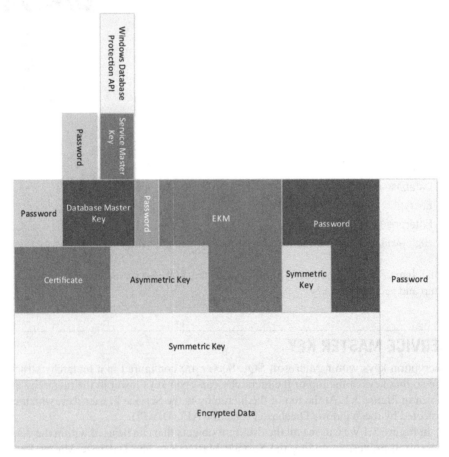

FIGURE 3.1 Encryption hierarchy within SQL Server.

secured via a Password or the Database Master Key. The Database Master Key can be secured via a Password or the Service Master Key and the Service Master Key can be secured via DPAPI.

The DPAPI is an operating system component that is used to encrypt and decrypt the Service Master Key. The Service Master Key is created automatically by the SQL Server instance at the time of installation. The Service Master Key can be regenerated if needed; however, this should be a rare event. Events which might require that the Service Master Key be regenerated would include if the Service Master Key was compromised, if the account which runs the SQL Server service is changed and the new account cannot read the old Service Master Key for some reason.

> **NOTE**
>
> **Changing the SQL Server Service Account**
>
> If you need to change the account that runs the SQL Server service, always use the SQL Server Configuration Manager. As part of the process of changing the service account within the SQL Server Configuration Manager access is granted to the Service Master Key through DPAPI to the new account by the old account so that when the SQL Server service restarts the Service Master Key is still usable. If any other method that the SQL Server Configuration Manager is used to change the SQL Server service startup account the change to the Service Master Key won't be done and the Service Master Key would need to be changed manually.

In some cases the SQL Server service can't regenerate the Service Master Key without losing access to data which has been encrypted. In this case there is a FORCE keyword which can be included in the ALTER SERVER MASTER KEY command which will force the SQL Server service to reset the Service Master Key even if it means that data can no longer be decrypted using the Service Master Key. If using the FORCE keyword be very careful as this may prevent access to some data forever as you can no longer decrypt the data using the Service Master Key. If you still have access to the password which secured the Database Master Key then the data is still decryptable. You would need to open the Database Master Key using the password then rebuild the Database Master Key using the new Service Master Key (this is discussed later in this chapter).

The Service Master Key is used to encrypt all other layers within the data encryption process, even if passwords are used as well. This Service Master Key is used so that the SQL Server service itself can open these keys when the SQL Server starts. As the SQL Server doesn't have access to the passwords that can also be used to encrypt these values, without the Service Master Key no encrypted data would be accessible until an administrator logged onto the server after each reboot in order to unlock the system.

The Service Master Key should be backed up using the BACKUP SERVER MASTER KEY statement each time the Service Master Key is changed. This should be done to ensure that if the Service Master Key is lost, due to a reinstallation of Windows and/or the SQL Server Service that the data which is encrypted within the database can be restored. The backup of the Service Master Key is encrypted by a password. This password should be a strong password with at least 16 characters in it to reduce the risk of anyone gaining access to the Server Master Key. The backup of the Service Master Key should be stored offsite in a secure location, when at all possible in a different physical location than the database backups as the Service Master Key gives an attacker access to all the encrypted data on the system.

DATABASE MASTER KEY

The Database Master Key is used to encrypt all the encryptable objects within the database that contains the Database Master Key such as Symmetric Keys, Asymmetric Keys, Certificates, etc. Each database which will contain encrypted data within it will have to have a Database Master Key created within the database before the objects needed to secure the data are created. The Database Master Key is created within the database by using the CREATE MASTER KEY command. The Database Master Key is secured by both the password, which is specified when running the CREATE MASTER KEY command, but also by the Service Master Key so that either the Service Master Key or the password can be used to open the Database Master Key.

In ultra-secure environments you can configure the Database Master Key to not be encrypted by the Service Master Key. Doing so will require that a Database Administrator log onto the SQL Server instance every time the database is closed and opened (reboots, if you have auto-close enabled, etc.) and use the OPEN MASTER KEY command to open the master key and allow other services to use the Database Master Key.

You can change the Database Master Key by using the ALTER MASTER KEY statement and using the REGENERATE WITH ENCRYPTION BY PASSWORD phrase as shown in Example 3.1.

ALTER MASTER KEY REGENERATE WITH ENCRYPTION BY PASSWORD = 'MyPassword';

EXAMPLE 3.1

Changing the password by the Database Master Key.

When the Database Master Key is changed all of the keys which it protects must be decrypted and re-encrypted using the new Database Master Key. If the objects which the Database Master Key protects cannot be decrypted the SQL Server instance will return an error message. The Database Master Key can still be regenerated by using the FORCE keyword as shown in Example 3.2. This will cause the objects which could not be decrypted to not be opened by the new Database Master Key.

ALTER MASTER KEY FORCE REGENERATE WITH ENCRYPTION BY PASSWORD = 'MyPassword';

EXAMPLE 3.2

Forcing the Database Master Key to be changed.

If the database server needs to be configured so that the SQL Server instance cannot open the Database Master Key automatically when the SQL Server restarts the encryption by the Service Master Key can be removed from the Database Master Key by using the ALTER MASTER KEY command as shown in Example 3.3.

> **NOTE**
>
> **Handling Broken Objects**
>
> If you have objects which are causing the Database Master Key to not be regenerated it is recommended to find and fix these objects instead of just forcing the Database Master Key to be regenerated. How this needs to be done depends on the object and why it can't be regenerated.

```
ALTER MASTER KEY DROP ENCRYPTION BY SERVICE MASTER KEY;
```

> **EXAMPLE 3.3**
>
> Removing the encryption of the Database Master Key by the Service Master Key.
>
> By removing the encryption of the Database Master Key via the Service Master Key a database administrator or other person who has the password for the Database Master Key will need to open the Database Master Key each time the database is closed and reopened, for instance when the database instance is restarted. In a situation like this, if the password for the Database Master Key is lost, all data which is encrypted by the Database Master Key will also be lost. Because of this it is typically recommended that you do not remove the encryption from the Database Master Key by the Service Master Key.
>
> If the encryption of the Database Master Key by the Service Master Key has been removed and needs to be restored, this can be done via the ALTER MASTER KEY statement as shown in Example 3.4.

```
ALTER MASTER KEY ADD ENCRYPTION BY SERVICE MASTER KEY;
```

> **EXAMPLE 3.4**
>
> Adding encryption of the Database Master Key via the Service Master Key.
>
> Because the Database Master Key is encrypted by a password and the Service Master Key if the database is restored to another SQL Server instance which would by default have a different Service Master Key, the Database Master Key cannot be opened without having the password and manually opening the Database Master Key. In this case the Database Master Key would need to be regenerated for the new Service Master Key by first opening the Database Master Key, then removing the Service Master Key, then adding the new Service Master Key as shown in Example 3.5.

```
OPEN MASTER KEY DECRYPTION BY PASSWORD = 'MyPassword';

GO

ALTER MASTER KEY DROP ENCRYPTION BY SERVICE MASTER KEY;

GO

ALTER MASTER KEY ADD ENCRYPTION BY SERVICE MASTER KEY;

GO
```

EXAMPLE 3.5

Changing the Database Master Key to use a new Service Master Key.

   Database Master Keys should be backed up when they are changed to ensure that the data can be recovered if the key is lost in the database. This is
done using the BACKUP MASTER KEY command that exports the Database Master Key to a separate file as shown in Example 3.6.

```
BACKUP MASTER KEY TO FILE = 'c:\backup\MyDatabaseMasterKey'

ENCRYPTION BY PASSWORD = 'DifferentPa33word!'
```

EXAMPLE 3.6

Backing up the Database Master Key.

   The password which is used to encrypt the backup of the Database Master
Key should be a different password from the password that secures the Database Master Key.

ENCRYPTION PASSWORD MANAGEMENT

The most important thing when encrypting data within a Microsoft SQL Server database is to properly manage the passwords, certificates, and any other identifier that
is used to secure the data. Without these securables for the encrypted data, the data is
lost and the application is useless.

   This presents a massive amount of risk, but this is a risk that we can manage by
properly securing the passwords and the backups for these keys. The most important step is to backup these keys when they are changed. The backups of these keys
should then be stored offsite. In a perfect world the keys will be stored in a different

physical location than the backups of the encryption keys so that if the backups are compromised from the offsite backup location only the backups are compromised and not the encryption keys.

Copies of the passwords for the various keys must be kept onsite as well as offsite. The passwords need to be stored in a secure location which is easy to access when needed, but not too easy to access. A perfect location for these passwords, is not to have them stored on a server in the data center or server room. Instead print them on paper, or put them in a text file and burn them to two different CDs or DVDs. The paper or CD/DVD should then be placed into an envelope (a padded envelope if using disks). The envelope should be sealed, the seal signed, and a piece of shipping tape placed over the signature. The envelope should then be secured in an executive's desk, or better yet a safe in someone's office (the Human Resources people usually have a safe in someone's office).

ENTERPRISE KEY MANAGEMENT

Enterprise Key Management (EKM) involves using a third-party platform to secure the database encryption keys. These keys are created and stored within the third-party platform and given to the SQL Server automatically when the SQL Server needs the key. There are a variety of Enterprise Key Management systems available on the market. Some are easy to setup, others are hard to setup. Some are physical appliances within the data center, others are software packages that can run within a VM either in your data center or in the Cloud.

One of these platforms that is available for all situations is the Alliance Key Manager from Townsend Security. This Enterprise Key Manager comes as a physical appliance that you can deploy as a single unit or as a highly available solution. It is also available as a virtual appliance which you can deploy to either Microsoft's Hyper-V or VMware's vSphere hypervisor platform. The virtual appliance is also easy to deploy to either Amazon's AWS cloud or to Microsoft's Azure cloud.

Enterprise Key Management systems give a more fine-grained control over the key creation process. This becomes very important in a lot of compliance situations. Enterprise Key Management solutions are built around the concept of dual control where one team setsup the key management system, while another uses the key management system to get a key and use that key. The team which manages the key management system that needs no access to the line of business system (Microsoft SQL Server in our case) and the database administrator needs no access to the key management system. This separation allows the data to stay secure because the team with the key can't access the data, and the team with access to the data can't access the keys. This also follows the concept of separation of duties. The dual control requirements also make it so that both the team that manage the keys and the team that uses the keys needs to be involved in order to create or change keys preventing any one person from being able to access data or prevent access to data by changing the keys.

Getting a Microsoft SQL Server instance setup to work with an Enterprise Key Management system is actually a pretty straightforward process. Before working with an Enterprise Key Management system ensure that you are using a version and edition that supports Enterprise Key Management. Enterprise Key Management support was added to the Microsoft SQL Server product starting in SQL Server 2008 and in SQL Server 2008 through SQL Server 2014 has only been available in the Enterprise Edition of Microsoft SQL Server.

Before you can start within SQL Server the security team who managed the Enterprise Key Management needs to create the key, which will be used within SQL Server. How this is done will vary depending on your Enterprise Key Manager. Within the Townsend product you connect to the Enterprise Key Manager and they have a branch within their menu specifically for Microsoft SQL Server as shown in Figure 3.2.

After selecting the "Create EKM Key" option from the menu shown on the left of Figure 3.2 the security administrator needs to give the key a name. This key should be unique within the Enterprise Key Management environment. After naming the key the length of the key is then selected. Longer keys are more secure but require more CPU power to encrypt and decrypt the data while shorter keys require less CPU power but are less secure. Whenever possible use a longer key for better data protection. After the fields are filled out the administrator who manages our Enterprise Key Management server clicks submit to create the key. The key then needs to be activated by using the "Enable Key for EKM" option from the menu on the left shown in Figure 3.2. The key name is then given to the database administrator so that the database administrator can tell the SQL Server where the key is and how to access it.

Before the encryption key can be setup within the Microsoft SQL Server instance, the instance needs to be configured to allow for third-party encryption keys. This is done using the sp_configure stored procedure and turning on the "EKM provider enabled" setting as shown in Example 3.7.

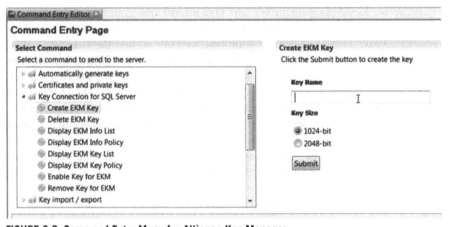

FIGURE 3.2 Command Entry Menu for Alliance Key Manager.

```
EXEC sp_configure 'show advanced', 1

GO

RECONFIGURE

GO

EXEC sp_configure 'EKM provider enabled', 1

GO

RECONFIGURE

GO
```

EXAMPLE 3.7

Configuring SQL Server to use an Enterprise Key Management Server.

Once the EKM provider setting is enabled the Enterprise Key Manager will have instructions on how to connect SQL Server to their specific EKM configuration. This will be done by taking a DLL provided by the EKM provider and placing that DLL on the SQL Server's hard drive. This DLL is then registered with the SQL Server using the CREATE CRYPTOGRAPHIC PROVIDER statement as shown in Example 3.8.

```
CREATE CRYPTOGRAPHIC PROVIDER My_EKM

FROM FILE = 'C:\SomeWhere\My_EKM_Providers_File.dll';

GO
```

EXAMPLE 3.8

Setting up an Enterprise Key Manager within a Microsoft SQL Server instance.

Once the SQL Server instance has been configured to use the Enterprise Key Manager, objects can be created using the keys within the Enterprise Key Manager. To create an asymmetric key using the key within the Enterprise Key Manager using the CREATE ASYMMETRIC Key statement as shown in Example 3.9. The name of the PROVIDER is the name created in Example 3.8 and the name of the PROVIDER_KEY_NAME is the name created by the administrator who manages the Enterprise Key Manager.

```
CREATE ASYMMETRIC KEY My_Key

FROM PROVIDER [My_EKM]

WITH PROVIDER_KEY_NAME = '<key_name>',

CREATION_DISPOSITION = OPEN_EXISTING;
```

EXAMPLE 3.9

Creating an asymmetric key using an Enterprise Key Manager.

The database which is the key which is created in Example 3.9 will depend on what you are using it for. If the key will be used for Transparent Data Encryption then the key must be created within the master database. If the key will be used for row level data encryption using functions such as SQL Server function EncryptByKey then the key should be created within the user database.

Once the asymmetric key is created it can be used just like any other asymmetric key. The key which is built using the Enterprise Key Manager does not store the key within Microsoft SQL Server. The key remains within the Enterprise Key Manager and is simply used by the SQL Server database engine as needed to encrypt and decrypt the data.

HIGH AVAILABILITY AND DISASTER RECOVERY FOR KEY MANAGEMENT

Our important applications have high availability and disaster recovery requirements. This means that our Enterprise Key Management solutions need to have the same high availability and disaster recovery requirements. Without having the Key Management Solution in place after a high availability or disaster recovery event there is no point in having the application online as without the key the application won't be available.

When using keys within SQL Server they will be failed over with the SQL Server instance. When using a third-party Enterprise Key Manager one that supports high availability within the data center as well as replication out to a unit or virtual machine at a second data center is a must as without the keys the application will be down even though the SQL Server service is up and running.

CONCLUSIONS

Key Management, and especially Enterprise Key Management, has typically been considered to be a complex solution to a complex problem. It doesn't have to be. Key management can be a straightforward process, provided that it's been done in a way that makes sense, is documented and the keys are backed up and securely stored in at least two sites both of which are properly secured.

Some Enterprise Key Management systems are more complex to setup than others, but much of this complexity comes around the job that they perform. Properly securing these systems is a complex problem, but like most complex problems when properly laid out and documented they don't have to be big complex and scary solutions.

Database Encryption

INFORMATION IN THIS CHAPTER:

- Database encryption
- Encrypting data within tables
- Encrypting data at rest
- Encrypting data on the wire
- Encrypting data with MPIO drivers
- Encrypting data via HBAs

This chapter talks about all the various ways of encryption and hashing data so that unauthorized users cannot access your data.

DATABASE ENCRYPTION

A key way to protect the data within your database is to use database encryption. However, no one encryption solution is correct for every database. The encryption requirements of your application will dictate which encryption solution you select. One thing to remember about database encryption is that the more data you encrypt and the stronger the encryption, the more CPU power will be required in order to encrypt and decrypt the data that is needed. So, be sure to balance the encryption requirements with the increased system load.

HASHING VERSUS ENCRYPTION

There are two techniques for protecting your data: hashing and encryption. Encryption is done using one of several different algorithms that give you a value that can be decrypted when using the correct decryption key. Each of the different encryption options provides you with a different strength of encryption. As you use a stronger level of encryption, you will be using more CPU load on the Microsoft SQL Server. Microsoft SQL Server only supports a subset of the available encryption algorithms; however, it does support some of the more popular algorithms, from weakest to strongest, which are DES, TRIPLE_DES, TRIPLE_DES_3KEY, RC2, RC4, RC4_128, DESX, AES_128, AES_192, and AES_256. The full list of available algorithms has not changed since Microsoft SQL Server 2005 and the newest version as of the writing of this book, which is Microsoft SQL Server 2014. The list gives you a variety of options that will provide an encryption option for just about everyone.

> **NOTE**
>
> **Algorithm Selection**
>
> Something to keep in mind when selecting the Data Encryption Standard (DES) algorithm is that the DES algorithm was incorrectly named when it was put into the product in Microsoft SQL Server 2005. Data that is encrypted with the DESX algorithm is not actually being encrypted with the DESX algorithm. The Microsoft SQL Server engine is actually using the TRIPLE DES algorithm with a 192-bit key. Eventually the DES algorithm within the Microsoft SQL Server engine will be removed, so future work using the DES algorithm should be avoided.

Triple DES

Triple DES or 3DES are the common names for the Triple Data Encryption Algorithm cipher. This cipher uses the Data Encryption Standard (DES) algorithm three times for each block of data that is to be encrypted. Triple DES actually uses three encryption operations to encrypt or decrypt the data three times for each 64-bit block of data that is to be encrypted or decrypted. The encryption and decryption processes can be expressed as shown in Example 4.1.

> **EXAMPLE 4.1**
>
> Expressions showing the encryption and decryption processes done using the 3DES algorithm. Processes marked with an E are encryption processes, while processes marked with a D are decryption processes.
>
> ```
> Encryption
> Encryptedvalue = Ek3(Dk2(Ek1(PlainValue)))
> Decryption
> PlainValue = Dk3(Ek2(Dk1(Encryptedvalue)))
> ```

As shown in the code block above, three keys are used, shown as k1, k2, and k3. Three keying options are used by the 3DES algorithm, which are defined by how many independent key bits are used. The strongest keying option has each of the three keys with different values of 56 bits, each giving a total of 168 bits represented within SQL Server as the TRIPLE_DES_3KEY algorithm or the DESX algorithm. The second keying option is a little weaker as keys k1 and k3 use the same key values and k2 uses a different value giving you 112 key bits, which is represented within SQL Server as the TRIPLE_DES algorithm. There is a weaker TRIPLE_DES algorithm, which is backwards compatible with the DES algorithm. In this case the TRIPLE_DES algorithm uses the same key values for all the possible keys.

RC Algorithms

Microsoft SQL Server supports two of the four common RC algorithms, RC2 and RC4. RC2 uses a 40-bit key size, making it a much weakened algorithm such as

RC4, which supports key sizes from 40 bits to 2048 bits depending on the needs of the application. In the case of Microsoft SQL Server, you can select from 40 bit and 128 bit configurations. There are some weaknesses in the RC4 algorithm, which have caused Microsoft to deprecate the RC4 algorithms in a future release of SQL Server. As such, new database applications should use another encryption algorithm. RC4 is probably the most widely used encryption algorithm, serving as the encryption algorithm that secures SSL (Secure Socket Layer) encryption for both SSH (Secure Shell) and HTTPS communications.

Advanced Encryption Standard

Three different sizes of cyphers can be used with Advanced Encryption Standard (AES) algorithm. These cyphers can be 128, 192, and 256 bits in size, which are represented by AES_128, AES_192, and AES_256, respectively, within Microsoft SQL Server. The variable key sizes are then used to combine data that are 128-bit blocks. Attackers have had some success in breaking the AES encryption algorithm when using the lower end AES encryption. To date, the higher end versions of AES have remained stable.

HASHING

Now on the flip side, you have hashing algorithms. Hashing algorithms provide you with a one-way technique that you can use to mask your data, with a minimal chance that someone could reverse the hashed value back to the original value. And with hashed techniques, every time you hash the original value you get the same hashed value. Microsoft SQL Server has supported the same hashing values from Microsoft SQL Server 2005 to Microsoft SQL Server 2008 R2. You can use MD2, MD4, MD5, SHA, or SHA1 to create hashes of your data. With the introduction of SQL Server 2012 the SHA2 hashing algorithm was added, which can be used as either a 256 bit of 512 bit hashing algorithm. There were no changed to hashing in SQL Server 2014. As long as you use the same hashing algorithm each time you hash a value, then you will always get the same hashed value back. For example, if you use the MD5 hash algorithm to hash the value "SampleValue," you will always give the value of "0x777E628ACB1D264A8CE4BC69427B3855" back.

Hashing is done, regardless of the algorithm used, via the HASHBYTES system function. The HASHBYTES function accepts two values: the algorithm to use and the value to get the hash for. The catch when using the HASHBYTES system function is that it does not support all data types that Microsoft SQL Server supports. The biggest problem with this lack of support is that the HASHBYTES function does not support character strings longer than 8000 bytes. When using ASCII strings with the CHAR or VARCHAR data types, the HASHBYTES system function will accept up to 8000 characters. When using Unicode strings with the NCHAR or NVARCHAR data types, the HASHBYTES system function will accept up to 4000 characters. When passing in binary data using the VARBINARY data type, the HASHBYTES function will accept up to 8000 bytes of binary data.

> **NOTE**
> **MD5 is Not Totally Secure**
> In 1996, collisions were first identified in hashed data against the MD5 algorithm causing the long-term usefulness of MD5 to be reduced. In 2005, researchers were able to create pairs of documents and X.509 certificates that, when hashed, produced the same hash value. Later that year the creator of MD5, Ron Rivest, wrote "MD5 and SHA1 are both clearly broken (in terms of collision-resistance)." Then in 2008, researchers announced that they were able to use MD5 and create a fake Certificate Authority certificate, which was created by RapidSSL and would allow them to create certificates for websites. Although these attacks do bring into question the long-term usability of the MD5 and SHA1 algorithms, these are the strongest hashing algorithms that Microsoft SQL Server supports natively. The other algorithms, which are weaker in nature than MD5 and SHA1, are considered to be severely compromised and should not be truly trusted to provide a hash which cannot be broken. In Microsoft SQL Server 2008, R2 MD5 and SHA1 are the most secure hashing algorithms that are available. However, in SQL Server 2012 Microsoft introduced the SHA2 hashing algorithm which is considered to be secure as of the writing of this book in the summer of 2014. The only way to support this more secure hashing algorithm in Microsoft SQL Server 2005 through 2008 R2 would be to use a .NET CLR assembly.

There are two ways that a hashed value can be used to find the original value. The first is rather simple: Simply create a database that stores all of the potential values. Then take the hashed value and compare it to the values in the database looking for matches. There are in fact websites such as http://tools.benramsey.com/md5/ that handle this lookup for you across several databases available on the Internet. The second attack method against MD5 is called a collision attack. A collision attack is when you find two different values that can be hashed to the same hash value, effectively allowing the check of the values to pass. Mathematically, you could express the attack as hash(value1) = hash(value2).

SHA2 and SQL Server
Starting with SQL Server 2012 Microsoft has introduced two new hashing algorithms. The first of the two is the SHA2_256 hashing algorithm and the second is the SHA2_512 hashing algorithm. The SHA2 hashing algorithm was written by the National Security Agency (NSA) and was published in 2001 by the National Institute of Standards and Technology (NIST) as a United States Federal Information Processing Standard. SHA2 while based on the older SHA1 hashing algorithm fixes the security issues which were identified by the SHA1 algorithm. As of this printing the SHA2 hashing function is still considered to be secure.

The first big difference between SHA2_256 and SHA2_512 is the amount of CPU power required when using the SHA_512 algorithm when compared to the SAH_256 algorithm. The second big difference between the SHA2_256 and SHA2_512 is the size of the hash which is returned. The SHA2_256 algorithm returns a 256 bit string (32 bytes) while the SHA2_512 algorithm returns a 512 bit string (64 bytes). Because of these size differences you must be sure that the table and variables which will be used with these values are large enough to hold the values.

> **NOTE**
> **Converting From MD5/SHA1 to SHA2**
> Besides having to increase the storage size of the column holding the data from 20 bytes to 32 or 64 bytes you also need to think about how to rehash the data in the table. If the data is stored in an encrypted form as well as a hashed form, then hashing with the new algorithm is pretty easy. Simply decrypt the data and hash it using the new algorithm. However, if the data is not stored in an encrypted form where you can decrypt it, then hash the decrypted value things will be a bit more complex.
>
> You will have a few options on how you want to do this. For the purposes of this example, we will use an authentication table with UserName varchar(255), Password varbinary(20)
>
> The first option would be to modify the table, adding a column which specifies which hashing function was used to store the hashed value as well as increasing the Password column with to 64 bytes. Then do the lookup on the UserName column looking to see if the username exists. If it does, look at the hashing function column and use the correct hashing function to then hash the value the user specified as the password comparing that value to the stored value.
>
> The second option would be to modify the password column from 20 to 64 bytes. Then change the password lookup to use something along the lines of WHERE UserName = @UserName AND Password IN (HASHBYTES("MD5," @Password), HASHBYTES("SHA2_256," @Password).
>
> Both of these techniques would allow you to store both values in the same password field without needing to rehash all the values in the column.

ENCRYPTING OBJECTS

Microsoft SQL Server allows database and application developers to encrypt the code behind specific objects to protect them from being viewed and modified by others. The objects which support encryption of the object are stored procedures and functions, including both table and scalar functions. Encryption of stored procedures and functions is done by adding the WITH ENCRYPTION statement within the header of the CREATE PROCEDURE or CREATE FUNCTION code as shown in Example 4.2.

> **EXAMPLE 4.2**
> Encrypting the code of a stored procedure.
>
> ```
> CREATE PROCEDURE MyStoredProcedure
> @Input1 as int
> WITH ENCRYPTION
> AS
> /*
> Normal code within the stored procedure goes here.
> */
> ```

Encrypting stored procedures and functions protects the code within the stored procedure from being changed by others who have db_owner access to the SQL Server database. The most common situation where stored procedures and functions are encrypted within a SQL Server database is when the application is going to be

> **NOTE**
>
> **Decryption of Encrypted Objects is Fast**
>
> The speed by which the third party applications can decrypt encrypted stored procedures and functions is pretty impressive. I have decrypted stored procedures at the rate of several thousand per minute without issue.
>
> One client I was doing some performance tuning work for had about 90% of the stored procedures in their database encrypted. This was the application which they wrote and had sent out to their clients to be installed on their clients servers. When I told them that the stored procedures needed to be decrypted so I can start gathering execution plans they told me that this was a problem because the developer who did all the SQL work was out on vacation and he had the only current copy of the stored procedures on his system. When I told my client that I could break the encryption pretty easily they were surprised as they assumed that the native SQL Server stored procedure encryption was as easy to break as it was.

deployed to a client's site, and the developer does not want the client to view or change the code behind the stored procedures. By encrypting the stored procedures and functions the customer is not able to modify the logic within the objects outside of the bounds of what the applications user interface supports.

By encrypting the stored procedures and functions the customer running the stored procedure may have problems troubleshooting performance problems on their server. Some of the side effects of encrypting the stored procedures include losing the ability to monitor for the SP:StmtStarting and SP:StmtCompleted SQL Profiler events. The person running the stored procedure or function also loses the ability to view the estimated or actual execution plan. When you query the sys.dm_exec_query_plan dynamic management function looking for the plan output the output which is returned is blank, and no plan is returned to the SQL Server Management Studio when a the execution plan is requested.

There are ways to get the code behind the encrypted stored procedures by connecting to the Dedicated Admin Connection then querying the system catalog. There are also third party applications available which can query for the encrypted values and then decrypt them. The encryption algorithm which is used by Microsoft to encrypt the code behind the stored procedures and functions was cracked many years ago allowing many third party vendors to create applications to handle this decryption for you.

ENCRYPTING DATA WITHIN TABLES

When it comes to encrypting data within your database table, there are a few different options. Where you encrypt the data within your application stack is just as important a question as is the technique you use to encrypt the data. Your choices for where to encrypt your data will typically be at the client side (in your fat client or within your web app) or within the database. Each option has pros and cons that have to be properly weighed before you make the decision.

When you handle the encryption within the database, you have the benefit of minimal to no changes to the front-end client (this assumes that you control all your database access via stored procedures). However, the downside here is that all the CPU load of the encryption is handled on the database server. Because all the encryption is handled on the database server, this can cause a bottleneck on the database server as the encryption and decryption of data will increase the CPU load of the database server. The other main disadvantage of encrypting the data with the SQL Server is that you have to store the decryption mechanism within the database. Granted the SQL Server will help mitigate these risks with object-level permissions and strong encryption of the certificates, but given enough time, any encryption scheme is crackable. The stronger the encryption that is used, the longer it would take an attacker to break the encryption with the strongest encryption levels, taking many years of CPU power to break the encryption.

On the other hand, you can handle all the encryption in the application tier (either the fat client or the web app). This gives you the benefit of spreading the entire encryption load across all the computers that run the application, but it gives you the downside of a load of application changes. Now while this does place a lot of extra work on the development team to implement these changes, the workload is spread across the application tier. When using a fat client on the user's desktop, this work is done on the client computer; when using a web application, this work is done on the web servers. In a web application environment, this increased CPU load on the web servers can be mitigated by adding more web servers to the web farm or by moving the encryption functions to another web farm that is only used to encrypt the data.

No matter where within your application you encrypt your data, and no matter what encryption technique you use your data storage requirements will typically increase by 10–20%. This is because encrypted data is larger due to the nature of encryption as well as any padding data that is put within the data. When planning for data encryption you also need to think about where in the application stack you want to encrypt the data, within the application, the web tier, the application server, or the database server. Adding encryption to the application will cause the CPU load within some part of the application to increase. Putting the encryption within the database server means that more and more powerful SQL Servers will be needed over time as more and more users are added to the system. Where if the encryption was done at the web or application server layer, scaling that workload out would be much easier and much less expensive.

ENCRYPTING WITHIN MICROSOFT SQL SERVER

When planning to encrypt data within Microsoft SQL Server, there is a clear dividing line that you have to keep in mind. Microsoft SQL Server 2000 or older does not include any usable techniques for encrypting functions natively. However, there are third party DLLs (Dynamic-Link Library), which can be used to encrypt and decrypt data. When using Microsoft SQL Server 2000 or older, the only hashing functions that you can use is pwdencrypt. It is highly recommended, however, that you not use

> **TIP**
>
> **Data Encryption Laws**
>
> Depending on where you live, where your company base is, and where your customers are located, you may have to deal with a variety of local, state, and federal (or national) laws that reference data protection. Most of these laws are very vague about how the data encryption needs to be implemented (which is considered to be a good thing by some), but some laws such as the state law in Massachusetts have some very serious consequences if your data is leaked. In the case of the law in Massachusetts, you will incur penalties if you have customer data that is not encrypted – even if the data is not breached and even if neither the company nor the data are within the borders of the state of Massachusetts. The Massachusetts state law is designed to protect the citizens of the state no matter where the company that the citizen does business with is located. Be sure to check with the laws in all the jurisdictions that you do business and in which your customers reside. Each state in the United States maintains a website that will have a list of all the available laws governing them. If you cannot locate the laws for your state, your company's legal department should be able to get a copy of these laws. When designing an encryption plan for company data, be sure to include the company's legal counsel in these planning meetings as the company's legal counsel will be the one responsible for defending the company in court in the event of a data breech or other legal action; as such, they should be involved in the planning phase.

this function, for the algorithms used by this function have changed from version to version of Microsoft SQL Server, and this function has been deprecated in the newer versions of Microsoft SQL Server. If you must use this undocumented system function, it accepts a single parameter and returns a varbinary (255) value (Example 4.3).

EXAMPLE 4.3

Showing how to use the undocumented system function pwdencrypt.

```
SELECT pwdencrypt('test')
```

Starting with Microsoft SQL Server 2005, you can use native hashing and encryption functions. When encrypting data within the Microsoft SQL Server, you can encrypt the data using one of three functions: EncryptByCert(), EncryptByKey(), and EncryptByPassPhrase().

When using the EncryptByCert() function, you are using a certificate that is created within the database in order to encrypt the data. Encrypting data with a certificate allows you to easily move the certificate from one platform to another or to use a certificate purchased from a third party such as VeriSign and GoDaddy.

When using the EncryptByKey() function, you use a symmetric key to encrypt the data. The symmetric key can be created using a password, a certificate, or another symmetric key. When you create the symmetric key, you specify the encryption algorithm that you want to use in order to encrypt the data.

When using the EncryptByPassPhrase() function, you specify a password when calling the EncryptByPassPhrase function. This passphrase is used to create a symmetric key, which is then used in the same manner as the EncryptByKey function is used.

As of the spring of 2014, none of the encryption functions shown in this section can be used with Microsoft Azure SQL Database. Microsoft Azure SQL Database does not support creating certificates, nor does it support using any of the encryption functions. The encryption functions will return an error saying that they are not supported in that version of SQL Server. The CREATE CERTIFICATE statement will return the same error message. All encryption would therefore need to be done within the web tier of your Microsoft Azure hosted application.

Encrypting Within the Application Tier

The most common (and usually the more scalable) place to encrypt data is within the application tier. Putting the encryption within the application tier probably requires the most changes to the application. However, it is the most scalable place to handle the encryption as the encryption workload is placed on all the web servers or the user's desktops (when using a fat client). The advantage of handling the decryption within the application tier is that the data is transmitted between the database server and the application tier in an encrypted form without having to configure and manage IP Sec within the network like it is when encrypting the data within the Microsoft SQL Server. These different techniques can be seen in Figure 4.1.

To encrypt data within your application tier, you will need to use the native encryption functions. For the purposes of this book all sample code will be written in VB.NET and C#. These same techniques can be used using other programing languages, but the syntaxes will be different.

Within .NET this is done using the System.IO.Cryptography namespace. The Cryptography namespace gives you access to a variety of hashing and encryption functions. The specific functions that are available to you will depend on the version of .NET framework that you are using; however, the basic technique will be the same no matter which hashing or encryption function you use. The sample code in Examples 4.4 and 4.5 shows how to use these encryption functions in C# and VB.Net, and in Examples 4.6 and 4.7 how to use the hashing functions in C# and VB.Net. The sample code shown in Examples 4.6 and 4.7 can be downloaded from http://www.securingsqlserver.com.

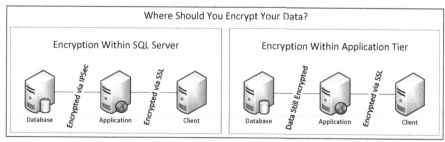

FIGURE 4.1 Where should you encrypt your data?

EXAMPLE 4.4

C# code showing how to encrypt and decrypt data within the application layer.

```
using System;
using System.IO;
using System.Security.Cryptography;
using System.Text;
namespace ConsoleApplication1
{
class Program
{
static void Main(string[] args)
{
Console.WriteLine(EncryptData("Test"));
Console.WriteLine (DecryptData(EncryptData("Test")));
Console.ReadLine();
}
static string EncryptData(string plainText)
{
//Setting the Passphrase, salting value, and vector which will be used to encrypt
the values.
These must be the same in your encryption and decryption functions.
string passPhrase = "YourStrongPassword!";
string SaltValue = "Your$altValue";
int passwordIterations = 2;
string initVector = "d83jd72hs0wk3ldf";
//Convert the text values into byte arrays
byte[] initVectorBytes = Encoding.ASCII.GetBytes(initVector);
byte[] saltValueBytes = Encoding.ASCII.GetBytes(SaltValue);
byte[] plainTextBytes = Encoding.UTF8.GetBytes(plainText);
//Create the password which will be used to encrypt the value based on the Passphrase,
salt value, SHA1 hash, and Password Iterations specified.
PasswordDeriveBytes password = new PasswordDeriveBytes(passPhrase, saltValueBytes,
"SHA1", passwordIterations);
//Create an array to hold the pseudo-random bytes for the encryption key.
byte[] keyBytes = password.GetBytes(32);
//Create an object to use for encryption.
RijndaelManaged symmetricKey = new RijndaelManaged();
//Set the encryption object for Ciopher Block Chaining.
symmetricKey.Mode = CipherMode.CBC;
//Generate the encryptor from the key bytes and the vector bytes.
ICryptoTransform encryptor = symmetricKey.CreateEncryptor(keyBytes, initVectorBytes);
//Create a memory stream object to hold the encrypted data.
MemoryStream memoryStream = new MemoryStream();
//Create cryptographic steam to do the encryption.
CryptoStream cryptoStream = new CryptoStream(memoryStream, encryptor,
CryptoStreamMode.Write);
//Begin the encryption.
cryptoStream.Write(plainTextBytes, 0, plainTextBytes.Length);
//Finish the encryption.
cryptoStream.FlushFinalBlock();
//Convert the encrypted value into a new byte array.
byte[] cipherTextBytes = memoryStream.ToArray();
//Close the streams.
memoryStream.Close();
cryptoStream.Close();
//Convert the encrypted value to a string value and return to the calling code.
return Convert.ToBase64String(cipherTextBytes);
}
static string DecryptData(string EncryptedValue)
{
```

EXAMPLE 4.5

VB.Net code showing how to encrypt and decrypt data within the application layer.

```
//Setting the Passphrase, salting value, and vector which will be used to encrypt
the values.
These must be the same in your encryption and decryption functions.
string passPhrase = "YourStrongPassword!";
string SaltValue = "Your$altValue";
int passwordIterations = 2;
string initVector = "d83jd72hs0wk3ldf";
//Convert the text values into byte arrays
byte[] initVectorBytes = Encoding.ASCII.GetBytes(initVector);
byte[] saltValueBytes = Encoding.ASCII.GetBytes(SaltValue);
byte[] cipherTextBytes = Convert.FromBase64String(EncryptedValue);
//Create the password which will be used to decrypt the value based on the Passphrase,
salt value, SHA1 hash, and Password Iterations specified.
PasswordDeriveBytes password = new PasswordDeriveBytes(passPhrase, saltValueBytes,
"SHA1", passwordIterations);
//Create an array to hold the pseudo-random bytes for the encryption key.
byte[] keyBytes = password.GetBytes(32);
//Create an object to use for encryption.
RijndaelManaged symmetricKey = new RijndaelManaged();
//Set the encryption object for Ciopher Block Chaining.
symmetricKey.Mode = CipherMode.CBC;
//Generate the decryptor from the key bytes and the vector bytes.
ICryptoTransform decryptor = symmetricKey.CreateDecryptor(keyBytes, initVectorBytes);
//Create a memory stream object to hold the decrypted data.
MemoryStream memoryStream = new MemoryStream(cipherTextBytes);
//Create cryptographic steam to do the decryption.
CryptoStream cryptoStream = new CryptoStream(memoryStream, decryptor,
CryptoStreamMode.Read);
//Create a byte array based on the size of the memorystream object
byte[] plainTextBytes = new byte[cipherTextBytes.Length];
//Decrypt the data
int decryptedByteCount = cryptoStream.Read(plainTextBytes, 0, plainTextBytes.Length);
//close the streams
memoryStream.Close();
cryptoStream.Close();
//Convert the decrypted value to a string value and return to the calling code
return Encoding.UTF8.GetString(plainTextBytes, 0, decryptedByteCount);
}
}
}
```

NOTE

What's Up With the Static Text in the Examples?

The sample code shown in Examples 4.4–4.7 is done using static text in order to show the concepts only. Using these examples with values from the database would simply be a matter of taking a value from the database or from the front-end application and placing it passing it into the correct function. This was not shown in order to keep the sample code shorter and simpler.

In the hashing examples a value from the application would simply be passed into the HashData function.

In the encryption examples a value from the database would be passed into the DecryptData function while the plain text value from the application would be passed into the EncryptData function.

EXAMPLE 4.6

C# code showing how to hash data within the application layer.

```
Imports System.Text
Imports System.Security.Cryptography
Imports System.IO
Module Module1
Sub Main()
Console.WriteLine(EncryptData("Test"))
Console.WriteLine (DecryptData(EncryptData("Test")))
Console.ReadLine()
End Sub
Function EncryptData(ByVal plainText As String)
'Setting the Passphrase, salting value, and vector which will be used to encrypt
the values.
These must be the same in your encryption and decryption functions.
Dim PassPhrase As String = "YourStrongPassword!"
Dim SaltValue As String = "Your$altValue"
Dim PasswordIterations As Integer = 2
Dim initVector = "d83jd72hs0wk3ldf"
'Convert the text values into byte arrays
Dim initVectorBytes() As Byte = Encoding.ASCII.GetBytes(initVector)
Dim SaltValueBytes() As Byte = Encoding.ASCII.GetBytes(saltValue)
Dim plainTextBytes() As Byte = Encoding.UTF8.GetBytes(plainText)
'Create the password which will be used to encrypt the value based on the Passphrase,
salt value, SHA1 hash, and Password Iterations specified.
Dim password As PasswordDeriveBytes = New PasswordDeriveBytes(PassPhrase,
SaltValueBytes, "SHA1", PasswordIterations)
'Create an array to hold the pseudo-random bytes for the encryption key.
Dim KeyBytes As Byte() = password.GetBytes(32)
'Create an object to use for encryption.
Dim SymmetricKey As RijndaelManaged = New RijndaelManaged()
'Set the encryption object for Ciopher Block Chaining.
SymmetricKey.Mode = CipherMode.CBC
'Generate the encryptor from the key bytes and the vector bytes.
Dim Encryptor As ICryptoTransform = SymmetricKey.CreateEncryptor(KeyBytes,
initVectorBytes)
'Create a memory stream object to hold the encrypted data.
Dim memoryStream As MemoryStream = New MemoryStream()
'Create cryptographic steam to do the encryption.
Dim CryptoStream As CryptoStream = New CryptoStream(memoryStream, Encryptor,
CryptoStreamMode.Write)
'Begin the encryption.
CryptoStream.Write(plainTextBytes, 0, plainTextBytes.Length)
'Finish the encryption.
CryptoStream.FlushFinalBlock()
'Convert the encrypted value into a new byte array.
Dim CipherTextBytes As Byte() = memoryStream.ToArray()
'Close the streams.
memoryStream.Close()
CryptoStream.Close()
'Convert the encrypted value to a string value and return to the calling code.
Return Convert.ToBase64String(CipherTextBytes)
End Function
Function DecryptData(ByVal EncryptedValue As String)
'Setting the Passphrase, salting value, and vector which will be used to encrypt
the values.
```

EXAMPLE 4.7

VB.Net code showing how to hash data within the application layer.

```
These must be the same in your encryption and decryption functions.
Dim PassPhrase As String = "YourStrongPassword!"
Dim SaltValue As String = "Your$altValue"
Dim PasswordIterations As Integer = 2
Dim initVector = "d83jd72hs0wk3ldf"
'Convert the text values into byte arrays
Dim initVectorBytes() As Byte = Encoding.ASCII.GetBytes(initVector)
Dim SaltValueBytes() As Byte = Encoding.ASCII.GetBytes(SaltValue)
Dim CipherTextBytes() As Byte = Convert.FromBase64String(EncryptedValue)
'Create the password which will be used to decrypt the value based on the Passphrase,
salt value, SHA1 hash, and Password Iterations specified.
Dim Password As PasswordDeriveBytes = New PasswordDeriveBytes(PassPhrase,
SaltValueBytes,
"SHA1", PasswordIterations)
'Create an array to hold the pseudo-random bytes for the encryption key.
Dim KeyBytes As Byte() = Password.GetBytes(32)
'Create an object to use for encryption.
Dim SymmetricKey As RijndaelManaged = New RijndaelManaged()
'Set the encryption object for Ciopher Block Chaining.
SymmetricKey.Mode = CipherMode.CBC
'Generate the decryptor from the key bytes and the vector bytes.
Dim Decrypter As ICryptoTransform = SymmetricKey.CreateDecryptor(KeyBytes,
initVectorBytes)
'Create a memory stream object to hold the decrypted data.
Dim memoryStream As MemoryStream = New MemoryStream(CipherTextBytes)
'Create cryptographic steam to do the decryption.
Dim CryptoStream As CryptoStream = New CryptoStream(memoryStream, Decrypter,
CryptoStreamMode.Read)
'Create a byte array based on the size of the memorystream object
Dim PlainTextBytes() As Byte = memoryStream.ToArray
'Decrypt the data
Dim decryptedByteCount As Integer = CryptoStream.Read(PlainTextBytes, 0,
PlainTextBytes.Length)
'close the streams
memoryStream.Close()
CryptoStream.Close()
'Convert the decrypted value to a string value and return to the calling code
Return Encoding.UTF8.GetString(PlainTextBytes, 0, decryptedByteCount)
End Function
End Module
```

MOVING FROM PLAIN TEXT TO ENCRYPTED VALUES IN AN EXISTING APPLICATION

In the perfect world we would only have to worry about encrypting data in new applications. However, in the real world we need to be able to take existing applications and change so that they support encryption without needing to completely replace the application. For small applications this can be done with a minimal outage to the application by encrypting the data in the tables within a single maintenance window. However, for applications which have huge amounts of data which needs

---

NAME

Downloading Source Code

The source code from this chapter as well as other resources can be found at http://securingsqlserver.com. This site will also have updated information and useful links that relate to this book.

---

to be encrypted this cannot be done within a single maintenance window. For these applications, the most complex part of the process becomes how to encrypt the data within the table so that the data which needs to be encrypted can be. In either case an application would need to be built to take the plain text values from the database, encrypt those values, then save the encrypted values to the database.

There are a variety of approaches which can be taken when designing the process which handles the data encryption. One method is to add an additional column to the table with the BIT data type called IsEncrypted, or something similar. It would then be recommended that an index be built on the table based on the primary key of the table, including the column to be encrypted, then a filter on the Index where the value of the IsEncrypted column is 0.

At this point the application should have its code modified so that if the value of the IsEncrypted column is 0 then the plain text value should be used. If the value of the IsEncrypted column is 1 then the encryption code should be used to encrypt and decrypt the value. The application should be configured so that if any value is updated in the table, weather it is encrypted when read from the table or not, the value is encrypted and the IsEncrypted column should be updated as well. In a nutshell we encrypt the table as the data is being used.

Once the production application code has been updated to read both encrypted and plain text data and to write encrypted data a separate application should be used to encrypt the plain text data from the table. The rows with the plain text data can be easily queried using the index which was created earlier in the process. Using this method, or a method like this, would allow tables with any number of rows, even into the billions or trillions, to be converted from plain text to encrypted data without any additional downtime to the application.

Once all the rows within the table have been encrypted the code which reads the IsEncrypted column as well as which returns the plain text value from the table can be removed. Once this code has been removed the IsEncrypted column can be removed from the database table and the data encryption project can be listed as completed.

ENCRYPTING DATA AT REST

Microsoft SQL Server 2008 introduced the Transparent Data Encryption feature of SQL Server. This feature allows the SQL Server to encrypt the data as it is written to the hard drive of the server, and the SQL Server decrypts the data as it is read from the hard drive into memory. The advantage of this system is that you are able to encrypt all data with no change to the data whatsoever. This feature also protects all your data when it is backed up as the backup is also encrypted. This encryption is done by encrypting the blocks of data instead of the data stored within the blocks. The difference between application level encryption and Transparent Data Encryption is that when the data is encrypted, only the data within the table is encrypted, while TDE will encrypt the metadata about the tables, the white space in the data pages, and so forth.

The downside to using Transparent Data Encryption is that if someone is able to access the SQL Server through normal means, or by using something like an SQL Injection, they will still be able to download the data from your SQL Server by simply querying the data.

Transparent Data Encryption will also increase the CPU load on the SQL Server because each data page being read from or written to the disk must be encrypted. On very high load systems this can turn into a great increase in CPU resources. Turning on Transparent Data Encryption is extremely easy, provided that you already have a master key within the database. From within SQL Server Management Studio simply right click on the database and select properties. Then select the options tab and scroll to the bottom of the option list. Locate the Encryption Enabled option and change it from False to True as shown in Figure 4.2 and click OK. This will enable

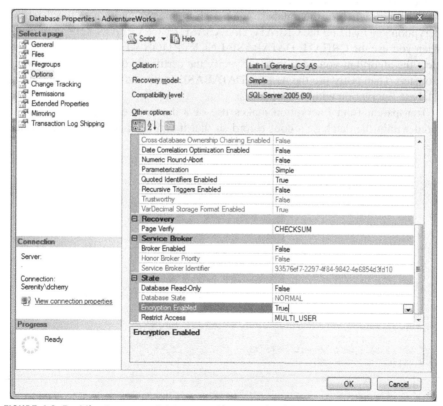

FIGURE 4.2 Enabling transparent data encryption on a database.

the Transparent Data Encryption setting for this database. If you do not have a master key created within the database the master key must be created using the CREATE MASTER KEY command before you can enable TDE. More information about the database master key can be found in Chapter 3 of this book.

When you enable Transparent Data Encryption as data is being written, the data within the page will be encrypted. As the SQL Server has free cycles available, it will read the unencrypted blocks from the disk, encrypt them, and then write the encrypted blocks to the disk. As data is written to the transaction log, it is also encrypted by the Transparent Data Encryption.

When you enable Transparent Database Encryption for any database within the instance, Transparent Database Encryption will also be enabled for the tempdb database for that instance. This will cause a performance impact to other databases within your instance that use the tempdb database for storing temporary data.

If you wish to enable Transparent Database Encryption with T-SQL, you will need to perform a few steps as shown in Figure 4.3. First, you will need to create a master key within the master database using the CREATE MASTER KEY command. Second, you will need to create a certificate within the master database using the CREATE CERTIFICATE command.

After this switch to the database, you wish to encrypt and create the database encryption key by using the CREATE DATABASE ENCRYPTION KEY command. When you use the CREATE DATABASE ENCRYPTION KEY command, you can select the algorithm you wish to use. Specify the certificate that you created in the prior step. Then lastly use the ALTER DATABASE command to enable Transparent Database Encryption within the database.

Transparent Data Encryption makes use of a database encryption key that is stored within the database's boot record so that it can be used for recovery when

```
SQLQuery1.sql - (l...nity\dcherry (53))*
    USE master;
    GO
    CREATE MASTER KEY ENCRYPTION BY PASSWORD = 'YourPasswOrdGoe$Here';
    go
    CREATE CERTIFICATE MyCertificate WITH SUBJECT = 'My TDE Certificate';
    go
    USE AdventureWorks;
    GO
    CREATE DATABASE ENCRYPTION KEY
    WITH ALGORITHM = AES_128
    ENCRYPTION BY SERVER CERTIFICATE MyCertificate;
    GO
    ALTER DATABASE AdventureWorks
    SET ENCRYPTION ON;
    GO
```

FIGURE 4.3 Enabling transparent data encryption on a database.

the database is first started. The database encryption key is a symmetric key, which is secured by a certificate stored in the master database of the instance. If you use a third party Enterprise Key Manager, such as the RSA Tokenization Server or the Cisco Key Management Center, then the database encryption key is an asymmetric key that is protected by the Enterprise Key Manager.

When you enable Transparent Data Encryption, you should be sure to backup the encryption keys immediately and store them securely. If you do not backup these keys and the database needs to be restored, you would not be able to read the backup because you will not have the key to the encrypted backup. If the key is downloaded by someone other than your company, that person would then be able to read your database backups, or attach the database to any server.

If you use database mirroring along with Transparent Data Encryption, then both the primary and the mirror will be encrypted. As the log data is moved between the instances, it will be encrypted for transport to preserve the security of the data within the transaction log as well as to protect the data from network sniffing.

If you use full-text indexing with Transparent Data Encryption, the data within the full text index will be encrypted by the Transparent Data Encryption process. This will not happen immediately, however. It is very possible that new data written to the full-text index could be written to the disk in an unencrypted form; therefore, Microsoft recommends not indexing sensitive data when using Transparent Data Encryption.

When using Transparent Data Encryption along with database backup encryption, you will notice a much lower amount of compression when you backup the database. This is because encrypted data cannot be compressed as the amount of unique data within the database greatly decreases when you compress the database.

If you replicate data from a database that has been encrypted by the Transparent Data Encryption, the replicated database will not be fully protected unless you enable Transparent Data Encryption on the subscriber and distributor as well as the publisher.

The big catch with Transparent Data Encryption is that it is an Enterprise Edition and up feature. This means that in SQL Server 2008, SQL Server 2012 and SQL Server 2014 the Enterprise Edition is required. With SQL Server 2008 R2 you can use either the Enterprise Edition or the Data Center Edition.

TDE AND FILESTREAM

If you use FILESTREAM within a database encrypted with Transparent Data Encryption, all data written via the FILESTREAM will not be encrypted. This is because the FILESTREAM data is not written to the actual database files. Only the data within the actual database files (mdf, ndf, ldf) is encrypted with TDE. The FILESTREAM files cannot be encrypted by the SQL Server engine because a user can access the FILESTREAM files directly via the Windows network share, so if the files that the FILESTREAM created were encrypted, the user would not be able to access the files. If you wanted to secure the data stored within the FILESTREAM, you would need to use a file system-based encryption process, as long as it is supported by the SQL Server Engine. The native Encrypting File Stream (EFS) encryption process that Windows 2000 and newer support is a supported encryption process for data stored by the SQL Server FILESTREAM.

LOG SHIPPING, DATABASE MIRRORING AND ALWAYSON AVAILABILITY GROUPS

In order for Transparent Data Encryption to be used on databases which are either logged shipped, Mirrored or protected by AlwaysOn Availability Groups requires that the encryption keys which are used by Transparent Data Encryption to first be restored to the destination server (I am using destination server to represent a log shipping target, Database Mirroring partner, or AlwaysOn partner). Without these encryption keys being first restored the destination server the destination instance would not be able process the initial database restore commands or will be able to process the transaction log entries.

In order for the destination database to be able to restore the backups of the TDE encrypted database the certificate from the master database which the database encryption key is created off of must be manually backed up and restored to the master database of the destination server. When performing this operation be very careful who has access to this backup of the certificate as anyone with the certificate can take your database backup and restore it to their server. Backing up the certificate requires the use of the BACKUP CERTIFICATE statement as shown in Example 4.8 which backs up the certificate named "TDE_Cert."

EXAMPLE 4.8

Showing the use of the BACKUP CERTIFICATE statement.

```
using System;
using System.IO;
using System.Security.Cryptography;
using System.Text;
namespace ConsoleApplication1
{
class Program
{
static void Main(string[] args)
{
Console.WriteLine (HashData("Test")));
Console.ReadLine();
}
static string HashData(string plainText)
{
UnicodeEncoding UnicodeString = new UnicodeEncoding();
//Convert the string into a byte array
Byte[] PlainTextByte = UnicodeString.GetBytes(plainText);
//Initalize the MD5 provider
MD5CryptoServiceProvider MD5 = new MD5CryptoServiceProvider() ;
//Computer the hash and store it as a byte array
byte[] HashBytes = MD5.ComputeHash(PlainTextByte);
//Convert the byte array and return as a string value
return Convert.ToBase64String(HashBytes);
}
}
}
```

After the certificate has been backed up the certificate should be moved to the destination server and restored by using the CREATE CERTIFICATE statement as shown in Example 4.9.

Once the certificate has been restored, delete the certificate backup file from both servers so that the file cannot be recovered. At this point the database backups which has been protected by Transparent Data Encryption can be restored and either Log Shipping, Mirroring or Always On can be setup and configured.

KEY PROTECTION

Protecting the certificate which is used for Transparent Database Encryption is extremely important. Without known good copies of the certificate which are stored in a secure location, there is no way to ensure that the certificate used by Transparent Database Encryption can be recovered in the event of a system failure. Backups of this certificate should not be kept sitting on random locations or really anywhere on the network as anyone who is able to access the backup file on the network is able to

---

EXAMPLE 4.9

Creating a certificate from a certificate backup.

```
Imports System.Text
Imports System.Security.Cryptography
Imports System.IO
Module Module1
Sub Main()
Console.WriteLine(HashData("Test"))
Console.ReadLine()
End Sub
Function HashData(ByVal PlainText As String)
Dim UnicodeString As New UnicodeEncoding()
'Convert the string into a byte array
Dim PlainTextByte As Byte() = UnicodeString.GetBytes(PlainText)
'Initalize the MD5 provider
Dim MD5 As New MD5CryptoServiceProvider()
'Computer the hash and store it as a byte array
Dim HashedByte As Byte() = MD5.ComputeHash(PlainTextByte)
'Convert the byte array and return as a string value
Return Convert.ToBase64String(HashedByte)
End Function
End Module
```

---

take your Transparent Data Encryption protected database backups and restore them to their own server, which would then allow the unauthorized person access to all the data within your database; effectively making your encryption useless.

While you have to be very careful to control where the backups of these keys are, having backups in secure locations is very important. It is recommended that there be two copies of the backups of these keys at all times. Both should be burned to a CD or DVD and each disk placed in a sealed envelope, preferably with the signature of the person sealing the envelope over the seal (as a method of tampering detection). One of these disks should remain onsite, locked in someone's desk drawer or office safe. The head of HR usually has an office safe that stuff like this can be put in. The second copy should be sent offsite to either another company facility such as a remote office, again being placed in a locked drawer or wall safe or sent to an offsite backup storage facility like Iron Mountain where the disk will hopefully sit for ever never needing to be recalled.

ENCRYPTING DATA ON THE WIRE

If your worry is that someone will sniff the network traffic coming into and out of your SQL Server, then you will want to encrypt the data as it flows over the network between the SQL Server and the client computers. This is typically done by either enabling SSL for the SQL Server connection or using IP Sec to secure all network

---

> **NOTE**
>
> **My Preferred Offsite Storage Locations**
>
> Personally, I prefer not to send the disk with these keys to the offsite tape backup site. The reason that I do not is because this is where all the backups are stored. This is kind of like storing the keys to the liquor cabinet in an unlocked drawer of the liquor cabinet. If someone wanted access to your backups and they broke into the offsite tape storage site to get the backups and your keys are sitting right there then they have got everything they need. Your backup security solution has just failed. If, however, the tapes are stored at your offsite backup company and your keys are in another state (or country) then you are covered.
>
> If you opt to send the encryption keys to another country, however, where you have another office, be sure to check the security export restrictions for both countries. There are some countries which high encryption keys cannot be exported to, and doing so is a pretty big deal when it comes to the penalties.

---

communication (or a subset of the network communication) between the client computer (end users' computer, web server, application server, etc.) and the database engine.

The upside to using SSL is that you manage the connection encryption between the SQL Server and the clients from within the SQL Server. This encryption is also more limited as only the SQL Server traffic is encrypted, while with IP Sec you have the option to encrypt all or some of the network traffic between the SQL Server and the client computer. The advantage of IP Sec is that there are Network Cards that can offload the IP Sec work from the CPU of the SQL Server to a processor on the network card. These IP Sec network cards will require a different configuration than the one shown later in this chapter.

When using Microsoft SQL Server Reporting Services, encryption over the wire is very important between the end user and the SQL Server Reporting Services server. When encryption is not used, the user's username and password are passed in plain text from the client application (usually a web browser) to the server, and any data that is returned is also returned in plain text. If the reports that are being viewed contain confidential information, this information could be viewed by an unauthorized person if they were to intercept the data between the SQL Server Reporting Services server and the user's web browser. When SQL Reporting Services is being used within an internal company network, this can be done by using SSL (which will be discussed in Chapter 5 within the section titled "Reporting Services") or IP Sec (which is discussed later in this section of this chapter). If the SQL Server Reporting Services instance is accessed directly over the public Internet (or another untrusted network), then SSL should be used, as the IP Sec policies may not be in place on both sides of the connection.

SQL SERVER OVER SSL

Before you can configure SQL Server over SSL, you will need to acquire an SSL certificate from a trusted Certificate Authority. If you have an internal Enterprise Certificate

Authority, you can get one from there; if not you will want to get one from a recognized Certificate Authority such as Verisign or GoDaddy, among others. After you have acquired the certificate, you will need to import it into the SQL Server. If you are using an SQL Server Cluster, then you will need to export the certificate from the server that you first requested the certificate be created for, and to import it into the other servers in the cluster. When you request the certificate, you will need to specify the name that your users will connect to the SQL Server as the subject of the certificate.

Microsoft SQL Server has some rather specific requirements when it comes to the certificate. The certificate must be stored in either the local computer certificate store or the current user certificate store (when logged in as the account that runs the SQL Server). The certificate must be valid when the valid from and valid to values are compared against the local system time. The certificate must be a server authentication certificate that requires the Enhanced Key Usage property of the certificate to specify Server Authentication (1.3.6.1.5.5.7.3.1). The certificate must also be created using the KeySpec option of AT_KEYEXCHANGE; optionally the key usage property will include key encipherment. SQL Server 2008 R2 and above support the use of wildcard certificates, while prior versions will require a specific name within the subject of the certificate.

Although you can use self-signed certificates to encrypt data connections between the client computers and the SQL Server, it is not recommended as this opens the server up to man-in-the-middle attacks where the user connects to another process; that process decrypts the connect and then forwards the connection along to the final destination while reading and processing all the traffic, exposing all your data you are attempting to protect to the third party process.

Before you can tell the SQL Server that you want to encrypt the connection, you need to request and install a certificate from your Certificate Authority. In the case of these examples, we will be using a local Enterprise Certificate Authority.

To request a certificate, open Microsoft Management Console (MMC) on your Windows 2008 R2 Server (other operating systems may have slightly different instructions than are shown here) by clicking Start > Run and typing MMC and clicking OK. This will open an empty MMC console. When the empty MMC console has opened, click on the File dropdown menu and select "Add/Remove Snap-in." From the list on the left select "Certificates" and click the Add button to move the snap-in to the right. You will then get the certificate snap-in properties, which asks if you want to manage certificates for your user account, a service account, or the computer account. Select the computer account and click next, then select the local computer and click Finish. Once you have closed the certificate snap-in properties wizard, click OK to close the Add or Remove snap-in page. At this point within the MMC console you should see the Certificates snap-in with a variety of folders beneath "Certificates (Local Computer)." Navigate to Personal > Certificates to view the list of certificates that are installed on the computer. By default there should not be any certificates listed here as shown in Figure 4.4.

To request a certificate from your Certificate Authority (CA), right click on Certificates (under Personal) and select "All Tasks" from the Context menu; then select

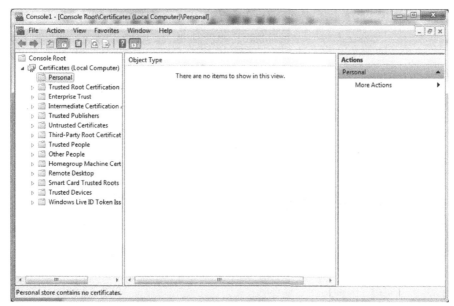

FIGURE 4.4 MMC with the certificates snap in showing no certificates installed.

"Request New Certificate." This will open the Certificate Enrollment wizard. Click next on the wizard to see the list of certificate templates. Check the box next to the "Computer" template and click the double down arrows next to Details on the right, then select properties. This will pull up the Certificate Properties window.

On the General tab set the friendly name to the DNS name of the SQL Server. In the case of our sample server, the domain name is ati.corp, and the server name is sql2008r2, so the friendly name is sql2008r2.ati.corp. On the subject tab, in the subject name section change the type dropdown to Common name and set the value to the same value as the friendly name, in this case sql2008r2.ati.corp. Click the add button to move the value to the column on the right, and then click OK. Back on the Certificate Enrollment page click the Enroll button to request the certificate. After the Certificate Enrollment window has closed, you should now see the certificate listed in the MMC console.

SQL Server 7 and 2000
In the older versions of Microsoft SQL Server, there is no User Interface (UI) to tell the SQL Server which certificate to use. By default the SQL Server will use the certificate that has the same name as the SQL Server. If you have multiple certificates or you wish to use a certificate that does not have the same name as the server, then you can force the SQL Server on which certificate to use by setting a registry key. This key can be found at HKEY_LOCAL_MACHINE\SOFTWARE\Microsoft\MSSQLServer\MSSQLServer\SuperSocketNetLib. Create a binary value called "Certificate" and place the thumbprint of the certificate as the value of the key.

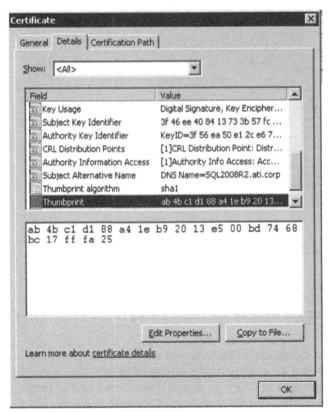

FIGURE 4.5 The thumbprint value of our sample certificate.

The thumbprint of the certificate can be found by viewing the certificate in the MMC console and looking at the Details tab as shown in Figure 4.5.

Configuring Microsoft SQL Server 2000 to use encryption is very easy to do. Open the SQL Server Network Utility by clicking on Start > Programs > Microsoft SQL Server, then Server Network Utility. When the Server Network Utility opens, simply select the instance you wish to configure and check the box that says "Force protocol encryption" as shown in Figure 4.5. Then click OK and restart the Microsoft SQL Server Services.

If the SQL Service does not start after making these changes, check the ER-RORLOG and application log. If the SQL Server cannot find the correct certificate, specify the certificate to use in the registry as shown above. The same applies if the SQL Service does start but you get messages back from the SQL Server saying that the name that you are connecting to does not match the certificate.

SQL Server 2005 and Up
After you have imported the certificate into the SQL Server open the SQL Server Configuration Manager by clicking Start > Programs > Microsoft SQL Server

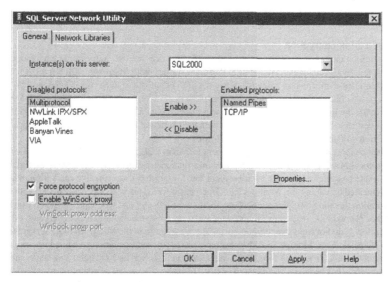

FIGURE 4.6 SQL Server Network Utility configured for encryption.

$200n$ > Configuration Tools. Expand the "SQL Server Network Configuration" menu (if you have installed the 32-bit build of SQL Server on a 64-bit server, then you will need to expand the "SQL Server Network Configuration (32-bit)" menu) and right click on "Protocols for {Instance Name}" and select properties. On the certificate tab select the certificate you wish to use to encrypt the network traffic. After selecting the certificate, switch back to the Flags tab. On the Flags tab you can force enable encryption or you can hide the instance. The screenshot shown in Figure 4.7 shows an instance configured to force encryption, while remaining visible to users on the network.

When you force encryption on an instance, the SQL Server will reject all connections that do not support encryption. If you do not force encryption, the SQL Server will accept both encrypted and non-encrypted connections, allowing you to set specific applications to use encryption via the applications connection string. This is done by putting the "FORCE ENCRYPTION = true" flag within the applications connection string. After you change the encryption settings you will need to restart the SQL Instance in order for the settings to take effect.

Certificate Strength Differences
The settings which were selected when creating the SSL certificate will determine the strength of the SSL protection of the data when sending it over the wire. If the certificate was purchased from a third party Certificate Authority (CA) such as Go-Daddy or Verisign then the certificate is most likely a 128 bit certificate, although older certificates could be as little as 64 bit certificates. If the certificate was created from an internal Certificate Authority (CA) then the encryption could be weaker than 64 bit or it could be much stronger than the 128 bit certificates.

> **NOTE**
>
> **Authentication Encryption**
>
> It is a common misconception that no network traffic between the SQL Server and client computer is encrypted. In all versions of Microsoft SQL Server starting with Microsoft SQL Server 2005, the authentication information passed between the SQL client and SQL Server is encrypted so that the passwords are protected when sent over the wire. For versions older than Microsoft SQL Server 2005, the username and password are sent in clear text. When using Microsoft SQL Server 2000, if you have Service Pack 3 installed on both the client and the server, then the authentication information will also be sent in an encrypted form.
>
> When connecting to versions of SQL Server older than SQL Server 2000 Service Pack 3 using Multiprotocol Net-Library, your authentication information is transmitted in an encrypted form. This is made possible because the Multiprotocol Net-Library has its own native encryption, which is implemented by calling the Windows RPC Encryption API. This is an independent encryption configuration that the SSL encryption talked about in this chapter and in Chapter 3. When using TCP/IP or Named Pipes to connect to the same instance, the authentication is not encrypted as these protocols do not support encryption using drivers older than the Microsoft SQL Server 2005 Native client. Because Multiprotocol Net-Library cannot be used to connect to named instances, no encryption of authentication information is supported on SQL Server 2000 named instances, unless SSL encryption has been configured on the named instance. This is not a problem for versions of Microsoft SQL Server 7.0 and older because these versions of Microsoft SQL Server do not support named instances.

FIGURE 4.7 Forcing Database Encryption for all connections to a SQL Server Instance.

The different in the protection comes from the length of the private key which is used to encrypt the data. The longer the private key is the more secure the data is, as it will take longer for an attacker to break the private key. This longer private key comes at a price, however, as it will require more CPU power to encrypt and decrypt the data using the longer private keys.

Selecting the right amount of protection in your key length is really a decision that management and the business need to make with technical guidance from the IT team. The reason for this is that it is the business unit whose data is being protected and they need to have a say in how secure the data is. If they insist on longest possible key for SSL encryption that is fine, as long as they understand that server upgrades will need to happen more frequently as the more load the system is placed under the harder the CPUs of the SQL Server will have to work in order to encrypt and decrypt this data.

An additional side effect of this longer encryption string is that the network will be used more by the SQL Server than it would before. Because the longer private key is used to encrypt the data as it goes out over the wire the data being transmitted over the wire will be larger than it was before. On the local LAN this probably would not be that big of a deal as the SQL Server probably has at least 1 1Gig uplink to the network and the network probably has multi-gig links between the switches. However, if you have remote users is a remote office this will this increase in network traffic will increase the amount of data flowing over the WAN link, and decrease its ability to handle more network traffic as the user base at the remote site increases. This will over time lead to increased costs of running the WAN links as they will need to be upgraded more often as well. The same goes for if there are users working from home connecting to the database on a regular basis. The more of them you add the faster the offices internet connection will become saturated faster, especially if these workers are VPNed in from home which will be taking the already encrypted traffic between the user and the SQL Server and encrypting it again for transport over the VPN.

NOTE

Picking the Right Tool for the Job

Knowing the various technologies in play throughout the enterprise is important to knowing when to encrypt data via SSL. If the security risk is people working from home that are using the application and we need to ensure that the data that they are accessing is protected, then setting up SSL encryption on the SQL server and requiring encryption for all users probably is not the best approach. It might be a better and more cost effective approach to require that those users VPN into the office and then launch the application which then connects to the SQL Server. This way all the data which is transmitted between the home user and the office network is encrypted between their home PC and the VPN endpoint. Once the data is within the office network and the network is considered secure maybe data encryption is not required at that point any more so SSL encryption might be overkill.

On the flip side the project at hand might have data which is so sensitive that the chance of anyone who is not supposed to view the data doing so must be avoided at all cost using SSL at the SQL Server and an encrypted VPN would be a reasonable approach. As would using IP Sec and a VPN. I guess the point that I am trying to drive home is that there are multiple way of doing things and having a good understanding of all of the available options will give you a much better long term solution.

Managing SSL Certificates

One of the downsides to configuring SSL over SQL Server is that you now have to manage the SSL certificate that the SQL Server clients use to connect to the SQL Server instance. This is because SQL Server certificates, and all SSL certificates, are created with specific start and end dates after which the certificate is no longer considered to be a valid certificate. Before this happens the certificate needs to be replaced with a new certificate.

If the certificate was purchased from a third party Certificate Authority (CA) then the new certificate will need to be purchased from either that CA or another CA (while you do not need to purchase the new certificate from the same CA that issued the first one it is usually easier to do so). If the certificate was issued from an internal Certificate Authority (CA) then the new certificate will probably need to be issued from the internal CA. In either case the process will be the same as getting a new certificate for the first time. Go through the same process which was described earlier in this chapter and then import the new certificate into the SQL Server.

Once the certificate is loaded into the OS then the SQL Server can be told to use the new certificate for connections. To do this, follow the instructions earlier in this chapter for either SQL Server 2000 and below and SQL Server 2005 and up. When you change the certificate that the SQL Server will use for SSL connectivity the SQL Server instance must be restarted in order for the SQL Server to begin using the new certificate.

The biggest reason for wanting to switch out to the new certificate before the old certificate has expired is to ensure that if there is a problem you have time to address the issue before the old certificate has expired. If you wait until the last day, and there is a problem importing the new certificate for some reason you will have a very short window to troubleshoot the issue.

NOTE

Your Certificate Authority may just go away

During late 2011 something happened which has not ever happened before. One of the major Certificate Authorities, named DigiNotar (a Dutch company), root key was compromised and the attacker was able to issue their own certificates for major sites like Google, Microsoft, Yahoo and the CIA to name just a couple. Unfortunately for the DigiNotar all of the major web browser developers (Microsoft, Mozilla, Google and Apple) quickly removed that Certificate Authority from the list of trusted Certificate Authorities that the browser would trust automatically. This caused users who went to websites that were secured by DigiNotar certificates to be prompted that the site may not be secure. Most of not all of the sites which were secured by DigiNotar's certificates promptly went and purchased new certificates from other Certificate Authorities. Because of this total lack of trust in DigiNotar the company files for bankruptcy, which was quickly approved by the courts with liquidation of the company's assets coming shortly after.

If your SQL Server certificates were issued by DigiNotar during all this your users could have started getting SSL warning messages every time they opened a connection to the SQL Server saying that the connection could not be trusted. This would cause one major headache for IT and the business until the problem was resolved.

HIDING THE INSTANCE

Microsoft SQL Server instance can be easily found by querying the network and using a specific feature within the SQL Server Native Client. When using the sqlcmd command line tool, this feature is exposed by using the -L switch, provided that the sqlcmd application is run from a client machine on the same IP subnet as the SQL Server instance. When using SQL Server Management Studio, this feature can be exposed by selecting the "<Browse for more…>" option from the Connection dialog box and selecting the "Network Servers" tab in the window that pops up. This feature can also be called via a custom .NET application. No matter which technique is used, the same result occurs, showing a list of all the SQL Server Instances that are available on the network.

It is possible to hide an instance of the database engine from reporting that it is there by changing the "Hide Instance" setting within the SQL Server Service's protocol properties, shown disabled (set to "no") in Figure 2.7. To hide the instance, change this setting from "no" to "yes" and restart the instance for the setting to take effect. After the setting is enabled and the instance has been restarted, the instance will not respond to queries by the Native drive querying for instance. Users will still be able to connect to the instance as before; however, they must know the name of the server name and the name of the instance, when not using the default instance.

IP SEC

IP Sec is the process by which all network communication between two computers is encrypted. IP Sec can be configured either on the local machine or on the domain via group policies. In the example local configuration will be shown, but the screens look very similar for a group policy configuration.

To configure IP Sec, open the Local Security Policy application by clicking on Start>Programs>Administrative Tools>Local Security Policy. Right click on the "IP Security Policies on Local Computer" option on the menu on the left and select "Create IP Security Policy." This will bring up the IP Security Policy Wizard.

On the first screen of the wizard, type a name and description of the policy. On the second screen you are asked to activate the default response rule. This default response rule tells the computer how to respond to requests for security when no other rule applies. The default response rule only applies when running against Windows Server 2003 and Windows XP. The third screen of the wizard asks you for the initial authentication method to use when negotiating the connection. You can select from Kerberos, a certificate from a CA, or a preshared key. If your SQL Server or any member of the communication is not a member of the domain (the SQL Server or web server is within a DMZ, for example), then you cannot select Kerberos as the Kerberos settings must come from a Windows domain. After this you have completed the wizard and the computer is configured for IP Sec communication. Once the wizard has been closed, you can see the rule listed in the list on the right-hand side of the window as shown in Figure 4.8.

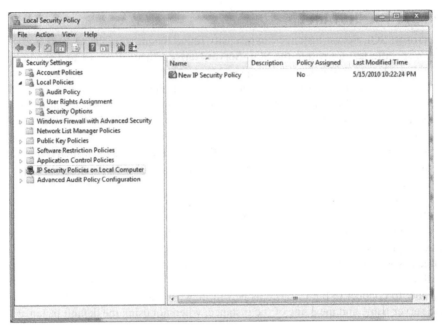

FIGURE 4.8 Local Security Policy with a newly created IP Sec Policy.

Once the blank policy has been created you need to tell the policy what IP Subnets this policy applies to and what it should do if it cannot set up a secure connection. To do this, right click on the policy and select "Properties" from the context menu. On the rules tab of the Policy Properties click the "Add" button to bring up the Security Rule Wizard. When the wizard opens, click next on the informational screen. The next screen of the wizard allows you to specify a tunnel endpoint. A tunnel endpoint allows you to specify a tunneling endpoint at the remote site, which will then pass the traffic unencrypted to the destination computer. For the purposes of this book, we will assume that you are not specifying a tunnel. After you click next you will be asked to specify the network type that this rule will apply to. Most people will want to select "All network connections" and click next. If you have the server configured as a VPN Endpoint or have dial-in via modem configured on this server (for a third party vendor to have access, for example) and if you do not want to encrypt these connections, you would then want to select the "Local area network (LAN)" option. If you only want to encrypt VPN or dial-in connections, you would select the "Remote access" option. The next screen shows the list of IP Address subnets to which this rule will apply. If this is the first rule you have created, the IP filter list will be empty; to add an entry, click the Add button, which will bring up the IP Filter List editor. When the IP Filter List editor opens, click the Add button, which will open another wizard. Click next on the information screen and enter a description if you would desire and unselect the Mirrored checkbox if desired and click next. On the next screen select

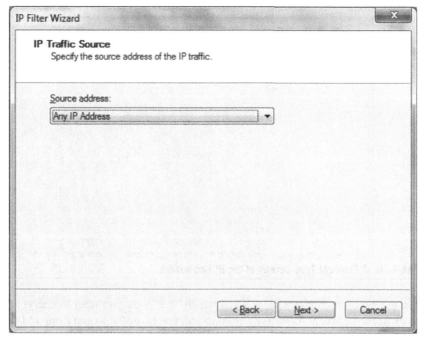

FIGURE 4.9 IP Traffic Source Screen of the IP Sec Policy wizard.

the source address you wish to use. The source address is the IP Address, which is the source of the connection. If you are trying to encrypt all traffic coming to this machine, select the "Any IP Address" option. If you are trying to encrypt all traffic from a specific subnet, then select the "A specific IP Address or Subnet" option and fill out the IP Address or subnet field with the correct information. For the purposes of this book we will assume you wish to encrypt all traffic to the server so you will have selected the "Any IP Address" option as shown in Figure 4.9.

After you have set the source address information and clicked the next button, you will be prompted for the destination address information. If you only want to encrypt the traffic to the SQL Server but not network traffic from the SQL Server to other machines, you will want to select the "My IP Address" option. If you want to encrypt access to and from the server, then select the "Any IP Address" option. As with the source address screen we looked at on the prior screen, this screen has several other options that can be used depending on your requirements. For the purposes of this book, we will assume that you have selected the "Any IP Address" option as you want to encrypt all network traffic in and out of the SQL Server. After setting your Destination IP Address information click next, which will allow you to configure which protocol should be encrypted. Assuming that you only wish to encrypt the connections to and from the SQL Server Service, select the TCP option from the protocol dropdown as shown in Figure 4.10 and then click Next.

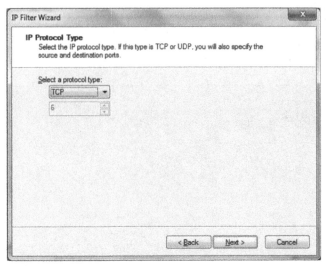

FIGURE 4.10 IP Protocol Type Screen of the IP Sec wizard.

On the next screen you will be asked which TCP ports you want to encrypt the network traffic between. As we only want to encrypt the traffic to and from a Microsoft SQL Server we select "From any port" and "To this port" and enter TCP port 1433 (or whichever TCP your SQL Server is configured for) in the text box under the "To this port" field as shown in Figure 4.11. Configuring the filter in this way will only encrypt the traffic to or from the SQL Server service. This will leave the

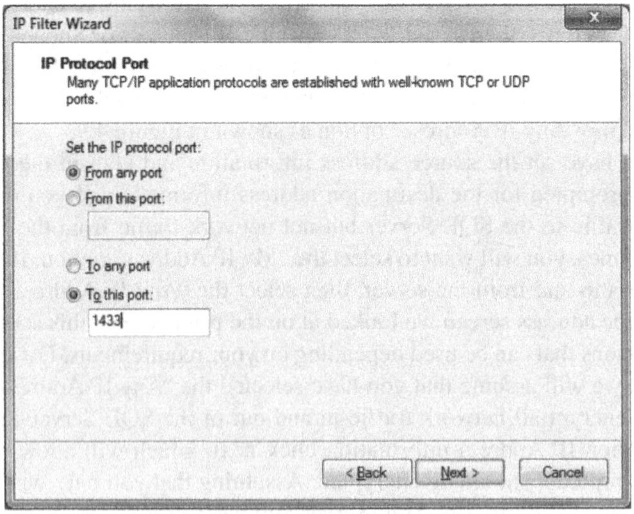

FIGURE 4.11 IP Protocol Port selection screen of the IP Sec wizard.

network traffic such as to and from Active Directory to be secured through the normal mechanisms and not through IP Sec.

After setting the TCP Port numbers, click next and then finish, which will complete the wizard. If you need to add additional connections to encrypt (such as if there are multiple SQL Server instances installed on the machine that you wish to encrypt traffic to), click the Add button again to run through the wizard and add additional configurations. Once you have completed all your IP Address filters to this filter list, click the OK button.

Back on the IP Filter List screen select the IP Filter List that you wish to apply to this IP Sec policy and click the Next button. The next screen in the wizard asks you for the filter action. By clicking Add you will tell the wizard how to handle the network traffic, what do you want to encrypt, what protocol should be used to encrypt the data, what traffic cannot be encrypted, and so on. After clicking on the Add button, click next on the first screen of the wizard to pass the information screen. On the next screen name your filter and provide a description, then click the next button. On the next screen you will be asked what to do with the network traffic: Permit it, Block it, or Negotiate Security. You will want to select the Negotiate Security option and click Next. On the next screen you can specify what to do with communications from computers that do not support IP Sec. The default is to not allow unsecured connections. If you change the option from the default to "Allow unsecured communication if a secure connection cannot be established," then users who do not have IP Sec configured correctly or that do not support IP Sec may put your SQL Servers data at risk. After making your selections click the next button.

On the next screen you are telling the policy what to do with the data. Three options are shown on this page of the wizard: "Integrity and encryption," "Integrity only," and "Custom." The "Custom" option allows you to select the algorithms that are used for the Integrity and Encryption options as well as how often new keys are generated. If you use Integrity only, then the information is validated upon transmission using the MD5 or SHA1 algorithms. What this means is that the data is hashed using the selected algorithm before it is transmitted. This hash is then transmitted along with the data, and the receiving computer hashes the data and compares the hashes. If they are different, the data has been modified in some way and is discarded. When you enable Encryption you can select from the DES or 3DES algorithms to decide what level of encryption should be used. This encryption setting is in addition to the Data Integrity option. When selecting the Data integrity and encryption option (from the customer editor), you can opt to disable the Integrity option if you prefer. You can also set the triggers, which will cause a new encryption key to be generated. You can trigger new key generation by either the amount of data that has been transferred, or based on the amount of time that the current key has been active, or both. Generally, accepted high security settings for IP Sec are shown in the screenshot in Figure 4.12.

If you have customized the settings, click the OK button. After setting the settings on the IP Traffic Security page, click the "Next" and then "Finish" buttons to close this wizard. This will take you back to the "Filter Action" page of the prior wizard. Select the "Filter Action" that you just created from the list and click "Next."

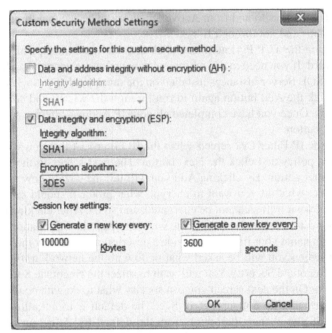

FIGURE 4.12 Generally accepted high security settings for IP Sec.

On the next screen select the initial security method for this rule. The default selection of Active Directory default should be the correct selection for most companies to use. If you prefer to use a certificate or preshared key, you can change the option here before clicking next. If your computer is not a member of a domain, you will need to select an option other than Active Directory as you cannot use Active Directory without both computers being a member of the same Active Directory forest. Complete the wizard using the "Next" and "Finish" buttons. Click OK to close the IP Sec policy properties window.

At this point the policy has been created, but it has not been assigned. To assign the policy, simply right click on the policy and select "Assign" from the context menu. This tells the computer that this policy is now active and should be followed. In order for IP Sec to encrypt the data between the SQL Server and the workstations, you will need to now create a corresponding policy on the workstations that need to connect to the SQL Server.

ENCRYPTING DATA WITH MPIO DRIVERS

Multipath Input Output (MPIO) drivers are only used when your SQL Server is connected to a Storage Array via either fiber channel or Internet Small Computer System Interface (commonly referred to as iSCSI). When you connect a server to a storage array, you typically do so over multiple cables (also called paths). This allows you

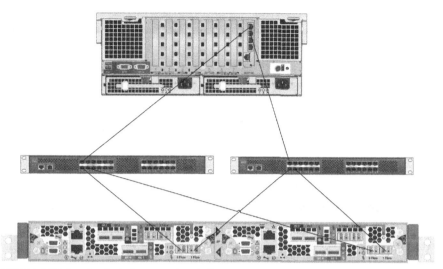

FIGURE 4.13 A redundant storage network diagram.

to connect the server to multiple controllers on the array and have multiple Host Bus Adapters (HBAs) on the server so that you have a redundant connection in the event of an HBA, cable, or Storage Controller failure. The most common way of making these connections is with two switches so that each HBA is connected to each storage controller. A sample diagram of these connections is shown in Figure 4.13.

Not all MPIO drivers are created equally. Some MPIO drivers, such as EMC's PowerPath include encryption features which allow the MPIO driver to encrypt and decrypt all the traffic between the server and the storage array. This is done by taking the write requests and encrypting the data portion of the write request (the data within the block, but leaving the block address unencrypted) so that when the data is written to the disk it is in an encrypted form. EMC was able to bundle this encryption into the PowerPath MPIO driver because of its purchase of RSA a few years ago.

FAQ

Options Besides PowerPath?

As of this writing in the spring of 2011, the only MPIO driver that can be used to encrypt data between the server and the storage array is EMC's PowerPath. You can use EMC's PowerPath even if you do not have an EMC Storage Array that you are connecting to. PowerPath supports a wide variety of other storage arrays such as IBM ESS, Hitachi, HP StorageWorks, and HPXP storage arrays. Other arrays maybe supported depending on the version of PowerPath you are looking to use. Check with an EMC reseller for more information as to if your array is supported by PowerPath. The array that you wish to connect to must be a supported array for EMC's PowerPath to manage the Logical Unit Numbers (LUNs) and allow you to configure the encryption. You can see this in Figure 4.14 where the PowerPath installer shows the various modules that can be installed so that the other storage array vendors' products can be installed.

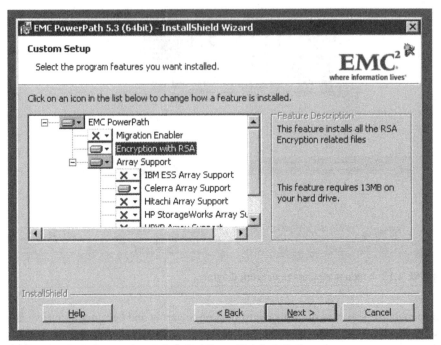

FIGURE 4.14 Updating an already installed PowerPath installation.

The upside to using this sort of technique is that everything gets written encrypted without any changes to any of your code, either in your stored procedures or in your application layer. The downside is that because this is a software package this means that the work to encrypt and decrypt the data has to be done by your SQL Server's CPU. So as the load on the SQL Server goes up, and the amount of IO being done by the SQL Server goes up, the amount of CPU power needed by the MPIO driver will also increase. The other downside to using your MPIO driver for encryption is that you now have to manage the certificate used by the MPIO driver for encryption. However, this certificate management is done through an Enterprise Key Management system such as RSA Key Manager (RKM).

POWERPATH ENCRYPTION WITH RSA REQUIREMENTS AND SETUP

The encrypting and decrypting of data with PowerPath is not as simple as installing the component and having it work. Using the PowerPath RSA Encryption requires installing and configuring some additional network components, including the RKM server software that is provided by RSA. Before you can begin configuring the system, you first need to request and install certificates from a certificate authority such as an internal Public Key Infrastructure (PKI). Both the server that will be encrypting the data using PowerPath and the server that will serve as the RKM server will need a certificate installed.

The certificates have some specific requirements that need to be met:

1. The certificate must be a password-protected PKCS#12 file, which contains the credentials that the PowerPath host uses. These credentials are the public key certificate and the associated private key that are used to secure the SSL communications.
2. The hosts are authenticated against the RKM server using a PEM (Privacy Enhanced Mail) encoded trusted root certificate.

After you have configured the RKM server and installed the needed certificates on the servers, the network administrator will need to configure a secure zone of the network for the servers that will be using PowerPath for encryption and the RKM server. A secure zone is a physical and logical area within a data center where all access to the devices within the zone is restricted. This restriction is implemented via a combination of user authentication and firewalls.

NOTE

Secure Zones are Ultra-secure

The Secure Zone within a company's network is going to be the most secured, isolated portion of the company network. This Secure Zone should be totally isolated using hardware firewalls preventing any unauthorized user from accessing the systems within it. General users would typically have no need to access the systems such as an Enterprise Key Management system, which would be housed within the secure zone. As users do not need access to this system, the firewall should be configured to block any request into the Secure Zone other than the specific systems that need access to these systems.

The access that machines would need between themselves and the RSA Key Manager server is very straightforward to set up. By default the RSA Key Manager is accessed via HTTPS on TCP port 443, although this TCP port number can be changed by the systems administrator during the setup of the RSA Key Manager system. The RSA Key Manger is accessed via a website, which is protected by standard SSL encryption.

Once the secure zone is configured, you can install the RKM server on a server within the secure zone of the network. Walking through the process of installing RKM is beyond the scope of this book, and it is assumed that the RKM server is already setup and in working order.

In order to configure PowerPath to do data Encryption and Decryption, you have to install a newer version of PowerPath. To use the Encryption, you will want to have the newest version of PowerPath. If you do not have access to the newest version, you will need to have PowerPath 5.2 or later. If when PowerPath was installed, the default options were used, then the Encryption with RSA option was not installed and it will need to be installed to be used.

To install the Encryption with RSA feature, launch the PowerPath installer on the server and click next on the information screen. The second screen will ask you if you wish to modify, repair, or uninstall PowerPath; select the modify option and click the next button. The next page shows the features to install. Enable the "Encryption with RSA" as shown in Figure 4.14 and click next. The next screen informs you that the installation is ready to continue; click the Install button on the screen to complete the installation. Once the installation has completed, you will be prompted to reboot the server.

If you have not net installed PowerPath, the installation will be very similar to the upgrade process, with two additional steps. During the installation you will be prompted for your PowerPath key as well as for the folder to which you wish to install PowerPath.

After you have installed the RSA encryption module, you can launch the RKM Client Configuration tool by clicking on the Start button, then the EMC Folder, and then the Configuration folder. This will launch a wizard that will assist you define the Key Manager Client configuration, initialize your encryption LockBox, and initialize the Key Manager Client for PowerPath Encryption on the server.

Before you can begin using PowerPath to encrypt your storage traffic, you need to tell the RKM how you wish to encrypt the data. You will want to start by creating a Key Class by logging into the RKM administration website and selecting the Key Class tab. If there is already a previously defined Key Class that you wish to use, then the process of creating a new class can be skipped; however, if you wish to use a class that is different from those that have already been created, you will need to create one. The Key Class stores the rules by which the keys that are generated for that key class must follow. This includes the algorithm, key size, and cipher mode, as well as the lifetime of the key.

Keys are controlled by Key Classes within the RKM. Optionally, these key classes can have the key specifications defined by a Crypto Policy (which is used by the Key Policy and is set when creating a new key policy later in this chapter). A crypto policy allows you to specify a fixed algorithm, key size, and cipher mode, as well as duration so that various classes have predefined values without having to set those values each time. To create a crypto policy, select the Create button on the Crypto Policy tab. Enter in the name of the Policy and set the values listed as shown in Figure 4.15.

To create a new key class, click on the Create button on the Key Classes tab that opens the first page of the five-page wizard as shown in Figure 2.16. On this first page you assign a name to the class, and assign the identity group that can use the Key Class. If the keys will expire, then you can check the box in the key duration option and optionally have the duration be controlled by a key class. This optional checkbox "Get Duration from a Crypto Policy" is shown in Figure 4.16 for reference only.

On the second page of the new Key Class wizard you will set the algorithm, key size, and mode of the cipher, as well as the duration of the key, and if the current key can be reused if needed or if a new key should always be created as shown in Figure 2.17. If on the first screen you did select that the duration should be gotten from the Crypto Policy, then the screen will look as shown in Figure 4.17. If you did not select this option, then this page will look as shown in Figure 4.18.

The next page of the wizard allows you to assign attributes to the key class, which is an optional step. The next page of the wizard allows you to assign specifications

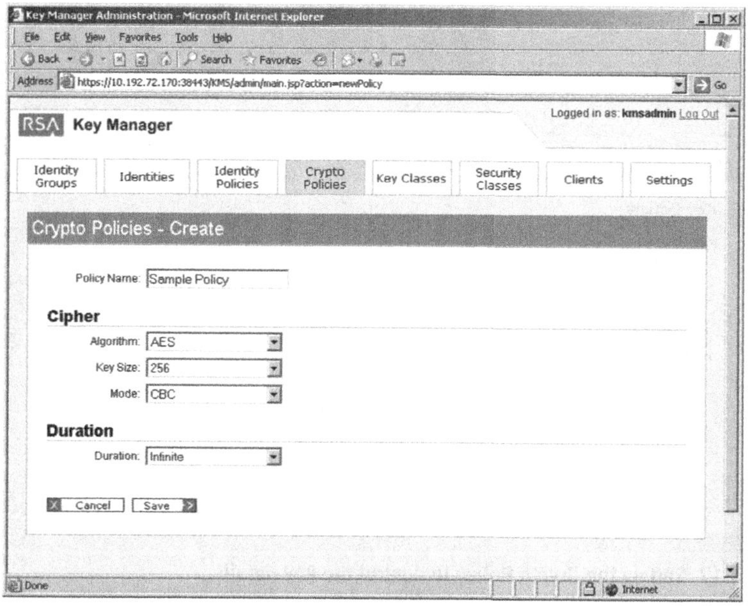

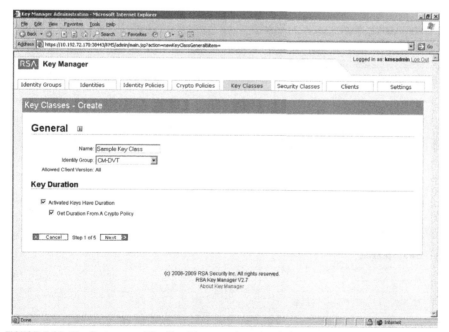

FIGURE 4.15 Creating a Crypto Policy in RKM's interface.

FIGURE 4.16 The first page of the Key Classes wizard setting the name and the identity group which can use the class.

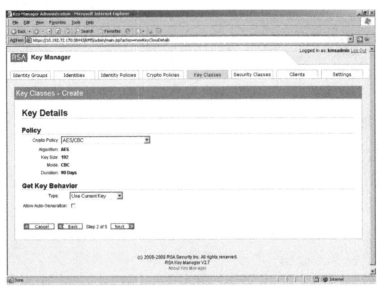

FIGURE 4.17 Setting the Crypto Policy to control the key details.

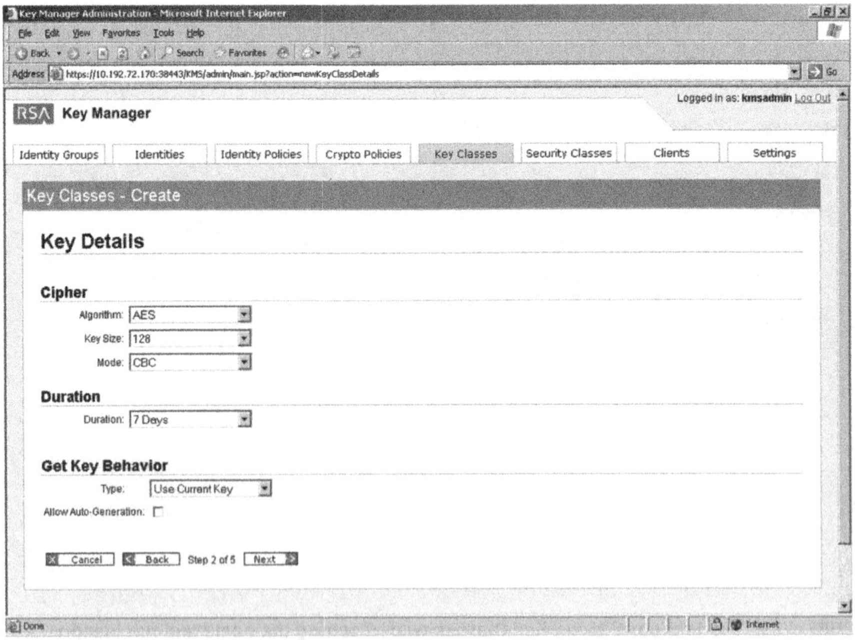

FIGURE 4.18 Setting the key details manually without the use of a Crypto Policy.

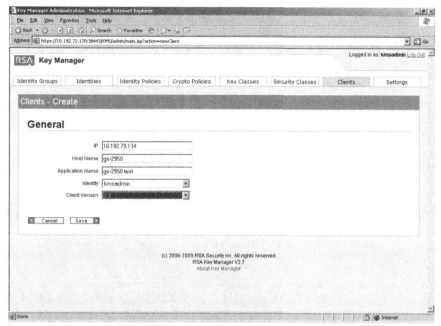

FIGURE 4.19 Showing the create client screen of the RKM.

to attributes, which is also an optional step. The last page of the wizard allows you to review all the various settings for the key class you are about to create.

After setting the key information into the system, you will need to configure the Key Management Server (KMS) to allow the client computer (in this case the SQL Server) to talk to it. This is done on the Clients tab of the RKM. After selecting the Clients tab, click the Create button and on the Create Clients page enter the IP Address, Hostname, and Application Name of the server. You will also want to select the identity of the user that the server will use to log into the RKM, as well as the version of the client software that will be used to talk to the RKM as shown in Figure 4.19. The client version that you select will depend on the version of the MPIO driver that you are using, so please check with your software vendor before selecting.

Once you have set up the needed resources within the RKM, you can configure the server's MPIO driver for encryption. On the server you will be using, open the RKM Client Configuration tool. This will allow you to configure the Key Manager Client, to initialize the LockBox for use, and then to initialize the Key Manager Client for PowerPath Encryption between the server and the storage array as shown in Figure 4.20. Once this has been done, Power Path will begin encrypting all the traffic between the server and the storage array so that when the data is written to the disk all the data will be written in an encrypted form.

To configure PowerPath open the RKM Client Configuration Wizard by clicking on Start > Programs > EMC > Configuration > RKM Client Configuration. This

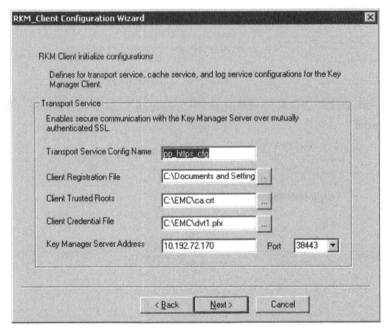

FIGURE 4.20 The first screen of the RSA configuration with EMC's PowerPath.

will bring up the wizard to configure PowerPath to talk to the RKM server. As part of the configuration you will need to supply the certificate and credential file to allow PowerPath to connect to the RKM Server. The Client Trusted Roots certificate and the Client Credential File will need to be exported from the RKM server by your systems administrator.

NOTE

The Names Have Been Changed to Protect the Innocent

The screenshots shown in Figures 2.20–2.23 can be changed to match your environment. The same goes with all the various network paths. The names and paths shown in these screenshots are simply the paths and names that are used in the lab where the screenshots were taken.

The next screen of the wizard will ask you for some information about the cache configuration for this server. The RSA client uses this cache to store keys locally after they have been downloaded from the RKM server. If you wish to enable logging of errors, warnings, and audit information to the system log, it is also configured on this page as shown in Figure 4.21.

The third screen of this wizard is the Client Registration Configuration screen. On this screen the registration state, polling intervals, and other registration settings are set as shown in Figure 4.22.

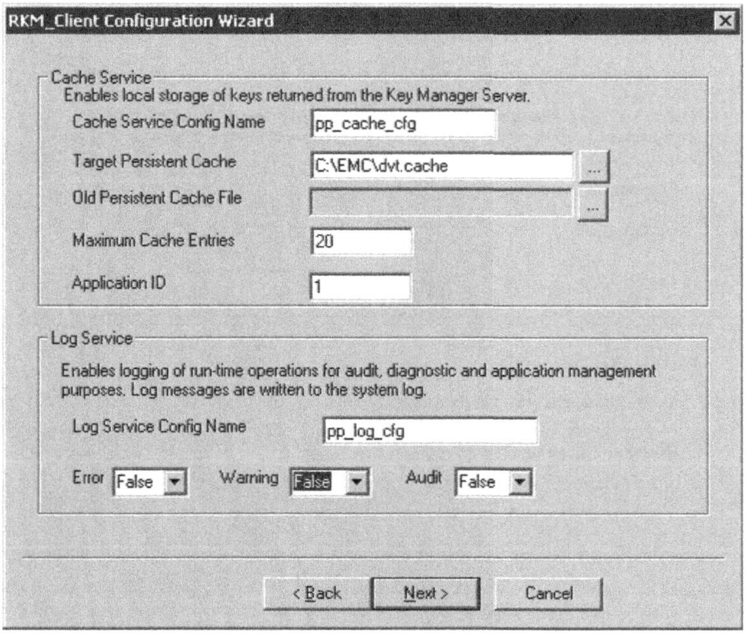

FIGURE 4.21 The cache and log configuration screen of the RKM setup for EMC's PowerPath.

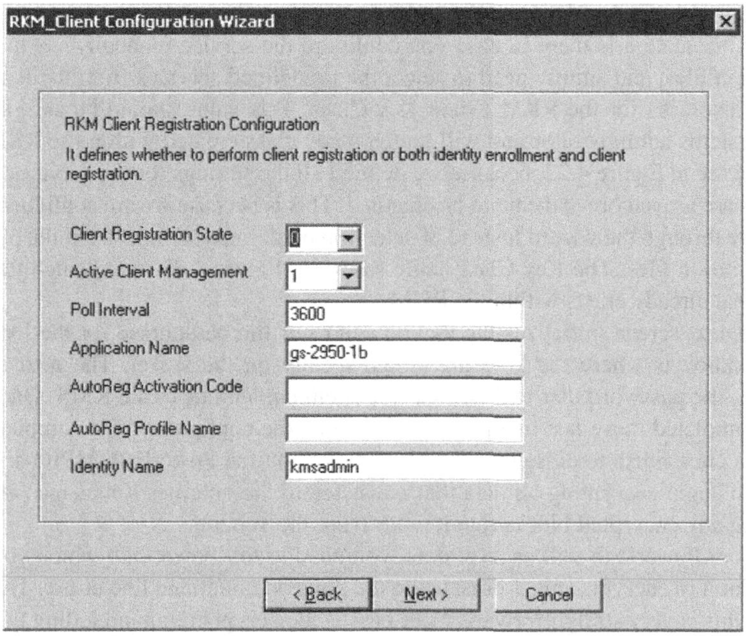

FIGURE 4.22 Screenshot showing the registration state, polling interval, and other registration settings.

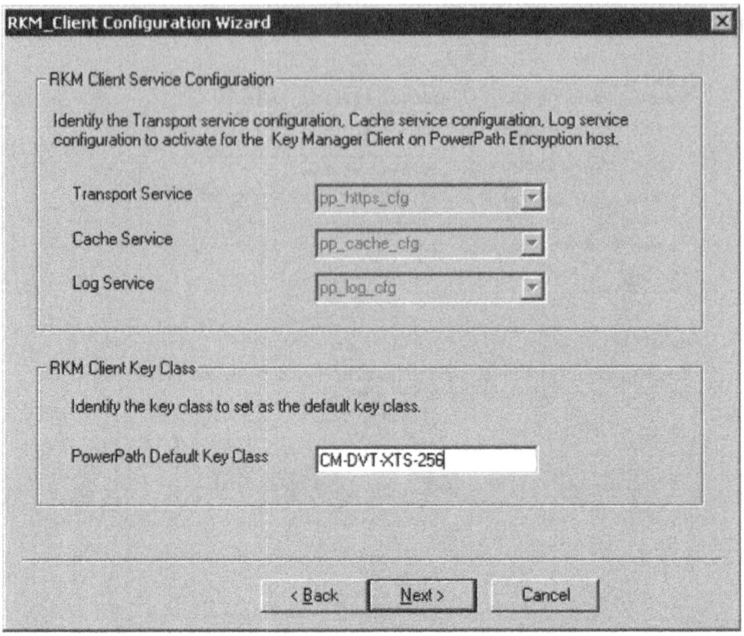

FIGURE 4.23 Assigning the default key class which will be used to encrypt the LUNs.

The fourth screen identifies the services based on the names you previously entered. This section is there in case you configure the service manually via the configuration files, and simply need to select the predefined services from the list. This screen also asks for the RKM Client Key Class. This value should be assigned by your systems administrator and will match a key class created within the RKM. As you can see in Figure 4.23, because we defined all the settings for the services, those options are grayed out and cannot be changed. This is because we are configuring the software through the wizard instead of selecting predefined settings from the prebuilt configuration files. The Key Class name shown in Figure 4.23 must match the Key Class that already exists within the RKM.

The next screen initializes the lockbox and sets the passphrase for the lockbox. The lockbox is where the keys are stored locally on the server. The next screen requests the password that will be used for client credentials to the KMS. Once you have completed these last two password screens, the configuration is complete and you can click finish to close the wizard. At this point the PowerPath MPIO driver is ready to begin encrypting all data that is written to the volumes it manages and decrypting any encrypted blocks that it reads from the volume.

Before PowerPath will encrypt data, you need to tell PowerPath which volumes you want it to encrypt. This is done using the powervt command line utility. The syntax for this is very straightforward. Your pass is the xcrypt command telling powervt that you want to manage encryption. You then use the –on switch to tell powervt that you want to enable encryption on a LUN (Logical Unit Number). The –dev parameter tells powervt you want to specify a device, and then specify the device name as shown in the Example 4.10.

EXAMPLE 4.10

Sample code showing how to enable encryption on device harddisk2.

```
powervt xcrypt - on - dev harddisk2
```

If you wish to view the status of a volume you also use the powervt command, this time switching the –on flag for the –info flag. This will return one of three return values. They are "encrypted," "encrypted with HBA assist," or "not encrypted." Not encrypted means that you have not encrypted the volume using PowerPath. A volume showing encrypted or encrypted with HBA assist means that the volume is being encrypted by PowerPath. Volumes that are encrypted with HBA assist are offloading the work of the encryption to the HBA, which is discussed later in this chapter.

FAQ

But Denny, My System is Very Complex and Some LUNs Need to be Encrypted with Different Levels of Encryption?

There is no easy way to do this, but it can be done. When working your way through the wizard within PowerPath enter the Key Class to encrypt the first set of LUNs with, and then use the powervt command to enable the encryption on those LUNs. After the encryption has been enEabled on those LUNs, find the rkm_keyclass.conf file (located in the "C:\Program Files\EMC\RSA\ Rkm_Client\config" directory by default) and open the file in notepad. Replace the value of the PowerPathDefaultKeyClass parameter with the name of the new Key Class that you want to use to encrypt the next set of LUNs. Repeat this process as needed until all your LUNs are encrypted with the correct Key Class.

If you use different Key Classes, you will need to document which Key Class is used for each LUN. As of the writing of this book in the spring of 2011, there is no way to query the system to find out which Key Class is being used to encrypt each LUN. PowerPath is able to do this because it writes some metadata to the front of the LUN where it stores which Key Class is used to encrypt that LUN; this is what allows you to encrypt different LUNs with different strengths of encryption.

ENCRYPTING DATA VIA HBAs

One of the newest ways to set up your encryption is to do the encryption via your HBA itself. This provides an interesting option for your encryption and decryption of data because all write and read requests are processed by the HBA so all the data stored on your disks is stored in an encrypted state (much like when you encrypt data via your MPIO driver). However, the workload of the actual data encryption and decryption is offloaded from the CPU of the SQL Server to the processors on the actual HBAs using a technique called HBA Assist.

Like everything else there is a potential downside to this. If you end up pushing so much IO through the HBA, you might overload the processor on the HBA, which would then slow down your IO requests that are queued by the HBA. However, if that were to become the case, you could simply add more HBAs to the server, giving you more processors to process the encryption and decryption of the data.

Another potential downside that you may see if encrypting data within the HBAs is that you are locked into a specific vendor's HBAs because, as of the spring of 2011, only one vendor can encrypt and decrypt data within the HBA, and that vendor is Emulex. Emulex currently supports only encryption and decryption of data when using the Emulex OneSecure adapters. This lock-in to a specific vendor maybe off-putting to some companies, but if you have already standardized on Emulex HBAs then this may not be a turnoff for you. If you need to replace the HBAs to HBAs that do not support encryption, the workload will then be pushed from the HBA back to the CPU of the server.

The Emulex OneSecure adapter encryption works with the PowerPath RSA Encryption configuration, so PowerPath will need to be configured to support encryption. The PowerPath encryption engine then hands off the Encryption work to the processor on the HBA instead of the CPU of the server being used to handle the encryption and decryption.

Setting up the encryption of the Emulex HBAs is incredibly easy. Once the encryption is configured through PowerPath, the HBAs will automatically begin encrypting the data. There is no configuration that must be managed or set up on the HBAs to begin the process. As you switch to the OneSecure HBAs, the output from the powervt command line utility will change from "encrypted" to "encrypted using HBA assist," which tells you that the HBAs are handling the encryption workload.

SUMMARY

Data encryption can be done at many, many different points in the application depending on the goal that you are trying to meet. Some of these configurations are more complex to configure, such as encryption using the PowerPath MPIO driver, than others, such as the Transparent Data Encryption. There is no single answer to the question "How should I encrypt my database?" because each database is different. This is why it is so important that there are so many options as to how you can encrypt your database. Each option will load on some part of the database-driven application; it just depends on which part of your database-driven application you want to put the additional CPU load on. You can select from the client computer, the middle tier, the database server's CPU, or the HBAs in the SQL Server as long as where you want to place the processor workload corresponds to the layer where you want to encrypt the data for the SQL Server database.

When using SQL Azure as your database instance, the encryption options are extremely limited as SQL Azure does not support most of the options described in this chapter. With SQL, Azure encryption can be handled within the application tier without issue. However, as of the spring of 2011, SQL Azure does not support any encryption within the SQL Azure database. SQL Azure does, however, support hashing using the same algorithms as the onsite SQL Server instances.

REFERENCES

Levy, S., 2002. Crypto: How the code rebels beat the government saving privacy in the digital age, 1st ed. Boston, Penguin (Non-Classics). Print.

Net-Library Encryption. *MSDN Microsoft development, subscriptions, resources, and more.* n.d. Web. August 22, 2010.

z/OS V1R9 Information Center – Beta "z/OS V1R9 Information Center – Beta." IBM Support and Downloads – United States. n.d. Web. October 21, 2010.

SQL Password Security

INFORMATION IN THIS CHAPTER:

- Login types
- SQL server password security
- Strong passwords
- Password change policies
- Renaming the "SA" account
- Disabeling the "SA" account
- Users versus logins
- Contained database users in SQL server 2012 and beyond
- Schemas
- Encrypting client connection strings
- Application roles
- Using windows domain policies to enforce password length
- Contained users

LOGIN TYPES

Any person or application which needs to get data from the SQL Server database engine needs to access the database engine via a login. SQL Server supports several different ways to authenticate against the database engine which include SQL Authentication logins, Windows Authentication Logins, Credentials, as well as Certificate Authentication options. Of these four options only SQL Authentication and Windows Authentication can be used by users and applications to gain access to the database engine. Credentials and Certificate Authentication are special purpose options which are explained in more details later in this chapter.

SQL AUTHENTICATION LOGIN

SQL Authentication Logins are logins which are defined within the SQL Server instance. With these logins the username and the password are both stored within the database engine. Logins within the database engine can be viewed by looking in the object explorer within SQL Server Management Studio or by querying the sys.server_principals system catalog view. No matter which method is used to view the login properties there is no way to view the password for the login. Passwords for SQL Server logins are stored as hashes which cannot be reverse engineered to get the original password. If the password for an account is lost and needs to be known the password for the account must be reset.

Creating logins is a very straightforward process when using either the object explorer within SQL Server Management Studio or when using T-SQL. When using the object explorer connect to the database instance and navigate to the instance, then the "Security" folder, then to the "Logins" folder. Right clicking on the "Logins" folder brings up the context menu which includes the "New Login" option. Selecting the "New Login" option from the context menu open the "New Login" dialog which allows you to create a new login as shown in Figure 5.1.

When creating a new Login the username goes into the "Login name" field. To create a SQL Server Authentication login change the radio button from the default of "Windows authentication" to "SQL Server authentication." The password should be placed into both the "Password" and "Confirm password" fields ensuring that the two values match.

By default in SQL Server only Windows Authentication is available. More can be read about enabling SQL Authentication later in this chapter.

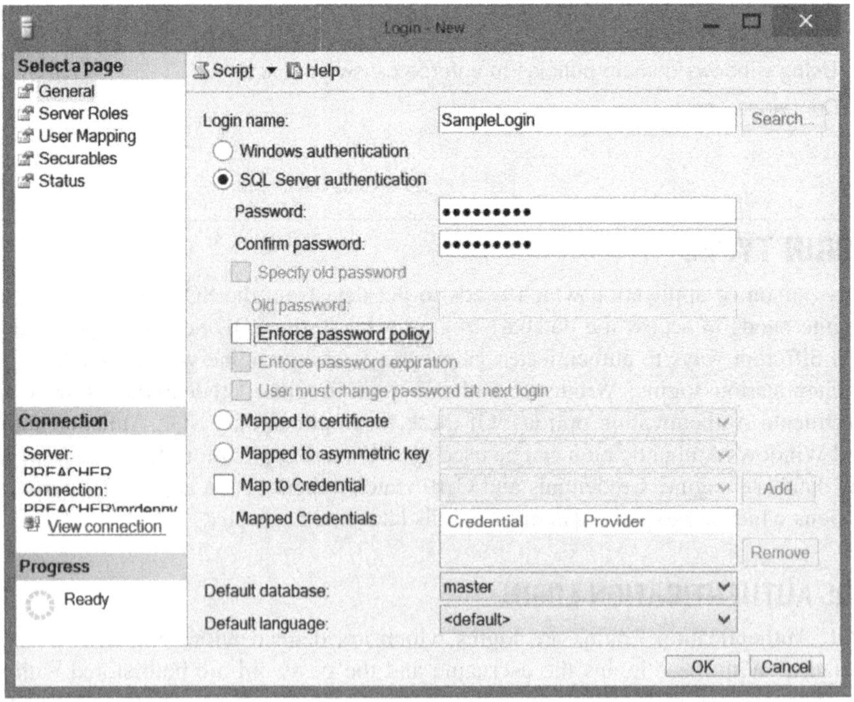

FIGURE 5.1 New login dialog from SQL Server Management Studio.

Table 5.1   Parameters Available When Creating a SQL Authentication Login

Parameter	Description
PASSWORD	Password which is used when logging into the SQL Server instance.
MUST_CHANGE	Specifies that the SQL Server will require that the password be changed the next time the login is used to log into the SQL Server instance.
DEFAULT_DATABASE	The default database parameter specifies which database the user should be connected to when logging into the SQL Server instance unless a database if specified within the applications connection string.
CHECK_EXPIRATION	Configures the password expiration checking for the login using domain password expiration policies.
CHECK_POLICY	Tells the SQL Server to check the domain's password policy when changing or setting the password.
DEFAULT_LANGUAGE	Specifies the language setting which the login should use when connecting to the SQL Server Instance.

Depending on the domain policies which should be enforced for this new login check or uncheck the two domain policy checkboxes. If you wish to force the user to change the password the next time the login is used then the two domain policies need to be checked. More can be read about the domain policy checkboxes later in this chapter.

SQL Authentication Logins can be created either using the SQL Server Management Studio User Interface as shown in Figure 5.1 of using T-SQL by using the CREATE LOGIN syntax. The CREATE LOGIN syntax accepts several parameters which all correspond to the options available in the User Interface shown in Figure 5.1. The most important parameter which is accepted is the PASSWORD parameter which sets the password for the new login. The other available parameters which are available are shown in Table 5.1.

Putting these parameters together is rather straightforward as shown in Example 5.1

EXAMPLE 5.1

Creating a SQL Authentication Login via T-SQL.

```
USE [master]
GO
CREATE LOGIN [SampleLogin]
WITH PASSWORD=N'test' MUST_CHANGE,
        DEFAULT_DATABASE=[master],
        CHECK_EXPIRATION=ON,
        CHECK_POLICY=ON
GO
```

WINDOWS AUTHENTICATION LOGIN

Windows Authentication Logins are SQL Accounts which are tied directly to a Windows account. The Windows account which the Windows Authentication Login is tied to can be either a domain account created within Active Directory, a domain group created within Active Directory, a local account created within the local Windows server, or a local group created within the local Windows server's operating system.

Creating a Windows login follows the same basic process as creating a SQL server Authentication login shown in the prior section of this chapter. When using the object explorer connect to the database instance and navigate to the instance, then the "Security" folder, then to the "Logins" folder. Right clicking on the "Logins" folder brings up the context menu which includes the "New Login" option. Selecting the "New Login" option from the context menu open the "New Login" dialog which allows you to create a new login as shown in Figure 5.1. When creating a new Login the username goes into the "Login name" field. To create a Windows authentication login leave the radio button as the default of "Windows authentication." The username should be entered using one of the two valid domain formats for usernames as either BACON\dcherry or dcherry@bacon.lab where BACON is the older Windows NT style of the domain name and bacon.lab is the DNS name for the domain and in either example "dcherry" is the username of the user. Either format is perfectly acceptable and neither works better than the other.

Like SQL authentication accounts, Windows authentication accounts can be created via SQL Server Management Studio's User Interface as shown in Figure 5.1 or T-SQL using the CREATE LOGIN statement. Only two parameters are used when creating Windows Authentication Logins which are the DEFUALT_DATABASE and DEFAULT_LANGUAGE parameters which are shown in Table 5.1. In the example shown in Example 5.2.

EXAMPLE 5.2

CREATE LOGIN statement which shows creating a Windows authentication login

```
CREATE LOGIN [BACON\dcherry]
        FROM WINDOWS
        WITH DEFAULT_DATABASE=[master],
        DEFAULT_LANGUAGE=[Español]
GO
```

DOMAIN ACCOUNTS

Domain accounts are accounts which are created within the Active Directory infrastructure. These accounts can be created within the Active Directory domain which the SQL Server belongs to, or in any Active Directory domain (or LDAP region)

which is trusted by the Active Directory domain which the SQL Server belongs to. More can be read about domain trusts in Chapter 6 in the side bar named "Domain Trusts."

Typically access is granted to SQL Servers via domain groups. This is done for a couple of different reasons. The first is to make granting access easier as access is granted to specific users by simply adding them into the domain group which grants them the access which they need. This makes it very easy for basic SQL Server access to be able to be managed by Help Desk teams or even self-service management applications which some companies use for granting access to resources which will assist with the separation of duties requirements which many companies have. The second reason for using domain groups is to keep the number of logins within the SQL Server to the minimum, which can sometimes be an audit finding for compliance auditors. This makes it much easier to audit the permissions within the SQL Server as they are typically very static at this point with only group membership changing as needed.

When creating Windows Authentication Logins an understanding of how domain groups works to ensure that users are able to access the SQL Server after. There are three different kinds of Windows domain groups which users can be a member of. These are:

- Domain Local
- Domain Global
- Universal

Each of these domain groups serves a different purpose within the domain infrastructure. For companies, which have a single Active Directory domain the majority of the domain groups will be Domain Local groups as this is the default.

When working in an environment which has multiple active directory domains using domain groups, becomes much more complex when users from one domain need access to resources within another active directory domain. This complexity comes from the fact that Domain Local groups can only contain users from within the same Active Directory domain that the domain group sits in. So if we had an Active Directory domain called BACON and that Active Directory domain had a domain group called BACON\DBAs which has a Domain Local group, that group could only contain resources (users, groups, computers, etc.) from within the BACON domain.

If our company which has the Active Directory domain called BACON purchased another company which had an Active Directory domain called STEAK and we wanted the DBAs from the STEAK domain to be able to be in the BACON\DBAs domain group we would not be able to add them, because the Domain Local domain group does not allow resources from another domain. In order to have a domain group with both the BACON and STEAK DBAs in a single group we would need to have a Global Group. The problem with the Global Group is that you cannot use Active Directory global groups to grant a user from another domain access to a SQL Server.

Understanding why this does not work requires understanding more about how Active Directory and SQL Authentication work. (The Windows Authentication process is fully documented later in this chapter in the section titled "SQL Server Password Security," you may want to review that section before continuing with this section.) A process within the domain controller called the KDC generates the Kerberos token when the user logs in to the domain. When this token is created is includes only the Domain Local and Universal domain groups.

This is because the Domain Global groups which the account belong in may be in other domains and it would be very expensive and time consuming to attempt to access all the other domains to see which Domain Global groups a user is a member of especially when accounting for the fact that there may be connectivity issues to the remote domain. Because of all the potential problems which getting the local of Domain Global groups Microsoft simply choose not to include the Domain Global groups in the Kerberos token. Because of this when a user logs in to the SQL Server if they are attempting to gain access via a Domain Global group the SQL Server will reject the connection request as the Domain Global groups are not in the token. SQL Server does not go out to the domain controllers to get a list of Domain Global groups for the same reason that the KDC service on the domain controller does not, it would be a very time consuming process with potentially slow network links, domain controllers which might be offline, etc. Because of this we are limited to only using Domain Local and Universal groups as they are listed within the users Kerberos token.

So the question becomes how to be get the users from the STEAK domain access to our BACON SQL Servers. Within the STEAK domain a Domain Local group should be created, in this case called STEAK\DBAs. The DBAs within the STEAK domain are then put into this domain group and this domain group is then added to the SQL Servers. This works because when the user from the STEAK domain attempts to connect to the BACON SQL Server the Kerberos token which was created when the user logged in contains the information for the STEAK\DBAs group, so when the token is handed to the BACON SQL Server the SQL Server verifies that the token is valid with the domain controller then matches the fact that the domain group STEAK\DBAs is listed as a Login within SQL Server and access is granted.

LOCAL ACCOUNTS

Local Windows accounts, which can be users or groups are a way to use Windows groups to grant access, but leave it within the control of the DBA without the DBA needing to have any enhanced permissions to Active Directory or any additional software installed on their workstations. The local Windows group is created within the operating system of the Windows server and domain or local Windows users are then placed within the local Windows group.

This works even though the local groups are not included in the Kerberos ticket because the SQL Server is able to ask its own operating system for a list of local groups that a user belongs to. The Windows operating system will respond very quickly to this request as everything is happening within the local server.

While local groups can be used, domain groups are a preferred solution. This is due to the fact that if the server fails the local group is lost when the server is rebuild. By using domain groups if the server fails the domain group membership is retained as the group membership lives in Active Directory and not on the SQL server's operating system.

CERTIFICATE AUTHENTICATION

Certificate Authentication in SQL Server is not quite as cool as it sounds unfortunately. There is no way from within SQL Server to issue a certificate and have the user use that certificate to authenticate against the SQL Server. The only way for a user to use a certificate to authenticate against the SQL Server is to use certificates to verify the user which is logging in is actually the correct user, typically by using a proxy card which is inserted into a card reader connected to the users workstation is by configuring Active Directory to support this sort of authentication and verification. This configuration is beyond the scope of this book, but is becoming more common in large organizations as it provides an additional layer of protection. When logging into the domain using a certificate the user is still granted access to the SQL Server via the Windows user account as shown in the prior section of this chapter.

Within SQL Server itself logins can be created which are tied to a specific certificate (you can see the certificate radio button in Figure 5.1). When this option is selected the login is not a SQL or Windows login so it cannot be used to log into the SQL Server. This type of login is mainly used to sign stored procedures and functions so that other users within the database can be granted rights to the stored procedures. More can be read about signing stored procedures and functions in Chapter 15.

To create a certificate login first create a certificate within the master database using the CREATE CERTIFICATE statement as shown in Example 5.3.

EXAMPLE 5.3

Example CREATE CERTIFICATE statement

```
CREATE CERTIFICATE SampleCert
WITH Subject='Sample Cert';
```

After the certificate is created you can create the login. When using the object explorer connect to the database instance and navigate to the instance, then the "Security" folder, then to the "Logins" folder. Right clicking on the "Logins" folder brings up the context menu which includes the "New Login" option. Selecting the "New Login" option from the context menu open the "New Login" dialog which allows you to create a new login as shown in Figure 5.1. When creating a new Login the username goes into the "Login name" field. Select the radio button toward the middle of the window which says "Mapped to certificate" and select the correct certificate to use for this login as shown in Figure 5.2.

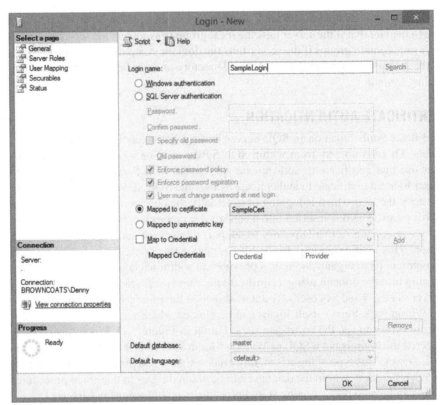

FIGURE 5.2 Creating a new login mapped to a certificate.

Logins which are mapped to certificates can be created using T-SQL as well as well as using the SQL Server Management Studio User Interface shown in Figure 5.2. Like the SQL authentication logins and Windows authentication logins the CREATE LOGIN statement is used to create Certificate mapped logins. The CREATE LOGIN statement does not accept any parameters when creating Certificate mapped logins as shown in Example 5.4 beyond the name of the certificate which the login is being mapped to.

EXAMPLE 5.4

CREATE Login example creating a Certificate mapped login.

```
USE [master]
GO
CREATE LOGIN [SampleLogin]
FROM CERTIFICATE [SampleCert]
GO
```

ASYMMETRIC KEY LOGIN

Logins can be created and mapped to Asymmetric Keys must like they can be mapped to certificates. Like the logins which are mapped to certificates, logins which are mapped to asymmetric keys cannot be used to connect to the SQL Server Instance and are instead used to sign stored procedures and functions.

When using the SQL Server Management Studio to create a login which is mapped to an asymmetric key being using the object explorer connect to the database instance and navigate to the instance, then the "Security" folder, then to the "Logins" folder. Right clicking on the "Logins" folder brings up the context menu which includes the "New Login" option. Selecting the "New Login" option from the context menu open the "New Login" dialog which allows you to create a new login as shown in Figure 5.1. When creating a new Login the username goes into the "Login name" field. Select the radio button towards the middle of the window which says "Mapped to asymmetric key" and select the correct certificate to use for this login as shown in Figure 5.1.

Like the other kinds of logins shown in this chapter logins which are mapped to an asymmetric key can be created via T-SQL as well. There are no parameters which are accepted beyond the name of the asymmetric key as shown in Example 5.5.

EXAMPLE 5.5

CREATE LOGIN command creating a login which is mapped to an asymmetric key.

```
USE [master]
GO
CREATE LOGIN [test]
FROM ASYMMETRIC KEY [SampleAsymmetricKey]
GO
```

CREDENTIALS

Credentials are a different kind of SQL Server object from a login, though credentials are mapped to a domain or local Windows user. With Windows Authentication logins we give the SQL Server the name of the user or group and the login is used to allow the user access to the SQL Server Instance. Credentials while also being bound to a Windows login are not used to grant access to the SQL Server Instance. Instead they are used to allow SQL Server Agent job steps to run under specific domain or local Windows logins (via proxies which are discussed later in this section of this chapter).

Creating a new credential can be done via the SQL Server Management Studio's User Interface or via T-SQL. To use SQL Server Management Studio's User Interface connect to the server in the object explorer. Navigate down the tree to the Security folder then the credentials folder. Right click on the credentials folder and select "New Credential" on the context menu.

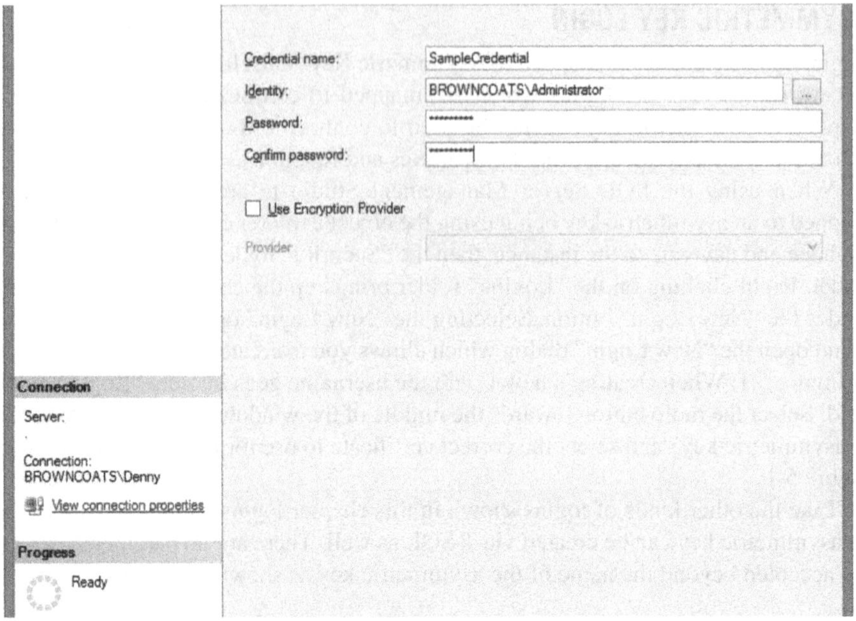

FIGURE 5.3 New credential window.

In the New Credential window there are 5 fields which can be filled out as shown in Figure 5.3. The first is the name of the credential which can be anything as long as it is a unique name within the instance. For simplicity it is recommended to name the credential the name as the Windows account which it is mapped to. In the Identity field the domain and username of the windows account should be specified. The next two fields are where the password for the domain account is put. The two passwords much match in order to create the credential. If you are using a hardware encryption provider which is configured within SQL Server you can check the "Use Encryption Provider" checkbox and select the provider from the dropdown menu (the checkbox is unchecked and the dropdown menu are grayed out in Figure 5.3).

Credentials can be created via T-SQL as well as via SQL Server Management Studio by using the CREATE CREDENTIAL command as shown in Example 5.6.

EXAMPLE 5.6

Sample CREATE CREDENTIAL command to create a new credential.

```
USE [master]
GO
CREATE CREDENTIAL [SampleCredential]
WITH IDENTITY = N'BROWNCOATS\Administrator',
      SECRET = N'DomainPassword!'
GO
```

In SQL Server 2014 Credentials are used to create a connection between the SQL Server Instance and the Microsoft Azure Blob Storage which allows on premise or SQL Server instances running within an Microsoft Azure Virtual Machine to backup to the Microsoft Azure Blog Storage. Creating a credential to the Microsoft Azure Blob Storage requires going to the Microsoft Azure Management Portal and getting your Azure storage name and Azure storage secret key. To create the credential place the Azure Storage Name in the Credential's username as shown in Figure 5.3 and Example 5.6 and the Azure Storage Secret Key in the Credential's password field shown in Figure 5.3 and Example 5.6. When connections are made between the SQL Server instance and the Microsoft Azure Blob Storage the credential's Azure Storage Name and the Azure Storage Secret Key are used to connect to the Microsoft Azure Blob Storage API.

SQL SERVER PASSWORD SECURITY

One of the key ways to protect your SQL Server is to use strong, secure passwords for your SQL Server login accounts. One of the biggest security holes in the SQL Server 2000 and older versions of Microsoft SQL Server was that the server installed with a blank system administrator (SA) password by default and would allow you to use a blank password, thereby permitting anyone to connect without much work at all.

Even with newer versions of Microsoft SQL Server, the SA account is still a potential weakness, as is any SQL Server Authentication based login. This is because SQL Accounts can be easily broken into by brute force password attacks. When using Microsoft Azure SQL SQL Database there is no SA account available to you the Microsoft customer work with. The SA account is reserved for the exclusive use of Microsoft.

When using Microsoft Azure SQL Database as your database instance, only SQL Authentication is available. As of the writing of this book in the Summer of 2014 Microsoft Azure SQL Database does not support Windows Authentication for use by Microsoft's customers as the Microsoft Azure SQL Database database server does not support being added to a company domain. The Azure database servers do support Windows Authentication buy only for use by the Azure administration team within Microsoft.

SQL Authentication Logins are more susceptible to these login attacks than a Windows Authentication login because of the way that these logins are processed. With a SQL Authentication login, each connection to the SQL database passes the actual username and password from the client computer to the SQL Server Engine. Because of this, an attacker can simply sit there passing usernames and passwords to the server until a connection is successfully made.

One of the big problems with modern password policies and the passwords which are generated from them is that the passwords which are generated become very easy for computers to figure out and they are very hard for people to remember.

For example if you require that your users use a password which has at least 8 characters with a number, character and upper- and lower-case characters the password will probably end up looking something like "P@ssw0rd" which fits the password policy but would not take a password cracking application long to figure out. However, if you teach your user to use a passphrase instead of a password, the users would be able to easily remember it and it would take months or years to guess the passphrase. A good passphrase to use would be something along the lines of "I like to have 4 really strong passwords!." This passphrase is very easy for the user to remember, would not take much longer to type in every day and will take forever to figure out with the password cracker. Even if the user never changes the password (personally I really hate password expiration policies) the password will easily stay secure for a very long time. Much longer than a password cracker application will be left running for.

With a Windows Authentication Login the process is much, much different from the SQL Authentication process. When the client requests a login using Windows Authentication, several components within the Windows Active Directory network are needed to complete the request. This includes the Kerberos Key Distribution Center (KDC) for when Kerberos is used for authentication, and the Windows Active Directory Domain Controller for when NTLM (NT LAN Manager) authentication is used. The Kerberos KDC runs on each domain controller within an Active Directory domain that has the Active Directory Domain Services (AD DS) role installed.

The process that occurs when a Windows Authentication connection is established is fairly straightforward once you know the components that are involved. When the client requests a connection, the SQL Server Native Client contacts the KDC and requests a Kerberos ticket for the Service Principal Name (SPN) of the Database Engine. If the request to the KDC fails, the SQL Server Native Client will then try the request for a ticket again using NTLM Authentication. This ticket will contain the Security Identifier (SID) of the Windows domain account, as well as the SIDs of the Windows groups that the domain account is a member of.

Once the SQL Server Native Client has received the ticket from the KDC, the ticket is passed to the SQL Server service. The SQL Server then verifies the ticket back against the Kerberos or NTLM server service on the domain controller to verify that the SID exists and is active, and was generated by the requesting computer. Once the Windows ID is confirmed against the domain, the SIDs for the local server groups that the user is a member of are added to the Kerberos ticket and the process within the SQL Server is started. If any of these checks fail, then the connection is rejected. The first thing that the SQL Server will verify is if there is a Windows Authenticated login that matches the user. If there is no specific Windows login, the SQL Server then checks to see if there is a Windows Domain Group or Windows Local Group to which the user belongs. The next check is to see if the login or domain group that has the login as a member is enabled and has been granted the right to connect. The next check is to ensure that the login or domain group has the right to connect to the specific endpoint. At this point the Windows Login has successfully connected to the SQL Server Instance. The next step in the process is to assign the Login ID of the Windows Login as well as any authorized domain groups. These login IDs are put together within an internal array within the SQL Server engine to be used by the last step of the authentication process as well as various processes as the user interacts with the objects within the SQL Server databases. The last step of the connection process takes the database name that was included within the connection string (or the login default database if no connection string database is specified) and checks if any of the login IDs contained with the internal array that was just created exist within the database as a user. If one of the login IDs exists within the database, then the login to the SQL Server is complete. If none of the login IDs exist within the database and the database has the guest user enabled, then the user will be connected with the permission of the guest user. If none of the login IDs exist within the database and the guest login is not enabled, then the connection is rejected with a default database specific error message.

EXTENDED PROTECTION

Extended Protection is a feature of the Windows operating system that was introduced with the release of Windows 2008 R2 and Windows 7. This new feature provides an additional level of pre-authentication protection for client-to-server communications when both the client and server software support it. As of the writing of this book, the only versions of the Microsoft SQL Server product that supports this new feature is Microsoft SQL Server 2008 R2 and higher. Patches are available from the website http://www.microsoft.com/technet/security/advisory/973811.mspx for the older Operating Systems. This new feature enhances the protection that already exists when authenticating domain credentials using Integrated Windows Authentication (IWA).

When Extended Protection is enabled, the authentication requests are both to the Service Principal Name (SPN) of the server which the client application is connecting to, as well as to the outer Transport Layer Security (TLS) channel within which the IWA takes place. Extended Protection is not a global configuration; each application that wishes to use Extended Protection must be updated to enable the use of Extended Protection.

If you are using Windows 7 and Windows Server 2008 R2 or later for both the client and server and if the SQL Server 2008 R2 Native Client or later are being used to connect to an SQL Server 2008 R2 SQL Server or later instance, and Extended Protection is enabled, then Extended Protection must also be negotiated before the Windows process can be completed. Extended Protection uses two techniques – service binding and channel binding – in order to help prevent against an authentication relay attack.

Service Binding is used to protect against luring attacks by requiring that as part of the connection process, the client sends a signed Service Principal Name (SPN) of the SQL Server service to which the client is attempting to connect. As part of the response, the server then validates that the SPN that was submitted by the client matches the one that the server actually connected to. If the SPNs do not match, then the connection attempt is refused.

> **NOTE**
> Authentication Relay Attack Details
>
> An authentication relay attack can take two different forms. The first, called a luring attack, refers to the situation where the client is tricked into connecting to an infected server passing its Windows authentication information to the attacked. The second is called a spoofing attack (or a man-in-the-middle attack) and refers to the situation where the client intends to connect to a valid service, but the connection is redirected to the attacker service via Domain Name Service (DNS) redirection or IP routing, and the spoofing server then captures the login information and passes the connection to the machine which the client is attempting to connect to.
>
> These Authentication Relay attacks allow the user to connect to the expected resource. However, the man in the attacking computer (the one to which the user's connection has been redirected) will then capture the username and password (or other authentication information) before passing the login information to the requesting computer. The attacking computer will then either store or forward the authentication information to the person who has set up the attack, allowing them to access the internal data with the authentication information that has been captured.

The service binding protection works against the luring attack as the luring attack works by having another service or application (such as Outlook, Windows Explorer, a .NET application, etc) connect to a separate valid compromised connection (such as a file server or Microsoft Exchange server). The attacking code then takes the captured signed SPN and attempts to pass it to the SQL server to authenticate. Because the SPNs do not match and the signed SPN is for another service, the connection to the SQL Server from the compromised server is rejected. Service binding requires a negligible one-time cost as the SPN signing happens only once when the connection is being made.

The channel binding protection works by creating a secure channel between the client and the SQL Server Instance. This is done by encrypting the connection using Transport Layer Security (TLS) encryption for all of the traffic within the session. The protection comes by the SQL Server Service verifying the authenticity of the client by comparing the client's channel binding token (CBT) with the CBT of the SQL Service. This channel binding protects the client from falling prey to both the luring and the spoofing attacks. However, the cost of this protection is much higher because of the TLS encryption, which must be maintained over the lifetime of the connection.

To enable Extended Protection, you first need to decide whether you wish to use service binding protection or channel binding protection. In order to use channel binding, you must force encryption for all SQL Server connections (more information about enabling SQL Server encryption can be found in Chapter 2). With SQL Server encryption disabled, only service binding protection is possible.

Extended Protection is enabled from within the SQL Server Configuration Manager for all editions of the Microsoft SQL Server 2008 R2 and higher database engine provided that you are also using Windows Server 2008 or newer. Within the SQL Server Configuration Manager select "SQL Server Services" from the left-hand pane and double click on the SQL Server Service you wish to enable Extended Protection for on the right, selecting the Advanced tab from the window that pops

> **NOTE**
>
> What Extended Protection Type Should I Select?
>
> The type of protection selected is completely up to the administrator depending on the needs of the specific environment. However, because of the CPU load differences that each option uses, the service binding protection is expected to become the more popular of the two. This becomes even more probable when it is noted that service binding protection requires the use of SSL encryption on the SQL Server connection.

up. The Extended Protection option has three values from which you can select. The setting of "**Off**" will disable Extended Protection and will allow any connection whether or not the client supports Extended Protection. The setting of "**Allowed**" forces Extended Protection from Operating Systems which supported Extended Protection, while allowing Operating Systems, which do not support Extended Protection to connect without error. The setting of "**Required**" will tell the SQL Server to accept from client computers only those connections that have an Operating System that supports Extended Protection.

If your SQL Server has multiple Service Principal Names (SPNs) requested within the Windows domain, you will need to configure the Accepted NTLM SPNs setting. This setting supports up to 2048 characters and accepts a semicolon-separated list of the SPNs that the SQL Server will need to accept. As an example, if the SQL Server needed to accept the SPNs MSSQLSvc/ server1.yourcompany. local and MSSQLSvc/ server2.yourcompany.local, then you would specify a value of "MSSQLSvc/server1.yourcompany.local;MSSQLSvc/server2.yourcompany.local" in the Accepted NTLM SPNs setting as shown in Figure 5.4. After changing any of the Extended Protection properties, you will need to restart the SQL Server Instance for the settings change to take effect.

As Windows Azure SQL Database servers are installed on Microsoft's domain and not the company's server, Extended Protection is not available when using Windows Azure SQL Database as of the writing of this book.

SERVICE PRINCIPAL NAMES

Service Principal Names (SPNs) are unique service names within a Windows domain that uniquely identify an instance of a service regardless of the system that the service is running on, or how many services are running on a single machine. While a single SPN can only reference a single instance of a service, a single instance of a service can have multiple SPNs registered to it. The most common reason for multiple SPNs for a service would be that a service needs to be accessed under multiple server names.

Before an SPN can be used by Kerberos authentication, it must be registered within the Active Directory. The SPN when created is registered to a specific account within the domain. The account to which the SPN is registered must be the one under which the Windows service will be running. Because an SPN can only be registered

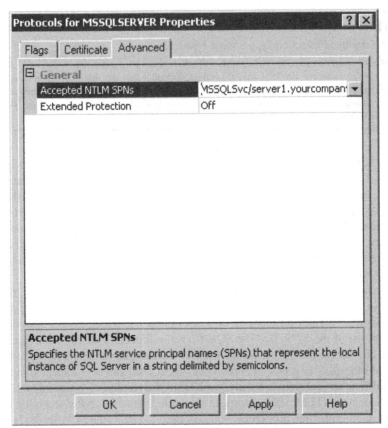

FIGURE 5.4 Configuring the Accepted NTLM SPNs setting in Microsoft SQL Server 2008 R2 or higher.

to a single service, this means that an SPN can only be registered to a single Windows account. If the account will be running Windows service changes, then the SPN must be removed from the original account and assigned to the new account. When the client software attempts to connect using Kerberos authentication, the client locates the instance of the service and creates the SPN for that service. The client software then connects to the remote service and presents the created SPN for the service to authenticate. If the authentication fails, the client disconnects returning an error message to the end user.

The client computer is able to create an SPN for the remote service very easily as the format for an SPN is very simple. The format for an SPN is <service class>/<host>:<port>/<service name>. The <service class> and <host> values are required while the <port> and <service name> values are optional. In the case of Microsoft SQL Server the <service class> value will be MSSQLSvc, while the <host> value will be the name that the client computers will use to connect to the SQL Server. As an example, for an SQL Server instance listening on the default TCP port 1433 on a server named DB1.contoso.local and a Windows account named CONTOSO\sqlserver would look like "MSSQLSvc/DB1.contoso.local:1433/CONTOSO\sqlserver." SPNs are created automatically when the SQL Service starts up, but only for the default name under which the service will be running. Typically this would be the name of the SQL Server. Other SPNs can be manually registered as needed by a member of the "Domain Administrators" group by using the setspn command line application with the -A switch followed by the SPN that should be created. If the DB1.contoso.local server needed to also support the name mydatabase.contoso.local, then the command as shown in Example 5.7 would be used.

EXAMPLE 5.7

Creating an SPN for mydatabase.contoso.local.

```
setspn -A MSSQLSvc/mydatabase.contoso.local:1433/CONTOSO\sql server
```

Once the SPN has been created and the SPN has replicated to all the domain controllers, the clients will be able to successfully authenticate against the new SPN. This replication can take anywhere from a few seconds to several hours, depending on how the domain replication is configured and the speed of the network links between sites.

SPNs do not need to be used with Microsoft Azure SQL Database instances as you must use SQL Authentication with Microsoft Azure SQL Database, and SPNs are used when using Windows Authentication with Kerberos.

STRONG PASSWORDS

Today there is no excuse for having an insecure password for your login to the SQL Server. Most websites to which you connect, such as your bank and credit card websites, all require that you use a strong password of some sort. It is shocking the number of companies that do not take these same techniques to heart for their internal security.

A strong password is typically defined as a password that contains at least three of the following four categories and is at least eight characters in length, although some companies may require longer passwords.

1. Lower-case letters
2. Upper-case letters
3. Numbers
4. Special characters

Passw☺rd

FIGURE 5.5 The word password with a smiley face in place of the letter "a."

Now when it comes to passwords for accounts like the SA account, which are rarely if ever actually used by people, there is no reason to stop limit yourself to just eight characters or the normal set of characters on your keyboard. The longer the password and the more special characters that you use in your password, the less chance that someone will be able to break into your SQL Server using this account. This same use of strong passwords should be used for any SQL Login that you create so as to better secure these SQL Logins against brute force attacks.

One thing that you can do to really secure your SA account is to use some high ASCII (American Standard Code for Information Interchange) characters within the password. This will basically make the account unbreakable to most of the people who use automated scripts to attack the SA password as all of them pretty much use the standard characters from the Latin alphabet. Inserting a character like a smiley face, which can be created by pressing <ALT>257 on your keyboard, will be outside the range of characters that are used by the password cracking program. By using this character, suddenly the word "Password" becomes a much more secure password as shown in Figure 5.5.

With a little creativity you could in fact turn the word "Password" into a truly strong and secure password. As shown in Figure 5.6, we have taken it to the extreme, replacing the letter S with the Hebrew Lamad, the letter O with a smiley face, and the letter D with a Dong Sign.

You can get more ideas on ways to replace characters with high ASCII characters from the character map that can be found within Windows. You can find the character map by clicking Start>Programs>Accessories>System Tools>Character Map. After the application loads, simply scroll down on the list of available characters until you find ones that you wish to use.

Now there is a catch with using these high ASCII characters for your SA password: If you ever need to log into the SQL Server using the SA account, you will either need to use the character map to get the characters, or you will need to know the <ALT> codes to access these characters.

FIGURE 5.6 The word password with the letters S, O and D replaced with high ASCII characters.

The SA account needs to be the most secured account on your SQL Server for a few reasons, the most important of which is that the SA account has rights to everything and you cannot revoke its rights to do anything that it wants. On SQL Server 2005 and below the SA account has a known username since you are not able to change the username from SA to something else. Because of this, someone who is trying to break into your SQL Server does not need to guess the username; he or she only needs to guess the password that reduces the amount of work needed to break into the SQL Server by half. Starting in SQL Server 2008 you can change the name of the sa account to another name to make using the sa account by someone who is not authorized much harder as they would need to figure out the new name for the sa account.

The most secure way to secure your sa account is to not enable SQL Authentication, which requires that all connections to the SQL Server come from a trusted computer that is authenticated against your Windows domain. Disabling SQL Authentication is a very easy change for you to make on your SQL Server. However, before you disable the SQL Authentication on an SQL Instance that is already in production, you will need to ensure that there are no applications logging into the SQL Server using SQL Authentication. Once this is done you can disable the SQL Authentication. Whenever possible, new SQL Server installations should be configured to use Windows Authentication only. SQL Authentication can be disabled by connecting the object explorer in SQL Server Management Studio to the instance in question, then right clicking on the Server and selecting properties. Select the Security tab on the right. In the Server Authentication section, select the Windows Authentication radio button as shown in Figure 5.7 and click OK. If you are using Enterprise Manager to configure SQL Server 7 or SQL Server 2000, the properties screen will look similar.

Now there is T-SQL code available to change this setting. However, the change is not a simple change via the sp_configure settings like most server wide settings. You have to update the registry using the xp_instance_regwrite system stored procedure from within the master database. The T-SQL code needed Figure 5.8. As with all changes made to the registry (either directly or via this T-SQL script), incorrect values or changes will cause the SQL Server to behave incorrectly or to not start at all.

If you find that you need to allow both SQL Server Authentication and Windows Authentication, then using T-SQL use the same code as shown in Figure 5.8, replacing the last parameters value of 1 with a value of 2.

When making changes to the Server Authentication mode, either with the UI (User Interface) or via T-SQL, you will need to restart the SQL Instance. This is because the setting is a registry setting that is only read on the start of the instance and is not refreshed by the instance while the instance is running.

When doing the initial install of the SQL Server 2005 or newer instance, if you select Windows Authentication only the SQL Server will automatically disable the sa account for you. It does this because you are not prompted for a password for the SA account during the installation wizard when installing using Windows only

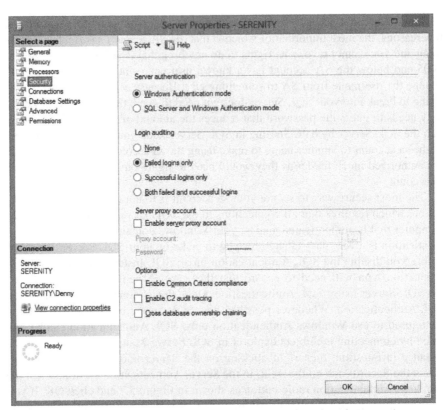

FIGURE 5.7 The security properties page of the server properties with Windows only authentication enabled.

```
SQLQuery1.sql - (l...nity\dcherry (54))*
  USE [master]
  GO
EXEC xp_instance_regwrite N'HKEY_LOCAL_MACHINE',
     N'Software\Microsoft\MSSQLServer\MSSQLServer',
     N'LoginMode',
     REG_DWORD,
     1
  GO
```

FIGURE 5.8 The T-SQL Script to enable Windows Only Authentication.

authentication. Thus, if you were to later change from Windows Authentication to SQL Server Authentication, you would have the SA account enabled with no password allowing the SQL Server to be easily broken into.

PASSWORD CHANGE POLICIES

After installing the SQL Server engine on the server, you will probably begin creating SQL Server accounts. Using SQL Server 2005 or newer, creating accounts that use SQL Server Authentication will give you a few checkboxes, shown in Figure 5.9, which you need to understand so that you know how these options work. If you are in a Windows NT 4 domain, then these options will not be available to you and they will be grayed out as Windows NT 4 domain's password policies are not used by Microsoft SQL Server. If you are using Windows Azure SQL Database these options will also not be available as Windows Azure SQL Database does not enforce domain

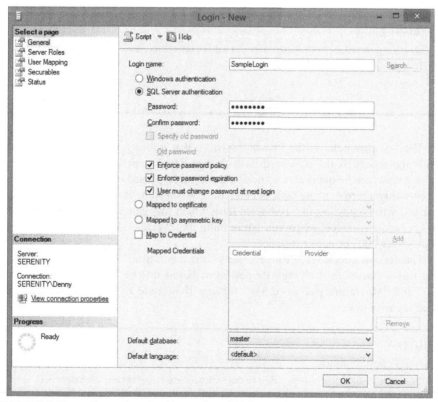

FIGURE 5.9 The policy option checkboxes for a SQL Authentication account created on SQL Server 2005 or higher.

policies. If you are using SQL Server within a Windows Azure Virtual Machine then the options will be available if the Virtual Machine is a member of your Active Directory domain.

The first checkbox, "Enforce password policy," tells the SQL Server that the password must fit within the password requirements of the Windows domain, or the local security policy defined on the server (if the server is not in a Windows domain). The password policies that are being enforced by the first checkbox are the "Enforce password history," "Minimum password length," and "Password must meet complexity requirements" policy settings.

The password policies cannot be checked after the login has been created. The password policies are only evaluated when a new login is created or when the password for an existing login has been changed. The system function PWDCOMPARE can be used to check accounts for known or blank passwords easily enough as shown in Example 5.8. The system function accepts three parameters, two of which are the most important and the third of which only needs to be used against a password hash from a SQL Server 2000 system.

EXAMPLE 5.8

Querying the SQL Server instance for all logins which have a blank password.

```
SELECT name
FROM sys.sql_logins
WHERE PWDCOMPARE('', password_hash) = 1 ;
```

The first parameter is the known password that is being checked in plain text, while the second is the password hash. Either a table, such as the sys.sql_logins catalog view, can be queried or a specific hash can be passed in. The third parameter accepts only a zero or a one with a default of 0. When a one is specified this indicates that you will be passing in a password hash which was generated by a SQL Server 2000 or older instance, when you are running the PWDCOMPARE statement on a SQL Server 2005 or newer instance.

The second checkbox, "Enforce password expiration," tells the SQL Server that this account must change its password based on the "Minimum password age" and "Maximum password age" settings that come from the domain or the local security policy.

NOTE

Group Policy Definitions

All six of the group policy settings – the five that SQL Server uses and the one that SQL Server does not look at – which control password policies within a Windows domain are explained in Chapter 3 in greater detail. Because they are covered there, they are only discussed at a high level in this chapter.

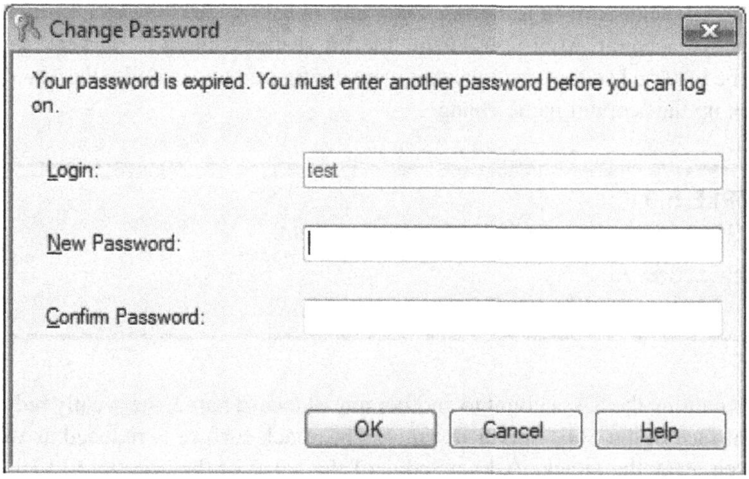

FIGURE 5.10 The Change Password dialog shown in SQL Server Management Studio.

The third checkbox shown in Figure 5.10 is the "User must change password at next login" option. In Figure 5.10 the option is disabled because the "Enforce password expiration" option is not selected. If the "Enforce password expiration" option were checked, then the "User must change password at next login" option would be available. By checking this option and clicking OK the next time the user attempts to log into the database engine, the user will need to change their password.

The advantage of having and using these policies is that all the SQL Authentication accounts that are configured to follow the policies meet the password policies that have been defined on the domain.

RENAMING THE SA ACCOUNT

Starting with SQL Server 2008, you have the ability to rename the SA account to another username to make the account more difficult for an attacker to use. This is an important security step to take, especially if the SQL Server is available on the public Internet. To rename the SA account use the ALTER LOGIN command as shown in

---

FAQ

How the Password Change Process Works

If the user connects to the SQL Server with an account that has an expired password, then they will need to be prompted to change their password. If the user is using SQL Server Management studio, they will be prompted to change they password automatically as shown in Figure 5.10. The same will happen when using the SQLCMD command line tool.

However, when using your own application to log into the database, such as a Windows Forms application, the application will need to know how to prompt the user for a new password, as well as what to do with the new password in order to change the password for the SQL Account.

Example 5.9. Microsoft SQL Server 2000 and older will not have the ability to re-name the SA account. After you rename the SA account, the SQL Server Agent will need to be restarted so that any jobs that were configured to run under the SA account will pick up the account name change.

EXAMPLE 5.9

T-SQL showing the renaming of the SA account.

```
ALTER LOGIN sa
WITH NAME = SomeOtherName
```

By renaming the SA account to another non-standard name, we greatly reduce the attack surface of the SQL Server Instance. The attack surface is reduced as we have now taken away the attacker's knowledge of the name of the account to login with. An attacker would now need to discover not only the password, but also the user-name for the account as well making a remote brute force attack very, very difficult to complete in any practical amount of time. The practical amount of time, however, is dependent on a variety of factors, including:

- How many computers the attacker has access to?
- How long the username is?
- How many characters the attacker starts with when attacking the SQL Server?
- If the user is able to get someone to tell them the username.

A typical attacker will start with the username SA and will try a large number of passwords before starting to try different usernames. The longer the username is the longer it will take an attacker to gain access to the database instance, with most at-tackers giving up long before finding the actual username and password. The biggest reason that this attack will take so long is that the SQL Server returns the same error message if the wrong username and password is used or if just the wrong username is used. In either case error 18456 will be returned with a level of 14 and a state of 1, with the wording of the error message simply stating "Login failed for user {username}" where {username} is the username that has attempted to log into the database instance.

DISABLING THE SA ACCOUNT

An important security procedure that many people do not follow is disabling the SA account. By having this account enabled, you have done half of the work for an at-tacker as the username for the SA account is well known by attackers. This means that the attacker just needs to figure out the password. While there is hopefully a very strong password on the SA account, with the account enabled the attacker can sit there and hammer away on the SA account until getting the password correctly. Where

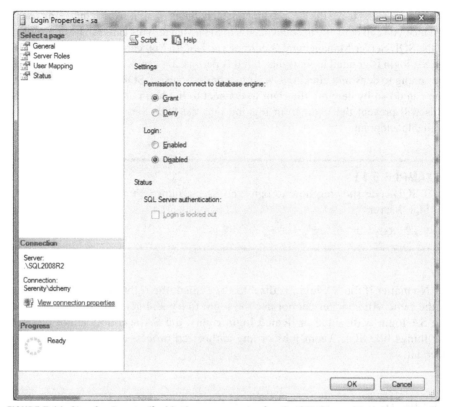

FIGURE 5.11 Showing how to disable the sa account using the SQL Server Management Studio.

you disable the SA account does not matter if the attacker gets the password correct; regardless, the account would not allow the attacker into the SQL Server instance.

If the SQL Instance is configured for Windows Only Authentication, then there is no need to disable the SA account as the SA account is an SQL login and when Windows Only Authentication is used the SA account cannot be used.

Disabling the SA account is a fairly easy process to complete. Connect to the server in question using the Object Explorer and expand the security node. Double click the SA account from the list and select the status tab. Select the disabled radio button and click OK as shown in Figure 5.11.

If you prefer to use T-SQL to disable the SA login you can do so with the ALTER LOGIN statement as shown in Example 5.10.

EXAMPLE 5.10

T-SQL showing how to disable the SA login.

```
ALTER LOGIN [sa] DISABLE
```

If you wish to leave the SA account enabled, but prevent it from connecting to the instance you can deny the account access to the instance. This can also be done either in the SQL Server Management Studio or via T-SQL. You can see in Figure 4.6 that the SA login is granted login rights, but this permission can be removed by changing the setting to deny and clicking OK. If you prefer to use T-SQL to make this change, you can do so by denying the right to connect to the login as shown in Figure 5.8. This will prevent the login from logging into the SQL Server instance using any available endpoint.

EXAMPLE 5.11

T-SQL code showing how to deny the SA account rights to connect to the SQL Server.

```
DENY CONNECT SQL TO [sa]
```

No matter if the SA login is disabled or denied, the right to connect the result is the same. An attacker cannot use the login to try and get into the instance. As the SA login is disabled or denied login rights, the SA account cannot be used for things like SQL Agent jobs or any authorized process that does use the SA account.

USERS VERSUS LOGINS

Users and Logins are related by different objects within the SQL Server database platform. They are both used to assign rights to allow access to various objects within the SQL Server database engine. Logins are used to connect to the SQL Server database engine as the login is used so that the person connecting is able to authenticate against the database engine. Permissions at the instance level can be granted to logins. This includes the permission to connect to the engine, alter other credentials (logins), create databases, restore databases, etc.

Users are created within databases so that the user is able to access specific databases. Permissions can then be granted to the user so that objects within the database can be accessed. When users are created they are typically mapped to a login so that when a user connects to the database engine using the login, they can then access the database.

This can be viewed within the system catalog views by looking at the sys.server_principals and the sys.database_principals catalog views as shown in Figure 5.12. Here in the first result set we see the output of the logins created at the instance level. In the second result set we see the output of the users created within a sample database. In the third result set we see the output of the name columns from each of the tables when the tables are joined together using the "sid" column. We can see that

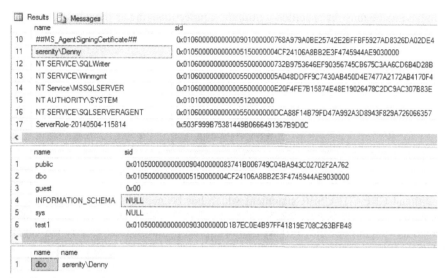

FIGURE 5.12 Output from the sys.database_principals and sys.server_principals system catalog views.

the login "serenity\Denny" at the instance level is mapped to the user "dbo" at the database level.

In SQL Server 2012 and above while logins and users do still exist within the database engine, there are some differences with the introduction of contained users. These contained users will be discussed later in this chapter.

CONTAINED DATABASE USERS IN SQL SERVER 2012 AND BEYOND

With the introduction of contained databases comes a new security piece which is known as the contained login. The biggest advantage to contained databases is the ability to move the contained database from one database instance to another without having to create new logins on the destination SQL Server instance first.

The way this works is that users can now be created within a contained database and that user has its own password assigned to it. These contained logins are not allowed to access resources outside of the specific database that they are in with the exception of a few global objects in master and temporary tables in the tempdb database.

From the connection string and application perspective contained logins work just like regular logins in that there is a username and a password which is specified. There is no special setting which needs to be specified to use a contained login, in fact the application does not need to be changed at all to use a contained login instead of a regular SQL Server Login; with one exception which is that the contained database name must be specified within the connection sting as the default database as shown in Example 5.12.

EXAMPLE 5.12

Showing the connection string used to connect to a contained database.

```
Data Source =MySQLServer; Initial Catalog =MyContainedDatabase;
User Id =ContainedLogin; Password =Pa$$wordForC0ntainedL0gin;
```

Creating a contained login within a contained database requires the use of the traditional CREATE USER statement which has been used to create users within databases since SQL Server 2005. To create a new contained user instead of a user linked to a login omit the "FROM LOGIN" portion and instead specify the WITH PASSWORD clause as shown in Example 5.13.

EXAMPLE 5.13

Showing the user of the CREATE USER statement to create a contained user within a contained database.

```
CREATE USER MyContainedLogin WITH PASSWORD = 'Pa$$wordForC0ntainedL0gin'
GO
```

Creating a contained login can also be done within the SQL Server Management Studio. To create a contained SQL user from within SQL Server Management Studio follow these steps.

1. Connect to the SQL Server 2012 or newer instance in the object explorer
2. Navigate to Databases
3. Navigate to *YourContainedDatabase* that you wish to create the contained login within
4. Navigate to Security
5. Right click on Security
6. Select "New User" from the context menu which appears

Within the "Database User – New" window which opens and change the User Type to "SQL user with password" and enter in the "username," password and "default schema" for the contained user as shown in Figure 5.13.

Contained users are not limited to SQL users. Windows account can also be created as contained users within a contained database. The principal of a contained Windows user (which is what a Windows account which has been set up as a contained user is called) is the same as that of a contained SQL user. The only change to the

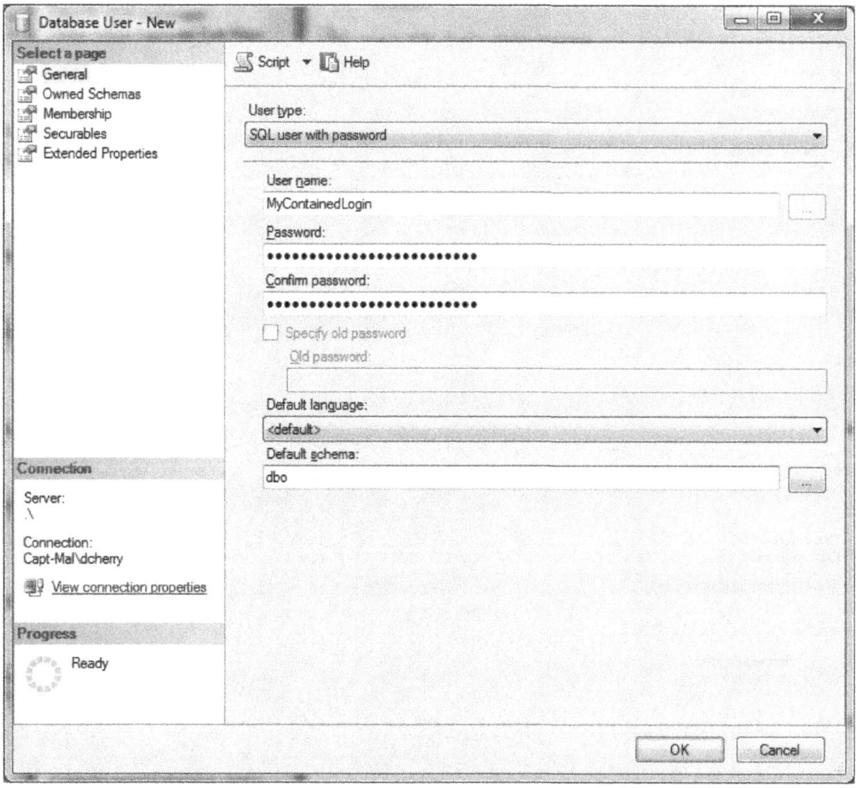

FIGURE 5.13 Then click OK to create the contained user within the contained database.

connection string needs to be that the default database is specified as the contained database which the user will be accessing.

Creating a contained Windows user via T-SQL is must like creating a contained SQL user in that the CREATE USER statement is used. Instead of specifying the users password simply specify the Windows domain and username as shown in Example 5.14 and the contained Windows user will be set up and mapped to the Windows account.

EXAMPLE 5.14

Showing the creation of a contained Windows user being created using the CREATE USER statement.

```
CREATE USER [CONOSO\dcherry]
GO
```

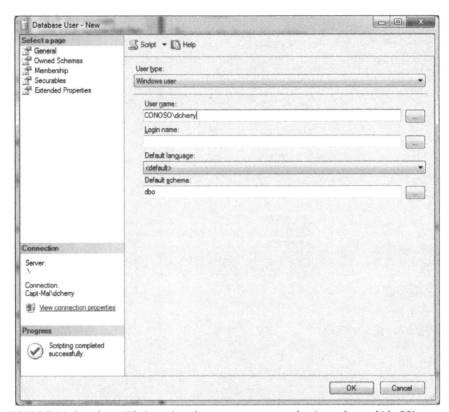

FIGURE 5.14 Creating a Windows domain account as a contained user from within SQL Server Management Studio.

Contained Windows users can also be created from within the SQL Server Management Studio user interface by following the same steps from above to open the "Database User – New" screen. Once opened change the user type to "Windows user" and set the "Username" field to the Windows account that you wish to setup as a contained user. Leave the "Login name" field blank and set the "default schema" to the needed schema as shown in Figure 5.14.

Once the contained user has been created it can be added to fixed and user defined database roles just like any other non-contained SQL Login. The big difference here is that contained users cannot be granted instance level rights such as the being a member of a fixed or user defined server role.

SCHEMAS

Within SQL Server 2005 and above we have the concept of schemas. When looking at a database object such as "dbo.users" the schema of the database is the portion "dbo." Schemas give a way to group objects together by functional unit within the company, module within the database, or really using any method that you want to.

SQL SERVER 2000 AND BELOW

In SQL Server 2000 and below the syntax was exactly the same, but these were not schemas, instead they were the username who owned the actual object. The big problem with having this be the actual object owner is that if a user created an object and then they left the company the object would still be owned by their account so in order to remote their user and login from the database engine you have to change the owner of all the objects within the databases. One of two things would need to happen before the login could be removed, either the objects needed to be assigned to another user which meant that code needed to be changed, or the login and user would need to be left in the database engine cluttering the database with un-needed entries possibly leading to a security issue if the login was a SQL Authentication login.

To fix this, developers would end up making all the objects owned by the "dbo" user as that user always exists and cannot be removed from the database. The other option available would be to create a loginless user and use that loginless user to be the owner of the objects.

In SQL Server 2000 all permissions are granted to the object on an object by object basis.

When creating objects which are owned by another user, such as the "dbo" user the object name must be specified by the person who is creating the object. If the name of the object owner is not included then the object will be owned by the user who created the object.

SQL SERVER 2005 AND ABOVE

Now that we have schemas in SQL Server 2005 and above object ownership is much easier to manage. While schemas do typically match usernames there is no requirement for this. Schemas are still owned by a specific user within the database, however, the ownership of this schema can be changed without impact the name of the objects, or without changing the name of the schema.

With the introduction of schemas the ability to grant permissions to schemas was also introduced. This gives the ability to grant SELECT permissions for example to the entire schema which would then allow the person who received the permissions on the schema the ability to query all the tables and views which are within the schema. More about object level permissions can be found in Chapter 15.

By default when users are created within the database their default schema is set to dbo, provided that the user who creates the new user has rights to the dbo schema. This means that any objects which are created within the database will be assigned to the dbo schema.

DOMAIN GROUPS AND DEFAULT SCHEMAS

In most companies rights to SQL Server instances are handled through domain groups so that the helpdesk or IT support desk can simply change domain group membership to grant users access to the databases which they need. The problem with domain groups in SQL Server 2005 through SQL Server 2008 R2 is that when domain groups are mapped to users the default schema is ignored. Starting in SQL Server 2012 the ability for domain groups to have default schemas is introduced.

If a user is a member of multiple domain groups which all have a default schema then the domain groups are sorted by creation date and the default schema for the domain group which was added to the database first is used. If the user wishes to use a different default schema then the domain groups would need to be removed and readded in the correct order so that the oldest one in the database is the one with the schema which the user wants to use. The other option would be to have the user specify the schema within their T-SQL scripts.

SETTING THE DEFAULT SCHEMA

Setting the default schema for a user, either a Windows Group (in SQL Server 2012 or higher) or a specific user is an easy process. When creating a new user on the general table of the new user screen, or edit an existing user, as shown in Figure 5.15,

FIGURE 5.15 Editing an existing user and setting the default schema.

> **NOTE**
>
> Encryption Is Not Just For Microsoft SQL Server
>
> This technique can be used for connection strings to all your database platforms. You could also be using a database server such as NoSQL, MySQL, which may or may not support Windows Authentication. This technique will work for all database platforms equally well as no matter what the database platform is, the connection string is always a weak spot.

and enter the default schema in the "Default schema" box. The default schema can either be typed in freehand, or searched for by clicking on the button with the ellipse (…) to the right of the "Default schema" box.

ENCRYPTING CLIENT CONNECTION STRINGS

While using Windows authentication is the best way to connect to the database server, this is not always possible because the client machine that is connecting to the database server may not be connected do the Windows Domain.

This is most often the case when the web server is located in a DMZ network and the database server is located within the internal network as shown in Figure 1.3 in Chapter 1. In a case like this, the application development team should take extra care to secure the web server's connection string. Without this extra protection, someone could break into the web server and find the database server's connection information sitting in the web.config file and simply log into the database using the username and password, which are stored in plain text in the configuration file.

One great technique to do this is to have the web application on startup read the web.config file looking for an unencrypted connection string. Then read that string into memory, delete that node from the web.config file's XML, and then add a new node labeled as being the encrypted string, encrypt the string, and place the encrypted string within the XML document, saving it when done. On subsequent loads of the XML file, the unencrypted connection string would not be found, and the application would then load the encrypted version, decrypting it in memory, thereby making it much, much harder for someone who has broken into the SQL Server to find any useful connecting string information.

If you do not want to give the web application access to write to the web.config file (as this would technically be a security hole unto itself), the application team could create a small standalone app that takes the normal connection string and outputs an encrypted value, which the Systems Administration could then put within the web.config file during deployment of the application by the Systems Administration team.

SQL REPORTING SERVICES

SQL Reporting Services does an excellent job of protecting the connection information to the repository databases, as well as the connection strings that the reports use to connect to the source databases. All database connection strings that are used by SQL Reporting Services are encrypted and stored within the web.config as the encrypted string. Within the SQL Server Reporting Services database, typically named ReportServer, all the connection information that the reports use to connect to the source databases is also stored as an encrypted value. Both of these encrypted values together form a very secure platform that makes it very difficult for an attacker to exploit the SQL Server Reporting Services platform to get any useful information from the database holding the Reporting Server catalog database, or the source data; getting access to the source data via the data stored within the SQL Server Reporting Service repository would require decrypting two layers of information.

APPLICATION ROLES

When using Windows Authentication, there is an unfortunate side effect that needs to be considered. The user can now log into the database using any Open Database Connectivity (ODBC)-based application such as Microsoft Access, Microsoft Excel, and SQL Server Management Studio, and they have the same rights that they would have if they were logged in via the application. If the user logs into the database by supplying the SQL Login username and password, this same risk is there. However, if the application contains the username and password hard coded within the application, then the user would not have this ability as they will not have the username and password. This is probably something that you do not want to happen. Before you go and switch all your applications to using SQL Authentication and hard coding the password within the application, there's another solution that gives you the best of both worlds. This solution is to use an application role.

The application role is not a very well understood, and therefore not very frequently used, security feature of Microsoft SQL Server, which allows a user to authenticate against the Microsoft SQL Server Instance, but not have any specific rights within the database. The rights to perform actions are granted to the application role, which would then need to be activated by the application before the user would be able to perform any actions.

Application roles are created by using the sp_addapprole system stored procedure in SQL Server 2000 and below or by using the CREATE APPLICATION ROLE statement in SQL Server 2005 and above. The application role has its own password that is used to ensure that only authorized applications are able to activate the application. The application role is activated by using the sp_setapprole system stored procedure, and then the application role is deactivated by using the sp_unsetapprole system stored procedure, or by simply closing the connection to the database engine.

> **TIP**
>
> sp_addapprole Has Been Deprecated
>
> If you are using SQL Server 2005 and above, you should use the CREATE APPLICATION ROLE statement as the sp_addapprole has been deprecated and will be removed in a future version of Microsoft SQL Server.

EXAMPLE 5.15

Sample code using the sp_addapprole system stored procedure and CREATE APPLICATION ROLE statement to create an application role.

```
EXEC sp_addapprole @rolename='MyAppRole', @password='MyPa$$word'
CREATE APPLICATION ROLE MyAppRole WITH PASSWORD='MyPa$$word'
```

The sp_setapprole system stored procedure has four parameters that are of interest. The first and second parameters are the @rolename and @password parameters to which you supply the name and password that were specified when you created the application role. The third parameter is the @fCreateCookie parameter, which is a bit parameter and tells the SQL Server if it should create a cookie when the application role is activated (I will explain the cookies in a moment). The fourth parameter is the @cookie parameter, which is a varbinary(8000) and stores the cookie that was created if the @fCreateCookie parameter was set to 1.

The @cookie parameter stores a cookie much in the same way that your web browser stores cookies when you browse the web, so that it can correctly identify the session that was used to activate the application role. Thus, when the application role is disabled, the SQL Server knows which session state to return the user's session to. If you do not plan to revert the application role and will simply close the connection to the SQL Server, then you do not need to set a cookie and can simply set the @fCreateCookie password to 0 telling the SQL Server to not create the cookie.

In the sample code shown in Example 5.16, we create a new database, and then we create an application role within that database. We then create a table within the database, as well as a user within the database. We next give the application role access to select data from the table. We then use the EXECUTE AS statement to change the execution context from that of the user we logged in with to that of the user defined within the EXECUTE AS, which we just created and which has no rights. Next we query the table, which returns an error message to us. After that we switch to using the application role and try and query the table again, this time receiving the output as a recordset. We then unset the application role using the cookie that was created by the sp_setapprole system stored procedure. We then use the REVERT statement so that we are no longer executing code as our MyUser database use, after which we drop the sample database.

EXAMPLE 5.16
Sample code showing the use of an Application Role.

```
USE master
GO
IF EXISTS (SELECT * FROM sys.databases WHERE name = 'AppRoleTest')
DROP DATABASE AppRoleTest
GO
CREATE DATABASE AppRoleTest
GO
USE AppRoleTest
GO
CREATE APPLICATION ROLE MyAppRole WITH PASSWORD='MyPa$$word'
GO
CREATE TABLE MyTable
(Col1 INT)
GO
CREATE USER MyUser WITHOUT LOGIN
GO
GRANT SELECT ON MyTable TO MyAppRole
GO
DECLARE @cookie varbinary(8000)
EXECUTE AS USER = 'MyUser'
SELECT * FROM MyTable
EXEC sp_setapprole @rolename=MyAppRole, @password='MyPa$$word',
@cookie=@cookie OUTPUT, @fCreateCookie=1
SELECT * FROM MyTable
EXEC sp_unsetapprole @cookie=@cookie
REVERT
GO
USE master
GO
DROP DATABASE AppRoleTest
GO
```

When we run this script as shown in text output mode from within SQL Server Management Studio, we see the output shown in Figure 5.16. The first SELECT statement that we issued was rejected because the user did not have rights to the table dbo.MyTable in the AppRoleTest database. However, the second SELECT statement

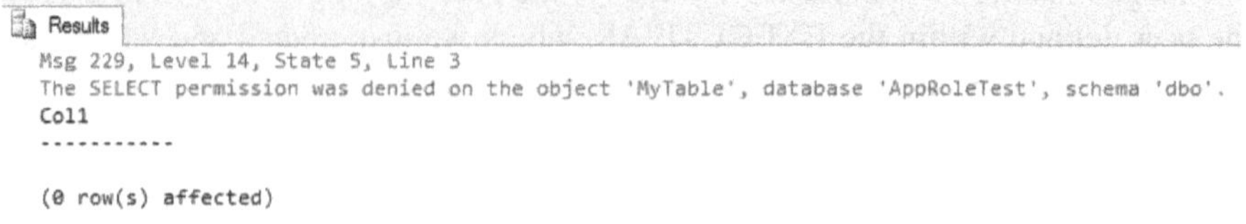

```
Results
Msg 229, Level 14, State 5, Line 3
The SELECT permission was denied on the object 'MyTable', database 'AppRoleTest', schema 'dbo'.
Col1
-----------

(0 row(s) affected)
```

FIGURE 5.16 Output from running code shown in Example 5.16.

> **NOTE**
>
> Application Roles and Linked Servers
>
> Application roles and linked servers can start giving you problems if you expect the Windows account to be passed across the linked server, as you are now executing within the context of the application role and not the Windows account. Any mapping being done through a linked server would need to be done globally or through the application role name. You can read more about linked servers and mapping logins in Chapter 6.
>
> In addition, system functions such as the login name functions will also return incorrect information for the same reason, i.e., the work is being done within the context of the application role, not within the user's context.

that we issued after we set the Application Role was accepted by the database, and the contents of the table were returned.

You can now see how use of the application role can enable the use of the very secure Windows authentication without requiring that the user's Windows account actually have rights to access any objects within the database directly, but the application can run once the application role has been activated.

Another technique that can be used along the same lines of the application role is to create a user with no attached login as done in Figure 5.17 and use the EXECUTE AS statement to run commands as that user. While this will allow you to run all your statements without the user needing to have rights to the database objects, the problem with this technique is that any logging that is done via the username functions returns the dummy user that you created and not the login of the actual user. This is shown along with sample code in Figure 5.17. As you can see in the sample code, we create a dummy user, then output my username using the SUSER_SNAME() system function, then switch to running under the context of the MyUser database user, and then output the value of the SUSER_SNAME() function again with the output being the SID of the MyUser database user account. You cannot even query the dynamic management views to get the correct username of the user logged in, because once the EXECUTE AS has been executed, the dynamic management views show the SID of the user instead of the name of the login that was originally connected to the database.

When using an application role, you do not have the database username return problem when using the system functions or the dynamic management views.

USING WINDOWS DOMAIN POLICIES TO ENFORCE PASSWORD LENGTH

Starting with Microsoft SQL Server 2005, Microsoft introduced a new level of password security within the product, as this was the first version of Microsoft SQL Server that could use the domain policies to ensure that the passwords for the SQL Authentication accounts were long enough and strong enough to meet the corporate

```
 1  USE tempdb
 2  GO
 3  CREATE USER MyUser WITHOUT LOGIN
 4  GO
 5  print 'normal login output'
 6  GO
 7  SELECT SUSER_SNAME()
 8  GO
 9  print 'Using EXECUTE AS'
10  GO
11  EXECUTE AS USER='MyUser'
12  SELECT SUSER_SNAME()
13  REVERT
14  GO
15  DROP USER MyUser
```

Results

```
normal login output
-----------------------------------------------------------------
Serenity\dcherry

Using EXECUTE AS
-----------------------------------------------------------------
S-1-9-3-2851743519-1315201071-3451601828-1822525857
```

FIGURE 5.17 Script and output showing how the **EXECUTE AS** statement is used with a user without a login.

standards as set forth by the SAs. By default, all SQL Authentication accounts created within the SQL Server instance must meet the domain password security policies. You can, if necessary, remove these restrictions by editing the SQL Authentication account.

Within the Microsoft SQL Server, two settings can be applied to each SQL Authentication Login, which are shown in Figure 5.18.

1. The "Enforce password policy" setting tells the SQL Server engine to ensure that the password meets the needed complexity requirements of the domain, and that the password has not been used within a specific number of days, which is defined within the domain policy, and is explained later in this chapter.

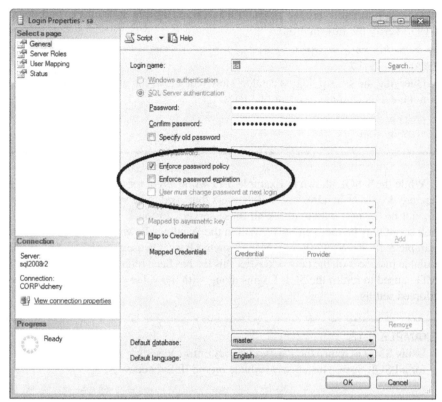

FIGURE 5.18 The SQL Authentication Login screen showing the two available domain policy settings with the "User must change password at next login" option disabled.

2. The "Enforce password expiration" setting tells the SQL Server that the password for the SQL Authentication Login should have expired based on the domain settings (also discussed in more detail later in this chapter).
3. The "User must change password at next login" option, shown disabled in Figure 5.18, will only become available when the logins password is manually reset and the "Enforce password policy" setting is enabled for the login.

Allowing the SQL Server to ensure that your passwords meet your domain policies has some distinct advantages, especially when it comes to auditing. Without this ability you would need to physically check each SQL server password to ensure that it meets the corporate standards when the Auditor asks you if all your SQL Authentication passwords meet the corporate standards. In a worst case situation, this would require that you either keep a list of all the usernames and passwords somewhere (which would probably cause you to fail the audit) or you would need to contact each person that uses the SQL Authentication login and ask them how long the password is, and if it meets the company policies, and so on. Now with this feature built into the product, a quick and simple SQL query is all that it takes to verify the information.

EXAMPLE 5.17

Querying the sys.sql_logins catalog view will show you any logins that may not meet the domain password policies.

```
SELECT name, is_policy_checked
FROM sys.sql_logins
```

While the T-SQL shown in Example 5.17 works great for a single SQL Server, if there are dozens or hundreds of SQL Servers that need to be verified, a T-SQL script may not be the best way to check all those servers. In this case a Windows Power-Shell script may be more effective. Within the Windows PowerShell script shown in Example 5.18, the SMO (Server Management Object) is used to get a list of all the available instances on the network. After this list has been returned from the network, SMO is used to return the SQL Logins along with the value of the PasswordPolicy-Enforced setting.

EXAMPLE 5.18

Using SMO to return the PasswordPolicyEnforced setting for all SQL Logins for all SQL Server Instances available on the IP Subnet.

```
[System.Reflection.Assembly]::LoadWithPartialName('Microsoft.SqlServer.Smo') |
out-null
foreach ($InstanceList in
[Microsoft.SqlServer.Management.Smo.SmoApplication]::EnumAvailableSqlServers())
{
$InstanceList;
$instanceName = $InstanceList.Name;
$instanceName;
$SMOserver = New-Object ('Microsoft.SqlServer.Management.Smo.Server')
$instanceName
$db = $SMOserver.Logins | where-object {$_.loginType -eq "sqllogin"} |.
select name,
PasswordPolicyEnforced
$db;
}
```

NOTE

Notes About the PowerShell Code

A quick note about the PowerShell code in Figure 5.18. This code will only show you the Logins for the SQL Server's on the local IP subnet which you run this on as the EnumAvailableSqlServers function which is used will have the same result as the –L switch for sqlcmd which was discussed earlier in this chapter.

By setting the is_policy_checked flag to true (shown as the number 1 when you run the sample query in Example 5.17), this tells you that any password that is assigned to the SQL Authentication Login must meet the password requirements of the domain. Expanding on the query shown in Example 5.17, an SQL Server Reporting Services report could be configured that runs against each SQL Server in the environment, giving a simple report that can be run as needed for auditing purposes.

When you have the is_policy_checked flag set to true, there are several domain wide settings that will be evaluated each time the password is changed. These policies can be found by editing the Group Policy Object (GPO) on the domain that holds these settings, or by editing the local security policies for the server in question if that server is not a member of a Windows domain. While you can set these settings on a server that is a member of the domain, doing so would not have any effect as the domain policies but will overwrite any local settings you have set.

If all the SQL Server Instances that need to be polled are registered within SQL Server Management Studio's Registered Server feature or within the Central Management Server, this select statement can be run against all the instances at once returning a single record with all the needed information. This can be done by opening the registered servers panel within SQL Server management studio by clicking on the View dropdown menu and then the "Registered Servers" menu item. Right click on the folder that contains the SQL Server Instances you want to execute the query against and select "New Query" from the context menu that opens. This opens a new query window which, when executed, will execute the query against all the servers that are within the registered servers folder with all the data from all the servers being returned as a single recordset. SQL Server Management Studio will automatically add in a new column at the beginning of the recordset, which contains the name of the instance; this will allow you to use the same query shown in Example 5.17 against all the SQL Servers at once and giving back a single recordset that can be reviewed or handed off as needed.

WINDOWS AUTHENTICATION GROUP POLICIES

There are a total of six policies that you can set within Windows that affect the domain or local password policy. However, Microsoft SQL Server only cares about five of them. The policy with which the SQL Server is not concerned is the "Store passwords using reversible encryption" policy. This policy tells Windows if it should store the user's password using a two-way encryption process, instead of a one-way hash. Enabling this policy presents a security vulnerability on your domain as an attacker could download the list of all users and passwords, then break the encryption on the passwords and have full access to every user's username and password. Due to the security issues with this setting, the setting is disabled by default and should remain so unless there is a specific reason to enable it. The typical reasons to enable it include using Challenge Handshake Authentication Protocol (CHAP) through Remote Access or Internet Authentication Services (IAS). It is also required if one or more Internet Information Service (IIS) servers within the Windows Domain are using Digest Authentication.

The five password policies that the SQL Server does recognize and follow are the following.

1. Enforce password history;
2. Maximum password age;
3. Minimum password age;
4. Minimum password length; and
5. Password must meet complexity requirements.

Each of these settings has a specific effect on what the passwords can be set to and should be fully understood before changing the password of an SQL Authentication Login.

The "Enforce password history" setting on the domain (or local computer) is not a boolean, although the name sounds as though it would be. It is in fact the number of old passwords for the account that the SQL Server should track so that passwords cannot be reused. The setting has a valid range of 0 (or no passwords) to 24 passwords. The more passwords that are kept, the greater the chance that the user will forget their password, but the lesser the chance that someone will break into the system via an old password. The default on the domain is 24 passwords.

The "Maximum password age" setting tells the SQL Server how many days a password is valid. After this number of days has passed since the last password change, the user will be prompted to change the password. If the password is not changed, the user will not be able to log into the database instance. This setting accepts a value from 0 (never expires) to 999 days, with a default value of 42 days.

The "Minimum password age" setting tells the SQL Server how many days from the time a password has been changed until it can be changed again. This setting prevents the user from rapid-fire changing their passwords to eat up the number of passwords specified by the "Enforce password history" setting. Without this setting, or with this setting set to 0, when the user's password expires, the user can simply change the password 24 times and then change it to the same password that it was before effectively breaking the password requirement feature. This setting accepts a value from 0 (allows immediate password changes) to 998 days, with a default value of 1; however, this setting has a practical upper limit of one day lower than the setting for the "Maximum password age." If you were to set this setting to the same value or higher than the "Maximum password age" setting, then the users would not ever be able to login until after their passwords had expired.

The "Minimum password length" setting tells the SQL Server how many characters need to be in the password for the password to be acceptable. This setting can be any value from 0 (allowing a blank password) to 14 characters, with a default value of 7 characters. It is typically recommended to increase this value from the default of 7 to a higher number such as 9 characters. While this will make the password harder for the user to remember, it will also make it exponentially harder for an attacker to guess. The "Password must meet complexity requirements" setting tells the SQL

Server that all passwords must be considered "strong" passwords. There are several requirements to having a strong password beyond what one would normally consider. By default this setting is enabled.

1. The password cannot contain the username within it.
2. The password must contain characters from at least three of these four categories:
   a. Lower-case letters (a–z);
   b. Upper-case letters (A–Z);
   c. Numbers (0–9);
   d. Symbols ($, #, @, %, ^, for example).

The "Minimum password length" setting and the "Password must meet complexity requirements" settings work together very nicely. Without configuring the "Minimum password length" setting the user would have the ability to have a three character password even with the "Password must meet complexity requirements" setting enabled. This is due to the fact that the "Password must meet complexity requirements" setting does not include a password length. The only length requirement which the "Password must meet complexity requirements" forces is a minimum of three characters do to the fact that the password much contain one character from each of the four groups listed earlier in this chapter.

When you enable the "Enforce password policy" setting for an SQL Authentication Login, this enforces the "Enforce password history," "Minimum password length," "Minimum Password Age," and "Password must meet complexity requirements" settings against that login. When you enable the "Enforce password expiration" setting for a SQL Authentication Login, this enforces the "Maximum password age" setting against that login. In order to enable the "Enforce password expiration" setting against an SQL Authentication login, you must also enable the "Enforce password policy" setting. However, you do not need to enable the "Enforce password expiration" setting if you enable the "Enforce password policy" setting.

When working on an Microsoft Azure SQL Database database, the login must meet the password complexity settings that Microsoft has defined. As of the summer of 2010, this means that the password must be 8 characters in length, and meet the complexity requirements shown above. There is no way to configure a login to an SQL Azure instance to not meet these requirements, for the SQL Azure instances do not support using the check_policy parameter to disable the policy checking.

NOTE

You May Have Noticed This Changed a Little…

It was pointed out to me while working on the second edition of this book that I had assigned the "Minimum Password Age" policy to the wrong SQL Server setting. After doing a lot of testing I have confirmed that it was incorrect in the first edition of this book, and it is now correct in the second edition. May thanks to Dr. Diana Dee for pointing out the issue.

WINDOWS DOMAIN REQUIREMENTS TO USE DOMAIN POLICIES TO MANAGE SQL AUTHENTICATION LOGINS

In order for these settings to be available, specific requirements from the Windows domain must be met. Notably, the domain must be a Windows 2003 domain or higher, and the domain functional level must be Windows 2003 Native or higher. If the domain is a Windows 2000 domain, or a Windows NT 4.0 domain (or older), then these settings will not be available for you to change and will effectively always be set to false.

There are two ways to configure these settings for an SQL Server login. You can use the SQL Server Management Studio to edit the login, or you can use T-SQL to change the settings. To edit a login within the SQL Server Management Studio, follow these five steps:

1. Connect to the server within the object explorer;
2. Navigate to Security;
3. From Security navigate to Logins;
4. From Logins navigate to the login that you want to configure;
5. Right click on the login, and select properties from the context menu which opens.

The window that opens, as shown in Figure 5.19, will allow you to configure which of the two properties you wish to enable.

If you prefer to use T-SQL to edit these settings, then you will need to use the ALTER LOGIN command as shown in Example 5.19.

EXAMPLE 5.19

T-SQL Code setting the policy and expiration settings for an SQL Authentication Login.

```
ALTER LOGIN YourLogin
WITH CHECK_POLICY = on,
CHECK_EXPIRATION = off
```

While you can configure these policy settings for a SQL Server Authentication login after the login has been created, the current password will not be checked against the policies until the next time that the password is changed. This is due to the fact that the SQL Server is storing a hashed copy of the password in its database and not the actual password which prevents the SQL Server database engine from being able to validate that the existing password meets the newly applied policies. If these policies are enabled for a login it is recommended that the password be changed in order to verify that the password meets the complexity requirements. This does not mean that the actual password needs to be changed. The password can in fact be changed to the same value as it was originally set for. Changing to

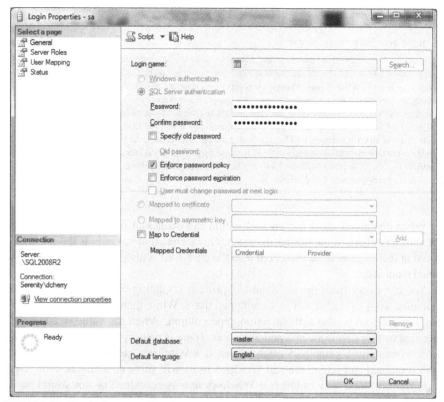

FIGURE 5.19 The login properties dialog box.

the password to any value after enabling the policy settings will cause the policy settings to be evaluated for the new value. The check policy settings can be enabled within the same T-SQL statement as the password change or it can be done within a separate T-SQL statement. If the password is being changed to verify that the existing password meets the password policy configuration it would be recommended that the policy setting be changed before attempting to change the password as the password failing would cause the policy settings change to also fail.

CONTAINED USERS

Contained databases which were introduced in SQL Server 2012 allow the administrator to create a database which can be quickly and easily moved from one SQL Server instance to another without the need to create logins at the instance level before moving the database thereby removing the need to realign user SIDs with login SIDs.

> **NOTE**
>
> Danger Will Robinson, Danger
>
> If using the UI to change the password and to enable the password policy settings all at once be very careful which checkboxes are checked when you click the OK button. If you change the password and check the "Enforce password policy" checkbox the SQL Server Management Studio dialog will automatically check the "User much change password at next login" checkbox. Unless the application which is connecting has been specifically written to know how to respond to the SQL Server's request to change the password, the application will fail to log into the SQL Server database and an error message will be returned to the end user causing an outage to the end users. In the event that the account being modified is in use by a Windows server and not a fat client or website there may be no indication of any problem for some time until users begin to complain that data is not being processed as expected.

When contained users are created within the contained database the user does not exist anywhere in the master database. This means that not only is the username stored in the contained database, but also the password is also stored within the contained database.

You can query from the sys.database_principals catalog view to see if users are contained users or traditional non-contained users. While there is no "is_contained" flag you can look at the authentication_type column. When the value is 2 the user specified by that row is a contained SQL user. There is no easy way to tell from within the sys.database_principals catalog view is a Windows user is contained or not. Both contained and non-contained Windows users will show an authentication_type of 3. The only real way to tell is a Windows user is contained or not would be to check the sys.server_principals catalog view to see if a matching row exists.

CONTAINED DATABASES AND AUTO-CLOSE

There are, however, a couple of problems that can come up when using contained databases from a security perspective, specifically if the contained databases are set with the auto-close setting enabled. With the auto-close setting enabled, if the contained database is not used very often the database will be closed most of the time. However, when a contained user attempts to log into the database, the database must then be opened, the user authenticated, and if authentication fails, the database must then be closed as per the auto-close setting. This opening and closing of databases does not take much in the way of resources when it is an occasional event, however, if someone was attempting to brute force the password for an account this opening and closing of the database will eventually take over the systems CPU resources and bring the server to its knees performance wise.

DB_OWNERS CAN NOW ADD NEW USERS TO THE INSTANCE

Another security issue when using contained databases is the fact that any member of the db_owners or db_securityadmin fixed database role can create additional contained users who can then allow other contained users into the contained database. This means that the ability to control who has the ability to log into the database instance has just left the control of the database and could now be in the hands of users that may not understand that not everyone in the company needs to be a member of the db_owner fixed database role.

PASSWORD POLICIES AND CONTAINED USERS

Unlike non-contained users, there is no way as of SQL Server 2012 to enforce domain password policies on contained SQL users. The reason for this is because the contained database may be moved from one Windows domain to another, and when the contained database was moved to the new domain the passwords may not follow the new Active Directory domain security policy. So instead of leaving SQL accounts which do not meet the new domain's security policy a decision was made to not allow contained SQL users to follow any domain security policies. There is no easy way to force the passwords for contained database users to follow a password policy except through written policies when creating newly contained users.

SUMMARY

One of the biggest problems in today's IT world is that once you have created your nice secure passwords, how do you track them? Those usernames and passwords are probably going to be documented somewhere, typically within an Excel sheet that is kept on a network share so that all the database administrators within the group have quick and easy access to them. However, by doing this you now have placed all the passwords that you have taken the time to ensure that are strong and secure within your web.config and app.config files are easily readable and usable by anyone who has access to the network share. Typically, not just the database administrators would have access to the network share. In addition to the database administrators, the SAs, backup software, and monitoring system would all have access to the network share. And this is in addition to whoever has found the lost backup tape for your file server. In other words, be sure to store that password list in a nice, safe place and not in the public arena available to everyone to read and network share. There are a variety of tools available for password management including applications which store those passwords in a secure file on your local network such as KeyPass, or applications which store passwords securely on a website such as the Password Vault available at http://dcac.co/go/pv.

REFERENCES

Choosing an Authentication Mode. Microsoft TechNet: Resources for IT Professionals.
Connecting to the database engine using extended protection. MSDN Microsoft development, subscriptions, resources, and more.

Securing the Instance

6

INFORMATION IN THIS CHAPTER:

- What to install and when
- SQL authentication and windows authentication
- Password change policies
- Auditing failed logins
- Renaming the SA account
- Disabling the SA account
- Securing endpoints
- Stored procedures as a security measure
- Minimum permissions possible
- Linked servers
- Using policies to secure your instance
- SQL azure specific settings
- Instances that leave the office
- SQL CLR
- Extended stored procedures
- Protecting your connection strings
- Database firewalls
- Clear virtual memory pagefile
- User access control (UAC)
- Other domain policies to adjust
- Reporting services

WHAT TO INSTALL, AND WHEN?

When building a new Microsoft SQL Server, proper security planning starts even before you launch the SQL Server installer. Each component of the Microsoft SQL Server product suite adds another piece that needs to be managed and patched regularly. Each additional component that is installed also provides a potential for additional security holes that could provide an attacker with an entry point into the SQL Server instance.

> **NOTE**
>
> **We Protect Against Potential Attacks**
>
> Fortunately, in the Microsoft SQL Server world, we are pretty lucky when it comes to security problems. In the last several versions of the database engine, Microsoft has done a very good job when it comes to securing the instance, and not having any security flaws that need to be patched. This is not to say that there have never been security issues within SQL Server, as there have been. However, as ultra-paranoid DBAs we do not guard against actual threats; we want to guard against any potential threat that we can conceive of. When this approach is taken, even if a security vulnerability is found, the SQL Server instances would not be susceptible to attack because the component that has the security problem is not installed or available on the server.

In Microsoft SQL Server 2000 and older, it was standard practice among most database administrators (DBAs) as well as Microsoft to install more components than were needed, such as the database engine, full-text search, DTS, and replication on the server hosting the database. This is because these subcomponents were not separate components but were all part of the database engine. This technique, however, leads to install components that you do not need; this can lead you to having security problems on the SQL Server's server that you may not realize are there because the component is not ever used.

In Microsoft SQL Server 2005 and later, this is becoming less and less the case, as each major function within the SQL Server product is now a separate component that can be installed or uninstalled as needed, so that only the minimum components that are needed are installed on the SQL Server. If you do end up with components installed that you do not need, for the most part you can simply stop the service that corresponds to this component, as without the service running, any potential security holes in that component are not available to the attacker. Only installing the services that are needed requires some additional planning and understanding of what will be used on the SQL Server so that the correct components are installed. This additional research and understanding is the price for reducing the potential attack surface.

This can be seen by default when a single instance of the Microsoft SQL Server 2008 engine (or newer) is installed as the default instance. When you install any instance of the Microsoft SQL Server engine, the SQL Browser is installed. When you only have a single instance installed, and that instance is the default instance, the SQL Browser is installed by default in a disabled state. This is because the SQL Browser is not used when connecting to the default instance.

There are two reasons that the SQL Browser is disabled by default when only a default instance is installed and that it should be disabled on older versions unless it is needed. The first reason is to reduce the number of components running on the server to reduce the attack surface. The second is to limit attacks like the SQL Slammer Worm that went around in 2003.

FAQ

What Does the SQL Browser Do?

The SQL 2000 driver and the SQL Native Client use the SQL Browser to identify the TCP port number that a named instance is listening on when a connection to a named instance is requested. This is because, by default, named instances are configured to use a dynamic port number.

When connecting to the default instance of Microsoft SQL Server, unless a specific TCP port is specified in the connection string, the SQL 2000 driver and the SQL Native Client will assume that the SQL Server is running on TCP port 1433. Because this assumption is made, the SQL 2000 driver and the SQL Native Client will not make a request to the SQL Browser to get the TCP port number. This assumption is made to save a round trip between the client and the server to save time when connecting to the default instance.

The SQL Browser works by listening on UDP port 1434 for connections from the SQL 2000 driver and the SQL Native Client. When the SQL 2000 driver or the SQL Native Client connects to the UDP port, they inform the SQL Browser of the name of the instance they are attempting to connect to. The SQL Browser will then respond with a TCP port number, which the SQL driver will then use to attempt to connect to the correct instance. As each Microsoft SQL Server instance on the server is started, it informs the SQL Browser of its name, and the TCP port number on which it is listening for requests.

NOTE

SQL Slammer Was a Major Embarrassment

The SQL Slammer Worm was unleashed on the world in January 2003 to the dismay of DBAs everywhere. The SQL Slammer attacked a vulnerability in the SQL Browser service, which was installed and running on every computer running Microsoft SQL Server 2000, including MSDE instances, which were installed by default by a variety of products including Visual Studio and Office Business Contact Manager.

The basic attack consisted of a 376-byte UDP packet being sent to the SQL Browser. Depending on the response from the SQL Browser, a remote privilege execution bug was used to grant the attacking code to upload the SQL Slammer Worm onto the server and launch it. Once infected, the server would begin scanning the local network and the Internet for other machines with which to infect, making the virus self-replicating. Because of the self-replicating nature of the virus, simply removing the virus from the SQL Server was not enough, for the server would become infected often within just a few minutes.

Fortunately, the SQL Slammer Worm did not have any additional payload other than to infect other machines with itself. It is assumed that the SQL Slammer worm was a test run to see how well the replication code would work. However, the replicate code worked a little too well, as within minutes of being infected, the Internet connection for the infected machine would run up to 100% utilization (or as close to 100% utilization as the worm could get) as the worm looked for more servers to infect. If the self-replication code was a little better behaved, it could have been months before anyone noticed the worm, this time with a dangerous payload running on SQL Servers and desktops in almost every company. The worm was able to make its way into most companies, not by going through corporate firewalls, but by infecting company laptops that had the MSDE edition installed on them (often without the user's or the DBAs' knowledge). The employee would then bring the infected laptop onto the company network where it would begin looking for internal and external SQL Servers to infect.

Microsoft's saving grace with regard to the SQL Slammer worm was that the patch for the problem had been released in October 2002. However, DBAs were slow to install the patch on their servers, leaving them open to SQL Slammer attack, which came three months later.

While the SQL Slammer worm did not do any damage with regard to data loss or data theft, several companies were unable to operate for days or weeks while they patched and cleaned hundreds or thousands of computers, all of which had been infected with the SQL Slammer worm. This included at least one of the major banks in the United States, which was unable to process debit card transactions for several days while the SQL Slammer cleanup proceeded.

You can read more about SQL Slammer by looking at the cert advisory published for the worm at http://www.cert.org/advisories/CA-2003-04.html or by looking at the Microsoft Security Bulletin MS02-061, which can be found at http://www.microsoft.com/technet/security/bulletin/MS02-061.mspx.

SQL Slammer was a wakeup call to SQL Server DBAs who, until this time, were known to install Service Packs only when there was a specific reason for installation. After the SQL Slammer was released on the world, DBAs became much more willing to install Service Packs and hotfixes more regularly on the database servers. Because of the extent of the problems, damage, and lost revenue that SQL Slammer caused, business users became more willing to accept the small amount of downtime that SQL Server patching required in order to protect themselves.

When installing a new Microsoft SQL Server, only install those components that are actually necessary for the application or applications that will be using the instance to function. If SQL Reporting Service and SQL Integration Service are not needed, then do not install those components. The same applies to the SQL Server Management tools. If you do not have a need to run the SQL Server Management Tools on the server's console, there is no need to install them. This is especially true on SQL Server 2005 and newer as installing the management tools also installs the Visual Studio shell, which gives yet another product that needs to be patched to ensure that it is safe to have installed.

SQL AUTHENTICATION AND WINDOWS AUTHENTICATION

Microsoft SQL Server has for many years now, going back to 6.0 if not further, given two different authentication methods when connecting to the SQL Server Engine. These authentication methods are SQL Authentication and Windows Authentication.

SQL Server Authentication takes place when the username and password for the account are both stored within the database engine. These accounts do not have any relation to any local or domain user account and can be used by any number of people to connect to the database engine.

Windows Authentication is based on an account being created and managed either on the operating system that is running under the SQL Server or on the Windows Active Directory domain that the server running the SQL Server is a member of, or has access to through domain trusts.

Windows Authentication is more secure than SQL authentication because with Windows Authentication the username and password are not sent between the client application and the SQL Server. Instead, a ticket is generated on the domain controller and passed to the client, who then passes it to the SQL Server instance for authentication. This ticket is then verified against the domain controller to ensure that it is valid and that it was passed to the SQL Server from the correct computer.

When you install SQL Server, several accounts are created by default. As for SQL Accounts, only one account has always been created, which is the system administrator (SA) account. Newer versions of SQL Server starting with SQL Server 2005 will create two additional accounts, which are "##MS_PolicyEventProcessingLogin##" and "##MS_PolicyTsqlExecutionLogin##." These logins, among others that may be created, depending on what features are installed on the instance, are for internal use by the database engine and should be left disabled. They should not be deleted, as the parts of the database engine that require them will not work correctly without them. These special logins that start with ## are certificate logins, so they are bound to a specific certificate each and that certificate is required in order to log in to the instance using that login.

FAQ

Domain Trusts?

Domain Trusts are used to allow multiple Windows domains access to each other. Several different kinds of trusts can be created between domains, the more advanced of which are beyond the scope of this book. The key points to remember about domain trusts is that any domains within the same domain tree (contoso.local and newyork.contoso.local, for example) have an automatic two-way transitive trust, which means that users in either domain can access resources in the other domain. The transitive part means that if the newyork.contoso.local domain had a child domain such as queens.newyork.contoso.local then because that domain has a two-way transitive trust to its parent, the trust is implied all the way up and down the tree. Thus, users in queens.newyork.contoso.com and contoso.com can access resources in the other domain as the authentication will be passed to the other domain via the newyork.consoso.local domain, as shown in the Active Directory diagram in Figure 6.1.

The same applies to domains that are within the same Active Directory forest, but are not members of the same Active Directory Tree. If you have a forest with two trees in it, contoso. local and adventureworks.local, the root domains of those trees would have a two-way transitive trust between them, automatically allowing any user in either domain, or any subdomain, to access resources within any domain or subdomain of the other tree as shown in the Active Directory diagram in Figure 6.2.

Systems administrators can also create external trusts between domains or forests to other domains or forests, allowing partner companies Windows Authentication to be used against internal resources. These trusts can be one way or two way, and can be either transitive or intransitive (the trust is not shared with other domains in the forest).

Now from a technical standpoint there are no two-way trusts. When a two-way trust is created (either a transitive or nontransitive trust), two one-way trusts are created between the two domains. There is no way to convert a two-way trust into a one-way trust. In order to do this, the two-way trust would need to be deleted and a new one-way trust created.

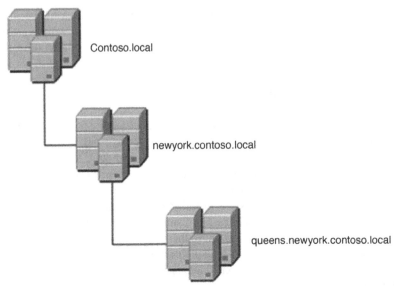

FIGURE 6.1 Showing a Windows domain tree with three layers having two-way transitive trusts between them.

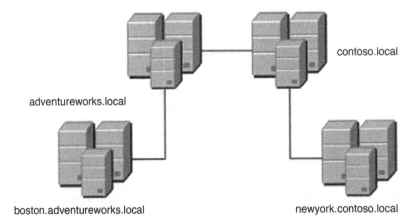

FIGURE 6.2 Showing a Windows forest tree with two domain trees having two-way transitive trusts between them.

Several Windows logins are created on a database instance by default. SQL Server 2005 and older will create a login for BUILTIN\Administrators, which allows anyone who is a member of the Administrators group on the Windows OS to log into the SQL

> **NOTE**
>
> **More Information about the Windows Authentication Process**
>
> The Windows Authentication process is rather lengthy when you include the various local and domain groups that are possible, as well as handling for both Kerberos and NTLM authentication. The process is fully documented in Chapter 5 of this book within the section titled "SQL Server Password Security" for your reference if you would like to read up further on the internal processes that happen between clicking connect and actually getting connected.

Server. By default, this group is a member of the sysadmin fixed server role, meaning that anyone in the local Administrators group is a member of the sysadmin fixed server role. When SQL Server 2008 and newer are installed they do not create this Windows login, as this login is considered to be a security violation in as much as it grants people other than the DBA system administrator (SA) rights to the database instance, and also allows people other than the DBA to grant other people SA rights on the database server by placing them within the local Administrators group. For database instances that have the BUILTIN\Administrators login, it is recommended that you, after granting SA rights to the DBAs, remove the BUILTIN\Administrators from the sysadmin fixed server role as well as removing the login from the instance. Some services such as the full-text service expect the BUILTIN\Administrators login to exist on older versions. If rights are removed from the BUILTIN\Administrators login, or the BUILTIN\Administrators login is removed, the "NT AUTHORITY\SYSTEM" login must be added so that these services will continue to function correctly.

While adding in "NT AUTHORITY\SYSTEM" will get services like the full-text service running again, it should be understood what the risks are with adding this login to the SQL Server. By adding this login to the SQL Server you give any application which is running under the local system account the ability to log into the SQL Server database instance. When the local system account has sysadmin rights great care should be taken to ensure that other applications are not installed on the server which are running under the local system account.

The versions of Microsoft SQL Server starting with the SQL 2008 version will also create other local Windows logins by default. While these logins should not be removed, they should be understood. These logins are as follows.

- NT AUTHORITY\SYSTEM
- NT SERVICE\MSSQLSERVER
- NT SERVICE\SQLSERVERAGENT

The "NT AUTHORITY\SYSTEM" service is used to allow applications running under the local system account access to the database instance. This is used for services such as the full-text indexing service that runs under the local system account. The "NT AUTHORITY\SYSTEM" login is a member of the sysadmin fixed server role, which can present a security risk because any application running under the local system account will have SA rights to the database instance. Unfortunately, the full-text service cannot be run under an account other than the local system account, as running under an account other than the local system account is an unsupported configuration. You can look to see what other applications will be running under the local system account by looking at the services which are configured to startup under that account, and any applications which are configured to be started by the scheduled tasks feature of the Windows operating system.

The "NT SERVICE\MSSQLSERVER" and "NT SERVICE\SQLSERVER-AGENT" Windows logins are service-specific logins that are used to run the SQL Service and the SQL Server Agent when the services are configured to run under the local system account. When the services are configured to run under a domain or local account, these logins will not exist; instead Windows logins will exist for the accounts that are running the services.

When installing SQL Server 2008 or higher, the installer will ask you to specify the Windows accounts, either accounts or groups, that should be members of the sysadmin fixed server role. The installer will add these Windows accounts as logins as the installation process is completed so that those Windows logins are members of the sysadmin fixed server role.

With SQL Accounts there is more to worry about than just having to protect from brute force attacks. Depending on what access someone can get to the database server there are other ways into the system. Some examples include shutting down the instance and editing the master.mdf file directly with a hex editor and changing the password to an encrypted value for a known password. Another technique that can be used is to attach a debugger to the SQL Engine process and capture the password as it comes into the engine and is processed.

In the event that all the accounts are removed from a SQL Server 2008 or higher instance the SQL Server does not need to be reinstalled in order to regain sysadmin rights to the SQL Server. The SQL Server can be restarted from the command line in single user mode. This will allow any member of the local Administrators group to log into the database instance as a member of the sysadmin fixed server role so that sysadmin permissions can be granted to other logins which need the rights allowing control of the instance to be restored.

EDITING THE MASTER.MDF FILE

Editing the master.mdf file to change the password is the least sneaky of the techniques, as it requires an outage to the database instance to complete, but it is the easiest. To break into the SQL Server using this technique simply backup the master database file, and restore it to another machine as a user database (called master_old or something similar). Query from another SQL Server Instance the hash for the password of an account that has a known password. The password can be queried from the syslogins catalog view in the master database. On the database that has been restored, update the password for the SA account in the master_old database to update the value to the password for the SA account (or other account that needs to be changed). Once the password has been changed, detach the master_old database. Stop the instance you wish to get into and replace the master.mdf with the

---

FAQ

More Information

The process of gathering passwords with a debugger is a rather complex process that does not explain well on paper. Fortunately, Sean and Jen McCown have published a video on the MidnightDBA.com website in which Sean walks you through the process of capturing a user's password as it comes through on the wire from a client. The video can be viewed or downloaded from http://bit.ly/RecoverSQLPasswords. The really interesting part of the video is about 6 min, which is where Sean finds the password in the memory dump.

   This trick will not work forever when it comes to getting passwords out of the database engine. Microsoft has been aware of this problem for some time now and is actively working on resolving this issue. While this has been fixed in Microsoft SQL Server 2012, the fix for this cannot be expected to be back ported to older versions of Microsoft SQL Server.

---

master_old.mdf file. When the instance starts up, attempt to log in to the SQL Server instance using the password you just changed.

USING A DEBUGGER TO INTERCEPT PASSWORDS

As the SQL Server Engine is just a computer process (albeit a very complex one), you can attach a debugger to the instance and get access to some of the data that the instance is passing around within the engine. This can be done by attaching a debugger to the instance and waiting for someone to log into the instance using an SQL Login. When this happens, the SQL Server will have the password in plain text in a variable that can be viewed through the debugger and used to now log into the SQL Server.

   You can use a memory debugger such as Olly Debugger, or even the sysinternals tools which are written by Microsoft, to capture the memory pages owned by the SQL Server process. Within these memory pages you can simply search for the login name that you want to find the password for.

PURCHASED PRODUCTS

All the truly lazy hacker needs is a copy of the master.mdf either by taking it from the database server itself or the backup server and a copy of a program like Advanced SQL Password Recovery by Elcomsoft, which allows you to view or reset the passwords in SQL Server 2000, 2005, or 2008. Once the hackers have the SA password, it is simple to now log into your servers and export and/or destroy the data that the server protects (Figures 6.1 and 6.2).

PASSWORD CHANGE POLICIES

After installing the SQL Server engine on the server, you will probably begin creating SQL Server accounts. Using SQL Server 2005 or newer, creating accounts that use SQL Server Authentication will give you a few checkboxes, shown in Figure 6.3, which you need to understand so that you know how these options work. If you are

FIGURE 6.3 The policy option checkboxes for a SQL Authentication account created on SQL Server 2005 or higher.

in a Windows NT 4 domain, then these options will not be available to you and they will be grayed out as Windows NT 4 domain's password policies are not used by Microsoft SQL Server.

The first checkbox, "Enforce password policy," tells the SQL Server that the password must fit within the password requirements of the Windows domain, or the local security policy defined on the server (if the server is not in a Windows domain). The password policies that are being enforced by the first checkbox are the "Enforce password history," "Minimum password length," and "Password must meet complexity requirements" policy settings.

The password policies within Windows Server cannot be checked after the login has been created. The password policies are only evaluated when a new login is created or when the password for an existing login has been changed. The system function PWDCOMPARE can be used to check accounts for known or blank passwords easily enough. The system function accepts three parameters, two of which are the most important and the third of which only needs to be used against a password hash from a SQL Server 2000 system.

```
SELECT name
FROM sys.sql_logins
WHERE PWDCOMPARE('', password_hash) = 1 ;
```

Querying the SQL Server instance for all logins which have a blank password.

The first parameter is the known password that is being checked in plain text, while the second is the password hash. Either a table, such as the sys.sql_logins catalog view, can be queried or a specific hash can be passed in. The third parameter accepts only a zero or a one with a default of 0. When a one is specified this indicates that you will be passing in a password hash which was generated by a SQL Server 2000 or older instance, when you are running the PWDCOMPARE statement on a SQL Server 2005 or newer instance.

NOTE

Group Policy Definitions

All six of the group policy settings – the five that SQL Server uses and the one that SQL Server does not look at – which control password policies within a Windows domain are explained in Chapter 3 in greater detail. Because they are covered there, they are only discussed at a high level in this chapter.

The second checkbox, "Enforce password expiration," tells the SQL Server that this account must change its password based on the "Minimum password age" and "Maximum password age" settings that come from the domain or the local security policy.

The third checkbox shown in Figure 6.3 is the "User must change password at next login" option. In Figure 6.3 the option is disabled because the "Enforce password expiration" option is not selected. If the "Enforce password expiration" option were checked, then the "User must change password at next login" option would be available. By checking this option and clicking OK the next time the user attempts to log into the database engine, the user will need to change their password.

The advantage of having and using these policies is that all the SQL Authentication accounts that are configured to follow the policies meet the password policies that have been defined on the domain.

FAQ

How the Password Change Process Works

If the user connects to the SQL Server with an account that has an expired password, then they will need to be prompted to change their password. If the user is using SQL Server Management studio, they will be prompted to change they password automatically as shown in Figure 6.4. The same will happen when using the SQLCMD command line tool.

However, when using your own application to log into the database, such as a Windows Forms application, the application will need to know how to prompt the user for a new password, as well as what to do with the new password in order to change the password for the SQL Account.

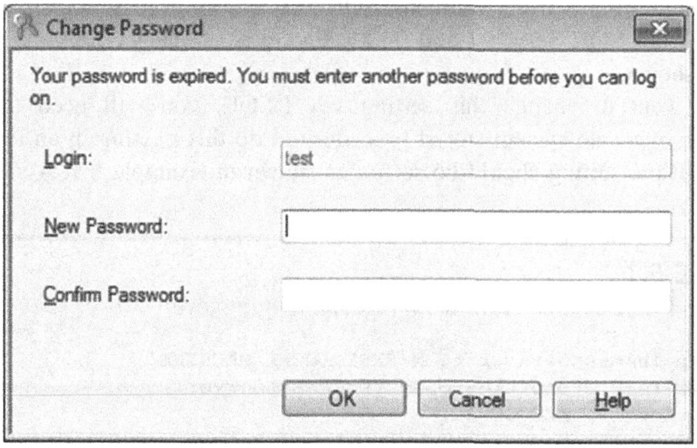

FIGURE 6.4 The Change Password dialog shown in SQL Server Management Studio.

AUDITING FAILED LOGINS

Microsoft SQL Server has, since at least version 6.5, included the ability to audit failed login connections to the ERRORLOG file. This auditing allows the DBA to know when someone is attempting to log into the database using an account for which they have no password. While this feature has been around for many versions, it was enhanced with the release of Microsoft SQL Server 2005 to include the IP Address of the computer that attempted the login. Before this change, the only information provided was the username that was being used to attempt to log into the database. This information is important to log so that you know when someone is attempting to break into the database.

You can also log successful login attempts to the database, which is information that can also be useful to track. If you do not track successful login attempts, you do not know why attempts to break into the SQL Server have stopped. If you do track this information and you see the login attempts stop, followed by successful logins, you know that the password was found and you need to change your password. If you see the login attempts stop, and no successful logins are found, then you know that the person gave up the attempt. The downside to logging the successful attempts is that all successful attempts are logged; thus on a very busy SQL Server instance that has hundreds or thousands of connections per second, the ERRORLOG file will get very full, very quickly.

Changing this setting is easily done via the Enterprise Manager or SQL Server Management Studio (depending on the version that you are using), as the setting is controlled via a registry key. When using Enterprise Manager, connect to the server and right click on the server and select properties. When using SQL Server Management Studio, connect to the server in the Object Explorer and select properties. Regardless of the version, then select the Security tab. Then look for the "Login auditing" section in the dialog box. Here you can select from None, failed only, successful only, or both failed and successful as shown in Figure 6.3. While the screenshot shown in Figure 6.5 is from Microsoft SQL Server 2008 R2s Management Studio, the dialog from SQL Server 7 and 2000s Enterprise Manager looks very similar to the one shown.

If you want to change this setting via T-SQL, you will need to use the xp_instance_regwrite system stored procedure to do this passing in an integer that defines what the setting should be set to, as shown in Example 6.1. A setting of 1

EXAMPLE 6.1

Sample T-SQL code on how to change the logging level.

```
EXEC xp_instance_regwrite N'HKEY_LOCAL_MACHINE',
N'Software\Microsoft\MSSQLServer\MSSQLServer',
N'AuditLevel', REG_DWORD, 2
GO
```

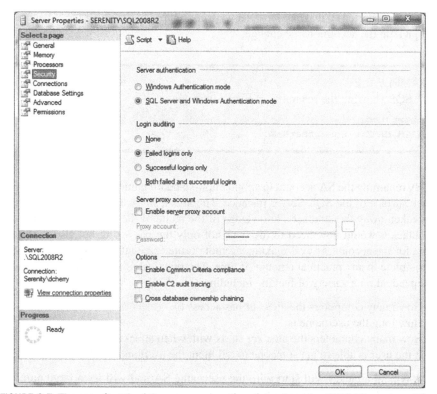

FIGURE 6.5 The security tab of the server properties dialog from the 2008 R2 version of the SQL Server Management Studio.

indicates that successful login only should be logged. A setting of 2 indicates that failed logins only should be logged. A setting of 3 indicates that both successful and failed logins should be logged. A setting of 0 indicates that neither failed nor successful logins should be logged.

No matter if you change this setting via T-SQL or the management tool, a restart of the SQL Instance is required before the setting change will take effect.

RENAMING THE SA ACCOUNT

Starting with SQL Server 2005, you have the ability to rename the SA account to another username to make the account more difficult for an attacker to use. This is an important security step to take, especially if the SQL Server is available on the public Internet. To rename the SA account use the ALTER LOGIN command as shown in Example 6.2. Microsoft SQL Server 2000 and older will not have the ability to rename the SA account. After you rename the SA account, the SQL Server Agent will need to be restarted so that any jobs that were configured to run under the SA account will pick up the account name change.

EXAMPLE 6.2

T-SQL showing the renaming of the SA account.

```
ALTER LOGIN sa
WITH NAME = SomeOtherName
```

By renaming the SA account to another non-standard name, we greatly reduce the attack surface of the SQL Server Instance. The attack surface is reduced as we have now taken away the attacker's knowledge of the name of the account to login with. An attacker would now need to discover not only the password, but also the username for the account as well making a remote brute force attack very, very difficult to complete in any practical amount of time. The practical amount of time, however, is dependent on a variety of factors, including:

- How many computers the attacker has access to;
- How long the username is;
- How many characters the attacker starts with when attacking the SQL Server;
- If the user is able to get someone to tell them the username.

A typical attacker will start with the username SA and will try a large number of passwords before starting to try different usernames. The longer the username is the longer it will take an attacker to gain access to the database instance, with most attackers giving up long before finding the actual username and password. The biggest reason that this attack will take so long is that the SQL Server returns the same error message if the wrong username and password is used or if just the wrong username is used. In either case error 18456 will be returned with a level of 14 and a state of 1, with the wording of the error message simply stating "Login failed for user '{username}'," where {username} is the username that has attempted to log into the database instance.

DISABLING THE SA ACCOUNT

An important security procedure that many people do not follow is disabling the SA account. By having this account enabled, you have done half of the work for an attacker as the username for the SA account is well known by attackers. This means that the attacker just needs to figure out the password. While there is hopefully a very strong password on the SA account, with the account enabled the attacker can sit there and hammer away on the SA account until getting the password correctly. Where you disable the SA account does not matter if the attacker gets the password correct; regardless, the account would not allow the attacker into the SQL Server instance.

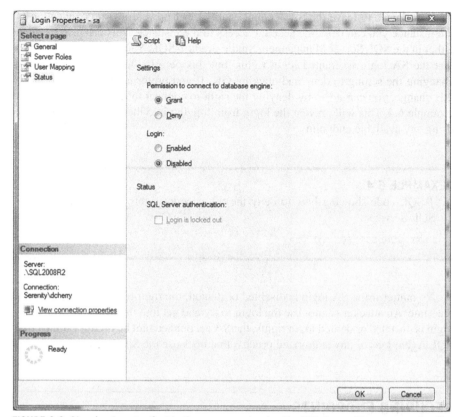

FIGURE 6.6 Showing how to disable the sa account using the SQL Server Management Studio.

If the SQL Instance is configured for Windows Only Authentication, then there is no need to disable the SA account as the SA account is an SQL login and when Windows Only Authentication is used the SA account cannot be used.

Disabling the SA account is a fairly easy process to complete. Connect to the server in question using the Object Explorer and expand the security node. Double click the SA account from the list and select the status tab. Select the disabled radio button and click OK as shown in Figure 6.6.

If you prefer to use T-SQL to disable the SA login you can do so with the ALTER LOGIN statement as shown in Example 6.3.

EXAMPLE 6.3

T-SQL showing how to disable the SA login.

```
ALTER LOGIN [sa] DISABLE
```

If you wish to leave the SA account enabled, but prevent it from connecting to the instance you can deny the account access to the instance. This can also be done either in the SQL Server Management Studio or via T-SQL. You can see in Figure 6.6 that the SA login is granted login rights, but this permission can be removed by changing the setting to deny and clicking OK. If you prefer to use T-SQL to make this change, you can do so by denying the right to connect to the login as shown in Example 6.4. This will prevent the login from logging into the SQL Server instance using any available endpoint.

EXAMPLE 6.4

T-SQL code showing how to deny the SA account rights to connect to the SQL Server.

```
DENY CONNECT SQL TO [sa]
```

No matter if the SA login is disabled or denied, the right to connect the result is the same. An attacker cannot use the login to try and get into the instance. As the SA login is disabled or denied login rights, the SA account cannot be used for things like SQL Agent jobs or any authorized process that does use the SA account.

SECURING ENDPOINTS

By default, Microsoft SQL Server 2005 and higher have several endpoints on each instance. These default endpoints are what users will normally be connecting to. If users are connecting using TCP, then they will connect to the "TSQL Default TCP" endpoint. If users are connecting using Named Pipes, then they will connect to the "TSQL Named Pipes" endpoint. If users are connecting using VIA, then they will connect to the "TSQL Default VIA" endpoint.

To provide an additional layer of security, you can create an endpoint that is an application-specific endpoint and configure it so that the endpoint will only allow the application account to use the endpoint. This way if an attacker is able to get into the web server and attempts to initiate his or her own connections to the SQL Server, the connection information coming from the applications connection string will reference an endpoint that the attacker cannot connect to with any account other than the application account. Attempted logins using other accounts to that endpoint would then fail to allow the user to connect.

By default, when you create a new endpoint on your SQL Server, the fixed server role public has its rights to connect to the T-SQL Default TCP endpoint removed as an additional security measure. You can correct this by running the code shown in Example 6.5.

EXAMPLE 6.5

T-SQL code showing how to restore the default connection rights to the default TCP endpoint.

```
GRANT CONNECT ON ENDPOINT::[TSQL Default TCP] to [public]
```

After you have created a new TCP endpoint for the application account to use for a connection, you will need to revoke the public rights to connect to the new endpoint, grant the application account rights to connect to that endpoint, and deny the application account rights to connect to the default endpoint as shown in Example 6.6.

EXAMPLE 6.6

T-SQL code showing how to secure an application account so that it can only connect to the specified endpoint.

```
/* Create the new endpoint*/
CREATE ENDPOINT SampleEndpoint AS TCP (LISTENER_PORT=12345,
LISTENER_IP=ALL)
FOR TSQL()
/*Grant rights back to the public endpoint*/
GRANT CONNECT ON ENDPOINT:: [TSQL Default TCP] to public
/* Remove default rights for all users to connect to the new endpoint.*/
REVOKE CONNECT ON ENDPOINT::[SampleEndpoint] to [public]
/* Prevent application account from connecting to default endpoint*/
DENY CONNECT ON ENDPOINT::[TSQL Default TCP] to [ApplicationAccount]
/* Allow application account to connect to Sample Endpoint.*/
GRANT CONNECT ON ENDPOINT::[SampleEndpoint] to [ApplicationAccount]
```

Regardless of what permissions that are granted to a T-SQL endpoint, all members of the sysadmin fixed server role can connect to the endpoint, as can the login who created the endpoint.

CERTIFICATE ENDPOINT AUTHENTICATION

There are certain processes which can use certificates to authenticate over endpoints. As of SQL Server 2014 these are all limited in scope to being internal SQL Server processes such as the SQL Service Broker, Database Mirroring, AlwaysOn Availability Groups, etc. These processes can be configured to authenticate to another SQL Server using certificates instead of domain accounts. This is needed in the case of SQL Service Broker or Database Mirroring when the servers which are talking

---

NOTE

Before Certificate Permissions

When exporting certificates from one SQL Server instance and importing them into another SQL Server instance be careful of the permissions which are created on the certificate backups by default. When SQL Server backs up the certificates the files which are created on the hard drive are by default secured so that only the SQL Server process and the account who backed the certificate up can read the certificate. If you then attempt to import the certificate to another machine which does not run under the same account the SQL Server would not be able to read the certificate backup and will fail with a file permission error. This is most common in test labs where everything may be running on a single server, but under different accounts, but it is possible in production as well.

Resolving the problem requires connecting to the server's console via the Remote Desktop Protocol (RDP) and changing the permissions on the backup file which was created so that the new SQL Server instance has access to the file.

---

to each other are not members of Windows Active Directory Domains which have domain trusts configured. When there is no Windows Active Directory domain trust configured the servers are not able to use their service accounts to authenticate so they must use another option, which in this case would be certificate authentication.

Setting up an endpoint for certificate authentication is a relatively straightforward process. A certificate is created on the two servers which need to communicate with each other. After the certificate has been created, the needed endpoint can be configured by specifying the "AUTHENTICATION = CERTIFICATE" option as shown in Example 6.8. Then the certificates are backed up from the master database in each SQL Server database instance and then restored to the other SQL Server instance.

Creating the certificates is done via the CREATE CERTIFICATE command as shown in Example 6.7. Each server should have a certificate with a unique name created so that there are no naming collisions when restoring the certificates to other servers. In the example shown in Example 6.7 the name of the server which this certificate is being created on is "ServerA" so the certificate is named "Auth-Cert_ServerA." If the server which ServerA was going to communicate with was called ServerB, then the certificate created on ServerB would be called "Auth-Cert_ServerB." Naming standards for certificates become critical so that the source machine for the certificate can be easily identified in the event that certificates need to be renewed.

EXAMPLE 6.7

Code to create a certificate for Endpoint Communication

```
CREATE CERTIFICATE AuthCert_ServerA
WITH SUBJECT = 'Auth Certificate',
     START_DATE = '1/1/2014',
     EXPIRY_DATE = '12/31/2016'
GO
```

Once the certificates have been created on each of the servers which will communicate with each other, the Endpoints can be created. Endpoints are created with the CREATE ENDPOINT command as shown in Example 6.8. In the example the certificate "AuthCert_ServerA" is used to secure the endpoint. This means that this is the certificate which will need to exist on the remote machine so that the remote machine can authenticate against this endpoint.

EXAMPLE 6.8

Creating an Endpoint for SQL Service Broker using a certificate for authentication

```
CREATE ENDPOINT [ServiceBrokerEndpoint]
        AUTHORIZATION [sa]
        STATE=STARTED
        AS TCP (LISTENER_PORT = 1234, LISTENER_IP = ALL)
        FOR SERVICE_BROKER (MESSAGE_FORWARDING = DISABLED,
                MESSAGE_FORWARD_SIZE = 10,
                AUTHENTICATION = CERTIFICATE AuthCert_ServerA,
                ENCRYPTION = REQUIRED ALGORITHM RC4)
GO
```

At this point if the SQL Server instances attempted to communicate using the endpoints on the remote instances the communication would fail. This is because ServerA does not have the certificate to authenticate against the endpoint on ServerB and ServerB does not have the certificate to authenticate against the endpoint on ServerA. Doing the certificate exchange requires backing up the certificate using the BACKUP CERTIFICATE command as shown in Example 6.9 followed by the CREATE CERTIFICATE command shown in Example 6.10. In these examples the code shown in Example 6.9 would be run on ServerA and would create the .cer file, while the code shown in Example 6.10 would be run on ServerB. Before running the code shown in Example 6.10 on ServerB the file c:\temp\AuthCert_ServerA.cer would need to be copied from ServerA to ServerB.

EXAMPLE 6.9

Backing up the certificate on ServerA

```
BACKUP CERTIFICATE AuthCert_ServerA TO FILE='C:\temp\AuthCert_ServerA.cer'
```

EXAMPLE 6.10

Restoring the certificate from ServerA on ServerB

```
CREATE CERTIFICATE AuthCert_ServerA
FROM FILE='c:\temp\AuthCert_ServerA.cer'
```

Making the code shown in Example 6.7, Example 6.8, Example 6.9 and Example 6.10 requires running this code twice on each server along with changing the certificate names so that they match correctly. If this code was laid out in a single large script to be run in SQLCMD mode within SQL Server Management Studio the script would look like that shown in Example 6.11. This example script uses the remote admin network shares of the remote machine to access the other server's certificate file. This is just one method of accessing the certificate, a remote network share which both servers have access to could be used as well.

EXAMPLE 6.11

Single code showing the order of operations for Examples 6.7–6.10 as a SQLCMD script.

```
:CONNECT ServerA
CREATE CERTIFICATE AuthCert_ServerA
WITH SUBJECT = 'Auth Certificate',
        START_DATE = '1/1/2014',
        EXPIRY_DATE = '12/31/2016'
GO
CREATE ENDPOINT [ServiceBrokerEndpoint]
        AUTHORIZATION [sa]
        STATE=STARTED
        AS TCP (LISTENER_PORT = 1234, LISTENER_IP = ALL)
        FOR SERVICE_BROKER (MESSAGE_FORWARDING = DISABLED,
                MESSAGE_FORWARD_SIZE = 10,
                AUTHENTICATION = CERTIFICATE AuthCert_ServerA,
                ENCRYPTION = REQUIRED ALGORITHM RC4)
GO
BACKUP CERTIFICATE AuthCert_ServerA TO FILE='C:\temp\AuthCert_ServerA.cer'
GO
:CONNECT ServerB
CREATE CERTIFICATE AuthCert_ServerB
WITH SUBJECT = 'Auth Certificate',
        START_DATE = '1/1/2014',
        EXPIRY_DATE = '12/31/2016'
GO
CREATE ENDPOINT [ServiceBrokerEndpoint]
        AUTHORIZATION [sa]
        STATE=STARTED
        AS TCP (LISTENER_PORT = 1234, LISTENER_IP = ALL)
        FOR SERVICE_BROKER (MESSAGE_FORWARDING = DISABLED,
                MESSAGE_FORWARD_SIZE = 10,
                AUTHENTICATION = CERTIFICATE AuthCert_ServerB,
                ENCRYPTION = REQUIRED ALGORITHM RC4)
GO
BACKUP CERTIFICATE AuthCert_ServerB TO FILE='C:\temp\AuthCert_ServerB.cer'
GO
CREATE CERTIFICATE AuthCert_ServerA
FROM FILE='\\ServerA\C$\temp\AuthCert_ServerA.cer'
GO
:CONNECT ServerA
CREATE CERTIFICATE AuthCert_ServerB
FROM FILE='\\ServerB\C$\temp\AuthCert_ServerB.cer'
GO
```

When more than two servers are involved in the application design, for example when database mirroring with automatic failover is used which requires three servers, this setup process gets more complex as each server needs to be able to authenticate against the other two servers. The larger the application configuration the more certificates need to be exchanged. If for example certificates were being used with AlwaysOn Availability Groups in a SQL Server 2014 Availability Group with 8 secondary replicas, then each server would have 9 certificates as every server needs to be able to authenticate with every other server in case that server have become the primary server.

STORED PROCEDURES AS A SECURITY MEASURE

Stored procedures make an excellent security measure for a couple of reasons:

1. Users do not need access to base tables to execute a stored procedure that uses the tables.
2. When calling stored procedures, the amount of access to the database is defined by the database developer.

ACCESS TO BASE TABLES IS NOT REQUIRED

When a stored procedure is run, the user account that runs the stored procedure only needs access to execute the stored procedure. No access to the underlying tables or views that are used by the stored procedure is needed for the stored procedure to execute. This is because of a concept within the database called a database permission chain. Database permission chaining is enabled by default and cannot be disabled.

Permissions chaining is what allows the user to access the tables via the stored procedure without the user having the ability to access the tables from outside the stored procedure. This is done because the SQL Server assumes that because the owner of the stored procedure has created the procedure to access these tables, and the stored procedure creator has access to the tables and views that are used by the procedure, so it is assumed that the user running the stored procedure should have access to those tables.

NOTE

Dynamic SQL versus Hardcoded SQL

Dynamic SQL within the stored procedure makes things work a little differently when it comes to permissions. When you run dynamic SQL, the dynamic SQL command is run outside the scope of the call to the stored procedure. Because the dynamic SQL is run out of scope, this breaks the permissions chain as permission chains cannot survive a change of scope. What this means is that the application account will need to have access to perform whatever operation the dynamic SQL specifies. If the dynamic SQL is a simple select, then the application account will need to have the select right granted to the table or view being accessed. The same goes for insert, update, or delete statements. Typically, the only commands that would be run through dynamic SQL are going to be select statements, as dynamic SQL is used to allow for dynamic sorting where the application layer can tell the database what column to sort the data with. However, in some cases, database developers have found reasons to use dynamic SQL for insert, update, and delete statements.

If the stored procedure needs to access tables or views within another database on the instance, the security chain can still be maintained. This is done by enabling cross database chaining, which was introduced in SQL Server 2000 Service Pack 3. When cross database chaining is enabled, it will allow the object security chain to pass from one database to another, removing the requirement of granting permissions to the tables and views that are being accessed in the second database.

Enabling Cross Database Chaining

By default, cross database chaining is disabled and needs to be enabled on the instance, as well as the databases that will be participating in the cross database chain. At the instance level this change is made by using the sp_configure system stored procedure, while the database level changes are made with the ALTER DATABASE command as shown in Example 6.12.

EXAMPLE 6.12

Enabling cross database chaining at the instance as well as the database level.

```
EXEC sp_configure 'cross db ownership chaining', 1
RECONFIGURE
GO
ALTER DATABASE YourFirstDatabase
SET DB_CHAINING ON
GO
ALTER DATABASE YourSecondDatabase
SET DB_CHAINING ON
GO
```

After enabling cross database chaining at the instance and database level, one last change to the database needs to be made. The login that will be using the stored procedure in the first database needs to be a member of the public fixed database role within the database that contains the tables. Without the login being mapped to a user within the second database, the user would not be able to log into the database to use cross database chaining. No other security permissions are needed in the second database.

MINIMUM PERMISSIONS POSSIBLE

A technique that has been alluded to in places throughout this book is the technique on giving users and applications only the minimal permission needed to get done whatever job needs to be done. By granting only the minimum permission

> **NOTE**
> **Lack of Security is not something to brag about**
> Recently a job posting came across my desk that I wanted to share with you. Its rather lengthy, so I will cut out the boring parts…
> "…We built our own platforms, i.e., for credit card transactions and order processing. We have a strong developer team that consists of 3 full time and 2 part time developers. And the CEO of the company is one of the most experienced developers in the industry. We do not have staging and QA servers, we work on production servers. …"
> Boy does not that sound like fun. Working on a credit card and order processing application without a dev and/or QA system. Being led by a "top" developer who apparently has no understanding of the risks that the company is under by not having Dev or QA systems. As all the development work is being done in production that can only lead to one security conclusion, that everyone is a member of the sysadmin fixed server role and can tweak everything as needed to get whatever they are working on working.
> At the very least this sort of setup is very irresponsible to your customers. As you are processing credit cards at the minimum this setup would not pass PCI compliance. At worst there might be criminal liability issues that need to be dealt with.

to the user account, the user is not able to accidentally (or intentionally) change data that they should not be able to, or to see data that they are not authorized to see.

The most complex part of granting minimum permissions is typically the discovery process where you work with the application developers or business users (when the business users have direct database access) to determine the correct permissions that the users need. This is because business users and developers often do not want to take the time to figure out what they *need* access to and will instead request what they *want* access to, which is everything. And everything usually translates to being a member of the dbo (database owner) fixed database role or the sysadmin fixed server role, both of which more than likely are more rights than are actually needed.

There is no easy technological solution to finding the permissions that users or applications need. You can use Microsoft SQL Profiler to help with this process. You can use SQL Server profiler to gather the commands that the user executes against the database. This captured information can then be used to document the objects that are being accessed. This documentation can then be used to determine what permissions the user or application needs, at which point the higher level permissions and rights that the user does not need are to be revoked. For this technique to work successfully, the SQL Profiler trace should be run for several weeks or months to ensure that all month-end, quarter-end, and year-end processes are captured to ensure that nothing is missed.

The other easy technique would be to start granting select permissions to the known table objects and then have a user begin using the application granting rights as needed to fix the various errors that come up. While this will eventually fix the permissions problem, it is a time-consuming and frustrating process, but it will work.

> **NOTE**
>
> **And How Many Members of the Sysadmin Fixed Server Role Do You Have?**
>
> The sysadmin fixed server role grants a massive amount of control to the database instance. A member of the sysadmin fixed server role has rights to everything within the database instance, and these rights cannot be revoked using any method. Due to the massive amount of power that can be wielded by the members of the sysadmin fixed server role, the number of SQL or Windows logins that are members of this role should be kept to a minimum. By keeping this to a minimum, it becomes much easier to see changes made to the membership of the sysadmin fixed server role.
>
> In a perfect world, the answer to the question "And How Many Members of the Sysadmin Fixed Server Role Do You Have??" is two. No more, no less. These two members should be the SA account (after having been renamed) and a Windows Domain (or local) group that allows the DBAs to have administrative rights to the instance. The Windows group that is a member of the sysadmin fixed server role should not be the BUILTIN\Administrators group, nor should it be the local administrators group referenced by the computer name or domain name. By using this group, other employees who have no business being within the database, such as the SAs, storage administrators, and network administrators, would have access to the database instance.

INSTANT FILE INITIALIZATION

Instant File Initialization was introduced in SQL Server 2005 much to the delight of Database Administrators everywhere. However, with Instant File Initialization comes some potential security risks as well. The way that Instant File Initialization works is that when the SQL Server database file is expanded the blocks on the disk are allocated to the database file, but the blocks are not actually written to. This allows the SQL Server to allocate massive amounts of space to a SQL Server database file very quickly, at rates of several hundred gigs of space in just a few seconds. Back in the SQL Server 2000 and earlier times (or when instant file initialization is disabled) as the database file's size was increased the new blocks which were allocated to the database file would be completely written with zeros.

The database file was filled with zeros for a couple of different reasons. The first is so that the data in the file is always formatted correctly in the known format that the SQL Server is expecting it to have. Another is to ensure that any data which already existed on the disk could not be read from the disk by someone who was not supposed to have access to it. This second reason is the security problem that comes into play with instant file initialization.

With instant file initialization enabled the SQL Server adds the blocks to the list of blocks which have been allocated to the database file, but if there was any data sitting on those blocks beforehand that data is still there, and can be read by the SQL Server. Say for example we have a 100 Gig hard drive which has two databases on it. One is the HR database and one is the reporting database and each database takes up 50 Gigs of space on the disk. Company policy states that no one should have access to read the data in the HR database except for the HR people. Because of this there are two instances installed on the SQL Server one for the HR database and one for the reporting database.

As time goes on the reporting database needs to grow, but it cannot because the HR database is taking up the rest of the space. The DBA and the HR staff work together to move the HR database to another server at the company allowing the reporting database to be grown to fill the hard drive. Without instant file initialization enabled the data pages which made up the old database are sitting there able to be read by using DBCC PAGE from the reporting instance. Until those pages are written to by the SQL Server, and by written to I mean new data is put down on the pages, any data which existed on those pages before would be easily readable from DBCC page. This means that with a little work and some patience anyone who has sysadmin rights on the reporting instance can now read the pages that used to make up the HR SQL Server database and view all the information which they were not supposed to be able to read.

Now there are a couple of different ways that we can protect ourselves from making the HR database be readable in the event that it is moved. The easiest would be to turn on Transparent Data Encryption (see Chapter 2 under "Encrypting Data At Rest") as TDE will encrypt the blocks on the disk preventing them from being readable. The nice thing about turning on TDE is that it, without a lot of overhead secures the database from prying eyes and it also protects the database backups from prying eyes as well; although it does introduce the complexity of key management to a system which according to the policy stated above does not have a normal DBA managing it.

The other good option would be to disable instant file initialization on the reporting instance. There are a couple of upsides to turning off instant file initialization. The first is that the data which was on the disk is gone as soon as the data file for the reporting database is expanded. The second is that the SQL Server now does not need to zero out the pages as it allocates them to objects. While you probably would not see any performance benefit from this, one can assume that if the SQL Server is going less work on page allocation that is probably a good thing. The big downside to having instant file initialization disabled is that when the database file needs to be expanded, this suddenly becomes a very expensive, and possibly offline operation. The reason that it is so expensive, is that, however, much space you just allocated to the database file needs to be filled with zeros before the space can be used and transaction which is expanding the database file can be completed. Now when manually expanding the database this "should not" be that bad of an operation as the users should still have space to work with so the only slow down should be as the new data pages are being written to disk (in one large 50 Gig chunk based on our scenario above). When the database has become full and SQL Server's auto-grow feature kicks in is where the real problems with not having instant file initialization come into play. When auto-grow kicks in it is because there are 0 unallocated pages in the database file, so in order to allocate a new page the file must expand. In order to do this the SQL Server pauses the users transaction and begins to grow the database file writing zeros to all the new pages which have been allocated. Once the zeros have been written to the database file the users transaction is allowed to continue. If the database growth event takes over 30 s, however, the users session will probably

> **NOTE**
>
> **Not All Database Files are Created Equal**
>
> Instant file initialization is only available for the data files of a SQL Server database. The Transaction Log file is not eligible for instant file initialization and must have zeros written to it before the transaction log can be used.

be killed by the calling application (.NET has a default command execution timeout of 30 s) which will cause their entire transaction to rollback, including the auto-grow. Then the next user comes in and tries to write data and the auto-grow kicks in again.

Typically, in these days it is recommended that instant file initialization is kept enabled unless there is a specific reason to have it disabled.

Instant file initialization is not just a setting that can be enabled or disabled from within SQL Server. It is part of a larger right which is granted at the operating system level. This operating system right is called "Perform volume maintenance tasks" and can be granted on a machine-by-machine basis, or it can be configured through Active Directory's group policy. In either case open the policy editor (either group policy editor via Active Directory or the local security policy editor). If editing via group policy navigate to "Computer Policies" then "Computer Configuration" then "Windows Settings." In either case then click on "Local Policies" then "User Rights Assignment." From there you will see "Perform volume maintenance tasks" on the right hand side of the window. Double clicking on this will display the list of users and groups that have this right assigned to them. By default only members of the local Administrators group (which includes the domain administrators group) have this right. If your SQL Server is not a member of the local administrators group (which it does not need to be) then this right will not be assigned and you will need to manually assign the right to the account which runs your SQL Server instance. If the SQL Server is running as a clustered instance for high availability this right must be granted on every node of the cluster otherwise instant file initialization will be enabled on some nodes and disabled on others providing an inconsistent performance and security experience between nodes.

LINKED SERVERS

Linked servers are a place where security problems can really pop up. Linked servers, which were introduced in SQL Server 7, allow a T-SQL statement or stored procedure to access database objects in the remote server. This remote server can be an SQL Server database, an Oracle database, an Excel sheet, and so on. The limits are basically driven by what ODBC (Open Database Connectivity) drivers are installed on the server.

When you configure a linked server, mappings are defined to grant security so that logins to the server to which the user is connected has a way to authenticate against the remote database instance. When you create a new login mapping, you specify the local login, as well as the remote login and password for the remote instance. Logins can be mapped from a Windows login or an SQL Login to a login of the same name by checking the Impersonate checkbox, or the login can be mapped to a different SQL login. When mapping to a different login, the remote login must be an SQL login and not a Windows login. The only way mapping to a Windows login can be done is when mapping is being done to the same Windows login, the user is logged into the system on the local server.

When a linked server is configured, a global mapping can be defined that covers all users that do not have specific mappings defined. Four options can be selected for this global mapping.

1. Not be made;
2. Be made without using a security context;
3. Be made using the login's current security context;
4. Be made using this security context.

When selecting the "Not be made" option, access to the remote server will be denied. Selecting the "Be made without using a security context," will attempt to log into the remote database instance without a username. When selecting the "Be made using the login's current security context" the Windows authentication credentials which the user used to connect to the database instance are passed to the remote SQL Instance. This option does not work when using SQL Authentication and requires that Kerberos (Kerberos is discussed in some detail within Chapter 3) be setup correctly for the authentication to be passed correctly to the remote server. The fourth option allows a specific SQL login to be used for all users that do not have specific login mappings defined.

Where linked servers can start to cause trouble is when some companies use linked servers to perform administrative tasks against all the SQL Servers within the environment from a central database server. Often when this is done the "Be made using this security context" option is selected, with a highly privileged account used as the remote login, often using a login that is a member of the sysadmin fixed server role, if not the SA account itself. This causes any user who connects to the database instance to then be able to connect via that linked server and execute tasks on that remote SQL Server with the high-level permissions of the mapped account.

NTLM Double Hop Problems

When configuring linked servers to pass Windows Authentication between instances, you can get into what is called the NTLM Double Hop problem. Where this problem comes into play is a limitation of the NTLM authentication process (some call it a bug, but it is really a design limitation) where NTLM does not allow a login token to be passed from the one server to another. The NTLM process will pass the login token from the user's computer to the database instance, which is the first hop. However, the database instance cannot pass that login token to the next database instance, which is the second hop. The second instance will reject the token because the token was created by a different computer other than the one that passed it the token. This is documented in Figure 6.7.

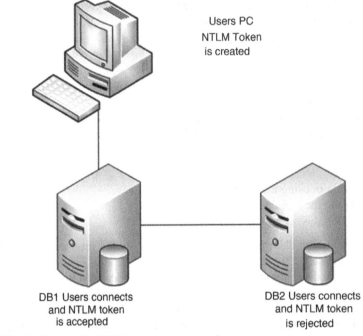

Users PC
NTLM Token
is created

DB1 Users connects
and NTLM token
is accepted

DB2 Users connects
and NTLM token
is rejected

FIGURE 6.7 Showing the NTLM process and rejection.

SECURING LINKED SERVERS

Security for linked servers is something that has not really changed very much for many releases now. When setting up a linked server there are only a couple of security settings which are called security login mappings where logins on one server are mapped to a login on another server. There is also a generic mapping which effects all logins which are not defined as a specific mapping.

One of the biggest problems with linked server security is that there is no support for domain or local Windows groups to exist in the list of mappings. This makes management of the linked servers quite difficult as when you add people to the SQL Server via domain groups, they would not get rights to the linked server automatically unless the global mapping is used when then grants rights to everyone across the linked server.

When setting up mappings between logins on one server and logins on another server only specific mappings between Windows and SQL Logins can be done as shown in Table 6.1.

Using SQL Server Management Studio for Linked Server Security Configuration

Setting up security mappings for a linked server can be done via the SQL Server Management Studio User Interface or via T-SQL. The easiest way to setup the mappings is via the SQL Server Management Studio User Interface as the changing of login mappings when done through T-SQL is done through a series of stored procedure calls.

Table 6.1 Showing which Authentication Types can Map to which Authentication Types

Source Server Login Type	Destination Server Login Type	
	SQL Server Login	**Windows Login**
SQL Server Login	Valid	
Windows Login	Valid	Valid

To change the security configuration on a linked server connect to the SQL Server with the linked server on it and connect to the SQL Server in the Object Explorer and navigate to "Server Objects" then "Linked Servers." Right click on the linked server and select properties on the context menu that opens; then click the Security page to view and change the security mappings as shown in Figure 6.8.

Figure 6.8 shows two different accounts which are specifically configured to access the linked server specifically. The first which is shown is the local SQL Login called "dcherry" which is mapped to another account on the remote SQL Server which is also called "dcherry" and has the password specified. The second login which is

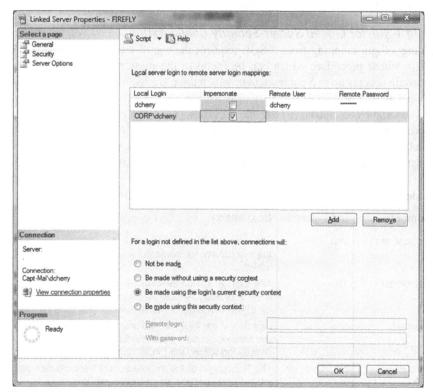

FIGURE 6.8 Showing the linked server security settings.

shown is a Windows account called "CORP\dcherry" which is configured to use the domain impersonation to access the remote server. For this remote impersonation to work correctly the servers must be configured with the correct Server Principal Names (SPNs) and Kerberos (see Chapter 3 for more information) must be working correctly.

A decision must then be made on how to deal with logins which attempt to access the linked server but are not listed in the list shown on the top half of Figure 6.8. This setting to controlled via the bottom half of the screen shown in Figure 6.8. The options are to block access to the linked server by using the "Not be made" option, connect without providing credentials (useful for things like Access) by using the "Be made without using a security context" option, using the same credentials which the user is currently logged in with by sing the "Be made using the login's current security context" or with a specific SQL Server login by selecting the "Be made using this security context" option and specifying a SQL Server login and password (Windows credentials cannot be entered here.

Using the "Be made without using a security context" option may or may not present a security issue depending on what kind of database the linked server is configured for, and how the security on that remote system is configured. If the remote system is a SQL Server database engine for example and no access has been granted to anonymous login attempts then this setting would not allow anyone access. However, if the remote database is something like Microsoft Access, then access may be granted to the remote data.

Using T-SQL for Linked Server Security Configuration
Adding a login mapping from T-SQL requires the use of the sp_addlinkedsrvlogin system stored procedure which can be found in the master database. This stored procedure accepts up to 5 parameters of which three are required and the last two are optional as shown in Table 6.2.

The sample code shown in Example 6.13 shows the T-SQL use to add linked server security for a SQL account, followed by a Windows account, followed by creating the default security setting for all accounts that do not have specific security settings. The code shown in Example 6.13 will configure the same settings as the screen shown in Figure 6.8.

Table 6.2 Showing the Parameters for sp_addlinkedsvrlogin

Parameter	Is Required	Description
@rmtsrvname	Yes	The name of the linked server to be edited as found in the sys.servers (or sysservers) catalog view (or system table).
@locallogin	Yes	The login which is having its mapping be configured. A value of NULL should be used to control the rights for logins which do not have specific mapping defined.
@useself	Yes	Specifies if the login should attempt to impersonate the same login on the remote SQL Server instance. Supported values are "True" or "False"
@rmtuser	No	The SQL Login of the remote account should be used when impersonation is not being used.
@rmtpassword	No	The password of the remote SQL Login specified in the @rmtuser parameter.

EXAMPLE 6.13

Showing the T-SQL syntax to create mapped security logins on a linked server.

```
USE [master]
GO
EXEC master.dbo.sp_addlinkedsrvlogin @rmtsrvname = N'FIREFLY', @locallogin =
N'dcherry', @useself = N'False', @rmtuser = N'dcherry', @rmtpassword =
N'SomePassword'
GO
EXEC master.dbo.sp_addlinkedsrvlogin @rmtsrvname = N'FIREFLY', @locallogin =
N'CORP\dcherry', @useself = N'true'
GO
EXEC master.dbo.sp_addlinkedsrvlogin @rmtsrvname = N'FIREFLY', @locallogin =
NULL , @useself = N'True', @rmtuser = N''
GO
```

Only Allowing Some Groups to Use a Linked Server

When all users that need access to the linked server access the SQL Server which has the linked server via their Windows login there are some tricks that you can do to ensure that the linked server works, even if the user should not have direct login rights to the remote SQL Server directly. This can be done by making use of the fact that SQL Server supports the use of different endpoints and that you can grant rights to various endpoints. To make this work a few things will need to be done. First, either a domain or local Windows group needs to be created which will hold all the Windows logins who will have access to the linked server. If the group is a Windows group it needs to be created on the remote SQL Server that the linked server will be connecting to. Populate this group with the logins who will need access to the linked server and create a login within the SQL Server that the users will be connecting to for that domain or Windows group. For example a domain group could be called CORP\SQLLinkedServerGroup with a SQL Login created for the same name. The second step is that on the remote SQL Server that the linked server will be pointing to a new TCP endpoint needs to be created. When the new TCP endpoint is created the permissions on the default TCP endpoint then need to be reset so that the default TCP endpoint will continue to work as shown in Example 6.14.

EXAMPLE 6.14

Creating a new TCP endpoint and correcting the rights on the default TCP Endpoint.

```
CREATE ENDPOINT LinkedServerEndpoint
STATE = STARTED
AS TCP (LISTENER_PORT=4567, LISTENER_IP=ALL)
FOR TSQL ()
GO
GRANT CONNECT ON ENDPOINT::[TSQL Default TCP] to [public]
GO
REVOKE CONNECT ON ENDPOINT::LinkedServerEndpoint to [public]
GO
GRANT CONNECT ON ENDPOINT::LinkedServerEndpoint TO [CORP\SQLLinkedServerGroup]
GO
```

The third step is that a logon trigger is created which will prevent people from logging into the server using any endpoint other than the LinkedServerEndpoint. As seen in Example 6.14 this logon trigger first looks at the sys.dm_exec_sessions dynamic management view to see which endpoint the user is connecting on. If the user has connected via an endpoint other than the one created in Example 6.13 we then examine the ways that the logon could have been granted access into the SQL Server instance by using the xp_logininfo extended stored procedure. If the user has been granted access to the SQL Server via only this domain group then we throw an error via RAISERROR (the new THROW syntax introduced in SQL Server 2012 could be used as well) and disconnect the connection via the ROLLBACK statement.

EXAMPLE 6.15

A logon trigger to prevent people from logging onto an instance when they should only be able to use a linked server to connect.

```
CREATE TRIGGER LinkedServerTrigger
ON ALL SERVER
FOR LOGON
AS

IF EXISTS (SELECT *
                    FROM sys.dm_exec_sessions
                    JOIN sys.endpoints ON sys.dm_exec_sessions.endpoint_id =
sys.endpoints.endpoint_id
                    WHERE sys.dm_exec_sessions.session_id = @@spid
                            AND sys.endpoints.name <> 'LinkedServerEndpoint')
BEGIN
        declare @user sysname = suser_sname()
        DECLARE @groups TABLE
        (account_name sysname, type varchar(5), privilege varchar(5), mapped_login_name
sysname, permission_path sysname)

        insert into @groups
        exec xp_logininfo @user

        IF @@ROWCOUNT = 1 and exists (SELECT * from @groups WHERE account_name =
'CORP\SQLLinkedServerGroup')
        BEGIN
                raiserror('Login does not have access via this TCP endpoint.', 16, 1)
                ROLLBACK
        END
END
GO
```

USING POLICIES TO SECURE YOUR INSTANCE

Starting with SQL Server 2008 you can now use Policy-based Management to ensure that users do not have permissions that they should not have. While Policy-based Management was introduced with Microsoft SQL Server 2008, Microsoft has made is possible to use Policy-based Management against Microsoft SQL Server 2005 and Microsoft SQL Server 2000 instances, as well just in a limited function.

Policy-based Management is a new feature that allows the DBA to create conditions and policies that can monitor hundreds of different metrics within the database

---

FAQ

Some Policy-based Management Features Do Not Work in Microsoft SQL Server 2000 and 2005

Because Policy-based Management is a new feature of Microsoft SQL Server 2008, not all the features of Policy-Based Management work on older versions of Microsoft SQL Server.

Policy Creation on an SQL Server 2008 or 2008 R2 instance can be done using the online technique shown within this section of the chapter. The second technique is called disconnected authoring. With disconnected authoring, the policies are saved to the file system of the SQL Server as an XML file. This disconnected authoring requires use of the Microsoft SQL Server 2008 (or higher) Management Studio, but does not require that the SQL Server 2008 database engine be installed, allowing you to deploy the policies to an SQL Server 2000 or SQL Server 2005 instance.

In SQL Server 2008 and higher, you can store the policies within the database instance or you can store the configuration within an XML file on the SQL Servers hard drive. SQL Server 2000 and 2005 can only store the configuration within an XML file.

SQL Server 2008 and up support the ability to automate policy evaluation. The automated policy evaluation requires features that are only available in SQL Server 2008 and higher, includ SQL CLR, SMO, SQL Agent, and DDL Eventing. Additionally, automated policy evaluation requires that the policy configuration be stored within the database instead of an XML document, which is a function which is only supported within SQL Server 2008 and higher.

---

instance either blocking changes or logging changes for later action by a DBA. Policy-Based Management can be configured through SQL Server Management Studio or through T-SQL. To configure Policy-Based Management follow these three steps.

1. Connect to the server in Object Explorer.
2. Navigate to the Management Folder.
3. Navigate to the Policy Management Folder.

In order to configure Policy-based Management, you first need to configure conditions. Conditions are logical checks that are made when the policy is evaluated. You can define multiple conditions within each instance of Microsoft SQL Server, and each policy can have one condition associated with it.

The second piece of Policy-based Management is the Facets. Facets are used when creating a condition so that the condition knows what part of the database instance the condition will apply to. There are 86 facets defined within the Policy-Based Management system in SQL Server 2014. The list of available facets can be found in the Facets folder under the "Policy Management" folder.

If you wanted to define a condition that checked to see if the logged in user was a member of the dbo fixed database role in the Object Explorer, select "Conditions" from the tree under the "Policy Management" folder. Right click on conditions and select "New Condition" from the context menu. This will open the "Create New Condition" dialog. In this example select "Database" from the Facet drop down menu. In the Field column select "@IsDbOwner" and set the Value column to "True" as shown in Figure 6.9. Name the policy as required in the Name field.

In addition to creating conditions through the SQL Server Management Studio UI, they can also be created using T-SQL by using the sp_syspolicy_add_condition stored procedure in the msdb database. This procedure takes a series of parameters,

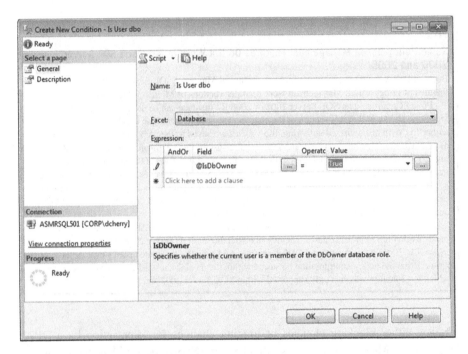

FIGURE 6.9 Showing the "Create New Condition" dialog box configured to log that a user is a member of the dbo fixed database role.

all of which are pretty straightforward with the exception of the @expression parameter, which takes an XML document showing how the condition should be evaluated as shown in Example 6.16.

EXAMPLE 6.16

Creating the same condition shown in Figure 6.8

```
Declare @condition_id int
EXEC msdb.dbo.sp_syspolicy_add_condition @name=N'Is User dbo',
@description=N'', @facet=N'Database', @expression=N'<Operator>
<TypeClass>Bool</TypeClass> <OpType<EQ</OpType>
<count>2</Count>
<Attribute>
<TypeClass>Bool</TypeClass>
<Name>IsDbOwner</Name>
</Attribute>
<Function>
<TypeClass>Bool</TypeClass>
<FunctionType>True</FunctionType>
<ReturnType>Bool</ReturnType>
<count>0</Count>
</Function>
</Operator>', @is_name_condition=0, @obj_name=N' ',
@condition_id=@condition_id OUTPUT
```

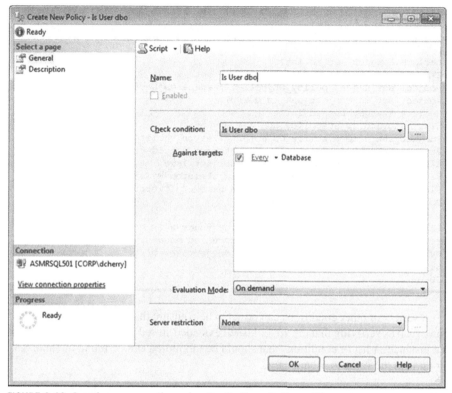

FIGURE 6.10 Creating a new policy using the "Is User dbo" condition.

After creating a condition, a policy needs to be created which uses the condition. Like the condition, this can be done either within the SQL Server Management Studio UI or by running a T-SQL script. Within the Management Studio UI, after navigating to the Policy Management folder, right click on Policies and select "New Policy" from the context menu. In the "Create New Policy" window name the policy and select the check condition that you wish to use as shown in Figure 6.10.

Policies can also be created using T-SQL instead of the SQL Server Management Studio using a series of stored procedures in the msdb database:

1. sp_syspolicy_add_object_set creates an object set which is an internal undocumented object;
2. sp_syspolicy_add_target_set creates a target set which says what type of condition target will be called, binding the object set to the target set;
3. sp_syspolicy_add_target_set_level assigns a target set level to the previously created target set;
4. sp_syspolicy_add_policy creates the policy specifying the object set name.

EXAMPLE 6.17

T-SQL code creating the same Policy as shown in Figure 6.9

```
Declare @object_set_id int
EXEC msdb.dbo.sp_syspolicy_add_object_set
@object_set_name=N'policy_ObjectSet', @facet=N'Database',
@object_set_id=@object_set_id OUTPUT
Declare @target_set_id int
EXEC msdb.dbo.sp_syspolicy_add_target_set
@object_set_name=N'policy_ObjectSet', @type_skeleton=N'Server/Database',
@type=N'DATABASE', @enabled=True, @target_set_id=@target_set_id OUTPUT
EXEC msdb.dbo.sp_syspolicy_add_target_set_level
@target_set_id=@target_set_id, @type_skeleton=N'Server/Database',
@level_name=N'Database', @condition_name=N' ', @target_set_level_id=0
GO
Declare @policy_id int
EXEC msdb.dbo.sp_syspolicy_add_policy @name=N'Is User dbo',
@condition_name=N'Is User dbo', @execution_mode=0, @policy_id=@policy_id
OUTPUT, @root_condition_name=N' ', @object_set=N'policy_ObjectSet'
Select @policy_id
GO
```

A variety of other conditions can be set to help ensure that an SQL Instance is secure, such as verifying that the xp_cmdshell extended stored procedure is disabled on the instance. A list of conditions that should be monitored can be found in Table 6.3, along with the value to monitor for.

Table 6.3 Various Conditions which Should be Monitored for to Ensure a More Secure SQL Server Installation

Facet	Field	Operator	Value
Server Security	@CmdExecRightsForSystem AdminsOnly	=	False
Server Security	@ProxyAccountEnabled	=	True
Server Security	@PublicServerRoleIsGranted Permissions	=	True
Server Security	@XPCmdShellEnabled	=	True
Database Security	@IsOwnerSysadmin	=	True
Login	@PasswordExpirationEnabled \ @LoginType	= \ =	False \ SqlLogin
Server	@AuditLevel	!=	All

NOTE

Conditions Can Have Multiple Checks Within Them

Table 6.3 shows the PasswordExpirationEnabled and LoginType values within the same line. This condition is configured in this way so that this condition only logs an issue when the password expiration is disabled and the user is an SQL Login. Setting this condition requires that two values be set within a single condition. The PasswordExpirationEnabled should be set to False, and the LoginType should be set to SqlLogin.

> **NOTE**
> **SQL Azure Is a Moving Target**
> Do keep in mind that in any book about Microsoft Azure SQL Database, including this one, the information about SQL Azure can get out of date very quickly as the SQL Azure product is a constantly moving target. This is because the SQL Azure team releases new versions of the database engine every few months, so what you see here may not be relevant after the Summer of 2014.

SQL AZURE SPECIFIC SETTINGS

Microsoft has done an excellent job of securing SQL Azure databases, but that does not mean that they cannot be screwed up by someone who does not know how to set up the SQL Azure instance correctly.

When you sign up for an SQL Azure account, you control the firewall to the database server. By default, no one has access to the instance, including other servers within the Microsoft Services platform. This is easy enough to change by checking the "Allow Microsoft Services access to this server" checkbox, as shown in Figure 6.11. You can access the Firewall settings by logging into SQL Azure and clicking on the Firewall Settings tab for the server you selected.

To add rules to the firewall list, click the Add Rule button, which will open a window that allows you to set an IP range that will have direct access to the database. When adding database rules, add as small sets of IP Addresses as possible in order to prevent unauthorized people from accessing the database. When the screen opens, it will display the public IP Address that you are using to access the management portal. The best firewall rules are the rules that only allow a single IP Address, as shown in Figure 6.12.

Configuring a firewall rule that allows all IP Addresses (0.0.0.0 to 255.255.255.255) would be a bad idea because any attacker would be able to attempt a brute force attack against the database engine.

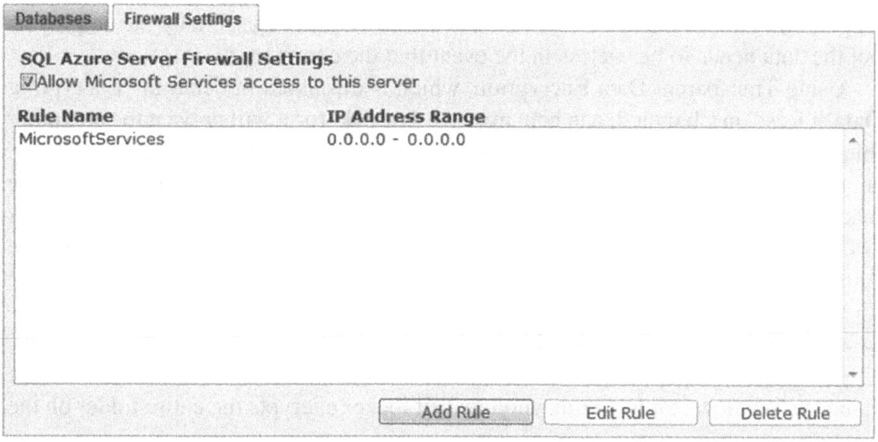

FIGURE 6.11 Showing how to enable the SQL Azure Firewall to other Microsoft Services servers.

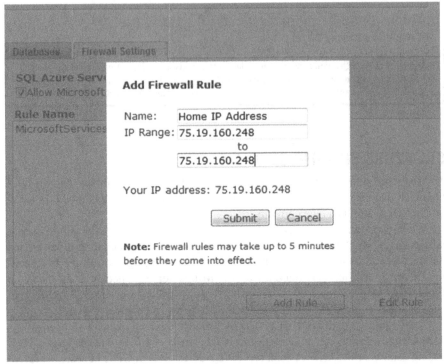

FIGURE 6.12 Showing how to allow a single IP address access to the SQL Azure database.

INSTANCES THAT LEAVE THE OFFICE

The most difficult instances within any company to properly secure are instances that leave the office on a regular basis. These instances are usually located on developers or DBAs laptops and are taken home daily. These laptops present an interesting challenge in that they need to be able to leave the office and be usable by the employee, but the data needs to be useless in the event that the computer is stolen.

Using Transparent Data Encryption, which is discussed in detail in "Encrypting Data at Rest" in Chapter 2, can help mitigate this risk, for it will prevent the computer thief from taking the database and attaching it to another instance of the SQL Server. As the laptop will more than likely be a member of the domain, the accounts on the machine will have a strong password, making it very hard to break into the Windows OS. This leaves the thief the option of removing the hard drive from the laptop and installing it within another computer as a secondary hard drive. This would allow the thief access to the physical files, but without the certificates from the master database, the attacker would not be able to attach the database.

An additional step that could be taken would be to secure the entire hard drive using the Windows bit locker technology. Bit locker encrypts the entire folder on the

FIGURE 6.13 Screenshot showing the "Encrypt contents to secure data" option.

hard drive so that only the OS that is installed on the computer can access the data within the folder. This prevents the laptop thief in this scenario from being able to access the files within the folder.

To enable the bit locker on a folder to navigate to the folder within the Windows Explorer, right click on the folder and select the Advanced button on the General tab. On the Advanced Attributes screen which opens, as shown in Figure 6.13, check the "Encrypt contents to secure data" and click OK and apply the changes to all subfolders if prompted (and desired).

SECURING ALWAYSON AVAILABILITY GROUPS

Using the new AlwaysOn high availability feature of SQL Server will require some careful planning to ensure that everything is working correctly from a security point of view. Any logins which are needed by the application to connect to the databases which are setup for use by AlwaysOn Availability Groups will need to be manually created on all the other instances which are availability replicas otherwise the application will not be able to connect to the SQL Server instance. If these logins are SQL Server logins then the logins will need to be first exported from the server they were created on so that they could be created on the other instances using the same SID as were created on the first instance. There is a better option available to us, which we will be discussing later in this chapter.

Another thing to keep in mind with AlwaysOn Availability Groups may include the need to give other users the ability to fail over an availability group without giving the user sysadmin rights to the database instance. If you were to do this it would require that the right to fail over the availability group on all instances which are hosting availability replicas. The best way to do this is to create a user defined server role (see Chapter 12) and grant rights for the user defined server role to be granted to the users who need to manage the AlwaysOn Availability Groups. This allows for the easy granting of rights to specific users the ability to failover the AlwaysOn Availability Groups without needing to grant the user sysadmin rights to the SQL Server. This is handy for allowing Windows Admins, NOC personal, and Junior DBAs the ability to failover the availability groups without needing to call a member of the sysadmin fixed server role.

There are four different rights which can be granted to a login for each Availability Group as well as two server wide rights which relate to Availability Groups. The two server side rights are the "Create Availability Group" and the "Alter Any Availability Group" rights. The first allows the user who has been granted this right the ability to create a new availability group while the second allows the user to make changes to any availability group on the instance. The four rights which can be granted against each availability group can be seen in Table 6.4.

Table 6.4 Permissions which can be Granted Against Each SQL Server Availability Group

Right	Description
Alter	The "Alter" right grants the user the right to make changes to the configuration of the AlwaysOn Availability Group.
Control	The "Control" right grants the other three rights to the user.
Take Ownership	The "Take Ownership" right grants the user the ability to become the ownership of the availability group.
View Definition	The "View Definition" right grants the login the right to view the configuration of the AlwaysOn Availability group.

NOTE

Incorrect Permissions Could Prevent Failback

If the permissions for an AlwaysOn availability group are not correctly setup on all of the AlwaysOn replica nodes the people who have triggered the failover may not be able to fail the node back to the original node. This could be a problem, or this could be by design. Do keep in this in mind when designing and implementing your AlwaysOn security policies.

When using SQL Server logins with an AlwaysOn database, it is critical that the logins all be created with the same SID on all the instances which host the AlwaysOn replicas. If this is not done then the SQL Server logins will not match up to the users within the AlwaysOn database and the SQL Server login would not be able to connect to the AlwaysOn database until the SIDs are matched backup. Typically, the way to do this would be to use the sp_change_users_login system stored procedure to change the SID of the user within the database to match the SID of the login on the server. However, when working with an AlwaysOn database this is not the way you will want to do this. With an AlwaysOn database you will want to query for the SID from the user within the database and then drop the login and recreate it specifying the SID of the login so that the SID of the login now matches the SID of the user within the AlwaysOn database. If there are other databases which use the login which the AlwaysOn database users, these databases will need to have their SIDs updated by using the sp_change_users_login system stored procedure so that the SIDs then match. The AlwaysOn database should be the master SID as that SID needs to exist on multiple instances correctly.

SECURING CONTAINED DATABASES

Contained Databases are another feature which was first introduced in SQL Server 2012 and have been a long looked for feature; specifically from a security perspective. Specifically the part of contained databases, which is most important is the ability to create a database user which has a password and does not need to have a login created on the database instance. This ability to create a contained user allows the database to be moved from one instance of Microsoft SQL Server to another without first needing to create logins on the destination server that have the same SID as the user on the initial server.

The ability to create a contained user requires that the instance first be configured to support contained users. This is done by using the sp_configure system stored procedure as shown in Example 6.18.

EXAMPLE 6.18

Using the system stored procedure sp_configure to enable contained database authentication.

```
exec sp_configure 'show advanced settings', 1
reconfigure
GO
exec sp_configure 'contained database authentication', 1
reconfigure
GO
exec sp_configure 'show advanced settings', 0
reconfigure
GO
```

Once the instance has been configured to support contained database users databases can be configured as a partially contained database then users can be created within the database. Changing a database from a non-contained database (all databases which are not contained or on older editions of Microsoft SQL Server are considered to be non-contained) requires using the ALTER DATABASE statement as shown in Example 6.19.

EXAMPLE 6.19

Making a database a contained database using the ALTER DATABASE statement.

```
ALTER DATABASE MyDatabase
SET CONTAINMENT = PARTIAL
```

Creating a contained database user can be done either using T-SQL or by using the SQL Server Management Studio User Interface. Creating a contained user using T-SQL, as shown in Example 6.20, uses the CREATE USER statement which has been available in Microsoft SQL Server for several versions now. The syntax which is used of the CREATE USER statement which is used to create a contained user is a combination of the legacy CREATE USER and CREATE LOGIN commands which have been in use for some time now.

EXAMPLE 6.20

Creating a contained user with the CREATE USER statement.

```
CREATE USER MyUser WITH PASSWORD='SomePAssword'
```

Creating a contained user with SQL Server management studio is almost as easy as using the CREATE USER statement. Connect to the instance using the Object Explorer. Navigate to the database, then to security, then to users. Right click on Users and select "New User" from the context menu which opens. Set the user type to "SQL user with password" specify the username and the password, as shown in Figure 6.14, as well as any group memberships which are needed any click OK.

Once the contained user has been created the application can be configured to use a contained user instead of the normal login based authentication. This is done by simply including the default database parameter in the connection string instead of relying on the SQL Server instance to know the default database which the application should be connecting to. For applications which already have a default database specified as a part of the connection string this should mean that no changes are needed to the application at all.

The Microsoft SQL Server instance can be queried to see if there are contained logins within the contained database easily enough. Simply query the sys.database_principals system catalog view looking for rows which have the value of 2 or 3 in the authentication_type column.

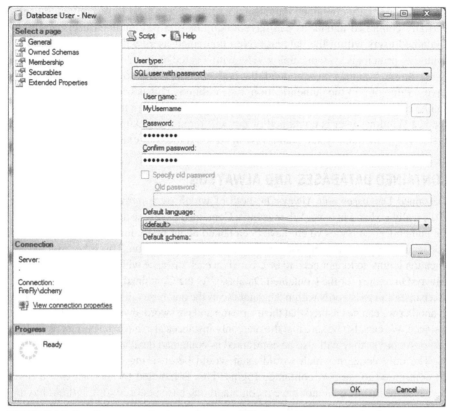

FIGURE 6.14 Creating a contained user by using SQL Server Management Studio.

NOTE

Why Partially Contained?

If you have been reading up on Partially Contained databases (there is much more to know than what is covered in this book as this book is only about security) you may have noticed that everyone references partially contained databases, but no other containment models. The reason for that is that when contained databases were introduced in SQL Server 2012 only the partially contained database model was included in the feature. The other containment model called "Fully Contained" was not ready in time for the SQL Server 2012 release of the product so Microsoft had to decide to pull the feature or only include the part of the feature that was ready.

Thankfully, they included the part of the feature which was ready namely the partially contained database. You can expect to see fully contained databases in a future release, although probably not until the next major release (Microsoft could always surprise us and introduce it as part of a Service Pack, but personally I would not expect that to happen).

With a partially contained database not all the users need to be contained users. Partially contained databases can have a combination of contained users and non-contained users within the database. Non-contained users will show up in the sys. database_principals system catalog view with a value of 1 or 3 in the authentication_type column. You may have noticed that both contained and non-contained users can have a value of 3 in the authentication_type column. This is because Windows users can be either contained or non-contained and type 3 users are the Windows users. To see if a Windows user is contained or not will require checking the user against the sys.server_principals system catalog view to see if the user exists as a login or not.

CONTAINED DATABASES AND ALWAYSON

Contained Databases and AlwaysOn, both of which were introduced in SQL Server 2012 really go hand in hand. When using a Contained Database and AlwaysOn many of the authentication issues where have been talked about pretty much disappear, so long as contained logins are being used for application authentication. This is because the application logins no longer need to be created on each instance which is functioning as an AlwaysOn replica for the Contained Database. As the Contained Database now has the usernames and passwords within the database as the database fails over from one replica to another we can be ensured that the username and password always exists on the active instance. We can also be sure that the read only instances also have the correct username and password as they will also be configured as contained databases.

The only concern which would exist would be ensuring that the instances are all configured to support contained logins. This is handled by the fact that a SQL Server 2012 instance cannot have a contained database restored to it without having the instance configured to support Contained Databases as shown in Example 6.18.

SQL CLR

When the SQL CLR was introduced in Microsoft SQL Server 2005, it was probably one of the most misunderstood and misused features of SQL Server. Part of this was due to the dual marketing message that Microsoft was putting out. When you spoke with those from the .NET and database developer side of Microsoft, they said that SQL supported the CLR and that you could use it to solve all your database problems. When you spoke with those from the Database Administration side of Microsoft, they said that SQL CLR was very limited and should almost never be used. This made proper implementation of the SQL CLR quite difficult, especially in environments where security was important. This has not really changed in the releases since the SQL CLR was introduced in SQL Server 2005 up through the SQL Server 2012 release.

The SQL CLR allows you to take an existing .NET CLR and load the compiled module into the SQL Server database as an assembly. Stored procedures and functions can then be created that call into the .NET assembly, allowing for the power and function of the .NET language to be used with the SQL Server database by calling

> ### STORY TIME
> #### Microsoft Has Not Always Told a Consistent Story About SQL CLR
> Back when SQL CLR was introduced to Microsoft SQL Server 2005, Microsoft had two very distinct stories they would present. The first story was being told to the database administrators and systems administrators, and the second to application and database developers. Neither story told the entire story, nor these different stories created a lot of arguments between developers who wanted to use the SQL CLR and database administrators who were scared to death of it.
>
> The story that the database administrators were being told was that the SQL CLR was very dangerous and that it had the ability to crash the SQL Server instance if things were not done correctly. Database administrators were told of limitations, but at the time most database administrators did not know much about programming, especially in .NET. Because of this lack of .NET knowledge, these limitations did not mean much to most database administrators.
>
> The story that the developers were being told was that SQL CLR was very safe to use and that it would be able to do anything that you needed it to do: Need to load data from a file, use the SQL CLR. Need to export data on the fly from a T-SQL stored procedure, use an SQL CLR procedure instead. Need to connect to a web service from a stored procedure, use an SQL CLR procedure to reach out to the web method. During the developer sessions, there was no mention of the limitations of the SQL CLR.
>
> Due to these massively different messages, some interesting "discussions" were held at companies all over the world between developers who wanted to implement SQL CLR procedures, but they did not understand the consequences of running SQL CLR assemblies in modes other than in the SAFE mode. Database administrators did not like the idea of running SQL CLR procedures that they did not have any visibility into, and even if they did, many of the database administrators would not know how to read the code even if they could see it.

them with T-SQL. When you create an assembly within the SQL Server database, you can choose from three security levels; these tell the SQL Server engine how much access the .NET assembly should have to the host system, which are SAFE, EXTERNAL_ACCESS, and UNSAFE.

T-SQL Assemblies that are considered to be safe are only allowed to access resources within the SQL Server Instance. These assemblies may not access the file system, system registry, variables, or network resources. These safe assemblies would typically be used to pass values into the procedure to do some sort of string manipulation or advanced math returning a value back to the database.

Assemblies that are created with the EXTERNAL_ACCESS permission have the same scalability and reliability features of the SAFE permission set, while giving the assembly rights to access the objects outside of the SQL Server instance. Unless impersonation is being used within the .NET assembly, the assembly will be launched under the same account that the SQL Server service is running. This means that the .NET assembly will have access to any object that the SQL Server service account has access to. If the SQL Server runs as a local administrator, and there is a .NET procedure within the assembly that accepts a file name to read, then the .NET assembly would have access to read any file on the server. If the SQL Server runs as a domain administrator with that same procedure, then the .NET assembly would have access to read any file (and probably write to any file) on the entire Windows domain.

Assemblies that are created with the UNSAFE permission can perform actions that could compromise the robustness of the SQL Server Instance. Procedures that

> **NOTE**
> **Debugging Can Kill You**
> Never ever, under any circumstance, attach a debugger to a .NET assembly that is running on a production SQL Server. The .NET assembly runs within the memory process space of the SQL Server process, which means that if you sent a breakpoint in the debugger to pause the execution of the .NET assembly, the entire SQL Server process would be paused, causing the SQL Server to stop all processing and stopping all new connection requests to the database engine. This debugging can be very handy when debugging SQL CLR procedures against a development instance, or against a developer's personal sandbox instance, but against a production instance it would be catastrophic.
> There are many horror stories of people attaching a debugger, setting a breakpoint in an obscure branch of code, then going to lunch waiting for the breakpoint to be hit and having the database come grinding to a halt for 30 min until the code can be restarted.

are run in the UNSAFE mode could potentially compromise the security features within the operating system or the SQL Server Instance. This is the case as assemblies that are run in the UNSAFE mode can reference any native or third party .NET assembly that allows them to have effectively unfettered access to the Windows operating system. Like assemblies that are created with the EXTERNAL_ACCESS permission, assemblies that are created with the UNSAFE permission run under the account that the SQL Server service is running unless impersonation is used to access objects under a different account.

The SQL CLR is governed by the more traditional CLR security policies which are in place at the computer level. For CLR 3.5 and below this is handled via three security policies which are the "Machine Policy," "User Policy," and "Host Policy" which together are called "Code Access Security" (CAS). More information about these security policies and Code Access Security can be found on MSDN at http://msdn.microsoft.com/en-us/library/sa4se9bc%28v=VS.85%29.aspx. With the release of version 4 of the .NET CLR the security policy functions have been removed from the CAS. More information about the security changes to the .NET framework can be found on MSDN at http://msdn.microsoft.com/en-us/library/dd233103.aspx.

It is recommended that assemblies be created using only the SAFE or EXTERNIAL_ACCESS permissions, preferably the SAFE permission, so that the assembly cannot cause problems or access .NET assemblies that are not considered safe. Only certain assemblies are thought to be safe for use in SQL CLR assemblies. As of the writing of this book, the list of assemblies to be SAFE are as follows.

- Microsoft.VisualBasic.dll
- Mscorlib.dll
- System.Data.dll
- System.dll
- System.Xml.dll
- Microsoft.VisualC.dll
- CustomMarshalers.dll
- System.Security.dll
- System.Web.Services.dll

> **NOTE**
>
> **Microsoft Has Special Support Policies for SQL CLR**
>
> Microsoft has special support policies for databases which have SQL CLR assemblies on them which have remained unchanged since SQL CLR was introduced through the introduction of SQL Server 2014. If a .NET assembly references assemblies that are not included on the list above and Microsoft's Support department feels that the SQL CLR assembly is related to the performance problem, then they may require that the assembly be removed from the SQL Server before troubleshooting can continue.
>
> In addition, Microsoft's support department may request that unsupported SQL CLR assemblies be temporally removed from the SQL Server instance while troubleshooting is performed. More information about the Microsoft support policy can be found at http://support.microsoft.com/kb/922672/en-us.

- System.Data.SqlXml.dll
- System.Transactions.dll
- System.Data.OracleClient.dll
- System.Configuration.dll

Assemblies can be created using either the SQL Server Management Studio User Interface (UI) or T-SQL via the CREATE ASSEMBLY statement. To create an assembly within SQL Server Management Studio, use these five steps:

1. Connect to the server in the Object Explorer.
2. Navigate to the database to put the assembly in.
3. Open the programmability folder.
4. Open the Assemblies folder.
5. Right click on the Assemblies and select "New Assemblies" from the context menu.

The screen that opens is the "New Assembly" window. Set the "Assembly owner," "Permission set," and "Path to assembly" similar to what is shown in Figure 6.15. The "Assembly name" and "Additional properties" values will be filled in automatically.

When you are creating an assembly using T-SQL, you use the CREATE ASSEMBLY statement. When using the CREATE ASSEMBLY statement, either the path to the assembly can be specified as shown in Example 6.21 or the bits that make up the binary can be included as shown in Example 6.22.

EXAMPLE 6.21

T-SQL code showing the creation of an assembly using the path to the .NET assembly.

```
CREATE ASSEMBLY [ATI.Net.Mail]
AUTHORIZATION [dbo]
FROM 'C:\Users\dcherry\Documents\Visual Studio 2008\Projects\Email
Labs Packages\mrdenny.Net.Mail.dll'
WITH PERMISSION_SET = SAFE
```

EXAMPLE 6.22

T-SQL code showing the creation of an assembly using the binary value of the assembly.

```
CREATE ASSEMBLY [mrdenny.Net.Mail]
AUTHORIZATION [dbo]
FROM 0x4D5A9000030000004000000FFFF0000B800000000000000
4000000000000000000000000000000

...
0000000000000000000000000000000
WITH PERMISSION_SET = SAFE
```

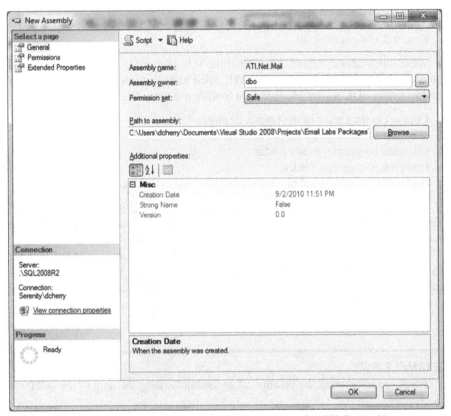

FIGURE 6.15 Showing the creating of a SAFE .NET Assembly using SQL Server Management Studio.

> **NOTE**
> **Sample Code Was Shortened to Save Dead Trees**
> This code, shown in Example 6.22, has been shortened for brevity. The binary representation of this .NET assembly is over 11 pages long. It was shortened for the sole purpose of saving dead trees that did not need to be chopped down.

When creating assemblies, specific rights need to be had. In order to create an assembly, the user creating that assembly must have the "CREATE ASSEMBLY" right within the database. In order to create an assembly with the EXTERNAL_ACCESS permission, the login must have the "EXTERNAL ACCESS ASSEMBLY" right at the instance level. In order to create an UNSAFE assembly, the login for the user must have the "UNSAFE ASSEMBLY" right at the instance level. These instance-level rights will allow the login that has the right to create an assembly at that level in any database that the user has the "CREATE ASSEMBLY" right assigned to it. Members of the dbo (database owner) fixed database role automatically have the "CREATE ASSEMBLY" right within those databases. Members of the sysadmin (System Administration) fixed server role automatically have the "EXTERNAL ACCESS ASSEMBLY" and the "UNSAFE ASSEMBLY" right within that instance. These high-level rights are not needed to run the procedures and functions within the assembly; they are only needed to create the assembly within the database.

> **NOTE**
> **Combining an Unsafe Procedure With an SQL Injection Attack Gives Some Interesting Possibilities**
> If an application account was configured with these higher level permissions and the application was susceptible to an SQL Injection attack, serious damage could be done very quickly and easily. An attacker could write a .NET dll, create an assembly within the database, and mark it as unsafe. Then an attacker could call the assembly and have the assembly download and install any software that the attacker wanted. The assembly could also log back into the database and elevate the permissions of the login that the application account uses, giving the attacker easier and greater access to the database instance.

EXTENDED STORED PROCEDURES

Extended stored procedures are DLL files which are referenced by the SQL Server by having the extended stored procedure created which then reference functions or procedures within the DLL. The DLLs which are behind the extended stored procedures are typically created in a lower level language like C or C++. Sample code to create an extended stored procedure can be found in Example 6.23. Even though Extended Stored Procedures are scheduled for removal from Microsoft SQL Server, they can still be a useful tool. When you create an extended stored procedure, the dll must physically exist on the database server, which makes it a little more complex for attackers to create an extended stored procedure on the fly as they can with an SQL Server Assembly.

> **NOTE**
> **Getting a New dll Onto the Server Is Not All That Hard**
> Once attackers have figured out that they can use SQL Injection attacks to gain access to the system, it is not hard to determine what sort of access they have to the database server. If the attacker is able to gain access to xp_cmdshell, even if it is without admin rights, the attacker can still do a decent amount of damage to the system.
>
> As an example, an attacker could create text file that has FTP (File Transfer Protocol) commands and then run ftp.exe using xp_cmdshell passing ftp.exe the name of the text file, which has the commands to run. The text file with the commands could be set up to log into the attacker's FTP server and download various files. If attackers have sysadmin rights to the SQL Server instance, then they can simply attack an extended stored procedure to the instance. If they do not have sysadmin rights to the instance, the attacker could install software on the machine and configure it to startup automatically either via a service (probably hidden by a rootkit), or in the run registry key for either one or all users. At this point this software could be configured to do anything the attacker wants to and will probably be hidden from the view of the database administrator and system administrators.

In order to create an extended stored procedure, the login that the user uses to log into the database must be a member of the sysadmin fixed server role. Extended stored procedures are always created within the master database, but can be referenced from any database. Typically, an extended stored procedure would be created with a name starting with xp_ or sp_ so that the database engine would automatically look in the master database for the object if there was no object with that name in the user database.

Like .NET assemblies, extended stored procedures can be written to access anything on the local system or the Internet, limited only by the coding knowledge of the developer who writes the dll that is attached as an extended stored procedure. Extended stored procedures run within the SQL Server, meaning that the code is executed within the SQL Server memory space. As the extended stored procedures run within the SQL Server process, bugs within the extended stored procedure can surface within the SQL Server and cause the SQL Server to crash or core dump, even causing the SQL Server engine processes to stop completely.

Extended stored procedures can be added to an SQL Server instance by using the sp_addextendedproc system stored procedure within the master database. The system stored procedure accepts two parameters, @functname and @dllname, as shown in Example 6.23. @functname is the name of the function to call within the DLL and is a nvarchar(517) parameter. @dllname is the full path to the DLL and is varchar(255). There can be multiple functions within a single DLL, each one with a different name and exposed as a separate extended stored procedure.

EXAMPLE 6.23
Adding an extended stored procedure to an SQL Server Instance.

```
EXEC sp_addextendedproc @functname='MyFunction',
@dllname='c:\Program Files\Microsoft SQL Server\MSSQL\binn\myfile.dll'
```

PROTECTING YOUR CONNECTION STRINGS

Applications use connection strings to identify the server instance and database to connect to and to determine what driver, login, etc. to use to connect to the SQL Server instance. Typically, the connection string will be stored in a configuration file somewhere within the application or web server. This connection string is typically stored in plain text to make it easy to edit and easy to change as the application is moved from development, to QA, to staging, and to production.

When the connection strings are stored in plain text, they provide a wealth of information to an attacker, typically everything that an attacker would need to break into a database. In order to protect the database, you have to protect the connection string, so that if an attacker is able to get access to the files on the web server or application server, the attacker is not able to use the connection string to attack the database. The best way to secure the database connection string is to encrypt the value within the configuration file. The application would then load the encrypted value from the config file, decrypt the value, and then use the decrypted value as the connection string to connect to the database.

Securing the connection string could be done through a separate application that the systems administrator could use during the deployment process to encrypt the string, or the application could be configured to automatically encrypt the string the first time the application launches. This automatic encryption of the connection string is a better method for the systems administrator because it does not require the systems administrator to use a separate application to encrypt the connection string.

In either case, troubleshooting the application is made a little bit harder as the connection string is not easily visible without decrypting the connection string to ensure that the connection string is correct, which would require a separate application.

Even with the connection string stored in the configuration file in an encrypted format, there is still a risk of an attacker getting the connection string. However, it is much more difficult for the attacker. For the attacker to get the connection string, the attacker would need to dump the memory for the application, be it a Windows Service, Win32 application, or web-based application, and read through the memory dump looking for the connection string. The application would have to store the connection string in a variable in memory, which means that it would be contained within a full memory dump.

DATABASE FIREWALLS

There is a special set of firewall products out there that are called Database Firewalls. These database firewalls monitor and track all connections that are made to the database engine. Many of them, such as "SecureSphere Database Firewall," can take proactive action if the firewall detects SQL injection attacks, buffer overflow attacks, and denial of service attacks. Depending on the Database Firewall, they can either monitor the network connection remotely, usually by using a feature on the network switch

> **NOTE**
>
> The catch to needing to have a database firewall application installed is that it means that you suspect that you have database applications which connect to the SQL Server which are not properly protected against SQL Injection attacks, or you are worried about purchasing applications which are not properly secured in the future. This puts you into a precarious position of needing to admit that you have applications which are not written to be protected from SQL Injection and that you would rather spend money on a database firewall than fixing the applications themselves.
>
> While the database application can be a much quicker and easier fix in the short term, however, in the long term it is better to fix the applications themselves which in turn gives the developers the training that they need to not make the same mistakes again.

called port mirroring where all network traffic going to one physical Ethernet port is sent to a second mirrored port for analysis. The second method involves installing an agent on the database server and using that agent to inspect all the database calls. The mirrored port method does not put any load on the database server at all, but this method typically does not allow for the monitoring of encrypted database connections.

These Database Firewall applications can go a long way toward preventing attacks as they monitor every command that is sent to the database server, no matter whether that statement is a DML (Data Modification Language) statement that is selecting, deleting, or updating data; or whether it is a DDL (Data Definition Language) statement that is dropping tables full of data. You can create policies that define which statements can be run, which would trigger an alert to be sent, or which statements should be blocked.

CLEAR VIRTUAL MEMORY PAGEFILE

When you have a server that can be accessed from the Internet, the possibility exists that an attacker could access a memory dump to gain access to data they normally would not be able to access. This includes the virtual memory page file, as well as system dumps that Windows has taken.

To protect the virtual memory page file, a policy setting can be enabled which upon shutdown of Windows will cause the page file to be rewritten with 0s. This setting is called "Shutdown: Clear virtual memory page file." It can be set via a group policy or via the "Local Security Policy" MMC (Microsoft Management Console) within the Administrative Tools menu off of the Start Menu. To set it on a single server, open the "Local Security Policy" and then navigate to the Local Policies folder and the Security Options folder. Then double click on the policy "Shutdown: Clear virtual memory pagefile" and set the setting to enabled as shown in Figure 6.16.

In order to set this setting on all computers on a domain (or a subset of computers on a domain), the setting should be enabled within a group policy that is applied to the computers, which should have the setting enabled. To do this, open the Group Policy Editor and edit the correct policy that affects the correct computers, then navigate to:

1. Computer Configuration
2. Policies

3. Windows Settings
4. Security Settings
5. Local Policies
6. Security Options

After navigating to the Security Options folder, locate and edit the "Shut-down: Clear virtual memory page file" policy, setting the value to enabled as shown in Figure 6.16. Closing the Group Policy Editor will save the settings back

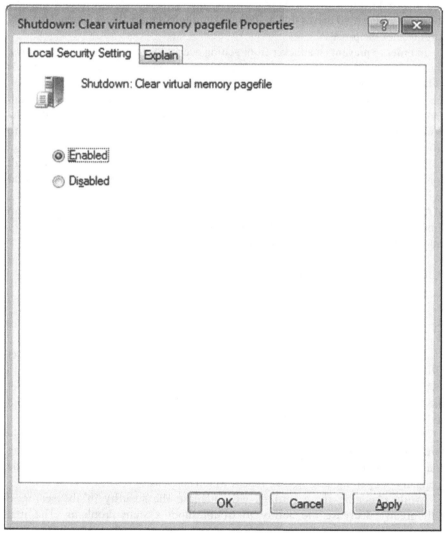

FIGURE 6.16 Enabling the "Clear virtual memory pagefile" setting on a single server.

to the domain controller, allowing the setting change to replicate to all domain controllers within the domain, then eventually to all the computers affected by the group policy.

There is a downside to enabling the "Shutdown: Clear virtual memory page file" setting: Notably, computers will begin taking a much longer time to shutdown or reboot. This longer time occurs because before Windows will complete the shutdown process, the page file will be overwritten with zeros so that no data from within the page file can be accessed. The more RAM a server has, the longer this process will take, with servers with a GB or two taking just a few minutes and servers with hundreds of GBs of RAM taking hours to complete the process. In addition to the amount of RAM in the server changing the amount of time it takes, the speed of the hard drives that hold the operating system will also impact the performance of the process.

In order to prevent an attacker from getting access to a memory dump, Windows' ability to dump the memory to disk should be disabled on a server unless it needs to be enabled for a specific reason. On a single server, this is done through the system control panel. After opening the system control panel, select the Advanced tab and click the Settings button within the "Startup and Recovery" section. In the new Window that opens, change the "Write debugging information" dropdown menu to "(none)" as shown in Figure 6.17.

There is no group policy setting that can be used to disable the setting over all computers in a domain. However, a group policy can still be used to make the needed registry change. The registry setting that needs to be changed is HKEY_LOCAL_MACHINE\SYSTEM\CurrentControlSet\Control\CrashControl\CrashDump Enabled. The setting is a DWORD value, which should be set to 0. To set a registry value within a group policy, edit the group policy and navigate to:

1. Computer Configuration
2. Preferences
3. Windows Settings
4. Registry

Right click on Registry and select "New" from the context menu then select "Registry Item." Set the Hive to HKEY_LOCAL_MACHINE and the key path to "SYSTEM\CurrentControlSet\Control\CrashControl" as shown in Figure 6.18. Set the "Value name" to CrashDumpEnabled, the "Value type" as REG_DWORD and set the "Value data" to 00000000 as shown in Figure 6.18.

No matter how this setting is disabled, either on the local server or globally through a group policy, the server(s) will need to be rebooted in order for the setting change to take effect. The reboot can either be done at the time the change is made manually or upon the next normal reboot which happens.

While changing these settings will increase the security of the server, it will greatly decrease the ability to troubleshoot system problems. The first

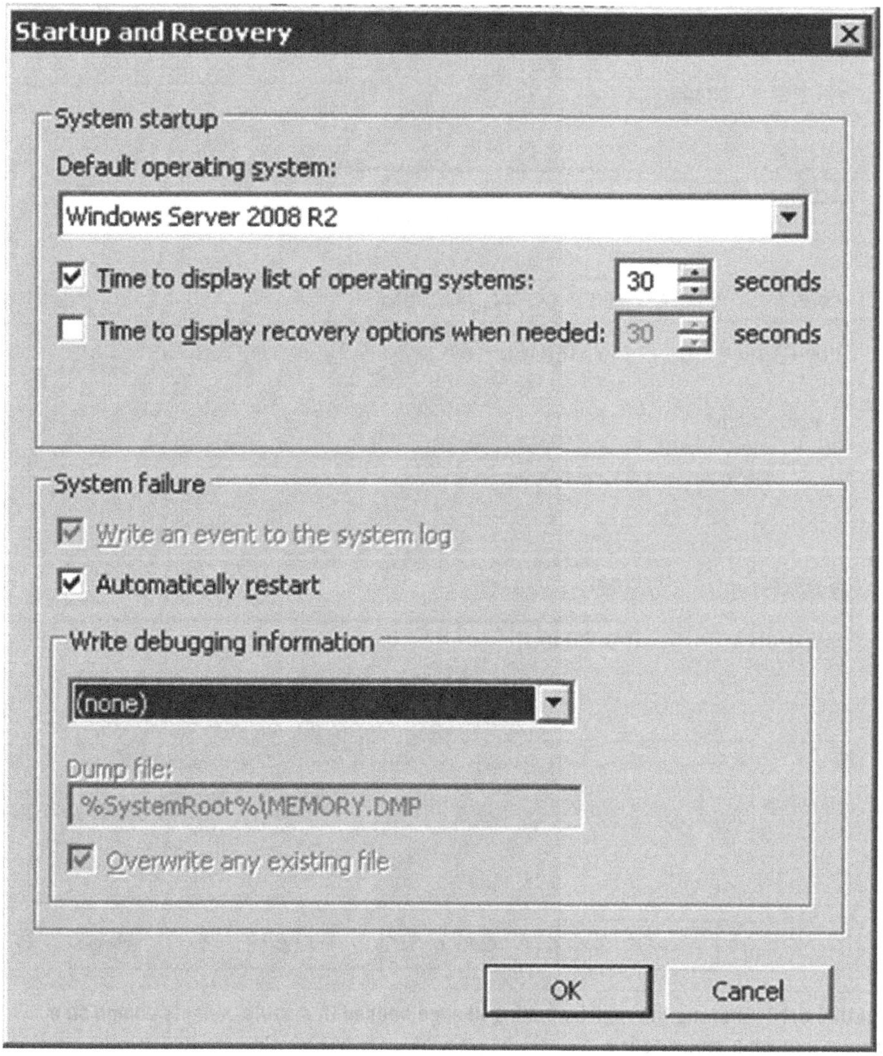

FIGURE 6.17 Showing how to disable the writing of memory dumps in Windows.

troubleshooting technique when attempting to resolve Windows instability issues would normally be to analyze the system memory dump. In the event that these memory dumps are not available, these settings will need to be reversed so that memory dumps can be created and used for debugging. After this debugging has been completed, the settings would then need to be put back into place in order to resolve the problem.

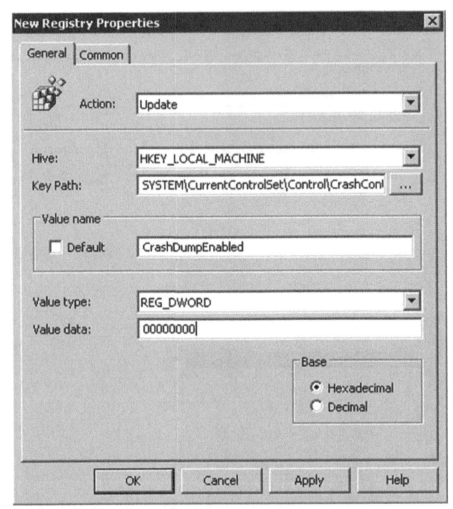

FIGURE 6.18 Showing the registry setting change needed to disable memory dumps on a server through a group policy.

USER ACCESS CONTROL (UAC)

User Access Control was first introduced to Windows in Windows 2008 and Windows Vista. UAC is often considered to be a pain and more trouble than it is worth. However, UAC serves an important function in that it requires a second approval to complete administrative actions on the computer, such as accessing the registry or various protected files and folders such as the Windows operating system and the Program Files folder. This extra approval is meant to prevent applications from being able to successfully access parts of the operating system that should not be accessed.

> **NOTE**
> **UAC Settings**
> Many people like to disable UAC on their servers and workstations so that it does not bother
> them with requesting permissions to do work. Personally I recommend that people increase the
> permissions not decrease them on production servers. When it comes to servers, extra permissions
> are almost never a bad thing.

While on the desktop this can be annoying at best and downright troublesome at worst, on a server this extra protection can prevent things from running that should not be running and making administrative level changes to the system such as installing applications, adding services, or making registry changes.

To make changes on a single computer, open the control panel and then the User Accounts control panel icon. From there click on the "Change User Account Control settings" link. From here you can adjust the level of interaction UAC will have with the desktop. On a production server this setting should be set as high as possible, as shown in Figure 6.19.

Beyond the simple slider setting shown in Figure 6.19, a variety of settings can be set via group policy. These can all be found under:

1. Computer Configuration
2. Policies

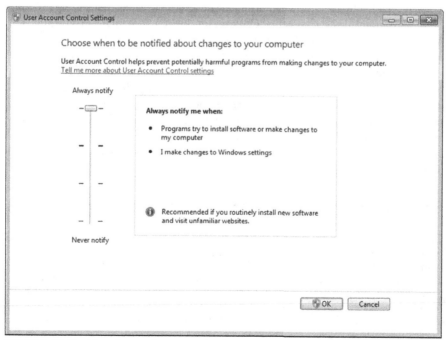

FIGURE 6.19 The User Access Control setting in the recommended setting for servers.

3. Windows Settings
4. Security Settings
5. Local Policies
6. Security Options

Within the Security Options folder there are 10 User Account Control settings that can be controlled for greater control of UAC than the normal control panel interface. Of these 10 settings, 3 of them will have a noticeable effect on servers. These settings are as follows.

1. User Account Control: Detect application installations and prompt for elevation
2. User Account Control: Virtualize file and registry write failures to per-user locations
3. User Account Control: Behavior of the elevation prompt for standard users

It is very important to enable the "User Account Control: Detect application installations and prompt for elevation" setting. When this setting is enabled, the UAC subsystem of the operating system will detect the installation of applications and will trigger a UAC authentication prompt when an installer is run. With this setting disabled, this check is not in place and installers are able to run without prompting.

The "User Account Control: Virtualize file and registry write failures to per-user locations" is another good setting to disable on production servers. This setting, which is enabled by default, when disabled causes applications that attempt to write to the %ProgramFiles% (typically "C:\Program Files\"), %WinDir% (typically "C:\Windows\"), and %WinDir%\System32 (typically "C:\Windows\System32\") folders and to the HKEY_LOCAL_MACHINE\Software registry key to fail instead of redirecting those writes to protected user-specific locations such as C:\UserData\. When the setting is enabled, the writes are automatically disabled, and when the setting is disabled, the writes will fail. Many rouge applications would be written to hide themselves and their data in the %WinDir% and %WinDir%\System32 folders. By preventing these rouge applications from writing to these protected locations, many of these rouge applications will fail to run correctly, causing them to simply crash.

> **NOTE**
> **Be Very Careful When Adjusting UAC Settings**
> Making changes to the UAC settings should not be done to production servers at random. These changes should first be fully tested on development and QA systems to ensure that all applications that are installed on the server can function as expected with these changes. There is nothing worse than changing settings to improve security and having the production systems crash days or weeks later after the next system reboot. As a result, large amounts of time are required to figure out what change, which happened days or weeks before (months possibly depending on how often you reboot), caused the problem.

A third setting that should be adjusted, assuming that the SQL Server service or the website is running under a non-administrator account, is the "User Account Control: Behavior of the elevation prompt for standard users." This setting controls how UAC will react when a standard user (a user who is not a member of the local Administrators group) attempts to perform an action that is protected by UAC. By default, UAC will prompt the user to enter a username and password that have the rights to perform the action. It is recommended that this setting be changed from "Prompt for credentials on the secure desktop" to "Automatically deny elevation requests," which will tell the Windows OS to simply fail the request to perform the protected action.

OTHER DOMAIN POLICIES TO ADJUST

Beyond User Account Control (UAC), other security policies should be adjusted in order to reduce the surface area that a potential attacker could use to attack the server. The more of these settings that are configured, the smaller the surface area of the server that can be attacked. These settings are as follows.

1. Accounts: Rename administrator account
2. Accounts: Guest Account Status
3. Accounts: Rename guest account
4. Devices: Prevent users from installing printer drivers

The "Accounts: Rename administrator account" policy allows you to globally change the username of the local Administrator account. This will help reduce the attack surface area by making an attacker guess the username of the local administrator account. Like the SA (system administrator) account in Microsoft SQL Server that has a known username, making it easier for an attacker to break into the database, leaving the Administrator account with the default name poses the same potential vulnerability. When selecting a new username to use for the local administrator account, the same syntax should be used that is used for the local administrator account. For example, if the company username syntax is first name dot last name, then a username of James.Kirk would be a good username to use. If the company username syntax is first initial followed by the last name, then a username of jkirk would be a good username to use.

The "Accounts: Guest Account Status" policy allows you to disable the guest account to ensure that no one is able to log into the server using the local guest account. While this is a very low privileged account that does not have rights to access much of the operating system, there is always the potential that an attacker could use this account along with a privilege elevation attack to increase their privileges. By forcing the account to always be disabled, no user can authenticate using the guest account even with the correct username and password.

The "Accounts: Rename guest account" policy allows you to globally change the username of the local guest account. It is recommended that you change the guest account so that the username is set to "Administrator." This way if someone attempts to log into the server using the local account with the name "Administrator" and that account is enabled, then the user will get a very low privileged account. If the account is disabled, then the potential attacker will receive a message about the account being disabled and the login will be denied.

The "Devices: Prevent users from installing printer drivers" privilege can be used to ensure that users do not have the right to install printer drivers on the server. One potential attack that could be used via a print driver would be to install an Internet print driver, which could then be used to print company documents to that print driver, sending the documents to a remote printer service. The service could then store the documents or print them on the attacker's printer. In either case, the attacker would have access to internal company documents, which they should not have.

SUMMARY

Properly securing a single instance of Microsoft SQL Server is not always the easiest task. However, with good company wide policies in place, as well as using newer features like Policy-based Management, securing all the instances within the enterprise becomes easier over time and eventually becomes second nature. When it comes to dynamic SQL and cross database object security time, a methodical approach, combined with closely working with application and database developers (as well as business users and data analysts who have direct database access) will be the best approach to keeping the database objects properly secured. New features like Contained Databases and AlwaysOn Availability Groups present new quirks and complexity to the setup and configuration of the database applications. However, these new features can help you easily bridge the worlds of high availability and high security.

Every server needs to be projected from those who have access to it. Servers that are customer (or Internet) facing need some extra protections in order to secure the server from attackers. This includes only hosting known code within an SQL Instance through the extended stored procedures and SQL CLR assemblies. The server can be further protected by limiting the amount of data that an attacker can gather by limiting the amount of memory data that can be written to the hard drive at any time through crash dumps and the Windows page file.

When working within Windows Azure SQL Database, the only section of this chapter that applies is that on securing your connection string. As of 2014, Windows Azure SQL Database does not support SQL CLR assemblies of any type, nor does it support extended stored procedures. The other information in this chapter is related to Windows-specific settings that must be set by logging into the Windows OS, which cannot be done on Windows Azure SQL Database instances. If the application requires SQL CLR or extended stored procedures, then Windows Azure SQL Database is not a good solution for hosting that application.

Analysis Services

7

INFORMATION IN THIS CHAPTER:

- Logging into analysis services
- Securing analysis services objects

LOGGING INTO ANALYSIS SERVICES

Microsoft SQL Server Analysis Services is a different kind of database engine from the traditional database engine that database administrators are used to working with. Analysis Services is designed as an Online Analysis Processing (OLAP) database engine. This database engine is especially designed for large amounts of data analysis and pre-aggregation of data.

Microsoft SQL Server Analysis Services was introduced in SQL Server 7 and it has been constantly improved release after release up through and including the SQL Server 2014 release. While the Microsoft SQL Server database engine supports both SQL Server authentication and Windows Authentication the SQL Server Analysis Services service only supports Windows Authentication. This creates a simpler and more secure service installation as only the one authentication model is required and the actual credentials are never passed from the user's workstation to the SQL Server Analysis Services service. Instead, the user's authentication token is passed from the users workstation to the Analysis Services server using either the Kerberos or NTLM protocols. More can be read on the authentication process in Chapter 3 under the heading "SQL Server Password Security" within this book.

Rights to log into the Microsoft SQL Server Analysis Services engine are handled in a much different way than in the SQL Server Database Engine. Traditionally database engine logins are created at the instance level and users are created within the databases which then map to logins within the instance. With SQL Server Analysis Services non-administrative users are granted rights directly into the specific SQL Server Analysis Services database which the user needs access to, much like the contained database functionality which was introduced in SQL Server 2012.

For administrative rights to the SQL Server Analysis Services database engine there are administrative users who have full control of the Analysis Services instance and who have full rights to all the databases and objects within the instance. Unlike the SQL Server database engine which has multiple system level roles for various levels of administrative access, the SQL Server Analysis Services engine has only a single level of administrative access unlike the traditional database engine which has several fixed server roles which a login can be a member of.

GRANTING ADMINISTRATIVE RIGHTS

Connecting to the SQL Server Analysis Services database engine is done is a very similar way to connecting to the traditional database engine. To connect to a SQL Server analysis services instance, open the Connect To dialog box by clicking the connection icon within the object explorer (if you do not see the object explorer you can enable the object explorer from the "View" dropdown menu in object explorer). In the Connect To screen which opens, change the "Server Type" dropdown menu to "Analysis Services," specify the server name and click connect. You may have noticed on this screen that there is no option to use anything other than SQL Authentication to connect as described earlier in this chapter.

To grant a user administrative rights into the SQL Server Analysis Services engine connect to the instance using the object explorer. Then right click on the server and select properties. When the server properties screen opens select the security page as shown in Figure 7.1. To add additional users to the instance click the "Add" button, while removing users from the list of administrators of the instance is done by selecting the user and clicking the "Remove" button.

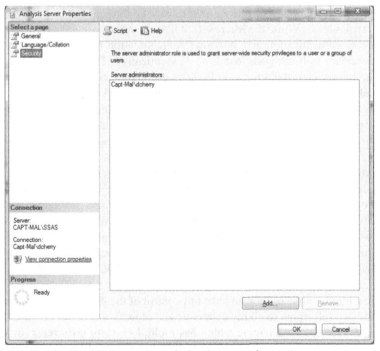

FIGURE 7.1 Showing the SQL Server Analysis Services security screen.

> **NOTE**
>
> Combining XMLA Scripts Together
>
> The various XMLA scripts which are shown in this chapter can be combined into a single XMLA script by putting each of the <ALTER> blocks into a single script with a single set of <BATCH> tags around all of the <ALTER> tags.

New administrative users can be added to the Microsoft SQL Server Analysis Services instance by using code as well as by using the SQL Server Management Studio User Interface. Microsoft SQL Server Analysis Services does not include a language like T/SQL which gives you the ability to manage the instance as well as query the database engine. In order to add users via code the Analysis Services code language of XMLA (XML for Analysis) is used add the user. XMLA is a rather verbose language as can be seen in Example 7.1 which shows the XMLA code required to add the user BACON\dcherry as a member of the Administrators group of the SQL Server Analysis Services instance. Like when doing most tasks within SQL Server Management Studio for the traditional database engine, when performing tasks against the Analysis Services engine, those tasks can be scripted out by clicking the "Script" button at the top of the various screens. This can make writing many of these scripts much easier, and make it easier to check administrative functions into source control.

EXAMPLE 7.1

Showing the XMLA code to change the membership of the Administrators group.

```
<Batch xmlns='http://schemas.microsoft.com/analysisservices/2003/engine'
Transaction='true'>
<Alter AllowCreate="true" ObjectExpansion="ObjectProperties"
xmlns="http://schemas.microsoft.com/analysisservices/2003/engine">
  <Object />
  <ObjectDefinition>
    <Server xmlns:xsd="http://www.w3.org/2001/XMLSchema"
xmlns:xsi="http://www.w3.org/2001/XMLSchema-instance"
xmlns:ddl2="http://schemas.microsoft.com/analysisservices/2003/engine/2"
xmlns:ddl2_2="http://schemas.microsoft.com/analysisservices/2003/engine/2/2"
xmlns:ddl100_100="http://schemas.microsoft.com/analysisservices/2008/engine/
100/100"
xmlns:ddl200="http://schemas.microsoft.com/analysisservices/2010/engine/200"
xmlns:ddl200_200="http://schemas.microsoft.com/analysisservices/2010/engine/
200/200">
      <ID>FIREFLY</ID>
      <Name>FIREFLY</Name>
    </Server>
  </ObjectDefinition>
</Alter>
```

```
<Alter AllowCreate="true" ObjectExpansion="ObjectProperties"
xmlns="http://schemas.microsoft.com/analysisservices/2003/engine">
  <Object>
    <RoleID>Administrators</RoleID>
  </Object>
  <ObjectDefinition>
    <Role xmlns:xsd="http://www.w3.org/2001/XMLSchema"
xmlns:xsi="http://www.w3.org/2001/XMLSchema-instance"
xmlns:ddl2="http://schemas.microsoft.com/analysisservices/2003/engine/2"
xmlns:ddl2_2="http://schemas.microsoft.com/analysisservices/2003/engine/2/2"
xmlns:ddl100_100="http://schemas.microsoft.com/analysisservices/2008/engine/
100/100"
xmlns:ddl200="http://schemas.microsoft.com/analysisservices/2010/engine/200"
xmlns:ddl200_200="http://schemas.microsoft.com/analysisservices/2010/engine/
200/200">
      <ID>Administrators</ID>
      <Name>Administrators</Name>
      <Members>
        <Member>
          <Name>BACON\SSIS_Admins</Name>
        </Member>
        <Member>
          <Name>BACON\dcherry</Name>
        </Member>
      </Members>
    </Role>
  </ObjectDefinition>
</Alter>
</Batch>
```

By default all members of the local administrators group of the Windows operating system are administrators of the SQL Server Analysis Services instance. Newer versions of SQL Server Analysis Services such as SQL Server 2014 will prompt your during the installation process for the list of Windows users and/or groups who should have administrative rights. For older versions which do not prompt for this during installation, this is fixed by changing an instance property within the Analysis Services instance. Before making the change be sure to grant yourself and the other administrators administrative rights within the Analysis Services instance.

To make the needed change, which needs to be made even on SQL Server 2014 instances where a server administrator was specified during installation, connect to the Analysis Services instance within SQL Server Management Studio's Object Explorer. Right click on the Analysis Services instance and select properties. Check the checkbox to "Show Advanced Properties" then locate the "Security\BuiltinAdminsAreServerAdmins" property within the list of permissions. Change this setting from True to False and click OK to save the change.

GRANTING RIGHTS TO AN ANALYSIS SERVICES DATABASE

Users are granted rights within the Microsoft SQL Server Analysis Services databases by adding their Windows account information to one or more roles within each

> **NOTE**
>
> Cubes?
>
> Cubes in SQL Server Analysis Services are objects which contain the data within the SQL Server Analysis Services database. These cubes are designed differently from tables in traditional databases. These cubes are designed with various levels of aggregation, with the aggregate values pre-calculated and stored within the cube so that users can simply retrieve them without having to go through the process of calculating the values on the fly.

specific Analysis Services database for which they need access. The roles which the users are members of then grant rights to the objects within the database. Within the database there are three permission levels which are granted to the role at the database level, and are separate from the object level rights. These three database level rights are "Full control" which is also known as "Administrator," "Process database," and "Read definition." The "full control" database level right gives the members of the role full access to the database. This includes the ability to create and delete objects, process the cubes within the database and change user permissions within the cube. The "process database" right gives the user the ability to process the cubes within the database but does not give the user the right to view the data within the database. The "read definition" right gives the user the ability to view the schema of the database including the cubes, dimensions, and other objects within the database but does not give the user the right to view the data stored within the Microsoft SQL Server Analysis Services database.

Granting a user rights into a Microsoft SQL Server Analysis Services Database can be done though either the SQL Server Management Studio User Interface, via XMLA or by creating the role within the SQL Server Analysis Services Project in the Business Intelligence Development Studio (BIDS) when using SQL Server 2005 or below, or SQL Server Database Tools (SSDT) when using SQL Server 2008 and above, and deploying it to the server with the project. To use SQL Server Management Studio to grant a user rights with the database connect to the SQL Server Analysis Services instance using the SQL Server Management Studio object explorer. In the object explorer navigate to the database then to roles. Right click on the database role that the user should be a member of and select properties from the context menu that opens. On the role properties page which opens select the membership page which brings up the list of users who are members of the role as shown in Figure 7.2. Adding a new member requires clicking the "Add" button while removing a login requires selecting a user from the database and clicking the "Remove" button.

Adding users to the database role can be done using XMLA as well as using the user interface. The advantage of using XMLA to add users to the database over the user interface is that XMLA files can be checked into source control so that the same permissions changes can be deployed between different environments such as dev, QA and production. The XMLA to add users to a database role would look similar to that shown in Example 7.2.

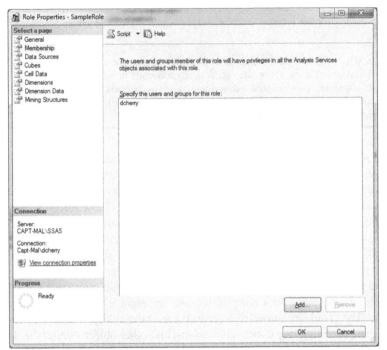

FIGURE 7.2 Showing the membership of a SQL Server Analysis Services Role.

EXAMPLE 7.2

Sample XMLA code to add a user to a role within a SQL Server Analysis Services database.

```
<Alter ObjectExpansion="ExpandFull" xmlns="http://schemas.microsoft.com/
analysisservices/
2003/engine">
    <Object>
        <RoleID>Role 1</RoleID>
        <DatabaseID>SampleDatabase</DatabaseID>
    </Object>
    <ObjectDefinition>
        <Role xmlns:xsd="http://www.w3.org/2001/XMLSchema"
xmlns:xsi="http://www.w3.org/2001/XMLSchema-instance"
xmlns:ddl2="http://schemas.microsoft.com/analysisservices/2003/engine/2"
xmlns:ddl2_2="http://schemas.microsoft.com/analysisservices/2003/engine/2/2"
xmlns:ddl100_100="http://schemas.microsoft.com/analysisservices/2008/engine/
100/100"
xmlns:ddl200="http://schemas.microsoft.com/analysisservices/2010/engine/200"
xmlns:ddl200_200="http://schemas.microsoft.com/analysisservices/2010/engine/
200/200">
```

```
            <ID>Role 1</ID>
            <Name>Admin</Name>
            <Members>
                <Member>
                    <Name>BACON\dcherry</Name>
                    <Sid>S-1-5-21-2407593644-4190971996-603350960-3150</Sid>
                </Member>
            </Members>
        </Role>
    </ObjectDefinition>
</Alter>
```

When the SQL Server Analysis Services project is under development, and before it has been deployed to a server and had data loaded into it rights can be configured as well. This can be done by opening the project with Business Intelligence Development Studio or SSDT depending on your development environment and the version you are using, and adding a new role to the project. To do this within the Solutions Explorer right click on "Roles" and select "New Role" from the context menu which opens. This will open the role editor as shown in Figure 7.3 which you can see looks very similar to the role editor from SQL Server Management Studio with the big difference being that the pages selector is along the top in Business Intelligence Development Studio and along the left hand in SQL Server Management Studio.

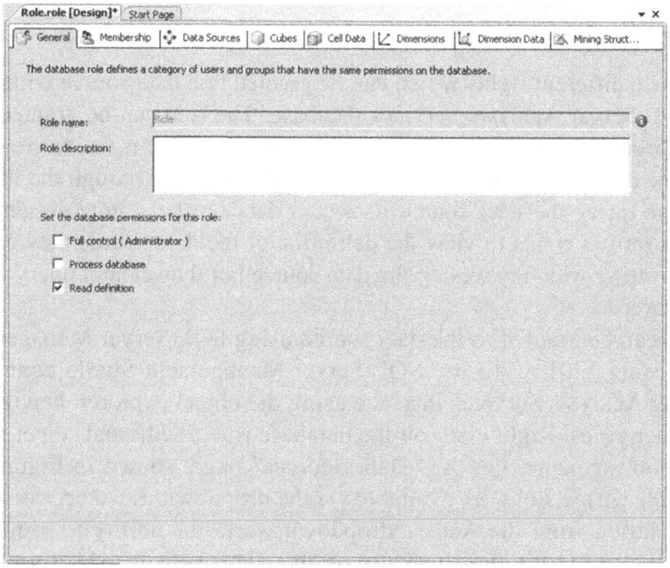

FIGURE 7.3 Showing the role designer from Business Intelligence Development Studio.

For the rest of this chapter only SQL Server Management Studio is referenced as a User Interface to edit the permissions of a role within SQL Server Analysis Services. All these same options are available within the BIDS designer and the screens look very similar with the big difference being that the navigation area in BIDS is at the top of the screen and in SSMS it is on the left hand side of the screen.

If changes were made to a role in BIDS, and then the project was redeployed to the server, the permissions changes would be uploaded to the SQL Server Analysis Services server as a part of this process. If changes were made to a role in SQL Server Management Studio then those changes would be overwritten the next time that the project was deployed to the Analysis Services instance.

The information within this chapter was made to reference SSMS only for brevity so that the chapter would not be twice as long providing the exact same information with only new screenshots.

SECURING ANALYSIS SERVICES OBJECTS

Granting rights to objects within the SQL Server Analysis Services database is done through the roles within the SQL Server Analysis Services database. Rights can be granted to a variety of objects within database. These objects include data sources, cubes, cell data, dimensions, dimension data, and data mining structures.

DATA SOURCES

There are two different rights which can be granted to a data source within the Microsoft SQL Server Analysis Services database. The role can be granted rights to read data through the data source, or the role can be granted rights to view the definition of the data source. When the user has rights to read through the data source the user can query the data source to access data on the source system directly. When the user has rights to view the definition of the data source they can see the connection string which makes up the data source but they cannot query data using the data source.

Access can be granted to the data source using SQL Server Management Studio or by using XMLA. To use SQL Server Management Studio connect to the SQL Server Analysis Services instance using the object explorer. Navigate to the database then roles. Right click on the database role to edit and select properties from the context menu. On the "Data Sources" page, shown in Figure 7.4, the two available permissions are available via the dropdown. Read access to the data source is chosen from the Access dropdown while the ability to view the read definition is granted via the checkbox on the right, both of which are shown in Figure 7.4.

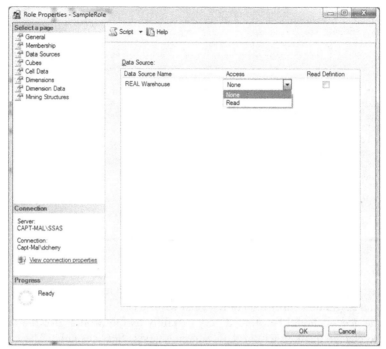

FIGURE 7.4 Showing the permissions of the data sources page of the database role properties.

When using XMLA to modify the database role permissions, as shown in Example 7.3, quite a bit of code is required to grant these simple permissions. The permissions being granted in the code in Example 7.3 grant access both to read the data source as well as to view the definition of the data source. To not grant these rights simply remove the line which grants these rights from the sample code.

EXAMPLE 7.3

Sample code showing how to grant permissions on a data source to a role using XMLA.

```
<Batch xmlns='http://schemas.microsoft.com/analysisservices/2003/engine'
Transaction='true'>
<Alter AllowCreate="true" ObjectExpansion="ObjectProperties"
xmlns="http://schemas.microsoft.com/analysisservices/2003/engine">
  <Object>
    <DatabaseID>SampleDatabase</DatabaseID>
    <DataSourceID>AdventureWorks2008R2</DataSourceID>
    <DataSourcePermissionID>DataSourcePermission</DataSourcePermissionID>
  </Object>
```

```
<ObjectDefinition>
  <DataSourcePermission xmlns:xsd="http://www.w3.org/2001/XMLSchema"
xmlns:xsi="http://www.w3.org/2001/XMLSchema-instance"
xmlns:ddl2="http://schemas.microsoft.com/analysisservices/2003/engine/2"
xmlns:ddl2_2="http://schemas.microsoft.com/analysisservices/2003/engine/2/2"
xmlns:ddl100_100="http://schemas.microsoft.com/analysisservices/2008/engine/
100/100"
xmlns:ddl200="http://schemas.microsoft.com/analysisservices/2010/engine/200"
xmlns:ddl200_200="http://schemas.microsoft.com/analysisservices/2010/engine/
200/200">
    <ID>DataSourcePermission</ID>
    <Name>DataSourcePermission</Name>
    <RoleID>Role 2</RoleID>
    <ReadDefinition>Allowed</ReadDefinition>
    <Read>Allowed</Read>
  </DataSourcePermission>
</ObjectDefinition>
</Alter>
```

CUBES

There are five rights which can be granted to a role with regard to a database cube. A role can be granted either read or read and write access to the cube. Granting read and write access should be granted very carefully as this would give the user the ability to change the data within SQL Server Analysis Services cube. The next two rights which can be granted is the right to "Drillthrough" or "Drillthrough and Local Cube." The "Drillthrough" right gives the user the ability to use the drill though function of the database cube to other cubes or the source database. The "Drillthrough and Local Cube" gives the user the rights to both drillthrough the database as well as to the local version of the data in the cube. The last right is the right to process the database cube which would give the user the right to update the data in the cube from the source location.

Granting permissions to cubes can be done via SQL Server Management Studio or via XMLA. To use SQL Server Management Studio connect to the SQL Server Analysis Services instance using the object explorer. Navigate to the database then roles. Right click on the database role to edit and select properties from the context menu. Select the Cubes page, as shown in Figure 7.5, from the menu on the left to show the list of available cubes in the menu on the right. In the access column the first two rights, being either Read or Read/Write, can be granted. In the "Local Cube/ Drillthrough Access" column the second two rights, being either "Drillthrough" or "Drillthrough and Local Cube" can be granted. In the "Process" column the right to process the cube can be granted.

Granting access via XMLA can be done as well as shown in Example 7.4. As you can see in Example 7.4 each of the permissions is listed out separately. To not grant a specific permission simply remove that line from the XML document which makes up the XMLA script.

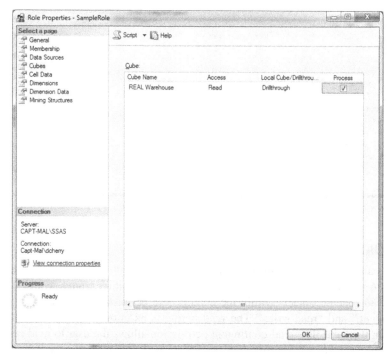

FIGURE 7.5 Showing the ability to change the various permissions on the cubes within the selected database.

EXAMPLE 7.4

XMLA script granting permissions to an OLAP cube.

```
<Batch xmlns='http://schemas.microsoft.com/analysisservices/2003/engine'
Transaction='true'>
<Alter AllowCreate="true" ObjectExpansion="ObjectProperties"
xmlns="http://schemas.microsoft.com/analysisservices/2003/engine">
  <Object>
    <DatabaseID>SampleDatabase</DatabaseID>
    <CubeID>Phreesia 6</CubeID>
    <CubePermissionID>CubePermission 1</CubePermissionID>
  </Object>
  <ObjectDefinition>
    <CubePermission xmlns:xsd="http://www.w3.org/2001/XMLSchema"
xmlns:xsi="http://www.w3.org/2001/XMLSchema-instance"
xmlns:ddl2="http://schemas.microsoft.com/analysisservices/2003/engine/2"
xmlns:ddl2_2="http://schemas.microsoft.com/analysisservices/2003/engine/
2/2"
xmlns:ddl100_100="http://schemas.microsoft.com/analysisservices/2008/engine/
100/100"
```

```
xmlns:ddl200="http://schemas.microsoft.com/analysisservices/2010/engine/200"
xmlns:ddl200_200="http://schemas.microsoft.com/analysisservices/2010/engine
/200/200">
     <ID>CubePermission 1</ID>
     <Name>CubePermission 1</Name>
     <RoleID>Role 2</RoleID>
     <Process>true</Process>
     <Read>Allowed</Read>
     <Write>Allowed</Write>
     <ReadSourceData>Allowed</ReadSourceData>
   </CubePermission>
  </ObjectDefinition>
</Alter></Batch>
```

CELL DATA

Rights can be granted within the specific cubes to specific objects within the SQL Server Analysis Services database engine. There are three rights which can be granted to specific objects within the cube. These permissions are "Read," "Read-Contingent," and "read/write." The read permissions allow the users to read data stored in the cube. The read-contingent permission allows the user to read cell content contingent on cell security. The read/write permission allows the user to both read and write the data within the objects.

Granting permissions to Cell Data can be done via SQL Server Management Studio or via XMLA. To use SQL Server Management Studio connect to the SQL Server Analysis Services instance using the object explorer. Navigate to the database then roles. Right click on the database role to edit and select properties from the context menu. Select Cell Data from the menu on the left which will show the screen shown in Figure 7.6.

Check the boxes for the permissions which should be granted, and enter the object names which the right should apply to using the MDX format as shown in Figure 7.6.

When granting permissions via XMLA the same information is needed as would be provided to the SQL Server Management Studio User Interface in much the same format as shown in Example 7.5.

> **NOTE**
> Read-contingent Is a Very Confusing Permission
>
> If you are not fully confused by the statement which says "The read-contingent permission allows the user to read cell content contingent on cell security" then you are not trying hard enough. In plain English what read-contingent permissions means is that measures which are based on other objects are only visible if the user has read rights on the underlying columns.

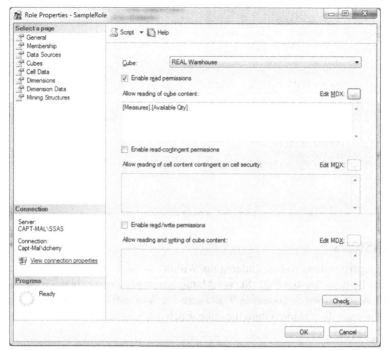

FIGURE 7.6 Showing the cell data permissions screen.

EXAMPLE 7.5

The XMLA to grant read access to the measure "Logs Count."

```
<Batch xmlns='http://schemas.microsoft.com/analysisservices/2003/engine'
Transaction='true'>
<Alter AllowCreate="true" ObjectExpansion="ObjectProperties"
xmlns="http://schemas.microsoft.com/analysisservices/2003/engine">
  <Object>
    <DatabaseID>SampleDatabase</DatabaseID>
    <CubeID>AdventureWorks 6</CubeID>
    <CubePermissionID>CubePermission 1</CubePermissionID>
  </Object>
  <ObjectDefinition>
    <CubePermission xmlns:xsd="http://www.w3.org/2001/XMLSchema"
xmlns:xsi="http://www.w3.org/2001/XMLSchema-instance"
xmlns:ddl2="http://schemas.microsoft.com/analysisservices/2003/engine/2"
xmlns:ddl2_2="http://schemas.microsoft.com/analysisservices/2003/engine/
2/2"
xmlns:ddl100_100="http://schemas.microsoft.com/analysisservices/2008/engine/
100/100"
xmlns:ddl200="http://schemas.microsoft.com/analysisservices/2010/engine/200"
xmlns:ddl200_200="http://schemas.microsoft.com/analysisservices/2010/engine/
200/200">
```

```
    <ID>CubePermission 1</ID>
    <Name>CubePermission 1</Name>
    <RoleID>Role 2</RoleID>
    <Read>Allowed</Read>
    <ReadSourceData>None</ReadSourceData>
    <CellPermissions>
      <CellPermission>
        <Access>Read</Access>
        <Expression>[Measures].[Logs Count]</Expression>
      </CellPermission>
    </CellPermissions>
  </CubePermission>
 </ObjectDefinition>
</Alter>
</Batch>
```

DIMENSIONS

Granting permissions to the dimensions within the SQL Server Analysis Services cube can be done via the SQL Server Management Studio, as shown in Figure 7.7, or XMLA, as shown in Example 7.6. There are four different rights which can be granted to each dimension within the cube. Each role can be assigned either "read," or

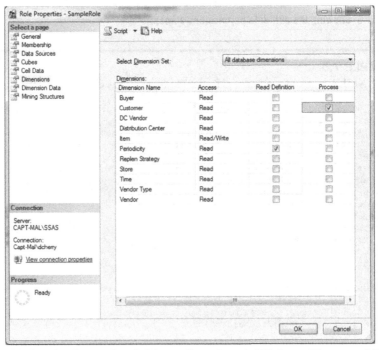

FIGURE 7.7 Showing the granting of rights to dimensions via SQL Server Management Studio.

"read/write" access to each specific dimension. Additionally the role can be granted rights to read the definition of the dimension by being granted the "read definition" right. The final right which can be granted against a dimension is the ability to "process" the dimension updating it from the source system.

EXAMPLE 7.6

Showing the XMLA used to grant permissions to dimensions.

```
<Batch xmlns='http://schemas.microsoft.com/analysisservices/2003/engine'
Transaction='true'>
<Alter AllowCreate="true" ObjectExpansion="ObjectProperties"
xmlns="http://schemas.microsoft.com/analysisservices/2003/engine">
  <Object>
    <DatabaseID>REAL Warehouse Sample V6 MT</DatabaseID>
    <DimensionID>Buyer</DimensionID>
    <DimensionPermissionID>DimensionPermission</DimensionPermissionID>
  </Object>
  <ObjectDefinition>
    <DimensionPermission xmlns:xsd="http://www.w3.org/2001/XMLSchema"
xmlns:xsi="http://www.w3.org/2001/XMLSchema-instance"
xmlns:ddl2="http://schemas.microsoft.com/analysisservices/2003/engine/2"
xmlns:ddl2_2="http://schemas.microsoft.com/analysisservices/2003/engine/2/2"
xmlns:ddl100_100="http://schemas.microsoft.com/analysisservices/2008/engine/
100/100"
xmlns:ddl200="http://schemas.microsoft.com/analysisservices/2010/engine/200"
xmlns:ddl200_200="http://schemas.microsoft.com/analysisservices/2010/engine/
200/200"
xmlns:ddl300="http://schemas.microsoft.com/analysisservices/2011/engine/300"
xmlns:ddl300_300="http://schemas.microsoft.com/analysisservices/2011/engine/
300/300">
      <ID>DimensionPermission</ID>
      <Name>DimensionPermission</Name>
      <RoleID>Role</RoleID>
      <Process>true</Process>
      <ReadDefinition>Allowed</ReadDefinition>
      <Read>Allowed</Read>
      <Write>Allowed</Write>
      <AttributePermissions>
        <AttributePermission>
          <AttributeID>Buyer ID</AttributeID>
        </AttributePermission>
      </AttributePermissions>
    </DimensionPermission>
  </ObjectDefinition>
</Alter>
</Batch>
```

DIMENSION DATA

One of the great things about Microsoft SQL Server Analysis Services is that rights can be granted to specific values within the dimension data. In the SQL Server core database engine this would be referred to as vertical permissions or row level permissions (more about row level permissions in Chapter 13) and is hard to build into applications in the database engine; however, SQL Server Analysis Services has this built into the database engine. Granting rights to the dimension data can be done via SQL Server Management Studio, as shown in Figure 7.8, as well as through XMLA code, as shown in Example 7.7. Rights on dimension data can be granted to all members, via the basic tab in SQL Server Management Studio or to specific values via the Advanced tab in SQL Server Management Studio as shown in Figure 7.9.

EXAMPLE 7.7

Showing the XMLA used to grant permissions to specific dimension data.

```
<Alter AllowCreate="true" ObjectExpansion="ObjectProperties"
xmlns="http://schemas.microsoft.com/analysisservices/2003/engine">
  <Object>
    <DatabaseID>REAL Warehouse Sample V6 MT</DatabaseID>
    <DimensionID>Buyer</DimensionID>
    <DimensionPermissionID>DimensionPermission</DimensionPermissionID>
  </Object>
  <ObjectDefinition>
    <DimensionPermission xmlns:xsd="http://www.w3.org/2001/XMLSchema"
xmlns:xsi="http://www.w3.org/2001/XMLSchema-instance"
xmlns:ddl2="http://schemas.microsoft.com/analysisservices/2003/engine/2"
xmlns:ddl2_2="http://schemas.microsoft.com/analysisservices/2003/engine/2/2"
xmlns:ddl100_100="http://schemas.microsoft.com/analysisservices/2008/engine/
100/100"
xmlns:ddl200="http://schemas.microsoft.com/analysisservices/2010/engine/200"
xmlns:ddl200_200="http://schemas.microsoft.com/analysisservices/2010/engine/
200/200"
xmlns:ddl300="http://schemas.microsoft.com/analysisservices/2011/engine/300"
xmlns:ddl300_300="http://schemas.microsoft.com/analysisservices/2011/engine/
300/300">
      <ID>DimensionPermission</ID>
      <Name>DimensionPermission</Name>
      <RoleID>Role</RoleID>
      <Process>true</Process>
      <ReadDefinition>Allowed</ReadDefinition>
      <Read>Allowed</Read>
      <Write>Allowed</Write>
      <AttributePermissions>
        <AttributePermission>
          <AttributeID>Buyer ID</AttributeID>
          <DeniedSet>{[Buyer].[Buyer ID].[All]}</DeniedSet>
        </AttributePermission>
      </AttributePermissions>
    </DimensionPermission>
  </ObjectDefinition>
</Alter>
</Batch>
```

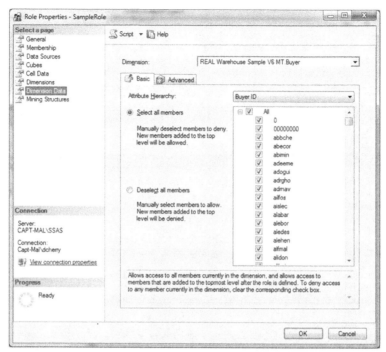

FIGURE 7.8 Granting rights to specific dimension data using the basic tab within SQL Server Management Studio.

When granting rights to specific values the XMLA is a little more complex than when granting rights to all the dimension values. The XMLA code to grant rights to all values is shown in Example 7.7, while the XMLA code to grant rights to specific values is shown in Example 7.8. The basic difference between the two is that when granting rights to specific values first the rights are first denied to all values, then the rights are granted to the specific value. This is shown in the XMLA in Example 7.8 within the <DeniedSet> tag. The <DefaultMember> tag is then used to grant rights to the specific values that the role should have access to.

EXAMPLE 7.8
Showing the XMLA code used to grant rights to specific dimensions members.

```
<Batch xmlns='http://schemas.microsoft.com/analysisservices/2003/engine'
Transaction='true'>
<Alter AllowCreate="true" ObjectExpansion="ObjectProperties"
xmlns="http://schemas.microsoft.com/analysisservices/2003/engine">
  <Object>
    <DatabaseID>REAL Warehouse Sample V6 MT</DatabaseID>
    <RoleID>Role</RoleID>
  </Object>
```

```xml
  <ObjectDefinition>
    <Role xmlns:xsd="http://www.w3.org/2001/XMLSchema"
xmlns:xsi="http://www.w3.org/2001/XMLSchema-instance"
xmlns:ddl2="http://schemas.microsoft.com/analysisservices/2003/engine/2"
xmlns:ddl2_2="http://schemas.microsoft.com/analysisservices/2003/engine/2/2"
xmlns:ddl100_100="http://schemas.microsoft.com/analysisservices/2008/engine/
100/100"
xmlns:ddl200="http://schemas.microsoft.com/analysisservices/2010/engine/200"
xmlns:ddl200_200="http://schemas.microsoft.com/analysisservices/2010/engine/
200/200"
xmlns:ddl300="http://schemas.microsoft.com/analysisservices/2011/engine/300"
xmlns:ddl300_300="http://schemas.microsoft.com/analysisservices/2011/engine/
300/300">
      <ID>Role</ID>
      <Name>SampleRole</Name>
    </Role>
  </ObjectDefinition>
</Alter>
<Alter AllowCreate="true" ObjectExpansion="ObjectProperties"
xmlns="http://schemas.microsoft.com/analysisservices/2003/engine">
  <Object>
    <DatabaseID>REAL Warehouse Sample V6 MT</DatabaseID>
    <DimensionID>Buyer</DimensionID>
    <DimensionPermissionID>DimensionPermission</DimensionPermissionID>
  </Object>
  <ObjectDefinition>
    <DimensionPermission xmlns:xsd="http://www.w3.org/2001/XMLSchema"
xmlns:xsi="http://www.w3.org/2001/XMLSchema-instance"
xmlns:ddl2="http://schemas.microsoft.com/analysisservices/2003/engine/2"
xmlns:ddl2_2="http://schemas.microsoft.com/analysisservices/2003/engine/2/2"
xmlns:ddl100_100="http://schemas.microsoft.com/analysisservices/2008/engine/
100/100"
xmlns:ddl200="http://schemas.microsoft.com/analysisservices/2010/engine/200"
xmlns:ddl200_200="http://schemas.microsoft.com/analysisservices/2010/engine/
200/200"
xmlns:ddl300="http://schemas.microsoft.com/analysisservices/2011/engine/300"
xmlns:ddl300_300="http://schemas.microsoft.com/analysisservices/2011/engine/
300/300">
      <ID>DimensionPermission</ID>
      <Name>DimensionPermission</Name>
      <RoleID>Role</RoleID>
      <Process>true</Process>
      <ReadDefinition>Allowed</ReadDefinition>
      <Read>Allowed</Read>
      <Write>Allowed</Write>
      <AttributePermissions>
        <AttributePermission>
          <AttributeID>Buyer ID</AttributeID>
          <DeniedSet>{[Buyer].[Buyer ID].[All]}</DeniedSet>
          <DefaultMember>[Buyer].[Buyer ID].&amp;[abecor]</DefaultMember>
        </AttributePermission>
      </AttributePermissions>
    </DimensionPermission>
  </ObjectDefinition>
</Alter>
</Batch>
```

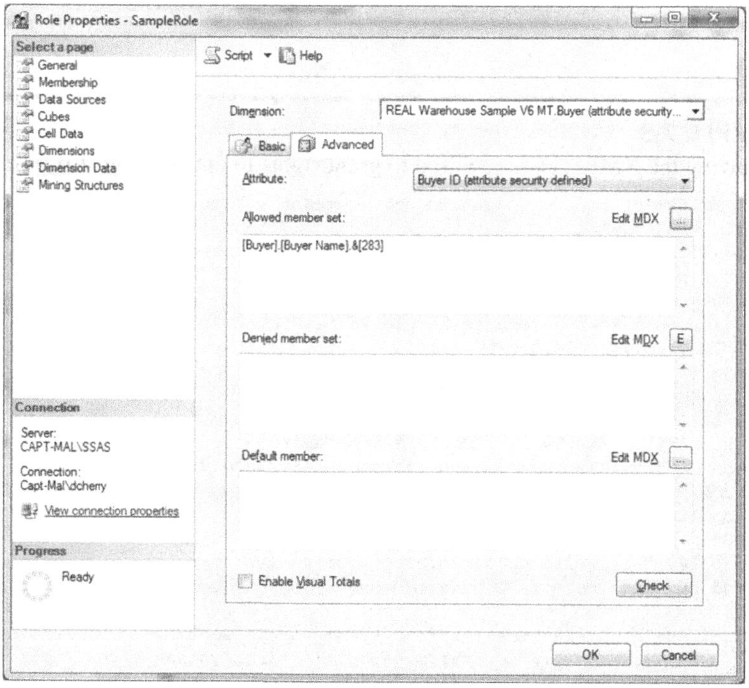

FIGURE 7.9 Granting rights to specific dimension data via the advanced tab within SQL Server Management Studio.

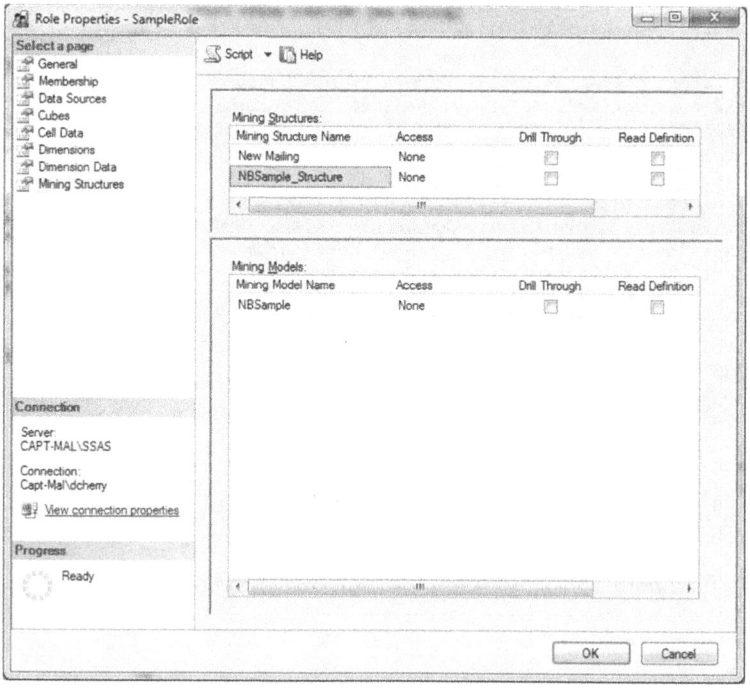

FIGURE 7.10 Granting rights to mining structures within SQL Server Management Studio.

EXAMPLE 7.9

Showing the XMLA code required to grant rights to data mining structures.

```
<Batch xmlns='http://schemas.microsoft.com/analysisservices/2003/engine'
Transaction='true'>
<Alter AllowCreate="true" ObjectExpansion="ObjectProperties"
xmlns="http://schemas.microsoft.com/analysisservices/2003/engine">
  <Object>
    <DatabaseID>REAL Warehouse Sample V6 MT</DatabaseID>
    <RoleID>Role</RoleID>
  </Object>
  <ObjectDefinition>
    <Role xmlns:xsd="http://www.w3.org/2001/XMLSchema"
xmlns:xsi="http://www.w3.org/2001/XMLSchema-instance"
xmlns:ddl2="http://schemas.microsoft.com/analysisservices/2003/engine/2"
xmlns:ddl2_2="http://schemas.microsoft.com/analysisservices/2003/engine/2/2"
xmlns:ddl100_100="http://schemas.microsoft.com/analysisservices/2008/engine/
100/100"
xmlns:ddl200="http://schemas.microsoft.com/analysisservices/2010/engine/200"
xmlns:ddl200_200="http://schemas.microsoft.com/analysisservices/2010/engine/
200/200"
xmlns:ddl300="http://schemas.microsoft.com/analysisservices/2011/engine/300"
xmlns:ddl300_300="http://schemas.microsoft.com/analysisservices/2011/engine/
300/300">
      <ID>Role</ID>
      <Name>SampleRole</Name>
    </Role>
  </ObjectDefinition>
</Alter>
<Alter AllowCreate="true" ObjectExpansion="ObjectProperties"
xmlns="http://schemas.microsoft.com/analysisservices/2003/engine">
  <Object>
    <DatabaseID>REAL Warehouse Sample V6 MT</DatabaseID>
    <MiningStructureID>New Mailing</MiningStructureID>
    <MiningStructurePermissionID>MiningStructurePermission
</MiningStructurePermissionID>
  </Object>
  <ObjectDefinition>
    <MiningStructurePermission xmlns:xsd="http://www.w3.org/2001/XMLSchema"
xmlns:xsi="http://www.w3.org/2001/XMLSchema-instance"
xmlns:ddl2="http://schemas.microsoft.com/analysisservices/2003/engine/2"
xmlns:ddl2_2="http://schemas.microsoft.com/analysisservices/2003/engine/
2/2"
xmlns:ddl100_100="http://schemas.microsoft.com/analysisservices/2008/engine/
100/100"
xmlns:ddl200="http://schemas.microsoft.com/analysisservices/2010/engine/200"
xmlns:ddl200_200="http://schemas.microsoft.com/analysisservices/2010/engine/
200/200"
xmlns:ddl300="http://schemas.microsoft.com/analysisservices/2011/engine/300"
xmlns:ddl300_300="http://schemas.microsoft.com/analysisservices/2011/engine/
300/300">
```

```
        <ID>MiningStructurePermission</ID>
        <Name>MiningStructurePermission</Name>
        <RoleID>Role</RoleID>
        <ReadDefinition>Allowed</ReadDefinition>
        <Read>Allowed</Read>
        <AllowDrillThrough>true</AllowDrillThrough>
      </MiningStructurePermission>
    </ObjectDefinition>
  </Alter>
<Alter AllowCreate="true" ObjectExpansion="ObjectProperties"
xmlns="http://schemas.microsoft.com/analysisservices/2003/engine">
  <Object>
    <DatabaseID>REAL Warehouse Sample V6 MT</DatabaseID>
    <MiningStructureID>NBSample_Structure</MiningStructureID>
    <MiningStructurePermissionID>MiningStructurePermission
</MiningStructurePermissionID>
  </Object>
  <ObjectDefinition>
    <MiningStructurePermission xmlns:xsd="http://www.w3.org/2001/XMLSchema"
xmlns:xsi="http://www.w3.org/2001/XMLSchema-instance"
xmlns:ddl2="http://schemas.microsoft.com/analysisservices/2003/engine/2"
xmlns:ddl2_2="http://schemas.microsoft.com/analysisservices/2003/engine/2/2"
xmlns:ddl100_100="http://schemas.microsoft.com/analysisservices/2008/engine/
100/100"
xmlns:ddl200="http://schemas.microsoft.com/analysisservices/2010/engine/200"
xmlns:ddl200_200="http://schemas.microsoft.com/analysisservices/2010/engine/
200/200"
xmlns:ddl300="http://schemas.microsoft.com/analysisservices/2011/engine/300"
xmlns:ddl300_300="http://schemas.microsoft.com/analysisservices/2011/engine/
300/300">
      <ID>MiningStructurePermission</ID>
      <Name>MiningStructurePermission</Name>
      <RoleID>Role</RoleID>
    </MiningStructurePermission>
  </ObjectDefinition>
  </Alter>
</Batch>
```

MINING STRUCTURES

Within SQL Server Analysis Services there are three rights which can be granted to data mining structures. These rights are the right to "read" the mining structure, the right to "Drillthrough" the data mining structure and the right to read the definition or the data mining structure which is done by granting the "Read Definition" right. These rights can be granted within SQL Server Management Studio as shown in Figure 7.10 or through code by using XMLA in Example 7.9.

Within the data mining structures are the data mining models, which have their own permissions which can be granted independently of the data mining structure. There are four rights which can be granted to the data mining models. The first two involve the actual data access via the "read" and "read/write" permissions. The third permission is the "Drillthrough" right which allows the members of the role to use the SQL Server Analysis Services drillthrough functionality on the data mining model. The last right is the "Read Definition" right which grants the members of the role the ability to read the definition of the data mining model without having the right to read the data within the data mining model.

The role property page which allows the editing of the data mining structures permissions and the data mining models permissions is shown in Figure 7.10, while sample XMLA code to modify the permissions via code is shown in Example 7.9.

SUMMARY

Microsoft SQL Server Analysis Services is a complex beast of an application. It has a complex, but extremely thorough security policy system. Understanding the security policies of SQL Server Analysis Services is key to providing customers with the most usable data analysis tool available, while still maintaining the integrity of the data within the system. Proper security within the SQL Server Analysis Services engine will increase the return on investment (ROI) on the SQL Server Analysis Services system as multiple departments can share a single SQL Server Analysis Services server while maintaining a separation of duties between the databases within the Analysis Services solution.

Reporting Services

8

Denny Cherry

INFORMATION IN THIS CHAPTER:

- Setting up SSRS
- Security within reporting services
- Anonymous authentication
- Forms authentication
- Report server object rights

SETTING UP SSRS

SQL Server Reporting Services is a web based report presentation tool which is included as a part of the SQL Server product. This allows for users to run pre-defined reports as need from a web interface. SQL Server Reporting Services is installed using the traditional SQL Server installer. After SQL Server Reporting Services is installed it needs to be configured by using the Reporting Services Configuration Manager. This application allows you to configure a variety of configuration options including several security related options.

When you first open the SQL Server Reporting Services Configuration Manager you will be prompted for the server name and report server instance to connect to as shown in Figure 8.1. As you can see in Figure 8.1 there is no place to put any sort of credentials when connecting to the Reporting Services service. This is because like SQL Server Analysis Services (discussed more in Chapter 7), SQL Server Reporting Services only supports Windows Authentication for managing and configuring the service.

After connecting to the reporting services instance you will be greeted with a screen which looks much like that which is shown in Figure 8.2. From this screen you can configure a variety of settings which are shown in Table 8.1. These various screens all look basically the same for all the various versions of SQL Server Reporting Services from its introduction in SQL Server 2000 through SQL Server 2014. The screenshots which are shown in this chapter are from SQL Server 2014 so they may look slightly different from the version you are using.

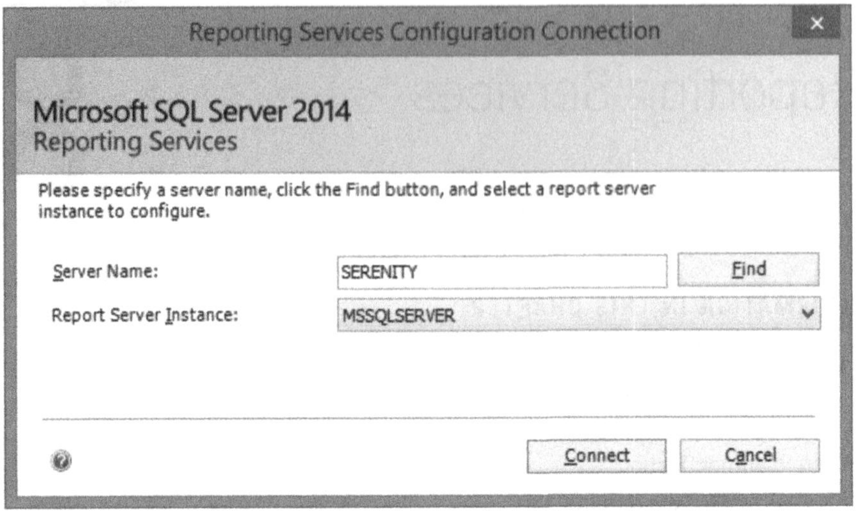

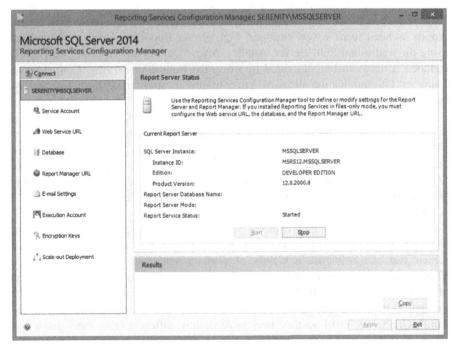

FIGURE 8.1 The SQL Server reporting services configuration connection dialog box.

FIGURE 8.2 Showing the home page of the SQL Server Reporting Services Configuration Manager.

> **NOTE**
>
> Report Server Mode
>
> There are two modes that a Reporting Service server can be installed in. The first is native mode which means that the instance is a standalone instance or a member of a reporting services web farm, in either case not being connected to a SharePoint farm. The second mode is SharePoint Integrated mode where the Reporting Services instance is a part of a SharePoint farm. For the purposes of this chapter it is assumed that Reporting Services is being installed in native mode. The security between native made and SharePoint mode is actually pretty different; however when running SQL Server Reporting Services in SharePoint mode all the security is controlled through the SharePoint farm and not through the native SQL Server Reporting Services site. There are a variety of SharePoint security books out there which will cover the SharePoint security model, which is unfortunately beyond the scope of this book.-

Table 8.1 Describing the Various Screens of the SQL Server Reporting Services Configuration Manager

Setting Name	Description
Service account	The Windows local or domain account which the SQL Server Reporting Services service will run under.
Web Service URL	The TCP port, SSL certificate and virtual directory which the Web Service will run under.
Database	This screen will show you two different sets of settings. The first is if the report server instance will be configured in Native Mode or in SharePoint integrated mode. The second is the SQL Server database engine which will host the reporting services databases (ReportServer and ReportServerTempDB by default) as well as the way that the SQL Server Reporting Services server connect to the SQL Server database engine.
Report Manager URL	The TCP port, SSL certificate and virtual directory which the Report Manager will run under.
Email Settings	The SMTP settings which the SQL Server Reporting Services will use to send emails
Execution Account	The local or domain account which is used to connect to database sources that do not require credentials or to connect to remote servers within the Active Directory network for accessing graphics, etc.
Encryption Keys	Screen which with the SQL Server Reporting Services symmetric keys can be backed up, restored, changed and encrypted content within the reporting services databases can be deleted.
Scale-out Deployment	Screen from which reporting services instances can be joined to the cluster.

SERVICE ACCOUNT

The "Service Account" screen within the Reporting Services Configuration Manager, shown in Figure 8.3, allows you to select from either a built-in account or a specific domain or local Windows account to run the SQL Server Reporting Services service under. The account which the service runs under that is used will depend on what

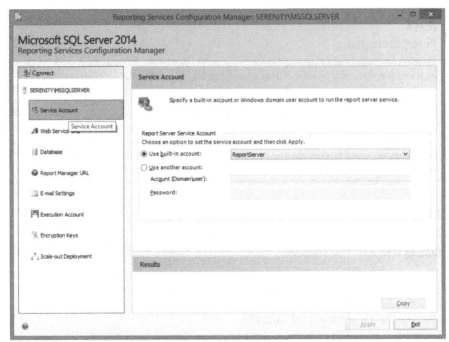

FIGURE 8.3 Showing the "Service Account" screen of the Reporting Services Configuration Manager.

features of SQL Server Reporting Services that you wish to use and how you wish to connect to the SQL Server instance which will host the SQL Server Reporting Services databases as well as how the SQL Server Reporting Services service will connect to the databases which hold the data which the reports will be built off of.

A domain user, which follows the "Minimum Permissions Possible" technique discussed in Chapter 4, should be used when the SQL Server Reporting Services service will be connecting to the database instance which holds the reporting services databases by using the Windows account which the Reporting Services Account is running as, and the SQL Server database instance will be running on a different server than the SQL Server Reporting Services instance. The SQL Server Reporting Services service can be configured to run under a local account when the Reporting Services service will be connecting to the database instance using a SQL Authentication login or when the SQL Server instance which hosts the Reporting Services configuration databases is on the same server as the SQL Server Reporting Services instance.

WEB SERVICE URL

The "Web Service URL" page allows you to set the IP Addresses, TCP ports, SSL Certificates and Virtual Directory which are used to host the Web Service URL for the Reporting Services instance as shown in Figure 8.4. The first field on the screen is the Virtual Directory. This field sets the path which is used from the root of the

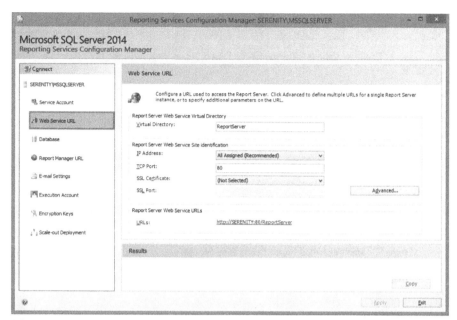

FIGURE 8.4 Web Service URL page of the Reporting Services Configuration Manager.

website which the web service will run under. By default this is the Report Server virtual directory. When configuring an Internet facing SQL Server Reporting Services instance this should be changed to a non-standard value to make it more difficult for unauthorized people on the Internet to attempt to access the URL.

The second section of the "Web Service URL" page configures the various IP addresses, TCP ports and SSL certificates which will be used for the Reporting Services service to listen for requests. If a single IP address should be used, or the Reporting Services service should listen on all IP addresses on the server then the Advanced button does not need to be used. If multiple specific IP addresses need to be configured then the Advanced button should be clicked allowing for multiple IP addresses to be selected as shown in Figure 8.5. If different websites need to be hosted on the same internal IP addresses, host headers can be configured by placing the host header in the "Host Header" column which can be seen on Figure 8.5. More information about Host Headers can be found in most web server books such as Windows Server 2008 R2 Unleashed by SAMS Publishing.

If SSL certificates need to be used in order to secure communications between the end user and the SQL Server Reporting Services server they should be configured on the screen shown in Figure 8.4. SSL certificates must be installed on the server which will be running the SQL Server Reporting Services service before the Reporting Services Configuration Manager is launched. If a certificate needs to be installed the Reporting Services Configuration Manager will need to be closed and reopened to reload the list of certificates. Multiple SSL certificates can be configured for multiple IP addresses from the screen shown in Figure 8.5 as well.

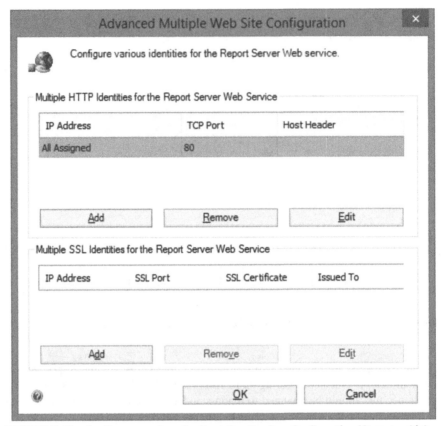

FIGURE 8.5 Showing the screen from the Reporting Services Configuration Manager which allows for multiple IP addresses and ports which SQL Server Reporting Services should listen on.

OUT OF SCOPE

Installing Certificates in Windows

SQL Server Reporting Services and the SQL Server database engine can both use SSL certificates. Certificates are requested and managed from within the Certificate plugin for Microsoft Management Console. Depending on the version of Windows which the various Microsoft SQL Server services are installed on will determine the method which should be used to install the certificate. Because of the variety of install options and the ways to request the certificate getting the certificates into Windows is outside the scope of this book. There is a wealth of information available on Microsoft's TechNet website (technet.microsoft.com) which documents how to install SSL certificates from both a public Certificate Authority as well as from an internal Certificate Authority.

At the bottom of the "Web Service URL" screen all the various URLs which can be used to connect to the ReportServer virtual directory. If multiple IP addresses are entered on the screen shown in Figure 8.5 then multiple URLs will be shown at the bottom of the screen shown in Figure 8.4.

Any time that the Web Service URL is exposed to the public Internet is should be secured via an SSL certificate. SSL Certificates, including how to request SSL Certificates, are discussed more in Chapter 4. The Web Service URL should also be protected by an SSL certificate even if the Reporting Services instance is an internal only Reporting Services instance and the instance is serving up reports which contain confidential or personally identifiable information.

DATABASE

The "Database" screen within the Reporting Services Configuration Manager allows for the configuration of the connection to the configuration database (ReportServer by default) and the cache database (ReportServerTempDB by default). On this screen, shown in Figure 8.6, the database server and database name are shown. To change the SQL Server instance or the database name the Change Database button should be clicked. This will present a wizard which will walk through the options needed to change the instance and/or database. During this wizard the user will be

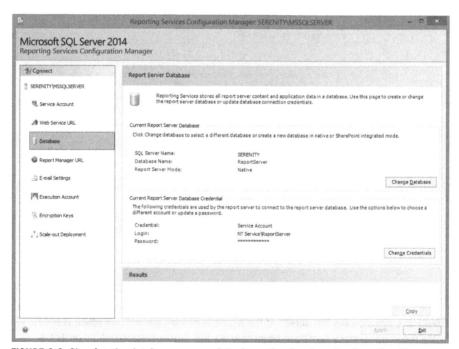

FIGURE 8.6 Showing the database screen of the Reporting Services Configuration Manager.

prompted for a set of credentials. These credentials are only used to connect to the instance while the wizard is running for the purposes of creating and verifying the needed databases. The credentials specified within this wizard should be members of the Database Creator (dbcreator) fixed server role and the Security Administrator (securityadmin) fixed server role if not a member of the System Administrators (sysadmin) fixed server role.

On the lower half of the screen shown in Figure 8.6 shows how the SQL Server Reporting Services service will connect to the SQL Server instance which is configured in the top half of the screen. Clicking the "Change Credentials" button starts the wizard to change the credentials. The wizard will ask for two sets of credentials. The first set of credentials that are asked for on the first screen, shown in Figure 8.7 specify how the user running the wizard should connect to the SQL Server instance. This user needs the ability to create a login by being a member of the Security Administrators Fixed Servers Role as well as being a member of the db_owner fixed database role within each of the Reporting Services databases.

The second screen of the "Change Credentials" wizard, shown in Figure 8.8, allows for the setting of the account which will be used to connect to the SQL Server instance which hosts the Reporting Services configuration databases. There are three options shown in the Authentication Type drop down menu, which are "Windows

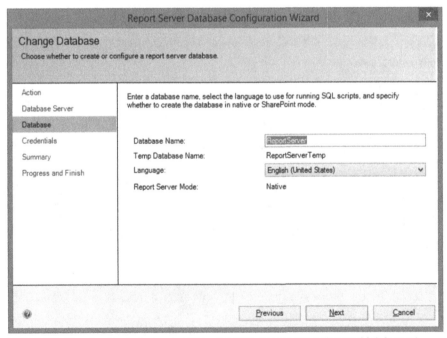

FIGURE 8.7 Showing the first screen of the wizard to change the account which is used by the reporting services service to connect to the SQL Server instance which hosts the configuration database.

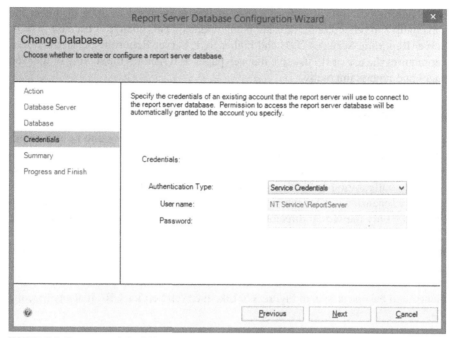

FIGURE 8.8 Page two of the "Change Credentials" wizard.

Credentials," "SQL Server Credentials" and "Service Credentials." When "Windows Credentials" is selected, as shown in Figure 8.8, a specific domain username and password can be used to connect to the SQL Server database instance. This account does not need to be the same account which the SQL Server Reporting Services server can run under. When "SQL Server Credentials" is selected from the drop down menu (not shown) a traditional SQL Server login credentials are used to connect to the SQL Server database instance which hosts the configuration database. While a username and password are being typed into the management console, and this information is saved to the app.config on the server, the information is encrypted within the configuration file. When "Service Credentials" is selected (not shown) the SQL Server Reporting Services service will use whatever Windows account the service is running under to connect to the SQL Server database instance which is hosting the configuration database.

The third screen of the "Change Credentials" wizard will show a summary of the settings which will be set. The fourth screen of the "Change Credentials" wizard will show success or failure of making the needed changes to the Reporting Services service. At this point the .config file for the SQL Server Reporting Services service is being updated with the new connection string. When using SQL Server Reporting Services 2000 or SQL Server Reporting Services 2005 the web.config file is what is being updated as those versions use IIS as the web server for serving the web pages and reports. When using SQL Server Reporting Services 2008 or higher the app.config and other .config files are being updated. This change is because in SQL Server Reporting Services 2008 and higher SQL Server Reporting Services no longer requires the use of IIS to serve the web pages as it handles the serving of the web pages and reports internally.

REPORT MANAGER URL

The "Report Manager URL" screen of the wizard services the same basic purpose as the Web Service URL in that it configures the IP address, TCP ports and SSL certificates that are used for access to the reporting services site. In this case however the configuration is for the end users to view and administer reports via their web browser instead of for the web service. When the screen appears, as shown in Figure 8.9 only the virtual directory and URL list is shown. With the "Web Service URL" screen it displays the basic connection information where on this screen clicking the Advanced button is required to make any changes to the IP addresses, TCP ports and SSL certificates which are used for end user connections. Clicking the "Advanced" button on the screen shown in Figure 8.9 bring up a screen which looks identical to the one shown in Figure 8.5. Like the Web Service URL if at any time the

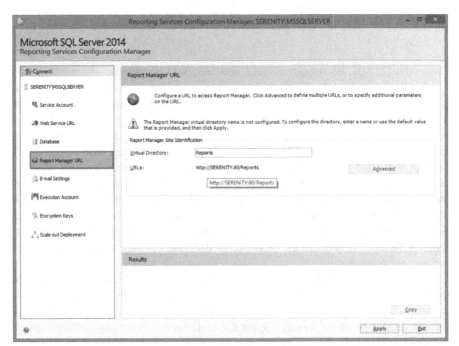

FIGURE 8.9 Showing the "Report Manager URL" screen of the Reporting Services Configuration Manager.

Reporting Services instance will be serving data over the public Internet or customer data is being transferred over any network including an office network the connection should be encrypted using the industry standard SSL encryption.

EMAIL SETTINGS

The email settings screen does not have any security related configuration on it, but I wanted to include it for completeness. On the "Email Settings" screen there are only two options available as shown in Figure 8.10. The first is the email address to send emails from and the second is the SMTP server to use to send emails.

EXECUTION ACCOUNT

The "Execution Account" screen, shown in Figure 8.11, allows you to specify a separate account which the SQL Server Reporting Services service should use to access objects within the domain such as graphics which are stored on file servers. Reports that are scheduled for execution can also be run under this account. If any reports will be including objects from file servers, or will be writing to file servers for scheduled delivery this account should be a domain account from the Active Directory domain.

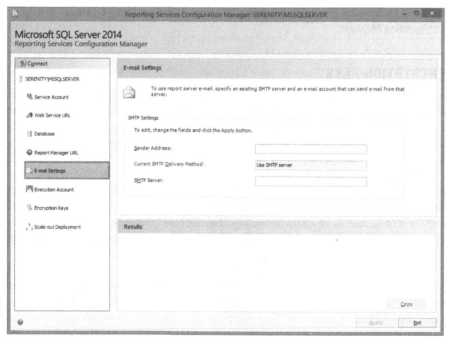

FIGURE 8.10 Showing the Email Settings screen of the Reporting Services Configuration Manager.

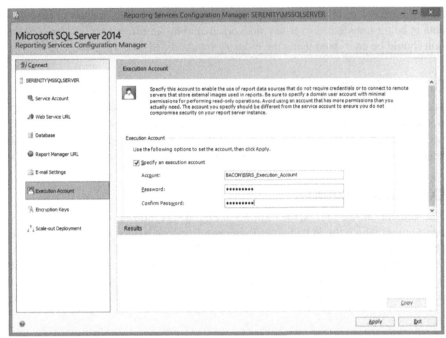

FIGURE 8.11 Showing the "Execution Account" screen of the Reporting Services Configuration Manager.

ENCRYPTION KEYS

SQL Server Reporting Services encrypts a variety of data within the SQL Server Reporting Services database (ReportServer by default) and the caching database (ReportServerTempDB by default) such as connection string, stored credentials among other sensitive data. This data is protected by a symmetric key which is created by the SQL Server Reporting Services during the initial configuration. From the "Encryption Keys" screen, shown in Figure 8.12, there are four operations which can be performed. The first operation is to backup the keys. This will protect the keys in the event of a total database failure. When the keys are backed up a password must be specified to secure the backup of the key. The second operation is to restore the encryption key. Restoring the key will require the password which was specified when the keys were backed up. Restoring the key replaces the existing key.

The third operation is to change the encryption key. Normally the encryption key should not need to be changed unless it becomes known that the encryption key has become compromised. If the encryption key is replaced the key should be immediately backed up and the backup placed in a safe place. The fourth operation is to delete the encrypted content. When the encrypted content is deleted all data sources within the Report Server environment will need to be recreated and all report subscriptions will need to be recreated.

NOTE

Backing Up the Keys

You will notice that there is a line in the first paragraph of this sub-section which says "The first operation is to backup the keys." When you get to this screen you need to backup the keys. Without a valid backup of the encryption keys you cannot connect another instance of Reporting Services to the configuration database (ReportServer by default) if your existing instance fails. The reason for this is that the new Reporting Services instance would not have the encryption keys needed to decrypt the data stored in the Reporting Services configuration database. Not only do you need to backup the keys, but they need to be stored somewhere safe which is not on the reporting services server.

A safe place is not someone on the network, or sitting on a thumb drive in someone's desk drawer. A safe place would be burned to a CD or DVD and stored in a safe on site, with a second backup copy being stored offsite at a remove storage facility much in the same way that database encryption keys need to be backed up as discussed in the "Key Protection" section of Chapter 2 of this book.

If there was a way for me to put flashing lights around that section of the page so really draw you to it, I would have. I am pretty sure that would increase the cost of printing the book a tad though. Would not it be awesome when we can have moving video in printed books?

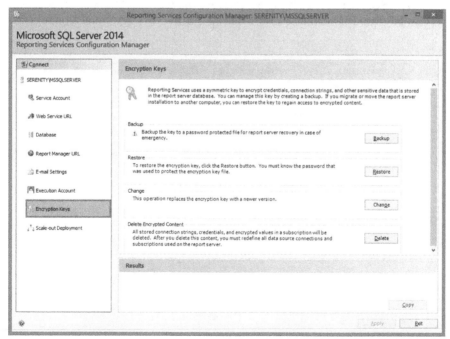

FIGURE 8.12 Showing the "Encryption Keys" page of the Reporting Services Configuration Manager.

SCALE-OUT DEPLOYMENT

The "Scale-out Deployment" screen, shown in Figure 8.13, is used to allow other Reporting Services servers into a farm configuration. Only servers which are known to be valid servers in the farm should be added into the farm. Once a server is a member of the reporting services scale out farm the server can run reports as well as add other server to the farm. If an attacker server became authorized as a member of the Reporting Services farm the attacker would have access to any data which the data sources which were configured within reporting services had access to. They would also be able to upload new reports into the Reporting Services farm which could give them access to more data than the current set of reports allow access to.

LOGGING ONTO SQL SERVER REPORTING SERVICES FOR THE FIRST TIME

The first time that you attempt to log onto SQL Server Reporting Services (especially versions 2008 R2 and higher) you will probably be greeted with a screen similar to that shown in Figure 8.14. This is because when User Access Control (UAC) is enabled on a computer running SQL Server Reporting Services even if the users account is a member of the local administrators group when IE (or FireFox or Chrome) runs the application is not running with administrative rights. In order to successfully connect to SQL Server Reporting Services for the first time the web browser will need to be started in administrative mode so that the ACL (Account Control List)

FIGURE 8.13 Showing the "Scale-out Deployment" screen of the Reporting Services Configuration Manager.

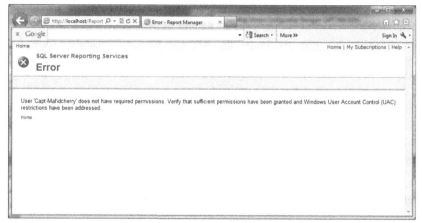

FIGURE 8.14 Showing the default error message when attempting to access SQL Server Reporting Services.

which says that the account is a member of the local administrators group to the Reporting Services server.

STORY TIME

UAC Can Just Be Evil Sometimes

When putting together this book, I used a Windows 7 workstation (my primary workstation as a matter of fact) to take all the screenshots. This required getting things which I normally do not have configured such as SQL Server Reporting Services and SQL Server Analysis Services configured and working correctly. Needless to say when I first opened by browser to connect to SQL Server Reporting Services and I saw the message shown in Figure 8.14. I was a little annoyed that it was not working correctly.

I checked all the settings in the Report Server Configuration Manager and everything looked correct as far as I could tell. I put together a pretty long email to my good friend Jessica Moss, who was kind enough to offer to help out with proofing the SQL Server Analysis Services and SQL Server Reporting Services chapters, about the error I was getting and what I had done to try and fix the problem (I almost started editing the dbo.Users table within the ReportServer database.

Just before I hit send (the entire 2 page email was completely written at this point) I remembered that I have UAC enabled and that even though my account is listed as an admin, I am not actually an admin. I fired up IE as an admin and got right into SSRS to finish the configure Needless to say I am sure that Jessica was glad to not get that lengthy email. Apparently everyone who works with SQL Server Reporting Services gets bitten by that little security "feature" every once and a while, meaning I can count myself in some pretty good company.

SECURITY WITHIN REPORTING SERVICES

When connecting to a brand new SQL Server reporting services instance the first thing that needs to be done is that rights need to be granted to the root folder of the Reporting Services website so that the users who need to view the Reporting Services site can. This is done by logging into the SQL Server by an account which has administrative rights to the reporting services site by default. If there is no way to get connected to the Reporting Services site the list of users who have administrative rights to the Reporting Services site can be found by querying the dbo.Users table from within the ReportServer database. If when configuring the Reporting Services site you are logged into the server which is running Reporting Services it may be necessary to run the web browser in administrative mode by right clicking on the web browsers icon in the start menu or the task bar and selecting "Run as administrator" as shown in Figure 8.15.

ITEM ROLES

After successfully connecting to the SQL Server Reporting Services website you should see a screen similar to that shown in Figure 8.16. From the home screen click

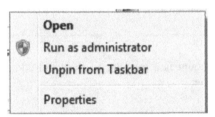

FIGURE 8.15 Context menu shown when right clicking on the Internet Explorer icon on the task bar.

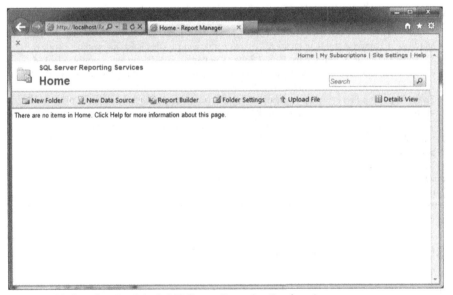

FIGURE 8.16 Showing the default SQL Server Reporting Services home screen.

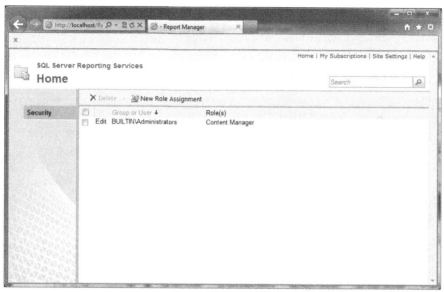

FIGURE 8.17 Showing the default permissions to the root folder of the SQL Server Reporting Services website.

on the "Folder Settings" option in the menu on the top in order to add new users rights to the home folder as shown in Figure 8.17.

After getting the permissions list, as shown in Figure 8.17, new rights can be added by clicking on the "New Role Assignment" button which can be seen in the middle-ish top part of Figure 8.17. The "New Role Assignment" screen, shown in Figure 8.18, allows for adding a Windows domain or local account rights to the SQL Server Reporting Services site.

There are five different roles which can be granted by default to users. The "Browser" role allows users to view folders, reports as well as to subscribe to reports. The "Content Manager" role allows the user to manage the content within the report server folder that the user has the right within. The "My Reports" role allows the user to publish reports, link to reports, manage folders, reports and resources within the users "My Reports" folder. The "Publisher" role allows the user to publish reports and create links to other reports. The "Report Builder" role allows the user to view the report definitions.

Users who will be managing the SQL Server Reporting Services Reports, probably the DBA staff and/or the system admin team and/or the BI developers should be added to the Content Manager role as this will give them full rights within the SQL Server Reporting Services website.

SYSTEM ROLES

There are two system-wide roles which can be assigned to users which are separate from the folder roles. These system roles are the "System Administrator" role and the

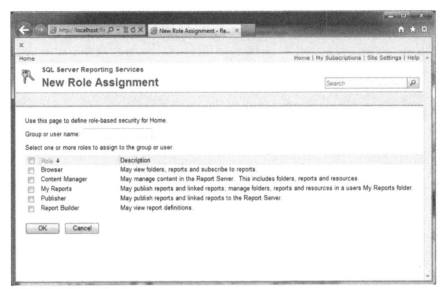

FIGURE 8.18 Showing the "New Role Assignment" screen within SQL Server Reporting Services.

"System User" role. The "System Administrator" role allows for total management of the SQL Server Reporting Services website, while the "System User" role allows for users to view system properties, shared schedules, and grants them the ability to use Report Builder or other clients that execute reports.

Adding users to the system roles is done by clicking on the "Site Settings" link in the upper right of any page, then by clicking on the "Security" tab on the left as shown in Figure 8.19. Adding users to system roles requires that the user making the change be a member of a system role which has the "Manage report server security" right granted to it (more about this right later in this section).

From the security tab new members of the system roles can be added by clicking the "New Role Assignment" button which will bring up the screen shown in Figure 8.20 which allows a Windows group name or Windows username to be entered as well as for the correct system role to be selected.

After clicking OK on the screen shown in Figure 8.20 the user will have the granted rights and will be added to the list of users shown in Figure 8.19.

ADDING SYSTEM ROLES

New System Roles can be added by using SQL Server Management Studio. To do so connect to the SQL Server Reporting Services instance with the SQL Server Management Studio object explorer. Then navigate to Security > System Roles to view the current roles and to add new ones. Adding a new role requires simply right clicking on System Roles and selecting "New System Role" from the context menu which

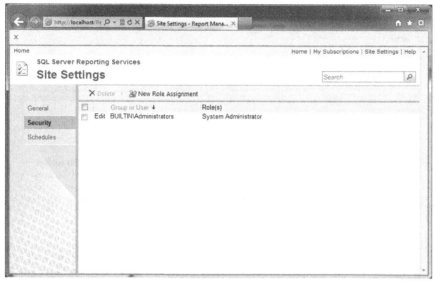

FIGURE 8.19 The Site Settings > Security page.

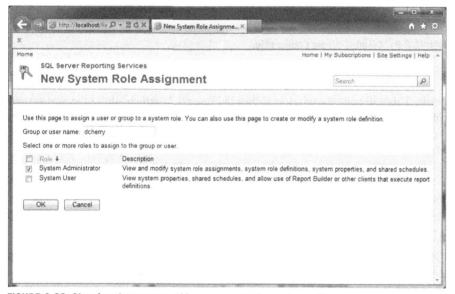

FIGURE 8.20 Showing the page to add new users to the system roles.

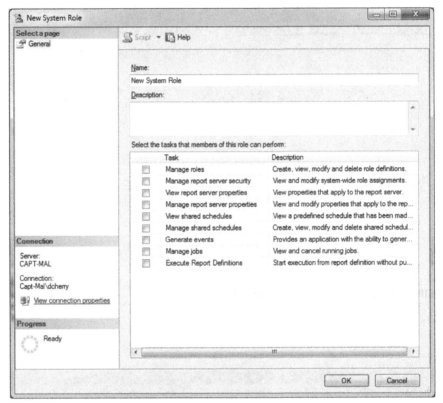

FIGURE 8.21 Creating a new system role.

opens. This will open the window shown in Figure 8.21 which allows the new system role to be named and the specific tasks to be granted to the role. Adding system roles within the SQL Server Reporting Services farm requires that the user be a member of a role which has the "Manage Roles" right granted to it.

There are 9 tasks which can be granted to system roles as shown in Table 8.2. While the rights to the pre-defined system roles can have their rights modified it is recommended that they not be changed and instead new system roles be created.

ADDING FOLDER ROLES

Like system roles, new folder roles can be added for customizing permissions within the Report Server Interface. Like the system roles new folder roles are created within SQL Server Management Studio. To do so connect to the SQL Server Reporting Services instance with the SQL Server Management Studio object explorer. Then navigate to Security > Roles to view the current roles and to add new ones. Adding a new role requires simply right clicking on Roles and selecting "New Role" from the

Table 8.2   System Roles Available in SQL Server Reporting Services

Task Name	Description
Manage roles	Create, view, modify and delete role definitions.
Manage report server security	View and modify system-wide role assignments.
View report server properties	View properties which apply to the report server.
Manage report server properties	View and modify properties that apply to the report server and to items managed by the report server.
View shared schedules	View a pre-defined schedule that has been made available for general use.
Manage shared schedules	Create, view, modify and delete shared schedules used to run reports or refresh a report.
Generate events	Provides an application with the ability to generate events within the report server namespace.
Manage jobs	View and cancel running jobs.
Execute report definitions	Start execution from report definition without publishing it to the Report Server.

context menu which opens. This will open the window shown in Figure 8.22 which allows the new system role to be named and the specific tasks to be granted to the role. Adding new roles requires that the user be a member of a system role which has the "Manage Roles" right assigned to it.

There are 16 tasks which can be granted to new folder roles which are listed in Table 8.3. While the rights to the pre-defined folder roles can have their rights modified it is recommended that they not be changed and instead new folder roles be created.

REPORTING SERVICES AUTHENTICATION OPTIONS

Other than the database engine (which hopefully is not ever configured directly connected to the Internet, as talked about in Chapter 1), SQL Reporting Services would be the only SQL Server Service that would be directly connected to the Internet. SQL Server Reporting Services can be directly connected to the internet so long as it is secured by using SSL encryption. As SQL Reporting Services provides a wide variety of information, it should be properly configured to prevent unauthorized access to the reports.

SQL Server Reporting Services 2005 and below require Internet Information Services (IIS) in order to function. When installing these older versions of SQL Server Reporting Services on Windows 2008 or newer, there is a much more granular control about what IIS features are being installed on the server. As with the SQL Server Services, only install the features that you will be using. If the server hosting the SQL

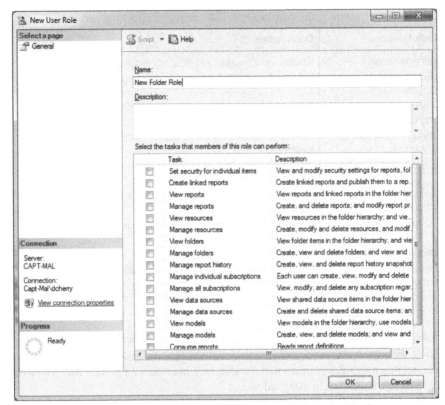

FIGURE 8.22 Creating a new folder role within SQL Server Management Studio.

Server Reporting Services will not be using classic ASP (as an example), then do not install and/or configure classic ASP. The same goes for the other native features that the Reporting Services does not need to use. The features that SQL Server Reporting Services uses that should be installed are the following:

- .NET Extensibility
- ASP.NET
- ISAPI Extensions
- Default Document
- Directory Browsing
- HTTP Errors
- HTTP Redirection
- HTTP Logging
- Request Filtering
- Windows Authentication

Other features can be installed as needed, but only when needed.

Table 8.3   Tasks Available for New Folder Roles

Task Name	Description
Set security for individual items	View and modify security settings for reports, folders, resources and shared data sources
Create linked reports	Create linked reports and publish them to a report server folder
View Reports	View reports and linked reports in the folder hierarchy; view report history snapshots and report properties
Manage reports	Create, and delete reports; and modify report properties
View resources	View resources in the folder hierarchy; and view resource properties
Manage resources	Create, modify and delete resources, and modify resource properties.
View folders	View folder items in the folder hierarchy; and view folder properties
Manage folders	Create, view and delete folders; and view and modify folder properties
Manage report history	Create, view and delete report history snapshots; and modify report history properties
Manage individual subscriptions	Each user can create, view, modify and delete subscriptions that he or she owns.
Manage all subscriptions	View, modify, and delete any subscription regardless of who owns the subscription.
View data sources	View shared data source items in the folder hierarchy; and view data source properties.
Manage data sources	Create and delete shared data source items; and modify data source properties.
View models	View models in the folder hierarchy, use models as data sources for a report, and run queries against the model to retrieve data.
Manage models	Create, view, and delete models; and view and modify model properties.
Consume reports	Reads report definitions

When configuring SQL Reporting Services to be accessed from the public Internet, it is always recommended to use SQL Reporting Services over SSL (or HTTPS) instead of HTTP. When using HTTP and SQL Reporting Services prompts for authentication, the username and password that the end user submits will be transmitted in plain text between the web browser (or other application that is calling the SQL Reporting Services website) and the web server. When SQL Reporting Services is configured to use SSL and the user uses SSL by putting HTTPS in front of the SQL Reporting Services website name, instead of HTTP, then the username and password are encrypted before being sent from the web browser (or other client application) and the web server that is hosting the SQL Reporting Services application. This holds true for SQL Reporting Services 2008 and higher, even though these versions do not rely on IIS in order to run.

ANONYMOUS AUTHENTICATION

Whenever possible, Anonymous Authentication should be disabled on all SQL Server Reporting Services instances. When Anonymous Authentication is enabled, anyone who connects to the reporting services instance will have access to the reports that are configured to be viewed by the account to which the Anonymous Authentication account is mapped. When using SQL Reporting Services 2000 or 2005, Anonymous Authentication can be easily enabled within the IIS Manager. However, when using SQL Reporting Services 2008 and above, Anonymous Authentication is very difficult to configure as SQL Reporting Services 2008 and above no longer are hosted by the Windows IIS. This is because SQL Reporting Services 2008 and above use the Windows APIs and host the web service within the SQL Reporting Services service directly. When configuring SQL Reporting Services 2005 and below, always ensure that Anonymous Authentication is disabled, as shown in Figure 8.23. This is done by following these X steps on Windows 2003:

1. Right click on the "Reports" or "ReportServer" virtual folder within IIS Manager (the folder names may be different depending on your configuration).
2. Select properties from the context menu that opens.

When using Windows 2008 or newer, the steps are a little different, with the final result shown Figure 8.24.

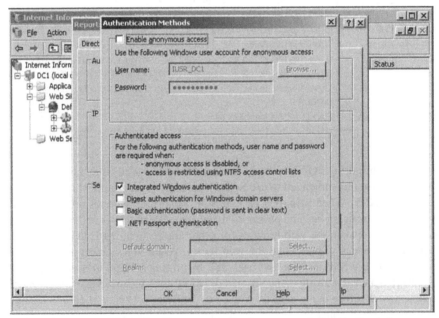

FIGURE 8.23 Internet Information Manager showing Anonymous Authentication being disabled for the Reporting Services web application when using Windows 2003 or lower.

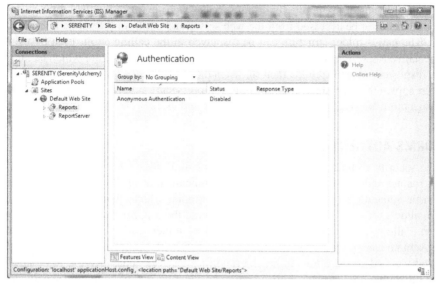

FIGURE 8.24 Internet Services Manager for Windows 2008 or higher showing Anonymous Authentication being disabled for the Reporting Services web application.

1. Navigate to the reports folder in the menu tree.
2. Double click Authentication from the menu on the left.
3. Select Anonymous Authentication from the new screen on the right.
4. From the "Actions" menu on the far right, select disable (this can also be found by right clicking on "Anonymous Authentication").

Once Anonymous Authentication has been disabled, ensure that some sort of authentication is used that requires the user to specify a username and password. Typically this would be done via domain authentication through active directory authentication, but it can also be done using a technique called forms authentication.

WORKING AROUND ANONYMOUS AUTHENTICATION REQUIREMENTS

Often we use Anonymous Authentication so that report services users can simply navigate to the reporting services website and browse the various reports which are available. Often this is done because the URL to access the reporting services website is imbedded within another website so it is assumed that all the authentication is being done at the parent application layer. However this still exposing the reporting services website potentially to the public Internet with some of your company's data therefore potentially being exposed to those who should not have access to the data.

A more secure option would be to build the reporting services reports directly into the application. This allows the web server which needs to display the reports to authenticate against the reporting services website using the web servers service account instead of allowing anyone to access the reporting services website. This has an added bonus of taking the reporting services website off of the public Internet as it only needs to be accessed from the web server and not from the public internet.

The native folder structure can be displayed in the calling application by using the native Reporting Services APIs to request the directory structure which can then be displayed, with the reports then shown in the report viewer object within the .NET web application. This presents not only a more secure report delivery method but also a more consistent user experience for the end users of the application.

FORMS AUTHENTICATION

The security technique called forms authentication allows for a database table of usernames and passwords to be used for the authentication against reporting services. Forms authentication is an advanced configuration which, though complex to set up, allows for greater flexibility when designing the reporting solution. The reason that it allows for greater flexibility is that forms authentication permits users to use a username and password that are stored securely within a database table, or LDAP database, and so on, allowing for the reporting services authentication to be keyed off of another application's authentication provider instead of being tied specifically to Active Directory authentication.

When using Windows credentials to handle Reporting Services authentication, the process is very straightforward. The login process happens in the same way that is described within the "SQL Server Password Security" section of Chapter 3. After

---

NOTE

What, No Sample Code?

Yep, you are correct, I have got no sample code to offer you here, but you can review the Microsoft document on the topic at http://securingsqlserver.com/go/ssrs-auth. That level of .NET code is unfortunately well beyond the scope of this book. Mostly this is because I am not a .NET programmer, never have been a .NET programmer and probably never will be a .NET programmer so anything which I can show you as far as .NET code here would simply be something which I have downloaded from the Internet which you can do easily enough yourself.

NOTE

Forms versus Active Directory Authentication

Forms authentication is a bit of a pain. While it provides you great flexibility in that you can use any authentication provider, it also takes away a lot of the flexibility that is provided by Active Directory. While it is great to be able to use different credentials to connect to the Reporting Services site than AD requires, this should not be the normal configuration. By default almost every shop would be using the native Active Directory authentication to authorize users to see and use objects within the Reporting Services farm. About the only time that it would be a good idea to use something like forms authentication is when a large portion of your users are not members of your Active Directory domain, and for some reason they cannot be added as members of your Active Directory domain.

the normal Windows Authentication process is completed, the Reporting Services ASP.NET application passes the user's information to the reporting services database to see what folders and/or reports the user should be able to view. When using forms authentication, however, the process is much different.

1. The user browses to the Reporting Services website.
2. The website redirects the user to the login form where the user enters in the username and password.
3. The username and password are passed from the website to the user-supplied security extension, which then checks against the database table or other authentication source.
4. Upon a successful authentication attempt, the Reporting Services ASP.NET application creates an authentication ticket (which is stored within a web browser cookie) and verifies the role that the user has been assigned to within the Reporting Services environment.
5. The cookie created in the prior step is passed to the user's web browser, and the user's reporting services page is displayed.
6. When the user navigates throughout the SQL Reporting Services website, the cookie is uploaded for each request, and the reporting services application checks with the user-defined security extension to determine whether the user has the right to perform the requested action.
7. If the user has the needed right, then the report or the menu is displayed to the user.

SECURITY WITHIN REPORTING SERVICES

Once SQL Reporting Services is set up and is prompting users for authentication, the security job is not done. In most Reporting Services environments, not all users have the need to view all the reports within the SQL Server Reporting Services environment. When this is the case, the native security should be used to enforce security on the folders and reports.

Probably the easiest way to secure the reports and folders is to create domain (or local) groups for each group of people who need access to a group of reports (you can use existing domain groups if those exist already). You can then edit the security

> **NOTE**
> Sample Source Code
>
> Putting sample source code for Forms Authentication into this book would take a very large number of pages full of C# code, which is not something the author is very good at writing. Fortunately, Microsoft has provided some excellent examples that can be referenced at "http://msdn.microsoft.com/en-us/library/aa902691(SQL.80).aspx." This page also includes several diagrams of the workflow that result when forms-based authentication is used to make understanding the workflow process easier when building your own forms-based authentication.

properties of the folders, or the specific reports, and remove the rights for all users to view the objects; you can also add in the specific groups that need to have access to the objects. When removing rights from the groups, be sure to leave in (or put in) the group that contains the database administrators (or other users who have the rights to deploy reports), so that report deployment is not blocked.

If forms-based authentication is being used, then the permission to view folders and reports must be controlled through the security provider, which is developed in house.

REPORT SERVER OBJECT RIGHTS

Once the System Roles and Folder Roles and created within SQL Server Management Studio (earlier in this chapter), not much administration of SQL Server Reporting Services is done via SQL Server Management Studio. Securing the reports and data sources is done from within the Report Manager itself where users and added to roles which rights users rights on various folders and if needed specific objects within the folders. Each object can have its security inherited from its parent object, the folder which it resides in, or rights can be granted to each specific object within the Reporting Services website so that specific users have rights to see specific reports. The default configuration is that all objects inherit their permissions settings from their parent making it very easy to change the permissions of an entire branch of the reporting services configuration quickly and easily.

Another neat feature of the Reporting Services website is the ability to hide objects from the default view. While this is at best "security by obscurity" this does give a quick way to change make objects not available for general users who would normally only use the object view but still making the objects available for the more advanced users who know how to view the list view.

CHANGING PERMISSIONS ON AN OBJECT

Changing rights on an object within the SQL Server Reporting Services web site is easy. The easiest way is to open the object you wish to modify then select the "Folder Settings" button if the object is a folder or the "Properties" button if the object is a report, then select the "Security" tab on the left hand side of the screen as shown in Figure 8.25.

After bringing up the security properties clicking the "Edit Item Security" button will bring up a screen similar to that shown in Figure 8.18. This will allow for adding or removing rights to the object.

HIDING OBJECTS

Hiding objects requires simply viewing the properties of an object. To do so open the folder or report and click the "Folder Settings" button if the object is a folder or

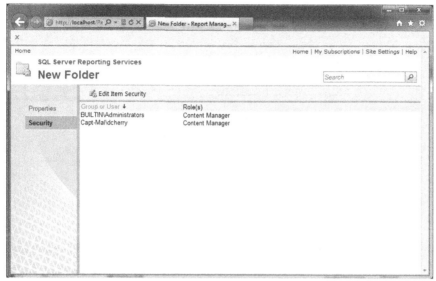

FIGURE 8.25 The security properties of a folder.

the "Properties" button if the object is a report. On the properties page which opens by default there is a "Hide in tile view" checkbox as shown in Figure 8.26. Checking this checkbox and clicking apply will make the object hidden in the default tile view for all users including administrators.

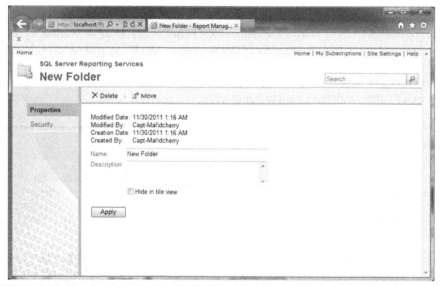

FIGURE 8.26 Showing the "Hide in tile view" checkbox on the properties of a folder.

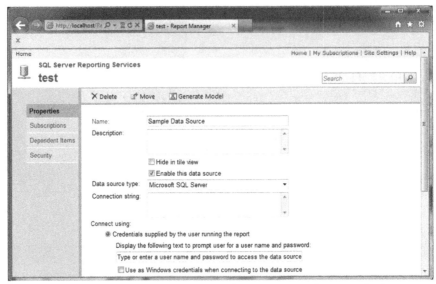

FIGURE 8.27 Showing the "Hide in tile view" setting on the properties page of a data source.

This "Hide in tile view" settings can also be applied to Data Sources by simply editing the data source by clicking on it as shown in Figure 8.27.

SUMMARY

Microsoft SQL Server Reporting Services can when properly configured provide a secure and safe report delivery system which is fully capable of delivering reports to users which contain sensitive data with no risk of data being leaked to unauthorized users. While the security configuration of SQL Server Reporting Services can seem complex at first, once you get used to the specific terminology and concepts it becomes rather straightforward rather quickly.

> ### NOTE
> #### Why So Few Changes in This Chapter?
> If you have read the second edition of Securing SQL Server you have probably noticed that this chapter has not really changed all that much. The reason for this is that SQL Server Reporting Services is basically unchanged between SQL Server 2008 R2 and SQL Server 2014. In fact if you look at the notes for the SQL Server 2014 release under the Reporting Services section it calls out that in fact there were no changes between SQL Server 2012 and SQL Server 2014 at all.
>
> Does this mean that Microsoft is abandoning SQL Server Reporting Services? No, not at all (I hope). It tells me that they have not figured out anything new to add to the product, they think that there is nothing to fix (which there are) or they are simply devoting resources (people and money) to other parts of SQL Server. My guess is the third option and that in the future we will be getting some sort of update to Reporting Services. Until then you can expect to see this chapter reprinted basically as is.

SQL Injection Attacks

9

INFORMATION IN THIS CHAPTER:

- What is a SQL injection attack?
- Why are SQL injection attacks so successful?
- How to figure out you have been attacked?
- How to protect yourself from a SQL injection attack?
- Cleaning up the database after a SQL injection attack

WHAT IS AN SQL INJECTION ATTACK?

An SQL Injection Attack is probably the easiest attack to prevent, while being one of the least protected against forms of attack. The core of the attack is that an SQL command is appended to the backend of a form field in the web or application front end (usually through a website), with the intent of breaking the original SQL Script and then running the SQL script that was injected into the form field. This SQL Injection most often happens when you have dynamically generated SQL within your front-end application. These attacks are most common with legacy Active Server Pages (ASP) and Hypertext Preprocessor (PHP) applications, but they are still a problem with ASP.NET web-based applications. The core reason behind an SQL Injection attack comes down to poor coding practices both within the front-end application and within the database stored procedures. Many developers have learned better development practices since ASP.NET was released, but SQL Injection is still a big problem between the number of legacy applications out there and newer applications built by developers who did not take SQL Injection seriously while building the application.

As an example, assume that the front-end web application creates a dynamic SQL Script that ends up executing an SQL Script similar to that shown in Example 9.1.

EXAMPLE 9.1

A simple dynamic SQL statement as expected from the application.

```
SELECT * FROM Orders WHERE OrderId=25
```

This SQL Script is created when the customer goes to the sales order history portion of the company's website. The value passed in as the OrderId is taken from the query string in the URL, so the query shown above is created when the customer goes to the URL http://www.yourcompany.com/orders/orderhistory.aspx?Id=25. Within the .NET code, a simple string concatenation is done to put together the SQL Query. So any value that is put at the end of the query string is passed to the database at the end of the select statement. If the attacker were to change the query string to something like "/orderhistory.aspx?id=25; delete from Orders," then the query sent to the SQL Server will be a little more dangerous to run as shown in Example 9.2.

EXAMPLE 9.2

A dynamic SQL String that has had a delete statement concatenated to the end of it.

```
SELECT * FROM Orders WHERE ORderId=25; delete from Orders;
```

The way the query in Example 9.2 works is that the SQL database is told via the semicolon ";" that the statement has ended and that there is another statement that should be run. The SQL Server then processes the next statement as instructed.

While the initial query is run as normal now, and without any error being generated but when you look at the Orders table, you would not see any records in the Orders table because the second query in that batch will have executed against the database as well. Even if the attacker omits the value that the query is expecting, they can pass in "; delete from Orders;" and while the first query attempting to return the data from the Orders table will fail, the batch will continue moving on to the next statement, which will delete all the records in the Orders table.

Many people will inspect the text of the parameters looking for various keywords in order to prevent these SQL Injection attacks. However, this only provides the most rudimentary protection as there are many, many ways to force these attacks to work. Some of these techniques include passing in binary data, having the SQL Server convert the binary data back to a text string, and then executing the string. This can be proven by running the T-SQL statement shown in Example 9.3.

EXAMPLE 9.3

Code showing how a binary value can be used to hide a T-SQL statement.

```
DECLARE @v varchar(255)
SELECT @v = cast(0x73705F68656C706462 as varchar(255))
EXEC (@v)
```

> **NOTE**
>
> **The Database Is Not the Only Weak Spot**
>
> If a file name is going to be generated based on the user's input, a few special values should be watched for. These values are Windows file system keywords that could be used to give attackers access to something they should not have, or could simply cause havoc on the front-end server.
> - AUX
> - CLOCK$
> - COM1-COM8
> - CON
> - CONFIG$
> - LPT1-LPT8
> - NUL
> - PRN
>
> By allowing an attacker to create a file path using these special names, attackers could send data to a serial port by using COM1 (or whatever com port number they specify) or to a printer port using LPT1 (or whatever printer port they specify). Bogus data could be sent to the system clock by using the CLOCK$ value, or they could instruct the file to be written to NUL, causing the file to simply disappear.

When data is being accepted from a user, either a customer or an employee, one good way to ensure that the value would not be used for an SQL Injection attack is to validate that the data being returned is of the expected data type. If a number is expected, the front-end application should ensure that there is in fact a number within the value. If a text string is expected, then ensure that the text string is of the correct length, and it does not contain any binary data within it. The front-end application should be able to validate all data being passed in from the user, either by informing the user of the problem and allowing the user to correct the issue, or by crashing gracefully in such a way that an error is returned and no commands are sent to the database or the file system. Just because users should be sending up valid data does not mean that they are going to. If users could be trusted, most of this book would not be needed.

The same technique shown in Example 9.3 can be used to send update statements into the database, causing values to be places within the database that will cause undesirable side effects on the websites powered by the databases. This includes returning javascript to the client computers causing popups that show ads for other projects, using HTML iframes to cause malicious software to be downloaded, using HTML tags to redirect the browser session to another website, and so on.

SQL Injection attacks are not successful against only applications which were built in-house, a number of third-party applications available for purchase are susceptible to these SQL Injection attacks. When purchasing third-party applications, it is often assumed that the product is a secure application that is not susceptible to the attack. Unfortunately, that is not the case, and any time a third-party application is brought into a company, it should be reviewed, with a full code review if possible, to ensure that the application is safe to deploy. When a company deploys a third-party application that is susceptible to attack and that application is successfully attacked, it is the company that deployed the application that will have to deal with the backlash for having an insecure application and their customer data compromised, not the company that produced and sold the insecure application.

Many people think that SQL Injection attacks are a problem unique to Microsoft SQL Server, and those people would be wrong. SQL Injection attacks can occur against Oracle, MySQL, DB2, Access, and so on. Any database that allows multiple statements to be run in the same connection is susceptible to an SQL Injection attack. Now some of the other database platforms have the ability to turn off this function, some by default and some via an optional setting. There are a number of tickets open in the Microsoft bug-tracking website http://connect.microsoft.com that are requesting that this ability be removed from a future version of the Microsoft SQL Server product. While doing so would make the Microsoft SQL Server product more secure, it would break a large number of applications, many of which are probably the ones that are susceptible to SQL Injection attacks.

Another technique that is easier to use against Microsoft SQL Server 7 and 2000 is to use the sp_makewebtask system stored procedure in the master database. If the attacker can figure out the name of the web server, which can usually be done pretty easily by looking at the sysprocesses table, or the path to the website, then the sp_makewebtask procedure can be used to export lists of objects to HTML files on the web server to make it easier for the attacker to see what objects are in the database. Then they can simply browse to the website and see every table in the database.

EXAMPLE 9.4

Code that an attacker could execute to export all table objects to an HTML file.

```
exec master.dbo.sp_makewebtask '\\web1\wwwroot\tables.html",
"select * from information_schema.tables"
```

If xp_cmdshell is enabled on the server, then an attacker could use xp_cmdshell to do the same basic thing just by using Bulk Copy Protocol (BCP) instead of sp_makewebtask. The advantage to sp_makewebtask is that xp_cmdshell does not need to be enabled, while the downside to sp_makewebtask is that it does not exist on Microsoft SQL Server 2005 and up. The downside to xp_cmdshell is that, unless the application uses a login that is a member of the sysadmin fixed server role, the xp_cmdshell procedure will only have the rights that are granted by the proxy account. An attacker can use the xp_cmdshell procedure to send in the correct commands to give the account that is the proxy account more permissions, or even change the account to one that has the correct permissions. At this point BCP can be used to output whatever data is wanted. The attacker could start with database schema information, and then begin exporting your customer information, or they could use this information to change or delete the data from the database.

> **NOTE**
>
> **There Are Lots of Protection Layers to Make Something Secure**
>
> Hopefully, by now you are starting to see how the various layers of the Microsoft SQL Server need to be secured to make for a truly secure SQL Server. In this case we look specifically at how the NTFS permissions, xp_cmdshell proxy account, the Windows account that the SQL Server is running under, the application account that logs into SQL having the minimum level of rights, and properly parameterizing the values from the web application all to create a more secure environment.
>
> To fully protect from an SQL Injection attack, the application account should only have the minimum rights needed to function; it should have no rights to xp_cmdshell. In fact xp_cmdshell which should be disabled (or removed from the server). The SQL Server service should be running under a domain or local computer account that only has the rights needed to run as a service and access the SQL Server folders. That Windows account should have no rights to the actual files that are the website files, and it should not be an administrator on the server that is running the SQL Server service or the web server. The resulting effective permissions that a SQL Server has are to access the database files and do nothing else. Any other functions that the SQL Server instance is expected to perform either via an SQL Agent job or a CLR procedure should be controlled through some sort of account impersonation.
>
> At the application level the actual SQL Server error messages should be masked so that they are not returned to the client. If you have done these things, then even if attackers were able to successfully complete an SQL Injection attack against the SQL Server they would not be able to do much to the server as they would not have any way to get information back from the SQL Server (as the error messages are masked) and they would not be able to get to the shell and get software downloaded and installed from the outside. Once these things fail a few times, attackers will probably just move on to an easier target.
>
> The amount of time that an attacker will spend trying to successfully use an SQL Injection attack against a web-based application will for the most part depend on the amount of value the target has. A smaller company such as a wholesale food distributor probably would not be attacked very often, and the attacker will probably leave after a short period of time. However, a bank or other financial company will provide a much more enticing target for the attacker, and the attack will probably last much longer, with many more techniques being tried, as well as many combinations of techniques until they successfully break into the database application.

The catch to either of these techniques is that the NT File System (NTFS) permissions need to allow either the SQL Server account or the account that the xp_cmdshell proxy account uses to have network share and NTFS permissions to the web server. On smaller applications where the web server and the database server are running on the same machine, this is much, much easier as the SQL Server is probably running as the local system account that gives it rights to everything.

WHY ARE SQL INJECTION ATTACKS SO SUCCESSFUL?

SQL Injection attacks are so successful for a few reasons, the most common of which is that many newer developers simply do not know about the problem. With project timelines being so short, these junior developers do not have the time to research the security implications of using dynamic SQL. These applications then get left in

---

NOTE

Leaving Notes for Future Generations

Would not it have been great if when you were first learning about writing application code that talked to the database, if someone had told you how to properly write parameterized code? Even if that did not happen, it can happen for the next guy. Leave some comments in the application source code that you maintain, that explain why you are parameterizing the database code the way that you are so that the next guy can learn from how you have done things.

---

production for months or years, with little to no maintenance. These developers can then move through their career without anyone giving them the guidance needed to prevent these problems.

Now developers are not solely to blame for SQL Injection attack problems. The IT Management should have policies in place in order to ensure that newer developers that come in do not have the ability to write dynamic inline SQL against the database engine; and these policies should be in forced by code reviews to ensure that things are being done correctly. These policies should include rules like the following.

1. All database interaction must be abstracted through stored procedures.
2. No stored procedure should have dynamic SQL unless there is no other option.
3. Applications should have no access to table or view objects unless required by dynamic SQL, which is allowed under rule #2.

WARNING

SQL Injection Happens at All Levels

Unfortunately, not just small companies can have problems with SQL Injection attacks. In 2009, for example, ZD Net reported that some of the international websites selling Kaspersky antivirus, specifically Kaspersky Iran, Taiwan, and South Korea, were all susceptible to SQL Injection attacks. In the same article (http://bit.ly/AntiVirusSQLInject) ZD Net also reported that websites of F-Secure, Symantec, BitDeffender, and Kaspersky USA all had problems with SQL Injection attacks on their websites.

These are some of the major security companies of the day, and they are showing a total lack of security by letting their websites fall prey to the simple injection attack. Considering just how simple it is to protect a website from an SQL Injection attack, the fact that some of the biggest security companies in the industry were able to have SQL Injection problems on their production customer facing websites is just ridiculous.

Because of how intertwined various websites are with each other, real-estate listing providers and the realtors which get their data from the listing providers, a lot of trust must exist between these companies and the people who use one companies site without knowing that they are using another companies data. This places the company that is showing the real-estate listings to their users in a position of trusting the advertising company to have a safe application. However, this trust can backfire as on a few occasions various partner companies have suffered from SQL Injection attacks, in some cases pushing out malicious software to the users of dozens, hundreds, or thousands of different websites that display the data.

---

4. All database calls should be parameterized instead of being inline dynamic SQL.
5. No user input should be trusted and thought of as safe; all user interactions are suspect.

With the introduction of Object Relational Mappings (ORM) such as Link to SQL and nHybernate, the SQL Injection problems are greatly lessened as properly done ORM code will automatically parameterize the SQL queries. However, if the ORM calls stored procedures, and those stored procedures have dynamic SQL within them, the application is still susceptible to SQL Injection attacks.

HOW TO FIGURE OUT YOU HAVE BEEN ATTACKED

There are two basics ways that SQL Injection attacks are used. The first is to query data from a database and the second is to change data within the database. When the attacker is performing a query only SQL Injection attack, detecting the SQL Injection attack is not the most straightforward thing to do. When an attacker does a good job executing a query only SQL Injection attack against your website there should be little to no evidence of a SQL Injection attack on the SQL Server database instance itself. The only evidence of the SQL Injection attack will be within the web server's logs, assuming that the web server is configured to log all requests to the website.

If logging is enabled then the web server will include within the logs any HTTP requests which are passed to the web servers. These requests will include the SELECT statements which were attempted to be executed against the database engine. Analyzing these logs should be done using some sort of automated process. Packages could be created in SQL Server Integration Services which could process the transaction logs for a smaller scale website which could be used to parse the log files looking for successful requests which include SQL Statements in the query string or POST requests. For larger websites it may be more efficient to process the logs using a NoSQL platform such as Hadoop or Microsoft's HD Insight version of Hadoop so that the workload can be processed by dozens or hundreds of nodes depending on the amount of web server log data which needs to be processed daily. Making the processing of the web servers logs harder is the fact that you need to look for more than just the SELECT keyword. Remember from Example 9.3 where binary values were passed in from the attacker to the web server which were then converted by the SQL Server back to dynamic SQL? This attack vector also needs to be watched for by looking for keywords such as EXEC and CONVERT or CAST. Due to the rapid complexity of searching through the web server's logs scaling out this processing on a distributed system quickly becomes a much more flexible and scalable option.

SQL Injection attacks which change data are easier to identify as they leave a trail behind in the changed data which resides on the SQL Server Instance. Typically if an attacker is making changes to data within the SQL Server database they are going to change large amounts of data at once. One way to initially detect this is to look for transaction logs which are suddenly larger than expected. This can give you a clue that may be a SQL Injection attack has modified large amounts of data within the database platform.

Other options include auditing data which should not be changing to see if that data has changed. If it has changed an alert can be sent to the database administrator or security team so that a person can visually inspect the data to see if it has been modified by normal processes or if invalid data, such as an HTML iframe tag has been injected into the data within the SQL Server's tables.

The third way to detect a SQL Injection attack against a SQL Server database where data has been changed is to monitor the web servers logs much like for the read only SQL Injection attack. While different key words may need to be evaluated this will still give you a good idea if something is attempting to attack the SQL Server instance.

There are unfortunately no standard SQL Server Integration Services packages of Hadoop queries which can be documented as each environment is different. These differences include the web server software which is used, the data points which are captured, the key words which need to be included or excluded based on the names of web pages, parameters which are expected, etc.

HOW TO PROTECT YOURSELF FROM AN SQL INJECTION ATTACK

Once the command gets to the database to be run by the database engine, it is too late to protect yourself from the SQL Injection attack. The only way to truly protect your database application from an Injection attack is to do so within the application layer. Any other protection simply would not be anywhere nearly as effective. Some people think that doing a character replacement within the T-SQL code will effectively protect you, and it might to some extent. But depending on how the T-SQL is set up and how the dynamic SQL string is built, it probably would not, at least not for long.

NET PROTECTION AGAINST SQL INJECTION

The only surefire way to protect yourself is to parameterize every query that you send to the database. This includes your stored procedure calls, as well as your inline dynamic SQL calls. In addition, you never want to pass string values that the front-end application has allowed the user to enter directly into dynamic SQL within your stored procedure calls. If you have cause to use dynamic SQL within your stored procedures (and yes, there are perfectly legitimate reasons for using dynamic SQL), then the dynamic SQL needs to be parameterized just like the code that is calling the stored procedure or inline dynamic SQL Script. This is done by declaring parameters within the T-SQL statement, and adding those parameters to the SQLCommand object that has the SQL Command that you will be running, as shown in Examples 9.5 and 9.6.

EXAMPLE 9.5

VB.NET code showing how to use parameters to safely call a stored procedure.

```
Private Sub MySub()
Dim Connection As SqlConnection
Dim Results As DataSet
Dim SQLda As SqlDataAdapter
Dim SQLcmd As SqlCommand
SQLcmd = New SqlCommand
SQLcmd.CommandText = "sp_help_job"
SQLcmd.CommandType = CommandType.StoredProcedure
SQLcmd.Parameters.Add("job_name", SqlDbType.VarChar, 50)
SQLcmd.Parameters.Item("job_name").Value = "test"
Connection = New SqlConnection("Data Source=localhost;Initial
Catalog=msdb;Integrated Security=SSPI;")
Using Connection
Connection.Open()
SQLcmd.Connection = Connection
SQLda = New SqlDataAdapter(SQLcmd)
Results = New DataSet()
SQLda.Fill(Results)
End Using
'Do something with the results from the Results variable here.
SQLcmd.Dispose()
SQLda.Dispose()
Results.Dispose()
Connection.Close()
Connection.Dispose()
End Sub
```

EXAMPLE 9.6

C# code showing how to use parameters to safely call a stored procedure.

```
private void MySub()
{
SqlConnection Connection = new SqlConnection("Data
Source=localhost;Initial Catalog=msdb;Integrated Security=SSPI;");
DataSet Results = new DataSet();
SqlCommand SQLcmd = new SqlCommand ();
SQLcmd.CommandText = "sp_help_job";
SQLcmd.CommandType = CommandType.StoredProcedure ;
SqlParameter parm1 = new SqlParameter();
parm1.ParameterName = "job_name";
parm1.DbType = DbType.String;
parm1.Precision = 255;
parm1.Value = "test";
SQLcmd.Parameters.Add(parm1);
Connection.Open();
SQLcmd.Connection = Connection;
SqlDataAdapter SQLda = new SqlDataAdapter(SQLcmd);
SQLda.Fill(Results);
//Do something with the results from the Results variable here.
SQLcmd.Dispose();
SQLda.Dispose();
Results.Dispose();
Connection.Close();
Connection.Dispose();
}
```

As you can see in the above, .NET code using a parameter to pass in the value is easy to do, adding just a couple of extra lines of code. The same can be done with an inline dynamic SQL string, as shown in Examples 9.7 and 9.8.

EXAMPLE 9.7

VB.NET code showing how to use parameters to safely call an inline dynamic SQL String.

```
Private Sub MySub()
Dim Connection As SqlConnection
Dim Results As DataSet
Dim SQLda As SqlDataAdapter
Dim SQLcmd As SqlCommand
SQLcmd = New SqlCommand
SQLcmd.CommandText = "SELECT * FROM dbo.sysjobs WHERE name=
@job_name"
SQLcmd.Parameters.Add("job_name", SqlDbType.VarChar, 50)
SQLcmd.Parameters.Item("job_name").Value = "test"
SQLcmd.CommandType = CommandType.Text;
Connection = New SqlConnection("Data Source=localhost;Initial
Catalog=msdb;Integrated Security=SSPI;")
Using Connection
Connection.Open()
SQLcmd.Connection = Connection
SQLda = New SqlDataAdapter(SQLcmd)
Results = New DataSet()
SQLda.Fill(Results)
End Using
'Do something with the results from the Results variable here.
SQLcmd.Dispose()
SQLda.Dispose()
Results.Dispose()
Connection.Close()
Connection.Dispose()
End Sub
```

EXAMPLE 9.8

C# code showing how to use parameters to safely call an inline dynamic SQL String.

```
private void MySub()
{
SqlConnection Connection = new SqlConnection("DataSource=
localhost;Initial Catalog=msdb;Integrated Security=SSPI;");
DataSet Results = new DataSet();
SqlCommand SQLcmd = new SqlCommand ();
SQLcmd.CommandText = "SELECT * FROM dbo.sysjobs WHERE name =
```

```
@job_name";
SQLcmd.CommandType = CommandType.Text;
SqlParameter parm1 = new SqlParameter();
parm1.ParameterName = "job_name";
parm1.DbType = DbType.String;
parm1.Precision = 255;
parm1.Value = "test";
SQLcmd.Parameters.Add(parm1);
Connection.Open();
SQLcmd.Connection = Connection;
SqlDataAdapter SQLda = new SqlDataAdapter(SQLcmd);
SQLda.Fill(Results);
//Do something with the results from the Results variable here.
SQLcmd.Dispose();
SQLda.Dispose();
Results.Dispose();
Connection.Close();
Connection.Dispose();
}
```

Once each parameter that is being passed into the database has been protected, the .NET code (or whatever language is being used to call the database) becomes safe. Any value that is passed from the client side to the database will be passed into the database as a value to the parameter. In the example code shown at the beginning of this chapter, the string value that has been passed into the application would then force an error to be returned from the client Microsoft SQL Server database as the value would be passed into a parameter with a numeric data type.

Using the sample query shown in the .NET sample code in Examples 9.7 and 9.8, if the user were to pass in similar attack code to what is shown in the SQL Server

---

NOTE

Do Not Trust Anything or Anyone!

The golden rule when dealing with SQL Injection is to not trust any input from the website or front-end application. This includes hidden fields and values from dropdown menus. Nothing should be passed from the front end to the database without being cleaned and properly formatted, as any value passed in from the front end could be compromised.

Hidden fields are probably the SQL Injection attacker's best friend. Because they are hidden from the end user's view and are only used by system processes, they are sometimes assumed to be safe values. However, changing the values that are passed in from a safe value to a dangerous value is a trivial matter for a script kitty, much less a skilled attacker.

When dealing with SQL Injection, the mantra to remember is NEVER, ever, trust anything that is sent to the application tier from the end user, whether or not the end user knows that he submitted the value.

sample code in Example 9.2, the query that would be executed against the database would look like the one shown in Example 9.9. This resulting query is now safe to run as the result which is executed against the database engine contains all the attack code as a part of the value.

EXAMPLE 9.9

Sample T-SQL code showing the resulting T-SQL Code that would be executed against the database if an attacker were to put in an attack code against the prior sample .NET code.

```
SELECT * FROM dbo.sysjobs WHERE name = 'test; delete from Orders';
```

In the sample code you can see that while the attack code has been passed to the engine, it has been passed as part of the value of the WHERE clause. However, because this is within the value of the parameter, it is safe because the parameter is not executable. If attackers were to pass in the same command with a single quote in front of it, in an attempt to code the parameter, and then execute their own code, the single quote would be automatically doubled by the .NET layer when it passed to the SQL Server database again, leaving a safe parameter value as shown in Example 9.10.

EXAMPLE 9.10

The resulting T-SQL code that would be executed against the database when an attacker passes in an attack string with a single quote in an attempt to bypass the protection provided by the .NET application layer.

```
SELECT*FROM dbo.sysjobs WHERE name = 'test''; delete from Orders';
```

PROTECTING DYNAMIC SQL WITHIN STORED PROCEDURES FROM SQL INJECTION ATTACK

When you have dynamic SQL within your stored procedures, you need to use a double protection technique to prevent the attack. The same procedure needs to be used to protect the application layer and prevent the attack from succeeding at that layer. However, if you use simple string concatenation within your stored procedure, then you will open your database backup to attack. Looking at a sample stored procedure and the resulting T-SQL that will be executed against the database by the stored procedure; we can see that by using the simple string concatenation, the database is still susceptible to the SQL Injection attack, as shown in Example 9.11.

EXAMPLE 9.11

T-SQL stored procedure that accepts a parameter from the application layer and concatenates the passed-in value to the static portion of the string, executing whatever attack code the attacker wishes against the database engine.

```
CREATE PROCEDURE sel_OrdersByCustomer
@LastName VARCHAR(50)
AS
DECLARE @cmd NVARCHAR(8000)
SET @cmd = 'SELECT*
FROM Orders
JOIN Customers ON Orders.CustomerId = Customers.CustomerId
WHERE Customers.LastName = ''' + @LastName + ''''
EXEC (@cmd)
GO
/*The command that will be executed when the attacker passed in ';
DELETE FROM Orders.*/
SELECT*
FROM Orders
JOIN Customers ON Orders.CustomerId = Customers.CustomerId
WHERE Customers.LastName = 'Smith'; DELETE FROM Orders '
```

Because of the value attack, the value being passed into the SQL Server Engine is passed in through the application layer, and the SQL Server engine does as it is instructed to do, which is to run the query. However, if we parameterize the dynamic SQL within the stored procedure, then the execute SQL code will be rendered harmless just as it would be if the dynamic SQL was executed against the database by the application layer. This is done via the sp_executesql system stored procedure as shown in Example 9.12.

EXAMPLE 9.12

T-SQL stored procedure that accepts a parameter from the application layer and uses parameterization to safely execute the query passing whatever attack code the users input safely against the database as a simple string value.

```
CREATE PROCEDURE sel_OrdersByCustomer
@LastName VARCHAR(50)
AS
DECLARE @cmd NVARCHAR(8000)
SET @cmd = 'SELECT *
FROM Orders
JOIN Customers ON Orders.CustomerId = Customers.CustomerId
WHERE Customers.LastName = ''' + @LastName + ''''
EXEC sp_executesql @cmd, '@LastName VARCHAR(50)', @LastName=@LastName
GO
/*The command that will be executed when the attacker passed in ';
DELETE FROM Orders.*/
SELECT *
FROM Orders
JOIN Customers ON Orders.CustomerId = Customers.CustomerId
WHERE Customers.LastName = 'Smith''; DELETE FROM Orders '
```

USING "EXECUTE AS" TO PROTECT DYNAMIC SQL

One of the best security related features within the SQL Server database engine is the "EXECUTE AS" T-SQL Syntax. This feature allows you to impersonate another login (at the instance level) or another user (at the database level) giving the administrator the ability to test commands and object access by using another, usually lower privileged, account without needing to have the password for the account. In order to impersonate another account within the SQL Server instance the login or user which is going the impersonation must have the right to impersonate the other account within the SQL Server instance. The IMPERSONATION right can be granted at the login level or the user level to Windows users, Windows groups or SQL Server users.

The "EXECUTE AS" feature is actually made up of two different commands. The first being "EXECUTE AS" and the second being "REVERT." The "EXECUTE AS" command (shown in Examples 9.12 and 9.13 later in this section) is used to begin the impersonation of another set of credentials; while the "REVERT" command (also shown in Examples 9.13 and 9.14 later in this section) is used to revert from the impersonated credentials back to the prior credentials. The prior credentials could be either the original credentials which were used to log into the database engine or a different set of credentials which were impersonated with a prior "EXECUTE AS" statement. It is important to note that "REVERT" may not always bring you back to the original credentials which the instance was logged into as "EXECUTE AS" statements can be nested several layers deep and there is no counter which can be used to identify how many iterations of "EXECUTE AS" have been entered through.

When using the "EXECUTE AS" the account remains impersonated for the lifetime of the session within the context of the execution of the "EXECUTE AS" statement. This means that if you run "EXECUTE AS" within a SQL Server Management Studio window all commands within that window will be executed within the context of those credentials until the "REVERT" command is run. When the "EXECUTE AS" statement is used within a stored procedure to impersonate an account the impersonated account will remain for the duration of the stored procedures execution or until the "REVERT" statement within the stored procedure, whichever comes first.

Impersonating a Login

As mentioned in the previous section, the EXECUTE AS statement can be used to impersonate logins at the instance level. This allows you to have the rights of the impersonated account within that query window. To demonstrate this functionality we can create a new login which has no extra permissions, and then use "EXECUTE AS" to impersonate this login then query for the list of available logins on the instance by querying the sys.server_principals system catalog view as shown in Example 9.13.

EXAMPLE 9.13

Sample code showing the creation of a new login then the use of that login using the "EXECUTE AS" T-SQL sytax.

```
IF EXISTS (SELECT * FROM sys.server_principals WHERE name =
'anotherLogin')
        DROP LOGIN anotherLogin
GO
CREATE LOGIN anotherLogin WITH PASSWORD='password1'
GO
EXECUTE AS LOGIN='anotherLogin'
SELECT * FROM sys.server_principals
REVERT
GO
```

When running the sample code as shown in Example 9.13 a result set will be returned which shows the "sa" login, the "anotherLogin" login and the various server roles (more about fixed server roles can be found in Chapter 12) on the instance. If the same select statement is run by a member of the sysadmin fixed server role that then more (possibly many more) logins will be shown including all the certificate logins which are created by default, and the various "NT SERVICE" accounts which are created automatically when the various SQL Server services are run under the local system accounts (more about these local accounts can be found in Chapter 12).

Impersonating a User

In addition to impersonating logins at the instance level, users can also be impersonated at the database level as well. This allows you access to the objects which the user has within the database as well as rights to objects which can be accessed in other databases via the public role or the guest account. In the example shown in Example 9.14 we create a new database, the change into the new database; creating a new loginless user within the database using that user to query the sys.databases system catalog view. The resulting record set includes only the master, tempdb and the new Impersonation databases as the modem and msdb databases are not accessable via through the public role.

EXAMPLE 9.14

Using the "EXECUTE AS" statement within a database to impersonate a database user.

```
use master
GO
IF EXISTS (SELECT * FROM sys.databases WHERE name = 'Impersonation')
        DROP DATABASE Impersonation
GO
```

```
CREATE DATABASE Impersonation
GO
use Impersonation
GO
IF EXISTS (SELECT * FROM sys.database_principals WHERE name =
'anotherUser')
        DROP USER anotherUser
GO
CREATE USER anotherUser WITHOUT LOGIN
GO
EXECUTE AS USER='anotherUser'
SELECT * FROM sys.databases
REVERT
GO
```

REMOVING EXTENDED STORED PROCEDURES

In addition to running all code from the application layer as parameterized commands instead of dynamically generated T-SQL, you should also remove the system procedures that can be used to export data. The procedures in question that you will want to remove are xp_cmdshell, xp_startmail, xp_sendmail, sp_makewebtask, and sp_send_dbmail. You may also want to remove the procedures that configure Database Mail such as sysmail_add_account_sp and sysmail_add_profileaccount_sp, so that attackers cannot use these procedures to give themselves a way to email out information from the database. Of course, you will want to make sure that you are not using these procedures in any released code and that you have Database Mail configured before removing your ability to configure it.

Of course, removing system stored procedures poses a risk of causing system upgrades to fail, so you will want to keep copies of these objects handy so that you can put the objects back before database version upgrades.

Unfortunately, this is not a surefire way to prevent an attacker from using these procedures. Crafty attackers can actually put these procedures back after they see that they have been removed. This is especially true of the extended stored procedures called DLLs (Dynamic Link Libraries), which must be left in their normal locations because other extended stored procedures that you do not want to remove are part of the same DLLs. The only saving grace is that you have to be a highly privileged user within the database engine to put an extended stored procedure into the SQL Server engine. Thus, the only way that an attacker could successfully put the extended stored procedures back would be to log into the database with a highly privileged account. If your application logs into the database engine using a highly privileged account, all bets are off as the attacker now has the rights needed to put the extended stored procedures back.

NOT USING BEST PRACTICE CODE LOGIC CAN HURT YOU

The application login process is probably the most important one that an attacker may want to take advantage of. Many times when developers are building a login process within their application, the front-end developer will use a query similar to the one shown in Example 9.15. After the query shown in Example 9.15 is run, if there is a record in the record set then the user logged in correctly so we grab the values from the first row and move on.

EXAMPLE 9.15

Sample query for authentication

```
SELECT * from dbo.Users WHERE username = 'Something'
and password = 'something'
```

Attackers wishing to exploit this situation would be able to get past the login screen, probably being logged in with a high level of permissions. This is done by adding a small text string in the username field such as "user OR 1=1 –"What this will do is change the code shown in Example 9.16 into the code shown in Example 9.17. Example 9.18 shows the T-SQL code that would be executed against the database engine.

EXAMPLE 9.16

The way a sample record set looks when validating a user account.

```
SELECT * FROM dbo.Users WHERE UserName = 'user' AND
Password = 'password'
```

EXAMPLE 9.17

The way the code looks when the attack code has been inserted.

```
SELECT * FROM dbo.Users WHERE UserName = 'user' OR 1=1 -- AND
Password = 'password'
```

EXAMPLE 9.18

The executable part of the code against the database engine from the prior sample code.

```
SELECT * FROM dbo.Users WHERE UserName = 'user' OR 1=1
```

Because of the OR clause in the prior sample code, it does not matter if there is a record where the UserName column equals user because the 1 = 1 section will tell the database to return every record in the database.

As you can see in the sample code above, the code that gets executed against the database engine would return the entire User table. Assuming that the front-end application simply takes the first record from the record set returned from the database, the attacker would then be logged into the application, probably with an administrative-level account. Preventing this sort of attack is easy; refer back to the beginning of this section of this chapter for the sample .NET code. Now that the user has been logged in, potentially with administrative rights, the user does not need to use any additional dynamic SQL to get access to your customer data, as he or she will now have full access through your normal administrative system.

To combat this problem the application should be verifying that the values within the record set which are returned are actually the values which are expected by comparing the value in the username column to ensure that it matches the username which the user entered. If the two values then match the user is allowed to continue. If the usernames do not match, then we know that something has gone horribly wrong, a generic error should be returned to the end user, and alerts should be triggered within the application which alert the systems administration team that something has gone wrong.

WHAT TO RETURN TO THE END USER

The next important thing to configure within the front-end application is what errors are returned to the end user. When the database throws an error, you should be sure to mask the error from the end user. The end user does not have any need to know the name of either the primary key or the foreign key that has been violated. You might want to return something that the end user can give to customer service or the help desk so that the actual error message can be looked up.

What this has to do with SQL Injection is important. If the attacker is able to send in code that breaks the query and returns an error, the error may well contain the name of a table or other database object within the error message. For example, if the attacker sends in an attack string of "Group by CustomerId–" to a query that looks like "SELECT * FROM Customers WHERE UserName = 'UserName' AND Password = 'Password'," creating the query "SELECT * FROM Customers WHERE UserName = 'UserName' Group by CustomerId– AND Password = 'Password'." The default error message that SQL Server would return gives the attackers more information than they had before. It tells them the table name. The attacker can use this same technique to figure out which columns are in the table. Overall, being able to see the actual SQL Server error message, even if the error does not give the attacker any database schema information, it tells the attacker that the attack attempt was successful. By using the sp_MSforeachtable system stored procedure and the raiserror function, the attackers could easily return the list of every table in the database, giving them a wealth of information about the database schema, which could then be used in future attacks.

There is more useful information that an attacker could get thanks to the error message being returned. For example, if the users were to run a stored procedure in another database that they did not have access to, the error message would return the username of the user – for example, if the attacker sends in an attack string "; exec

> **NOTE**
>
> Why Are SQL Injection Attacks Still Possible?
>
> One major reason why SQL Injection attacks are still possible today is that there is so much bad information circulating about how to protect yourself from an SQL Injection attack. For example, an article published by Symantec at http://www.symantec.com/connect/articles/detection-sql-injection-and-cross-site-scripting-attacks says that all you need to protect yourself is to verify the inputs using a regular expression that searches for the single quote and the double dash, as well as the strings "sp" and "xp." As you can see throughout this chapter, SQL Injection attacks can occur without tripping these regular expressions, and considering the high number of false positives that looking for a single quote would give you (especially if you like doing business with people of Irish descent), the protection would be minimal at best. If you were to read this article and follow its instructions you would be leaving yourself open to SQL Injection attacks.

model.dbo.Working –." It does not matter if the procedure exists or not, for the attacker would not get that far. The error returned from this call is shown in Example 9.19.

EXAMPLE 9.19

Error message returned by an attacker running a stored procedure that does not exist.

    Msg 916, Level 14, State 1, Line 1

    The server principal "test" is not able to access the database "model" under the current security context.

The model database is an excellent database to try this against, as typically no users have access to the model database. If the attacker gets an error message saying that the procedure does not exist, the attacker now knows that the login that the application is logging into the database has some high-level permissions, or the model database has some screwed-up permissions.

After finding the username, the attacker can easily enough find the name of the local database that the application is running within. This can be done by trying to create a table in the database. This is because the error message when creating a table includes the database name. For example, if the attack code "; create table mytable (c1 int);--" is sent, the error message shown in Example 9.20 will be returned.

EXAMPLE 9.20

Error message returned when creating a table when you do no have rights returning the name of the database to the attacker.

    Msg 262, Level 14, State 1, Line 1

    CREATE TABLE permission denied in database "MyApplicationDatabase."

These various values can be used in later attacks to clear the database of its data or to export the data from the database.

DATABASE FIREWALLS

There are products available on the market today which are called database firewalls. These database firewalls are either software packages which run on the server which is running the SQL Server service, or they are an appliance which runs on its own hardware (or virtual machine). In either case the concept of these applications is simple, they intercept every SQL query which the application sends to the SQL Server's endpoint and if the application feels that the query is a SQL Injection query, based on the text of the query being sent in, the query will be terminated before the query ever gets to the SQL Server database engine.

While these appliances can do a good job with most basic SQL Injection attacks their ability to prevent more complex attacks is not well known. Because of this variable in the effectiveness of the database firewalls they should be part of the solution not the only solution for SQL Injection attacks.

TEST, TEST, TEST

One of the most important things that must be done when protecting a SQL Server database against a SQL Injection attack is to test the application regularly for SQL Injection vulnerabilities. This is can be done either internally by in house personal by using penetration testing applications or by outsourcing this function to trusted vendors who specialize in penetration testing. At the minimum penetration testing should be performed every time there is a major software package release, as well as quarterly to ensure that none of the minor releases which have been released during the quarter are susceptible to SQL Injection attacks.

In a perfect world penetration testing would be performed at every software release. But these penetration tests take time and resources, and the reality is that most companies do not have the resources available to do this sort of constant and consistent penetration testing.

CLEANING UP THE DATABASE AFTER A SQL INJECTION ATTACK

There are a few different attacks that an attacker can perform against an SQL Server database. As shown so far in this chapter, delete commands can be passed into the SQL engine. However, other commands can be executed as well. Usually, attackers do not want to delete data or take a system offline; they instead want to use the SQL Server to help launch other attacks. A simple method is to identify tables and

---

FAQ

IFRAME Versus PopUp

Often people ask if a popup blocker would prevent this iframe attack from affecting the end user, and the answer is no, it would not. An iframe does not show a web browser popup on the users screen. An iframe is an inline frame which shows within the displayed webpage. An iframe with a height of 0 would be totally invisible to the end user, but it could be requesting data from a webpage on another website, passing information from the user's computer back to this unknown website. The website that is called from the iframe could then exploit vulnerabilities in the end user's web browser to install key loggers or command and control software turning the end user's computer into a member of a bot-net.

> **NOTE**
>
> Notes About Using This Sample Code
>
> Before running the included T-SQL code, be sure to make a full backup of the database in case of accidental data modification. The larger the database that you run this against, the longer it will take. When running this sample code, it is recommended that you change the output type from the default output style of grid to text by pressing <CTRL > + T, in order to reduce the resources needed to run the query. The included code will execute against all versions of Microsoft SQL Server from version 7 to 2014.

columns that are used to display data on the website that uses the database as a back-end. Then extra data is included in the columns of the database, which will allow attacking code to be executed against the database. This can be done using an update statement that puts an HTML iframe tag into each row of a table. This way when customers view the website, they get the iframe put into their web browser, which could be set to a height of 0 so that it is not visible. This hidden iframe could then install viruses or spyware on the user's computer without their knowledge.

Once this attack has occurred and viruses or spyware have been installed on the customer's computer, the most important thing now is to stop additional users' computers from being attacked. This means going through every record of every table looking for the attack code that is pushing the iframe to the customer's web browser. Obviously, you can go through each table manually looking for the records in question, or you can use the included sample code, shown in Example 9.21, which searches through each column in every table for the problem code and removes it. All you need to do is supply the variable with the attack code. The only columns that are not cleaned by this code are columns that use the TEXT or NTEXT data types. This is because the TEXT and NTEXT data types require special attention as they do not support the normal search functions.

> **NOTE**
>
> SQL Injection is Serious Business
>
> In case you had not guessed after reading this chapter, SQL Injection attacks are a very serious threat. Normally when an SQL Injection attack is launched, it is not launched against a single website. An attacker will often write a program that will check as many websites as possible before the attacker is taken off the Internet. The last successful large-scale attack on the Internet (as of the writing of this book) successfully changed the data in tens of thousands of separate databases that run tens of thousands of different websites. At the time of the attack, this was verified by searching on Google for the text of the code that was inserted into the attacked databases and looking at the number of domains that Google returned with matches.
>
> Falling prey to these attacks puts users and customers at major risk, as these attacks often are trying to install viruses or Trojan horses on the end user's computer, so that confidential data such as credit card numbers, and banking usernames and passwords can be gathered by the attacker and used to commit future fraud against the users and customers of the attacked websites. This can lead to months or years of credit report problems and the like.
>
> One final point to keep in mind: If you use your own company's websites or services, then the SQL Injection attacker is attempting to attack you as you are also a customer. So do yourself a favor and protect the database so that you do not get viruses or Trojan horses installed on your computer through your own company's website.

EXAMPLE 9.21

T-SQL Code that will clean a database that has had its values updated to send unvalued code to users.

```
DECLARE @injected_value NVARCHAR(1000)
SET @injected_value = 'Put the code which has been injected here.'
/*Change nothing below this line.*/
SET @injected_value = REPLACE(@injected_value, '''', '''''')
CREATE TABLE #ms_ver (indexid INT, name sysname, internal_value INT, character_value
VARCHAR(50))
INSERT INTO #ms_ver
EXEC xp_msver 'ProductVersion'
DECLARE @database_name sysname, @table_schema sysname, @table_name sysname, @column_name
sysname, @cmd NVARCHAR(4000),
@internal_value INT
SELECT @internal_value = internal_value
FROM #ms_ver
DECLARE cur CURSOR FOR SELECT TABLE_CATALOG, TABLE_SCHEMA, TABLE_NAME,
COLUMN_NAME
FROM INFORMATION_SCHEMA.columns c
JOIN systypes st ON c.DATA_TYPE = st.name
WHERE xtype IN (97, 167, 175, 231, 239, 241)
OPEN cur
FETCH NEXT FROM cur INTO @database_name, @table_schema, @table_name,
@column_name
WHILE @@FETCH_STATUS = 0
BEGIN
SET @cmd = 'SELECT NULL
WHILE @@ROWCOUNT <> 0
BEGIN
'
IF @internal_value > 530000
SET @cmd = @cmd + ' SET ROWCOUNT 1000
UPDATE'
ELSE
SET @cmd = @cmd + ' UPDATE TOP (1000)'
SET @cmd = @cmd + ' [' + @database_name + '].[' + @table_schema + '].[' +
@table_name + ']
SET [' + @column_name + '] = REPLACE([' + @column_name + '], ''' +
@injected_value + ''', '''')
WHERE [' + @column_name + '] LIKE ''%' + @injected_value + '%''
END'
exec (@cmd)
FETCH NEXT FROM cur INTO @database_name, @table_schema,
@table_name, @column_name
END
CLOSE cur
DEALLOCATE cur
DROP TABLE #ms_ver
```

OTHER FRONT END SECURITY ISSUES

Any time the general public is invited to touch your servers (usually via a web browser, but it could be via any application which talks to a server) there is the potential for problems. This is because of the simple fact that people write the code, and people access the application. The first group of people are perfectly capable of making mistakes, or just being junior level professionals (even if they have senior level titles) and taking shortcuts in the code to get the project they are working on done. These shortcuts can lead to exploits which the second group of people can easily (though sometimes not so easily) exploit to get access to information that they should not have, or to damage in some way the information stored in the SQL Server (or other) database.

THE WEB BROWSER URL IS NOT THE PLACE FOR SENSITIVE DATA

One shortcut, which only the truly inexperienced developer will use is to put sensitive information into the URL bar of the client web browser. Some things, which should never be placed into the URL bar as part of the websites query string include:

- Username
- Password
- Account Number
- Social Security Number (or other national ID number)
- Driver's License Numbers
- Any kind of identifying information

The reason that you do not want to put this information into the URL bar is that would make it very easy for someone to change the value. This includes storing these values as hidden form fields being passed from one page to another. Proper secure application development practices tell us that we should only be storing this

---

WARNING

The SQL Server Session State Database Is Evil, Evil I Tell You

While there is no security issue with using the Microsoft Session State Database functionality which comes with Internet Information Server (IIS) and Microsoft SQL Server there is a major performance issue once the site starts to really grow. SQL Server was not designed to be a good key value store which is exactly what the session state database is. As the session state database begins to grow you will see all sorts of performance problems including ghost records, locking and blocking problems, index fragmentation issues (the indexes become basically 100% fragmented very quickly), IO problems, massive page splitting to name just a few. To get the best performance from Session State look at one of the in memory session state providers. The .NET framework includes one by default on all Windows Servers, it just needs to have its service started and there are several other options available. You may have noticed that I did not mention using the session state database in this chapter, and now you know why.

> **STORY TIME**
>
> **It Is Not Just The Small Companies or the Junior Developers Who Make These Mistakes**
>
> In the middle of 2011, there was a little data disclosure issue at a small credit card and banking company called CitiBank. In the infinite wisdom of the developers at CitiBank they decided to include the account number of the person who was signed into the CitiBank portal in the URL bar, then use this handy piece of information to do lookups for the account information instead of relying of the username and password, or a session variable to hold this information.
>
> Needless to say the results were pretty predictable. Someone figured out that once you signed into the CitiBank portal you could simply change the account number at the top and view someone else's account information. Based on all on and off the record answers it appears that the people that did this only gathered customer information, but the results could have been much, much worse. New credit cards could have been issued, accounts could have been closed, I general massive havoc could have been rained down upon the customers of CitiBank; all because a developer decided to stick a value in the URL bar and then trust that value.

information in a server side variable which is accessed via the automatically generated session information which the web server creates and manages.

The first excuse that people usually make at this point is that they need multiple web servers and the session information would not be available is the end user switches to another web server. The answer to this situation is actually very simple, its called using the .NET session state service (there are other third party session state services available as well).

If the website which is being developed continues to grow to MySpace (in its heyday, not today), Facebook, or Twitter sized then you need to find another solution than an in memory session state server. If you do not the in memory session state server will quickly become your bottleneck and another solution will need to be found as a single session state server (or even a session state farm) probably cannot effectively manage having hundreds of millions of records being accessed and modified regularly. In these cases it might make sense to either tie the user to the web server in question for the duration of the session visit, or store some small piece of information in an encrypted form, as well as the checksum or hash of that value in a cookie on the users system which can then be used to find the rest of the information that the user is looking for.

USING xEVENTS TO MONITOR FOR SQL INJECTION

Extended Events, also known as xEvents, are typically thought of as a performance monitoring tool not a security monitoring tool. However, there is not anything that says that Extended Events cannot be used to monitor for SQL Injection attacks.

While doing this in SQL Server 2008 or SQL Server 2008 R2 is not very easy, SQL Server 2012 introduced a bit of new xEvents functionality which makes this

---

NOTE

xEvents is Out of Scope of This Book

While diving into xEvents a little bit, this is not an xEvents book. For more information about xEvents look for any of the current books on xEvents such as THIS BOOK by Jonathan Kehayias.

---

possible. That functionality is the ability to define a filter against the text of the SQL Statement as shown in Example 9.22.

EXAMPLE 9.22

Creating an Extended Events Session to capture keywords in queries which may be issued against the SQL Server Database Instance in a SQL Injection Attack.

```
CREATE EVENT SESSION SQL_Injection_Trap
ON SERVER
ADD EVENT sqlserver.sql_statement_completed
        (ACTION (sqlserver.sql_text, sqlserver.plan_handle,
package0.collect_system_time)
        WHERE (sqlserver.sql_text LIKE '%SELECT%*%FROM%sys.tables%'
                    or sqlserver.sql_text LIKE '%DROP%'
                    or sqlserver.sql_text LIKE '%SQL_Injection_Trap%')
                )
ADD TARGET package0.asynchronous_file_target
    (SET FILENAME = N'c:\xEvents\SQL_Injection_Trap.xel', METADATAFILE =
N'c:\xEvents\SQL_Injection_Trap.xem')
WITH (EVENT_RETENTION_MODE = ALLOW_MULTIPLE_EVENT_LOSS)
GO
ALTER EVENT SESSION SQL_Injection_Trap
ON SERVER
STATE=start
GO
```

As the code in Example 9.22 is reviewed, special attention should be paid to the where clause within the ACTION portion of the declaration. This is where the clause that separates the functionality of SQL Server 2012 from the earlier releases of xEvents.

NOTE

Monitor for the xEvent Name

Whenever setting up anything which monitors for an attack like this, you should always monitor for the name of the monitor to see if anyone attempts to make changes to the monitor. In the case of the same code in Example 9.22 we monitor for the name of the event session so that if someone turns the session off we would capture the command which turns it off.

Viewing the data which is captured by this extended event is easy enough using the query shown in Example 9.23. A query like this could be scheduled to run hourly or nightly (changing the WHERE clause as needed) and if there are records returned send an alert to the database administration team or whoever is responsible for ownership of the SQL Server instance with the output of the query so that they can take action on the potential intrusion.

EXAMPLE 9.23

Showing sample code which reads the xEvents session capture.

```
SELECT *, data.value('(event/@timestamp)[1]', 'datetime'),
        data.value('(event/action[3])[1]', 'varchar(max)')
FROM
    (SELECT CONVERT (XML, event_data) AS data FROM sys.fn_xe_file_target_
read_file
        ('c:\xEvents\SQL_Injection_Trap*.xel', 'c:\xEvents\SQL_Injection_
Trap*.xem', NULL, NULL)
    ) entries
WHERE data.value('(event/action[3]/text)[1]', 'datetime')  BETWEEN
DATEADD(dd, -1, getutcdate()) AND GETUTCDATE()
order by data.value('(event/@timestamp)[1]', 'datetime') desc
GO
```

Sadly as of the writing of this book in Early 2014, Extended Events are not available in the Microsoft Azure SQL Database offering so this type of monitoring would not be available to users of the Microsoft Azure SQL Database platform.

SUMMARY

SQL Injection attacks pose some of the greatest dangers to the database and customers because they are typically used to directly affect the information that the customer sees and can be rather easily used to attempt to push malicious code to clients' computers. These attacks are very popular with attackers because they are a relatively easy way to exploit systems design. They are also popular because they are easy to reproduce once a site is found to be easy to compromise, as it usually takes a long time to correct all the potential attack points in a website. This length of time leaves the website and database open to attack for a long period of time as companies are usually unwilling to shut down their customer facing websites while the website design is being repaired.

Because of the way that the SQL Injection attacks work, the Database Administrator, Database Developer, Application Developer, and Systems Administrator all need to work together to ensure that they are correctly protecting the data within the database and the company network at large. As the database and application developers begin getting in the habit of writing code that is not susceptible to SQL Injection attacks, the current project will become more secure, as will future projects that the team members work on.

SQL Azure is just as susceptible to an SQL Injection attack as any other SQL Instance. What the attacker can do within the instance is much less dangerous simply because there are many fewer features available. For example, protection against xp_cmdshell is not a priority because xp_cmdshell is not available on an SQL Azure instance. Neither are features such as database mail or SQL mail, so protecting against attackers that plan to use these vectors does not need to be done. As time goes on, and more features are added to Windows Azure SQL Database, this may change; however, as of this writing, this information is accurate.

With proper planning (such as proper object security design) and proper monitoring (such as using xEvents to capture suspect statements) we can prevent many of the potential SQL Injection problems and when those problems do show up, we can track the statements to see that something happened and what happened.

REFERENCE

Wall Street Journal, Others, Hit in Mass SQL attack – SC Magazine US. *IT Security News and Security Product Reviews – SC Magazine US*. n.d. Web. October 21, 2010.

Database Backup Security 10

Denny Cherry

INFORMATION IN THIS CHAPTER:

- Overwriting backups
- Media set and backup set passwords
- Backup encryption
- Transparent data encryption
- Compression and encryption
- Offsite backups

All too often people spend all their time securing the database while it is active within the database engine, without providing protection for the database backups. Not securing the database backups provides an easy way for a data thief to get access to all the information stored within the database. This is because the database backups are the least secure portion of the database. They are so insecure because they actually leave the building on a regular basis. This is because the database backups are typically put on tape and shipped offsite to another location, such as Iron Mountain or another secure facility. Where problems can occur is that the number of tapes that end up being lost is a lot higher than any of these offsite storage companies want to admit.

There are some key things you need to remember no matter which encryption solution you select for your backup (and you should be encrypting your backups). The first of these needs is to balance the encryption protection with the amount of time and CPU power that encryption solution will take to implement. While stronger encryption will better protect your data, it will also increase the load on the server that is processing the encryption. If the application that is using the database requires 24 x 7 uptime, you may not be able to implement the stronger levels of backup encryption because while the backups are running, the database engine may not be able to service requests quickly enough to maintain your service levels.

OVERWRITING BACKUPS

When setting up backup policies, it is very important to ensure that the backups do not simply overwrite the prior backup file each time a backup is taken. If the backups are done to the same file over and over, and the backup fails, there is no longer a useful backup that can be used to restore the database in the event the database fails. This rule applies to full backups, differential backups, as well as the transaction log backups. When you use the FORMAT key word within the BACKUP DATABASE command, this tells the database engine to remove any backups that exist within the backup media – either the file when backing up to disk or the tape when backing up to tape. If you do not use the FORMAT statement, the backup is appended to the backup media. When you do not include the FORMAT key word and you backup to disk, there is no way to remove the old backups from the backup media. Because of this behavior, writing each backup to its own backup file is highly recommended. When using the SQL Server Maintenance plan to manage backups, the Maintenance plan will use this behavior automatically. When writing custom T-SQL backup scripts using the BACKUP DATABASE and BACKUP LOG commands, this adjustment must be done manually. The easiest way to handle this is to declare a variable and set that variable to a date string and then use that date string as part of the backup file name as shown in Example 10.1.

EXAMPLE 10.1

T-SQL code showing how to backup the database to a different file each time the backup is taken.

```
DECLARE @FileName AS NVARCHAR(255)
SET @FileName = 'D:\backups\MyDatabase-' +
convert(varchar(20), getutcdate(), 127)
 + 'bak'
BACKUP DATABASE MyDatabase TO DISK=@FileName
```

The same technique that is shown in Example 10.1 to backup the full database can be done for a differential backup by adding the DIFFERENTIAL keyword or for a transaction log backup by using the BACKUP LOG statement as shown in Example 10.2.

EXAMPLE 10.2

T-SQL code showing how to backup the log to a different file each time a log backup is taken.

```
DECLARE @FileName AS NVARCHAR(255)
SET @FileName = 'D:\backups\MyDatabase-' +
convert(varchar(20), getutcdate(), 127)
 + 'bak'
BACKUP LOG MyDatabase TO DISK=@FileName
```

The code shown in Examples 10.1 and 10.2 can be a little difficult to read at first glance. We take the value of the UTC date and time, and convert it into format 127 which outputs the date and time with no spaces with the date as year-month-day for easy sorting of the files.

DELETING OLD BACKUPS

Once each of the backups is being done to a separate file, the older files will need to be deleted at some point. If the backups are not deleted, eventually the backups will fill the hard drive they are being written to, causing new backups to fail to function. If a database maintenance plan is being used to backup the databases, it can be configured to remove the database backups after a specified number of days. In the SQL Server 2000 maintenance plan (Figure 10.1), this can be done by checking the checkbox and setting the value to the required number of days as shown in Example 10.1. In the SQL Server 2005 and above maintenance plan, this can be done by adding a "Maintenance Cleanup Task" to the maintenance plan and setting the path for the backup files as well as the file extension to be deleted as shown in Figure 10.2.

As shown in Figure 10.2, which presents the SQL Server 2005 and higher, the "Maintenance Cleanup Task" only supports cleaning up one file extension at a time. If transaction log backups are backed up with a different file extension, then a second "Maintenance Cleanup Task" will need to be added to the maintenance plan for the second file extension.

The "Maintenance Cleanup Task" in SQL Server 2005 and above is not all that complex as a function, as can be seen by clicking the View T-SQL button at the bottom of the "Maintenance Cleanup Task" dialog. This operator simply calls the xp_delete_file extended stored procedure, which can be found in the master database. This procedure, when the correct parameters are passed to it, will automatically delete any backup files in the specified path, as well as subfolders. The extended stored procedure xp_delete_file accepts five parameters:

1. Reports or Backups = Uses a 1 for reports and 0 for backups;
2. Path = The path to the backup files;

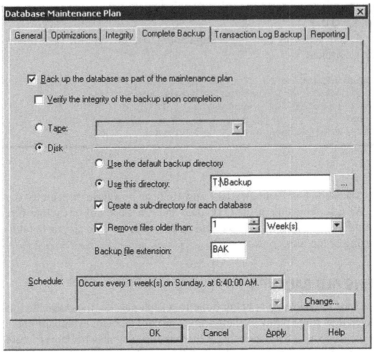

FIGURE 10.1 Showing the page of the SQL Server 2000 maintenance plan which controls the deletion of database backups.

3. Extension = The extension of the backups to process;
4. Date to delete to = The newest backup to keep; and
5. Search subfolders = 0 only searches the specified folder, 1 searches the specified folder and the first level of subfolders.

This procedure can be easily called passing a variable into the procedure for the value of the date to stop deleting files, as shown in Example 10.3.

EXAMPLE 10.3

The use of the xp_delete_file extended stored procedure to delete older backup files.

```
DECLARE @date DATETIME
SET @date = DATEADD(dd, -28, getdate())
EXEC master.dbo.xp_delete_file 0,N'd:\backups',N'bak',@date,1
EXEC master.dbo.xp_delete_file 0,N'd:\backups',N'trn',@date,1
```

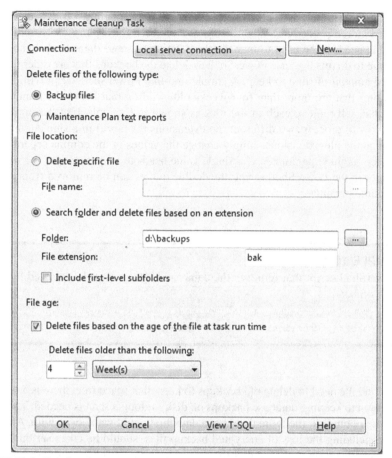

FIGURE 10.2 Showing the page of the SQL Server 2005 and up maintenance plan which controls the deletion of database backups.

There are a couple of catches when using the xp_delete_file extended stored procedure. The first is that this is technically an undocumented stored procedure and its use may change at any time at Microsoft's whim. The second is that the procedure can only be used to delete valid database backups that are created using the native CREATE BACKUP and CREATE LOG commands. This is because the xp_delete_file extended stored procedure opens each file before deleting it to ensure that the file is a valid Microsoft Tape Format (MTF) file. If the file is not a valid MTF file, then the xp_delete_file will not delete the file. This can become a problem when using one of the third-party backup utilities such as Dell's LiteSpeed for SQL Server, or Red Gate SQL Backup, as these backup utilities do not use the native

MTF file format, and as such these backups are not recognized by xp_delete_file extended stored procedure. When using one of these third-party tools, a different technique needs to be used to manage the deleting of these database backups. One technique to do this is to use PowerShell to delete the backups that are older than the required amount of time to keep. A simple one-line PowerShell script will identify all the files that are more than four weeks old, sending that list to the remote-item applet that will remove each of the files as shown in Example 10.4. Example 10.4 shows how to process two different file extensions (or more) in a single command. To change the file extensions, simply change the values in the comma separated list within the -include parameter. If a single value needs to be passed into the -include parameter in the PowerShell script, the double quotes can be removed from around the -include parameter.

EXAMPLE 10.4

PowerShell script that removes the database backups that do not need to be kept on hand.

```
Get-ChildItem "d:\backups\" "-include *.BAK,*.trn" -recurse | where
{((get-date)-$_.creationTime).weeks -ge 4} | remove-item -force -recurse
```

Beyond the need to delete old backups to keep disk space free, there is a security implication to keeping database backups on disk for longer than is needed. The more files that are on disk, the more data that a data thief could walk away with. Any data breach, including the loss of encrypted backup files, should be taken seriously. The fewer files to maintain, the smaller the risk in keeping those files around. For those worried about having to restore the database from older files, the files should never be removed from the local disk until they have been archived to a tape backup system that would allow the backup files to be restored to disk and then restored to the SQL Server engine.

NOTE

SQL Server Analysis Services Does Not Use MTF

Only two components of the SQL Server product suite require that backups be made of the data they keep: the SQL Server engine and the SQL Server Analysis Services engine. However, the SQL Server Analysis Services engine does not create its database backups using the MTF format. This means that, like the third-party SQL Server engine database backups, the SQL Server Analysis Services backups cannot be deleted by using the xp_delete_file extended stored procedure. A process such as the PowerShell script shown in Example 10.4 must be used to remove these older backups.

MEDIA SET AND BACKUP SET PASSWORDS

When you backup your Microsoft SQL Server database, you have the option of specifying a backup set password as well as a media set password. These passwords provide a very basic level of protection of your database backups. The backup set password is designed to prevent accidental restore of the database, while the media set password is designed to prevent the media from being accidently overwritten. Even with this most basic level of security, these passwords will give you some level of protection, for, without the passwords, the backups cannot be restored to another SQL Server.

When you password protect the media, no additional backup sets can be created on that media without supplying the correct password, and no backup can be restored from the media without supplying the media password. You can password protect both the media and the backup set, or just one or the other. Obviously, the more passwords that are in place, the more secure the data within the backup is. However, because the format that is used to store these passwords within the backup and/or the media are well documented and have been around for decades, it is quite easy for someone to read the value, and reverse engineer the source password, or to simply write a new password into the media and then use this new password value to then restore the data from the backup.

While these passwords are not the most secure method available, for older versions of Microsoft SQL Server these passwords are your only native option for securing your database backups. The most common way to use these passwords would be within a T-SQL script so that the backup of the database can be scheduled. Password protected databases are backed up using the BACKUP DATABASE command like a normal database backup as shown in Example 10.5.

EXAMPLE 10.5

T-SQL script to backup a database with a backup set password and media password.

```
BACKUP DATABASE YourDB TO DISK='D:\YourDB.bak'
WITH MEDIANAME='YourMediaPassword',
PASSWORD='YourBackupSetPassword',
FORMAT
```

NOTE

Backup Set Passwords and Media Set Passwords Are Going, Going, Gone

It should be noted that both the backup set password and the media set password are scheduled to be removed in a future version of Microsoft SQL Server. Because of this scheduled removal, these passwords should not be used in new database instances that are configured, and they should be removed from current policies.

BACKUP ENCRYPTION

Encrypting your database backups is probably the most reliable way to secure your database backups from prying eyes. There are a few different ways to encrypt your database backup. In SQL Server 2012 and below you need to use a third-party backup application such Dell's LiteSpeed for SQL Server, or Red Gate Software's SQL Backup to encrypt your database backups as they are written to either disk or when they are written directly to tape. SQL Server 2014 introduces a native database encryption function for encrypting database backups. This new native data encryption option works when backing up to a local drive or network share, as well as when backing up to the Microsoft Azure Blob Storage.

If you use a media library such as CommVault, IBMs Tivoli, or another of the large Enterprise Class tape backup solutions where you backup the database directory from the database to the tape library, then these third-party tape backup options may not work for you. In these cases you will need to look at encrypting your SQL Server backups using the native functions of your existing tape backup solution.

NATIVE ENCRYPTION IN SQL SERVER 2014

Backup encryption using traditional encryption algorithms such as AES was first introduced to the SQL Server product in SQL Server 2014. This allows the SQL Server to backup a database and write it as an encrypted backup without having to enable Transparent Data Encryption, which until now was the only way to create a native encrypted backup.

Creating an encrypted backup using T-SQL is as simple as including the EN-CRYPTION parameter in the BACKUP DATABASE command along with the encryption options you wish to use. Encrypting your backups using the SQL Server's native BACKUP DATABASE command does have a prerequisite which is that you must have a certificate or asymmetric key created to use to encrypt the backups. Like Transparent Data Encryption, which was discussed in Chapter 4, great care must be taken to protect the certificate which is used to encrypt database backups. If the certificate which is used by the SQL Server to encrypt the backups is lost then there will be no way to recover the backups and restore them to a SQL Server database instance.

As can be seen in Example 10.6 turning on backup encryption for database backups is a very straightforward change to the BACKUP DATABASE command. The addition of a single set of parameters turns the backup encryption on. In Example 10.6 a certificate is used to encrypt the database backup.

EXAMPLE 10.6
Encrypting a database backup using native backup encryption

```
BACKUP DATABASE AdventureWorks2014
TO DISK='D:\Backups\AdventureWorks2014.bak'
WITH ENCRYPTION (ALGORITHM=AES_256, SERVER CERTIFICATE =
MyBackupCert);
```

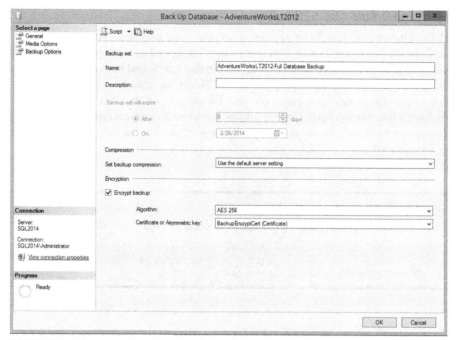

FIGURE 10.3 "Backup options" page of the backup database window.

Encrypted backups can also be taken using the SQL Server Management Studio interface. Log onto the SQL Server and connect to the SQL Server database instance using the object explorer. Right click on the database and from the context menu which opens select "Tasks" then "Backup." On the "Backup Options" tab, shown in Figure 10.3 check the check box next to the "Encrypt backup" toward the bottom of the window. Then select the encryption algorithm which should be used as well as the certificate or asymmetric key which should be used to secure the backup.

The native backup encryption feature can be used when backing up to Microsoft Azure Blob Storage as well as to a local network location on the network or on the server itself. Simply change the backup location from a on site location such as D:\ Backups\File.bak or \\FileServer\Share\Folder\File.bak to a valid Azure Blob Storage location such as http://AzureStorageURL/backup/file.bak. The backup will then be encrypted as it leaves the SQL Server instance and will be transferred to the Microsoft Azure Blob Storage container already encrypted allowing you to store your backups securely in the Windows Azure cloud without any risk that Microsoft can access the data.

LITESPEED FOR SQL SERVER

Using LiteSpeed to handle encryption is actually quite easy once you have the products installed and configured. If you are using LiteSpeed to backup your databases, you will need to edit each database backup job that LiteSpeed has created, adding in the @encryptionkey or the @jobp parameter. The @encyrptionkey parameter allows you to provide a plain text password that LiteSpeed can then use to encrypt your backup, while the @jobp parameter allows you to pass in an encrypted value so that you do not have to store an unencrypted password in your backup scripts as shown in Example 10.7.

EXAMPLE 10.7

A sample SQL LiteSpeed job designed to encrypt a database backup.

```
EXEC master.dbo.xp_backup_database @database='YourDatabase',
@backupname='YourDatabase Backup', @encryptionkey='YourKey',
@file='D:\Backups\YourDatabase.bak';
```

In order to get the encrypted value for use with the @jobp parameter, use the extended stored procedure xp_encrypt_backup_key that SQL LiteSpeed creates in the instance. The extended stored procedure accepts a single-input parameter of @key and returns a single value as a recordset. The value that is returned is the encrypted version of the password.

When restoring a database from a LiteSpeed for SQL Server encrypted backup, simply pass in the @encryptionkey or @jobp parameter so that LiteSpeed is able to read the database backup and write the data back to the SQL Server engine.

RED GATE SQL BACKUP

Red Gate software has two backup products available that can handle encryption. Red Gate SQL Backup is configured and used very much like LiteSpeed for SQL Server Enterprise. Red Gate SQL Backup uses an extended stored procedure to run the backup process. Unlike LiteSpeed for SQL Server Enterprise where a parameter is passed to the extended stored procedure, Red Gate SQL Backup takes a single parameter with a variety of parameters passed within that single-text parameter.

To enable encryption of your backup, two values must be specified: KEYSIZE and PASSWORD. The KEYSIZE is the size of the encryption key that will be used. Red Gate SQL Backup supports either a 128-bit key or a 256-bit key. The PASSWORD is the key phrase that allows the encryption to be used as shown in Example 10.8.

As with other backup products, you can pass in an encrypted password or a plain text password. Like always, passing in an encrypted value is more secure as this does not require storing the password in plain text within the Red Gate SQL Backup Job.

EXAMPLE 10.8

T-SQL code showing how to create a Red Gate SQL Backup Job using both an encrypted password and a plain text password.

```
EXECUTE master.dbo.sqlbackup '-SQL "BACKUP DATABASE [AdventureWorks]
TO DISK = "D:\Backup\<AUTO>.sqb" WITH PASSWORD =
"<ENCRYPTEDPASSWORD>o1a5dA==</ENCRYPTEDPASSWORD>",
DISKRETRYINTERVAL = 30, DISKRETRYCOUNT = 10, COMPRESSION = 0,
KEYSIZE = 256, THREADCOUNT = 2"';
EXECUTE master..sqlbackup '-SQL "BACKUP DATABASE [AdventureWorks] TO
DISK = "D:\Backup\<AUTO>.sqb" WITH PASSWORD = "test", DISKRETRYINTERVAL =
30, DISKRETRYCOUNT = 10, COMPRESSION = 0, KEYSIZE = 256,
THREADCOUNT = 2"';
```

When you encrypt your SQL Server databases (or any backups) using any technique, you will need to take special care to protect the keys that you use when backing up the data. If the keys are lost or are unavailable when it comes time to restore the backups, then the backups are effectively useless as there will be no way to decrypt the backup and restore the data. A common practice is to place a copy of the key on a USB drive or other portable media such as a CD. This media should then be placed into a sealed envelope and stored in a secure location such as a safe in the Human Resources Department or the Legal Department. If possible, this location should be at a facility other than the primary facility that you are attempting to backup data from. The tapes should be stored at a second facility so that in the event of a major failure of the primary facility such as an earthquake, flood, or hurricane, which destroys the primary facility, the backup tapes are still available to restore the data and get the business backup and running.

Regardless of the encryption technique you use, there is a CPU overhead to process this encryption, and this overhead must be taken into account when you configure your backup encryption solution.

THIRD-PARTY TAPE BACKUP SOLUTIONS

Dozens of enterprise class tape backup solutions are available. Each one of these solutions has its own method of encrypting data. For the most part, they all work basically the same way. They use the SQL Server API to create a virtual backup tape device within the SQL Server, which sends the data to the application installed on the SQL Server. This then directs the data stream to the tape backup server, which then sends the data to be backed directly to tape (or written to disk, then moved later on to tape).

In these backup environments, there are typically a huge variety of encryption options. Before selecting your encryption options with these larger platforms, it is important to know where the encryption will take place. The documentation that came with your backup and recovery application (BURA) should be able to tell you at what layer the encryption is done. Typically, the encryption will be done in one of two locations; either within the backup application running on the SQL Server or within the service running on the tape backup control server.

The preference for performance of the SQL Server is to have the encryption handled at the tape backup server's level as this takes the CPU load of the encryption away from the SQL Server's CPU. However, the systems administrator will prefer to have the encryption done on the SQL Server because this distributes the encryption load back to each SQL Server instead of putting all that very expensive data encryption on the backup server. The problem of putting all the backup encryption on the backup server's CPUs can be offset by running various systems backups at various times of the day and night, instead of backing up all the databases at the same time.

Not all enterprise backup solutions support encryption within the backup solution. If the enterprise backup solution does not support encryption of data as it is written to the tapes, care must be taken to ensure that the enterprise backup solution does support having SQL Server backup the data in an encrypted form. If the backup solution cannot tell the SQL Server to backup the data with encryption (either using the native SQL 2008 and higher encryption or a third-party tool), then the backups should be first configured to backup to disk in an encrypted form, and then those backups should be moved from the disk to the tape backup array without the need to worry about encryption, as the database encryption has already been handled by the database engine.

For an extra layer of protection, if the tape backup solution does support encryption and it supports using either the native SQL Server 2008 and up or third-party encryption options, then the database can encrypt the data before it is sent to the tape backup solution, which can then encrypt the data again. This would provide an extra layer of protection, as for someone to read the backup tapes they would first need to break through the encryption on the backup tape itself, and then they would need to break the encryption that the SQL Server or third-party tool placed on the data. This double layer of encryption increases the complexity of the solution because now two different sets of keys will need to be maintained and safely stored. Nonetheless, this would be a more secure solution.

TRANSPARENT DATA ENCRYPTION

Using Transparent Data Encryption (discussed in the "Encrypting Data at Rest" section of Chapter 2 of this book) protects not only your data at rest on the production server's hard drive, but also your SQL Server backups when taken with either the native backup process or one of the third-party backup tools that have been discussed in this chapter. Transparent Data Encryption does this by ensuring that each data page is encrypted as it is written on disk. Then when the data page is transferred to the backup file, the page is still encrypted.

Transparent Data Encryption is configured by creating a database master key in the master database. After creating the database master key, a Certificate is created in the master database. Then a database encryption key is created in the user database, and this database encryption key is secured using the certificate that was created within the master database. After the database encryption key has been created, the ENCRYPTION option on the user database can be enabled telling the Transparent Data Encryption engine to begin the background encrypting of data. Much more information on this topic is available in Chapter 2 of this book.

This means that in order to restore the backed up database to the same SQL Instance or to another SQL Instance you will first need to export the Certificate from the source instances master database and then restore the key into the destination instance's master database. Without having this certificate restored, you will be unable to restore the database to the SQL Instance. Because of this, backing up these certificates is critical. Without backups of the certificates, you will NOT BE ABLE TO RESTORE YOUR DATABASE that is being encrypted.

SECURING THE CERTIFICATES

Securing the certificates which are used by Transparent Database Encryption is very important. If someone was able to get a copy of the certificate which is used to create the database encryption key as well as the database backup they would be able to restore that database backup file to their own SQL Server and therefore have full access to the data within the SQL Server database.

After backing up the certificate from the master database by using the BACKUP CERTIFICATE command security best practices dictate that the certificate backup be burned onto two different CDs (or DVDs, or whatever the standard single write media is when you are reading this). Each CD should be placed into a large envelope which identifies the system which the certificate is for. The envelope should be sealed, with the person sealing it signing their name over the sealed edge. Then a piece of clear shipping tape should be placed over the signature from edge to edge of the envelope. This makes the envelope virtually impossible to open without causing damage to the envelope making it obvious that the envelope was opened. One envelope should be placed in the office safe of a manager or executive at the company. Typically, the Human Resources department will have a safe which only they have

> **NOTE**
>
> But Does Not This Put the Key in the Same Location as the Backups?
>
> Yes it does. Which I admit is a problem. In a perfect world the company would have a second account with a second offsite storage facility and this second facility would store only the CDs which have the various certificate backups. However, this is not always the most practical solution as maintaining this second contract is very expensive.
>
> Now some companies will store their tape backups at one location and their paper documents (legal papers, human resource documents, etc.) at a second site. If this is the case, ask for a box at the paper storage location to be allocated for IT and use this to store the envelopes which contain all the CDs.
>
> If your company has multiple offices the second copy could be stored at another office, provided that the second office is far enough away that whatever natural disaster destroyed the first office would have no possibility of destroying the second office. In the United States this would mean offices at least 500 or 1000 apart (and that are not in the same basic storm path, so do not use two offices on the eastern sea board that might be hit by the same hurricane even though one is in Florida and one is in New York). In Europe, South America or Africa this probably means an office in a different country (depending on the size of the countries and the natural disasters that you have to deal with regularly).

access to, and you can have this disk stored in that safe. The second safe should be sent offsite to another secure location.

The reason for the two copies, one stored securely onsite and the second stored securely offsite is so that if the certificate is needed to perform a restore you can get the certificate quickly from the onsite copy. If, however, there is a major disaster and the entire office is destroyed you need to have that second copy available so that you can recall it and restore using it.

These certificate backups should never be left on a network share, or on the server's hard drive. Leaving the certificate backup sitting on the server's hard drive is basically the same as buying a very expensive lock for the door to your house and leaving the key sticking out of the lock when you go on vacation.

COMPRESSION AND ENCRYPTION

Two of the most important concepts in today's IT world are encryption and compression or deduplication. Encryption stores the data in a safe and secure manor, while compression and deduplication reduce the amount of physical data being stored. Unfortunately, however, these two concepts usually do not play well together. This is because compression or deduplication of data requires lots of duplicates within your data, but encryption tends to make your data very unique.

Not all is lost, however, there is a way to make compression or deduplication and encryption work together. The trick is to compress the data before the data is encrypted. This allows the duplicates to be removed, allowing for maximum compression, and then the data can be encrypted providing the needed protection.

> **NOTE**
>
> Working Together Gets the Best Results
>
> Deciding at what level the compression and the encryption are going to be done will require working with the systems administrator in charge of the tape backup system. By working together on the solution design, you can get the best results out of the solution.
>
> If the tape backup system takes an already encrypted backup and tries to compress it, the tape backup system would not get any acceptable level of compression, which will lead to wasted tape and wasted time and CPU power while attempting to compress the backup. However, if you can compress first and then encrypt the backup within the SQL Server (or use a third-party tool) and write that backup to disk and have the tape backup solution move the backups to tape without trying to compress, then time and CPU power will be saved.
>
> If, however, the tape backup solution has to compress and encrypt, then your best bet may be to backup a non-encrypted database backup. This way the backup server can handle the entire compression and encryption process.

The third-party tools that have been discussed all do an excellent job of compressing and encrypting within a single step. If you are using one of the larger enterprise solutions to backup to tape directly from the SQL Server, in order to do compressions and encryption the compression must be done before the data is sent to the tape library. This requires that when the tape library performs the BACKUP DATABASE operation against the SQL Server database it must know how to tell the SQL Server to compress the database backup. If the tape library does not know how to use the COMPRESSION option, it will attempt to do the decryption after the data has been encrypted and as it is written to tape. At this point it is too late, as the level of compression will drop to 1–2% compression compared to the normal 40%+ compression that the native backup or the third-party software compression backups can provide.

ENCRYPTION AND DATA DEDUPLICATION

In the backup world there is another data size reduction technology besides compression, which is called data deduplication. Data deduplication differs from compression where compression attempts to find the duplicate values within a single file by removing those duplicate values; while data deduplication works across files looking for duplicate blocks of data within each file. Because data deduplication works between different files on the file system even data which is encrypted can be deduplicated. This is especially true of encrypted data which is stored within a SQL Server database.

When data is stored as an encrypted string, as long as the value does not change when the data is backed up to a backup system which supports data deduplication, the backup system should be able to deduplicate some of the data stored within the database. The lower the data change rate of the database backup the higher the percentage of the data which will be deduplicated.

There are two different techniques available for data deduplication. The first is fixed length deduplication and the second is variable length deduplication. Fixed

> **NOTE**
>
> Deduplication and Compression
>
> Deduplication and database backup compression typically will not work very well together as there is no guarantee that the SQL Server database will write out the compressed data pages exactly the same every time.

> **NOTE**
>
> Other Things Which Can Effect Deduplication
>
> While this is not a data deduplication book, there are not a whole lot of resources out there for SQL Server professionals to read up on data deduplication that is not from the marketing departments of the various vendors. Because of that I thought this information was important enough to include in the book even though it is pretty far off topic.
>
> When it comes to using data deduplication compression, the page verify option that you have selected will actually impact the ability to deduplicate the database backups. The use of "torn page detection" will decrease, possibly dramatically, the success rate of data deduplication. This is because when data is written to these rows, even if the row is updated with only minor (or no) changes the torn page detection bits will be flipped. This means that even if only a single bit column of a single row within the page is changed the torn page detection bits which reside every 512 bytes within the database page are changed meaning that for data deduplication to work correctly on that page the string length must be less than 512 bytes. With a fixed length data deduplication process the odds of this being the case are basically 0.
>
> The database index rebuilding schedule will also greatly impact the success of data deduplication. This is because every time an index is rebuild the index is rewritten to different data pages within the database file which causes the header of the page to be changed making the data deduplication process less successful.

length is typically much less expensive to purchase (license fees) and to implement (less CPU power on the deduplication appliance) than variable length deduplication is. However variable length deduplication is much more efficient when it comes to deduplication of data which has a high change rate. This is because the variable length deduplication will look at the data and work with a variety of string lengths as it attempts to deduplicate the data.

As an example a fixed length deduplication process may work in 8192 byte blocks, which within the context of Microsoft SQL Server would be a single database page. So if a single bit within the page is changed between backups that page cannot be deduplicated between the two backups because the backup system is using a fixed length string. However with a variable length string deduplication platform the system will compare various smaller strings within the database page and see that only the one bit has changed, so it would deduplicate the first part of the database page and then as a separate deduplication process deduplicate the second part of the database page leaving only the one bit as needing to actually be written to the backup device (in addition to the two pointers which refer back to the original 8192 byte page.

OFFSITE BACKUPS

Offsite backups of your SQL Server backups are probably the biggest weakness in database backup security. This is because by the nature of the offsite backup, you are trusting another company and that company's employees to keep your backup data safe and secure. While these offsite backup companies are expected to keep the backup tapes, there have been many cases (both published in the news and heard about through word of mouth) where tapes have been lost or returned to the wrong company when recalled.

Companies with multiple offices may use different offices to store their offsite tapes. This is fine provided that wherever the tapes will be stored at the remote office are secured. The last thing that you will want to do is to insecurely store tapes in a remote office when the data would be well secured if it were still within the data center. When tapes are stored in a remote company office the same level of security

---

STORY TIME

I am Sorry to Inform You of This, But We Have Lost the Backup Tape with All Your Customer Information on It

A quick search on Google, Bing, or your favorite search engine for "lost backup tapes" will give you a pretty clear idea of what can happen when backup tapes go missing.

In June 2005, CitiGroup, one of the largest financial companies in the world, reported that a backup tape was lost. This was not just any old set of backup tapes either; these specific tapes were being shipped via UPS from the financial giant to one of the credit bureaus in the United States. These tapes, which were most likely sent without any sort of encryption in place to protect the data, included customer information for about 3.9 million of CitiGroup's customers. The data on the tapes included the customer's name, Social Security number, account history, and loan information about current and former customers. Basically, they had just about everything a data thief would need to begin a massive amount of identity theft.

CitiGroup was not the only large company to lose tapes in 2005. In February of that same year, Bank of America reported that it lost backup tapes that contained personal information on 1.2 million credit card customers. Not to feel left out, Time Warner reported in May 2005 that it lost information (one can easily enough assume backup tapes) with information relating to 600,000 current and former employees.

The companies that own the data and the tapes are not the only ones that can lose backup tapes. In 2005 Iron Mountain, a company that specializes in storing backup tapes, reported that it "lost track" of four sets of customer backup tapes during the first four months of the year. While admitting that the tapes were lost, Iron Mountain says that it loses only a very small number of tapes as it ships more than 5M tapes annually.

More recently, in June 2010, the insurance broker Marsh and Mercer reported that in April of that year they lost tapes that were being shipped between their offices. Although the total number of people affected was not disclosed, the company reported to the New Hampshire Attorney General's office that information on 131 New Hampshire residents was on the tapes that were being transferred.

These few items are just a few of the articles that can be found with a couple of quick searches online. Considering the frequency with which tapes disappear during shipping and long-term storage, the issue of protecting data stored on tape becomes extremely important. The data should be encrypted and password protected at the very minimum.

> **NOTE**
>
> Ditch the Tape
>
> Another way that these risks can be mitigated is by using a virtual tape library (VTL) instead of a physical tape library. A VTL connects to a traditional enterprise backup solution, but instead of backing up to a tape drive the backup is written to a hard drive. The advantage of the virtual tape library is that the backups run much, much faster.
>
> When using a VTL, a second virtual tape library can be placed in a second data center. The first virtual tape can then be configured to replicate data over the Wide Area Network (WAN) to the second virtual tape library. This gives the VTL the offsite backup capabilities that traditional tape libraries can provide by getting the backups out of the primary data center facility while continuing to use the existing backup server infrastructure.

should be used as if the tapes were within the data center. This includes hardened locks, minimal access to the room which stores the tapes, etc.

Because there is no guarantee that the tapes you send out would not be sent to another company, you need to ensure that when another company gets these tapes they are completely worthless to whoever receives them. Although one would hope that whatever company that receives your tapes would simply return them when they find that the tapes are not theirs, there is no way to know that this company is not a competitor who would love to have access to your company's proprietary information.

Tapes being returned to the wrong company are not the only thing that can go wrong. There have been stories about tapes literally falling off the truck between the customer's office and the remote storage facility. In this case, you have no way of knowing who has your tapes or what their end goal of having the tapes might be. If your offsite storage facility is an employee's or manager's home, there is an even higher chance of tape loss. This is not due to any fault of the employees, but rather to the fact that cars get stolen and houses get broken into with much more frequency than happens with professional offsite service.

With all the potential problems that come with moving database backups offsite, still offsite backups are a necessary evil in order to meet the organization's disaster recovery and business continuity requirements. The key to taking your database backups offsite is to mitigate these risks by using database encryption best practices.

SUMMARY

Just because the data has left the SQL Server or even the office does not mean that the DBA's responsibilities have ended. Some of the primary responsibilities of any DBA is to secure the data, while maintaining the ability to keep the system up and running, and having the ability to restore the data as needed so that the system can be restored quickly in the event of a failure. In order to accomplish this, security best practices need to be followed not just in the production environment but within your back solution as well.

As you work with older and older versions, you have much fewer options available to you. On the native function side, Microsoft began introducing compression in Microsoft SQL Server 2008, and native encryption with Transparent Data Encryption was introduced in Microsoft SQL Server 2008. When using older versions of Microsoft SQL Server, you will need to use a third-party solution to encrypt your backup solution. Check with your backup solution provider to see what options are available to you based on the version of Microsoft SQL Server.

Beginning around early 2014 Microsoft Azure SQL Database begin supporting backups of the Microsoft Azure SQL Databases. As of the writing of this book in the summer of 2014 backups of Microsoft Azure SQL Databases are supported for the Basic, Standard and Premium databases. For each of these databases sizes backup retention is different with the basic size database supporting 7 days of retention, the standard size database supporting 14 days of retention and the premium size database supporting 35 days of backup retention.

The backups within Microsoft Azure SQL Database can be thought of like transaction log backups where point in time recovery is available for the databases. There are some limitations to what the Microsoft Azure SQL Database backups can do. For the most up to date information from Microsoft visit http://securingsqlserver.com/go/azure-backups.

REFERENCES

CNN. Citigroup Division Tells 3.9M Customers Personal Info Lost, Jun. 6, 2005. *Business, financial, personal finance news – CNNMoney.com.* June 5, 2005. Web. September 25, 2010. http://money.cnn.com/2005/06/06/news/fortune500/security_citigroup.

"Marsh and Mercer Report Lost Backup Tape (update 1) | Office of Inadequate Security." *Office of Inadequate Security.* June 12, 2010. Web. September 25, 2010. "SQL Server tools, Oracle tools, .NET developer tools, Email archiving tools—Red Gate Software." *SQL Server tools, Oracle tools, .NET developer tools, Email archiving tools—Red Gate Software.* n.d. Web. September 25, 2010.

Storage Area Network Security

11

INFORMATION IN THIS CHAPTER:

- Securing the array
- Securing the storage switches

Securing of the data does not end with the Windows server which runs the SQL Server service. It also includes properly securing the storage array and the storage area network. Because each storage array and switch vendor does things differently this chapter talks only about basic concepts instead of providing specific walk through information for specific platforms.

SECURING THE ARRAY

Data security does not end with the SQL Server service or the Windows OS. There are plenty of other ways that an intruder could access the data which is stored in your SQL Server database. One potential attack vector is the storage array itself. This can be done through a variety of techniques which include the following.

- Logging into the storage array
- Disks being presented to multiple servers
- Snapshots being presented to servers
- Accidental LUN (Logical Unit Number) deletion
- Accidental removing of LUNs
- Attacking the OS of the storage array

> **NOTE**
>
> **What Are All the Strange Terms in This Chapter?**
>
> This chapter is full of terms which are not specifically SQL Server related. During this chapter I will do my best to explain as many of these terms and concepts as possible, however some of them may simply be too complex to explain in a SQL Server book. I encourage you to talk to your storage and/or sysadmin team about these concepts so that you have a better understanding of these terms and concepts. There are online courses made available by companies like SSWUG (www.sswug.org) on their Virtual Conference site (www.vconference.com) which are designed specifically around teaching these storage concepts to database administrators.

> **NOTE**
>
> What is a LUN?
>
> While this is not a storage book, I wanted to explain what a LUN is. A LUN is a SAN term which describes the block of storage which has been carved up from the storage array and is to be presented to a server for use. While the way that LUNs are created is different for each storage array the concept of a LUN exists on every storage array. When the LUN is presented to Windows, Windows sees it as a blank disk which a partition is then created on. Within that partition a volume is then created and a drive letter assigned so that the disk can be used.

LOCKING DOWN THE MANAGEMENT PORTS

Storage arrays are simply powerful computers which have large amounts of storage connected to them (granted there is often some custom hardware in there). Storage arrays are configured in such a way that they can present storage to multiple servers, typically over a dedicated network. These networks can either use fiber channel or iSCSI in order to present the storage from the storage to the server. These storage arrays may run typical operating systems on them such as Windows or Linux or other more custom OSs such as Cisco's SAN-OS or FreeNAS. Older storage arrays did not have very strong storage authentication security or auditing capabilities built into them. Because of this it is highly recommended that the software which runs the storage array be kept up to date with the newest versions which are supported on the hardware platform. This will provide the greatest possible level of authentication by introducing more enhanced security processes into the storage arrays. This includes multiple storage admin roles allowing for logins which have minimal rights to the array such as read only rights, or security administrator rights where users only have the right to manage security but not the actual storage array itself.

While the storage arrays may run traditional operating systems on them, keeping this operating systems fully patched with the OS provided patches is typically not recommended. This because the storage vendor does not test every patch against their hardware. The only patches which should be installed on the storage array should be patches which have been approved by the storage array vendor. Typically the storage array vendor would publish the list of patches which can be installed via their website or bulletins which the vendor sends out. They only test specific builds of the operating system to be compliant with their hardware and software packages. Because of this it is recommended that the Ethernet ports which host the management of the storage array be configured on their own VLAN with access to connect to those ports limited to only the personal who need to manage the equipment and only via the specifically needed network ports. Many storage arrays are introducing integration features between the VMware vCenter server in virtualization environments which use the VMware platform. Due to this integration access between the vCenter server and the storage array would also be needed. While each storage array may need different TCP ports open between the administrators and the storage array typically the storage array communication is done over TCP ports 80 (http), 443 (https) and/or 22 (ssh).

> **STORY TIME**
>
> Yes, This Has Really Happened
>
> While it should go without saying that the storage array's management ports should not ever be connected to the public Internet with public IP addresses, I have seen it done which is why it is listed in here.
>
> I was doing some work with a client doing a SQL 2000 to SQL 2005 upgrade. They were not sure about what the configuration of the storage was, or if it was done correctly so they asked me to connect to the storage array. They told me that it was an EMC array and gave me two public IP addresses to connect to (one for each storage processor). When I logged into the storage array I took a look at what IP address the storage array thought that it had, and it was configured with the actual public IP address that I was connected to. In other words the very expensive EMC storage array was directly connected to the public Internet for all to attempt to connect to. I advised them that this was not the best idea from a security standpoint, which is when I noticed that the SQL Server also had a public IP address and was directly connected to the Internet.

Check with your storage array vendor to find out exactly which network ports are required to be opened for this software to function as expected.

Some storage arrays will run software on the servers which are connected to the servers to assist in the failover from one storage processor to another within the storage array. This software will need access to the storage array, typically via the management ports on specific TCP ports. These ports will need to be opened between the servers and the storage array, often in both directions. Consult with your storage vender to determine which TCP ports need to be opened and in which direction.

The management ports for the storage array should never be connected to the public Internet; no matter how much security is in place on the storage array.

AUTHENTICATION

Every administrator who needs access to the storage array should have their own login, preferably one which is tied directly to Active Directory. There is always a default login on the storage array, typically called admin, administrator, or root (the username may vary depending on the storage array vendor which you use) which should be secured with a very long, secure password and which should never be used. If possible the username for this account should be changed and recorded. This account should not be disabled, especially if all other accounts are using Active Directory for authentication because if there is a problem with using Active Directory for authentication you do not want to lose connectivity to the storage array.

USER ACCESS TO THE STORAGE ARRAY

It should go without saying that only currently employed systems administrators who are qualified to manage the storage array should have logins to the storage array. All accounts on the storage array should be either configured with very strong passwords, or preferably configured to use Active Directory logins so that the authentication is handled by the Windows Active Directory domain allowing for the logins to be disabled automatically when the employee leave the company. In the event that an employee who has rights to the storage array leaves the company their account should be immediately disabled to prevent any accidental logins to the storage array.

LOCKING DOWN THE ISCSI PORTS

If the storage array supports iSCSI then there are additional Ethernet ports which should be secured to prevent a potential attacker from attacking the iSCSI target on the storage array. The only TCP port which should need to be accessed on the iSCSI ports on the storage array is TCP ports 860 and 3260. Access to any ports besides this TCP port should be blocked from any computer on the network and access to any TCP network ports including ports 860 and 3260 should be blocked from any IP address which is not a computer on the iSCSI network. This includes admin workstations, other server IP addresses, etc. If possible the iSCSI network should be totally isolated with no network routes from the iSCSI network to the rest of the company network to prevent users from accessing the iSCSI ports of the servers or the storage, and to prevent any possible network flooding with the data from the iSCSI network.

Fiber Channel over Ethernet (FCoE) ports are not as susceptible to this sort of attack because they do not use traditional IP (Internet Protocol) Addresses on the FCoE ports like iSCSI ports do. While FCoE ports use the same kinds of Ethernet cables as iSCSI and traditional networking the data is transferred using the Fiber Channel protocol instead of using TCP (Transmission Control Protocol).

LUN SECURITY

LUNs should be configured in such a way that they can only be presented onto a single server (or cluster when using clustering) at a time. By default LUNs are presented to servers in read/write mode which allows the LUNs to be written to by the server. However it is possible to present LUNs to an additional server or servers where the other server(s) could have the LUN mounted as a read only LUN. This would allow this server to read all the files from the LUN without the source system knowing that this was happening. In the case of SQL Server database files which are normally locked for exclusive use by the SQL Server service, this locking would not be honored on the additional server(s) which had the LUNs mounted in read only mode as the OS of the additional server(s) would not know about the request to lock the files. This would allow someone who was logged into that LUN to copy the database files to another disk or server, or upload the files to their favorite file sharing site so that they could later attach the database files to a SQL Server instance and get the information from the database.

If LUNs were incorrectly mounted to multiple servers at once in read/write mode and more than one server attempted to write to the disks, which Windows will often do as soon as the drive is opened in the "My Computer" window, the file system on the LUN can become corrupt causing all the data which is on the LUN to instantly be lost.

Moving LUNs

Whenever a LUN is being moved from one server to another, extreme care must be taken to ensure that the LUN is only presented to one server at a time. It only takes a few seconds for the file system of a LUN to become corrupt and typically the only way to restore is from a full backup typically requiring hours of downtime.

Deleting LUNs

When a LUN is being removed from a server and the LUN is being deleted the storage administrator and the database administrator need to work together to ensure that only the correct LUN is removed and deleted. Whenever possible LUNs should be removed from the server and placed into a holding area for at least a couple of days to ensure that the correct LUN was removed before the LUN is deleted. This is because storage arrays do not have a recycle bin like Windows does. When the storage array is told to delete the LUN there is typically a single confirmation followed by the LUN being completely deleted. Once a LUN has been deleted the only way to recover the data would be from a backup.

SNAPSHOTS AND CLONES

Snapshots and clones should be carefully protected within the storage array. These virtual LUNs contain copies of the data from the source LUN and the snapshots and clones can be presented to other servers for reading and writing. This can lead to someone copying the data from the snapshot or clone without ever needing to touch the production LUNs. Snapshots and clones should only be kept around for as long as needed for space, performance and security reasons.

SECURING THE STORAGE SWITCHES

The storage switches which pass the storage network traffic should be secured to prevent someone from watching the storage traffic or reconfiguring the network switch to redirect a copy of the storage traffic to another machine. While this is easiest to do in iSCSI and Fiber Channel over Ethernet (FCoE) environments as in these cases the network traffic is using more traditional Ethernet switches, it is possible to do this in a traditional Fiber Channel environment.

> **NOTE**
>
> Snapshots, Virtual Snaps, Clones, Instant Snapshots, Virtual Clones, etc.
>
> Different vendors have different names for what I call clones and snapshots. In all cases, no matter the underlying technology the concepts are the same. What I call a snapshot is a point in time view of the source LUN. What I call a clone is a full copy of the source LUN. Clones can be kept in sync with their source LUN or the replication from the source LUN to the clone LUN can be broken or administratively fractured. No matter what they are called they run a security risk as they can be presented to another server.

FIBER CHANNEL

Within fiber channel networks the risk of an attacker viewing data which is being passed across the fiber channel switch is minimal as to do so the attacker would need to be able to physically connect a fiber optic cable to the fiber channel switch. If the attacker is able to get into the data center and connect a computer to the fiber channel switch using a fiber optic cable the attacker could configure the fiber channel switch for port mirroring. Like the name sounds port mirroring is a special configuration where every bit of data which is sent to the port which is being mirrored is duplicated and is also sent to the second port which was configured to be the mirror. Data capture software can then be run on the machine which is connected to the mirror port which would then receive and store all the data which is being sent to the port. An example of a network switch is shown in Figure 11.1 which shows a storage array connected to port 1 and port 2, and servers connected to ports 3, 4, 5, and 6. The attacker then connects to the network switch and configures port 3 to be mirrored to port 10 which the attacker has connected a laptop to.

In the configuration shown in Figure 11.1 the attacker would see all reads and writes which were made between the SQL Server connected to port 3 and the storage array which is connected to ports 1 and 2.

iSCSI

iSCSI network traffic is a little easier to intercept than fiber channel traffic by an attacker. While the attack vector is the same, using port mirroring, Ethernet switches have had port mirroring for a much longer period of time. In additional to this it may be less suspicious looking within the data center to have a laptop connected to a network switch than it would to a fiber channel switch.

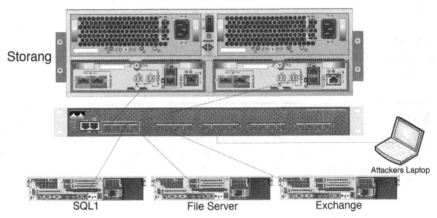

FIGURE 11.1 Showing a fiber channel switch.

There are some Ethernet switches which have implemented a virtual Ethernet port which can be used for port mirroring which would then allow the attacker to not need to be physically connected to the network switch in order to configure the port mirroring. The virtual Ethernet port would then be configured to redirect the network traffic to a different IP address on the network, potentially allowing the attacker to place the device anywhere on the network, possibly even on the Internet at another site if the virtual port was configured to route the network traffic to a public IP address.

Because iSCSI uses TCP as the protocol for the data transfer between the server and the storage array, any TCP data capture application can be used on the attackers computer to capture the iSCSI traffic from the mirrored port and safe it to disk.

FIBER CHANNEL OVER ETHERNET

Capturing Fiber Channel over Ethernet (FCoE) is the hardest method of exchange to capture data. While the same port mirroring which can be used to capture iSCSI traffic is possible Fiber Channel over Ethernet traffic is not transferred by TCP like the iSCSI traffic is. There for the data being transferred by the fiber channel protocol cannot be simply rerouted like the iSCSI traffic can. Instead the same kind of fiber channel capture software that would be used for a fiber channel switch must be used, and the device must be directly connected to the FCoE switch. Because Fiber Channel over Ethernet is not a routable protocol there would also be no need to connect the Fiber Channel over Ethernet switches to the rest of the routable network which would also cause the attacker to need physical access to the network switches in order to connect and capture the data.

MANAGEMENT PORTS

No matter the technology to get from the servers to the storage array, the switches which handle the transport will have management ports. These management ports should be isolated from the rest of the network with only the users who need to manage the switches having access to the network ports. This access can be blocked at the switch level through the use of Access Control Lists (ACLs) or via a firewall between the subnets which the general company users are on and the subnet which the management ports for the switches are connected to. Like the storage array management ports these ports should not be connected to the public internet.

AUTHENTICATION

Ever administrator who needs access to the switches which carry the storage traffic should have their own login, preferably one which is tied directly to Active Directory. There is always a default login on the switches, typically called admin, administrator, or root (the username may vary depending on the switch vendor which you use) which should be secured with a very long, secure password and which should never be used. If possible the username for this account should be changed and recorded. This account should not be disabled, especially if all other accounts are using Active Directory for authentication as if there is a problem with using Active Directory for authentication you do not want to lose connectivity to the network switches.

ZONE MAPPING

The zone mapping or zone configuration files are what tell fiber channel switches which ports are allowed to talk to which ports within the fiber channel storage area network. These zone files should be backed up and stored in a location other than the default location within the switches in the event that an attacker was to break into the switches and damage or erase the zone configuration. Without the zone file the fiber channel switch would have no idea which servers were allowed to talk to which servers and would prevent all traffic within the switch. Having a backup of the zone file stored outside of the switch would allow for this mapping to be quickly put back in place after an attack.

SUMMARY

There are a variety of attack vectors which an attacker can use to gain access to data or to cause problems within the storage environment. This includes attacking both the storage array as well as the switches which pass the traffic from the servers to the storage array. While using encryption (as talked about in Chapter 2) can make any data which was captured useless, if an attacker can get into the system to gather data they can get into the system to reconfigure the system to prevent reads and writes from functioning as expected causing major system downtime which can be very hard to troubleshoot.

Auditing for Security

12

INFORMATION IN THIS CHAPTER:

- Login auditing
- Data modification auditing
- Data querying auditing
- Schema change auditing
- Using policy-based management to ensure policy compliance
- C2 auditing
- Common criteria compliance

Setting security policies is a great start, but you need to ensure that the system remains secure. This is where auditing comes into play. Auditing by itself is not good enough; someone needs to review the auditing information that has been collected in order to ensure that the system has remained as secure as expected. This includes monitoring the logins into the database, the data that has been changed, and any changes to the schema.

As you move from the newer versions of Microsoft SQL Server into older versions of the product, there are fewer and fewer auditing features available to you. Microsoft really began putting auditing features into the SQL Server product starting with Microsoft SQL Server 2008. Prior to SQL Server 2008, the auditing options are very limited and have to be mostly done through third-party products or homegrown systems.

NOTE

Auditing in SQL Azure

At the time of this writing, if you are working with an SQL Azure database, none of the auditing options discussed in this chapter are available to you. Hopefully, the SQL Azure team will be able to include auditing features into the product in the future.

Do keep in mind that in any book about SQL Azure, including this one, information about SQL Azure can get out of date very quickly as the SQL Azure product is a constantly moving target. This is because the SQL Azure team releases new versions of the database engine every few months so what you see here may not be relevant after the Fall of 2014.

LOGIN AUDITING

Login auditing in SQL Server falls into two categories: SQL Server 2005 and prior and SQL Server 2008 and newer. SQL Server 2005 and older only provides very basic information, and that information is written to the SQL Server ER-RORLOG file and to the Windows Application log. The only configuration option is to enable login failure logging, successful login logging, logging of both successful and failed logins, or logging of neither. SQL Server 2008 and newer allow for a much more granular level of auditing controlled through "Server Audit Specifications."

SQL SERVER 2005 AND OLDER

In the older auditing version, a change was made between SQL Server 2000 and SQL Server 2005. While this was a relatively small change, it is a very important one. The change was to include the source IP Address that was attempting to log into the database engine. Before the change to the login auditing specification, the logged messages looked like that shown in Example 12.1, while the post-change audit message looks like that shown in Example 12.2.

EXAMPLE 12.1

Sample auditing information for a successful login into an SQL Server 2000 or order instance.

```
2010-09-06 18:50:01.28 Logon Login succeeded for user 'DOMAIN\UserName'.
Connection made using Windows authentication.
```

EXAMPLE 12.2

Sample auditing information for a successful login into an SQL Server 2005 or newer instance.

```
2010-09-06 18:50:01.28 Logon Login succeeded for user 'DOMAIN\UserName'.
Connection made using Windows authentication. [CLIENT: 10.3.30.84]
```

Changing the auditing level setting for the SQL Server instance is most easily done through the Enterprise Manager or SQL Server Management Studio (depending on the version you are using) as the setting is controlled via a registry key. When using Enterprise Manager, connect to the server and right click on the server and select properties. When using SQL Server Management Studio, connect to the server in the object explorer and select properties. Regardless of which version is used,

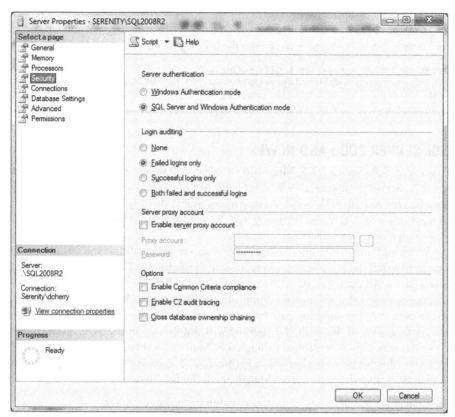

FIGURE 12.1 The security tab of the server properties dialog from the 2008 R2 version of the SQL Server Management Studio.

then select the Security tab. Next look for the "Login auditing" section in the dialog box. Here you can select from None, failed only, successful only, or both failed and successful, as shown in Figure 12.1. While the screenshot shown in Figure 12.1 is from Microsoft SQL Server 2008 R2s Management Studio, the dialog from SQL Server 7 and 2000s Enterprise Manager looks very similar to the one shown.

If you want to change this setting via T-SQL, you will need to use the xp_instance_regwrite system stored procedure to do this passing in an integer, which defines what the setting should be set to as shown in Example 12.3. A setting of 1 indicates that successful login only should be logged. A setting of 2 indicates that failed logins only should be logged. A setting of 3 indicates that both successful and failed logins should be logged. A setting of 0 indicates that neither failed nor successful logins should be logged.

No matter if you change this setting via T-SQL or the management tool, a restart of the SQL Instance is required before the setting change will take effect.

EXAMPLE 12.3

Sample T-SQL code: how to change the logging level.

```
EXEC xp_instance_regwrite N'HKEY_LOCAL_MACHINE',
N'Software\Microsoft\MSSQLServer\MSSQLServer', N'AuditLevel', REG_DWORD, 2
GO
```

SQL SERVER 2008 AND NEWER

Starting in SQL Server 2008, Microsoft introduced SQL Server Audit, which allows the SQL Server to capture a wide variety of information into audit files. The files can then be viewed with SQL Server Management Studio directly, or they can be loaded in mass into a central repository using SQL Server Integration Services for long-term storage, querying, and trending.

When auditing information using the new server-side auditing specification, you first need to tell the SQL Server where to store the audit log. This is done by defining a new audit. An audit can be written to a file on the SQL Server's local hard drive, a network share, to the Windows Application Log, or to the Windows System Log. In the event that the audit log gets full, one of two things will happen; depending on the configuration of the audit, the auditing will simply stop or the SQL Instance will be shut down. This is controlled through the "Shut down server on audit log failure" checkbox that is shown unchecked in Figure 12.2. The easiest way to create an audit is to do so within the SQL Server Management Studio. To do so:

1. Connect to the SQL Server Instance within the object explorer.
2. Navigate to Security.
3. Navigate to the Audits folder under Security.
4. Right click on Audits and select "New Audit" from the context menu which pops up.

In the Create Audit screen that opens, give the audit a name, specify the queue delay in milliseconds, and select the audit destination as shown in Figure 12.2. Using a delay of 0 milliseconds indicates that the audit data should be written synchronously to the disk as the commands are executed.

Like all new features with Microsoft SQL Server, you can also create an audit using T-SQL. This is done by using the CREATE SERVER AUDIT command. The command creates the same server audit destination that is created from within SQL Server Management Studio as shown in Example 12.4.

EXAMPLE 12.4

Creating a server audit using the CREATE SERVER AUDIT statement in T-SQL.

```
CREATE SERVER AUDIT [Login Audit]
TO FILE
```

```
(FILEPATH = N'D:\Program Files\Microsoft SQL
Server\MSSQL10_50.MSSQLSERVER\MSSQL\Log'
'MAXSIZE = 0 MB
'MAX_ROLLOVER_FILES = 2147483647
'RESERVE_DISK_SPACE = OFF
)
WITH
( QUEUE_DELAY = 1000
'ON_FAILURE = CONTINUE
)
GO
```

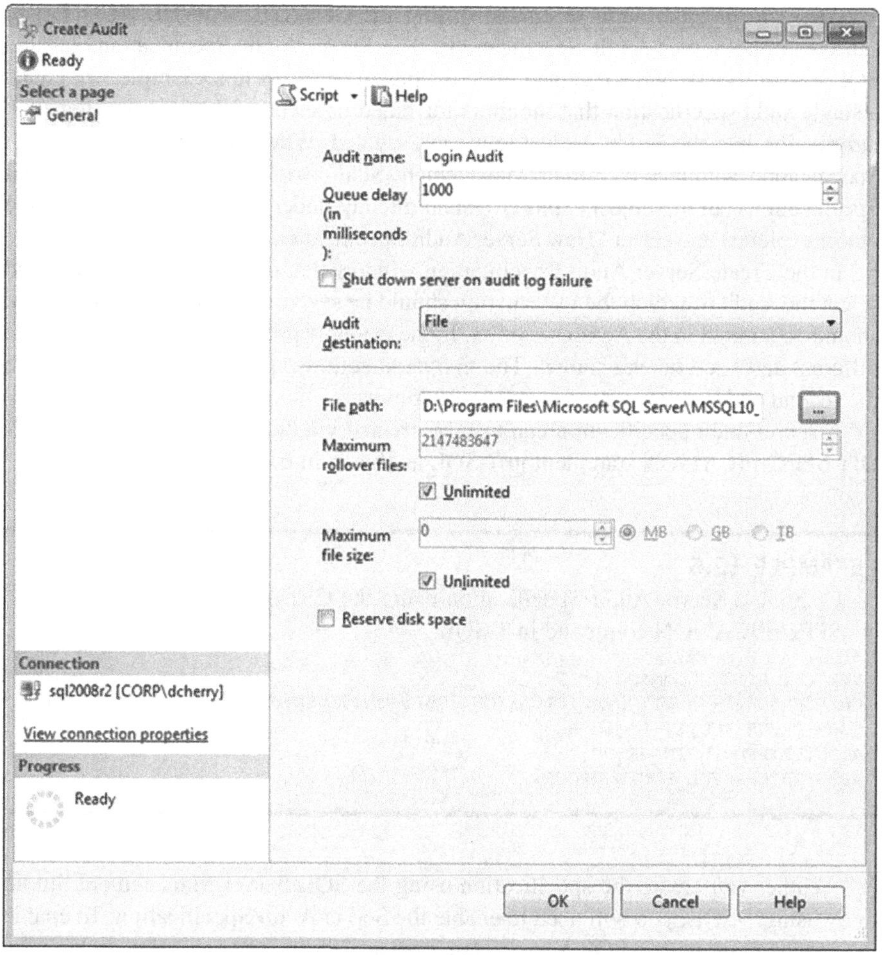

FIGURE 12.2 The filled out Create Audit screen creating a new audit file in SQL Server.

Weather you create the audit using SQL Server Management Studio or T-SQL, you need to enable the audit. You can do this either by right clicking on the Audit within the object explorer and selecting "Enable Audit" or by using the ALTER SERVER AUDIT statement in T-SQL as shown in Example 12.5.

EXAMPLE 12.5

Enabling a server audit using the ALTER SERVER AUDIT statement.

```
ALTER SERVER AUDIT [Login Audit]
WITH (STATE = ON)
GO
```

After creating the audit destination using the CREATE SERVER AUDIT, you can create the Server Audit Specifications. The Server Audit Specifications tell the SQL Server exactly what instance wide actions to audit. In this example, we create a single audit specification that monitors for failed or successful logins and logs that information into the Login Audit file we just created. When creating a Server Audit Specification within SQL Server Management Studio, right click on "Server Audit Specifications" in the object explorer (found directly under the "Audits" folder in the object explorer) and select "New Server Audit Specification."

In the Create Server Audit Specification window that opens, name the audit and select the Audit to which the information should be saved, as well as the actions that should be audited in the Actions section. In the example presented in Figure 12.3 two different audit actions are shown. The first audit action captures failed logins, while the second audit action captures successful logins.

A server audit specification can also be created via the CREATE SERVER AUDIT SPECIFICATION statement in T-SQL as shown in Example 12.6.

EXAMPLE 12.6

Creating a Server Audit Specification using the CREATE SERVER AUDIT SPECIFICATION command in T-SQL.

```
SPECIFICATION command in T-SQL.
CREATE SERVER AUDIT SPECIFICATION [ServerAuditSpecification-LoginAudit]
FOR SERVER AUDIT [Login Audit]
ADD (FAILED_LOGIN_GROUP),
ADD (SUCCESSFUL_LOGIN_GROUP)
```

Weather you create the specification using the SQL Server Management Studio or by using T-SQL, you will need to enable the Server Audit Specification. To enable the specification within SQL Server Management Studio, you can right click on the

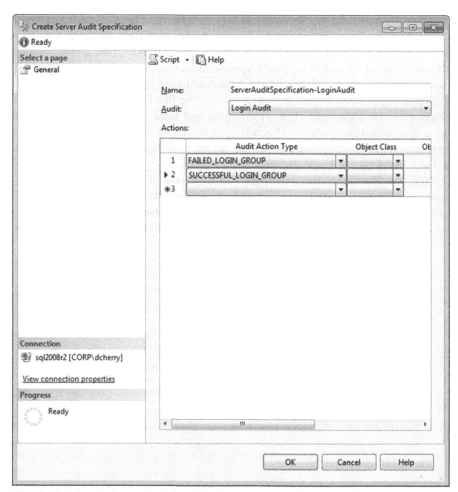

FIGURE 12.3 Create Server Audit Specification screen capturing both failed and successful logins and writing the data to the "Login Audit" audit file.

specification and select "Enable Server Audit Specification" from the context menu. To enable the specification using T-SQL, you can use the ALTER SERVER AUDIT SPECIFICATION statement as shown in Example 12.7.

EXAMPLE 12.7

Enabling a Server Audit Specification using T-SQL.

```
ALTER SERVER AUDIT SPECIFICATION [ServerAuditSpecification-LoginAudit]
WITH (STATE=ON)
```

Once the Audit and the Server Audit Specification have been enabled and a user logs into the database, instance data will begin being logged into the Audit file. If the Server Audit Specification is enabled but the Audit is disabled, then no information will be collected for any of the Audit Specifications which are writing to that Audit. Both the Server Audit Specification and the Audit need to be enabled for data collection to begin. To view the information within the file, locate the Audit within the object explorer. Then right click on the Audit and select "View Audit Logs" from the context menu that pops up. This will open the log file viewer reading the log file information into the grid for easy viewing, filtering, sorting, and searching, as shown in Figure 12.4.

You can also query the data using a T-SQL statement by using the fn_get_audit_file function as shown in Example 12.8. The guide shown in the file path can be found in the audit_guid column of the sys.server_audits system catalog view. The guide shown in your database will be different from that shown in Example 12.8.

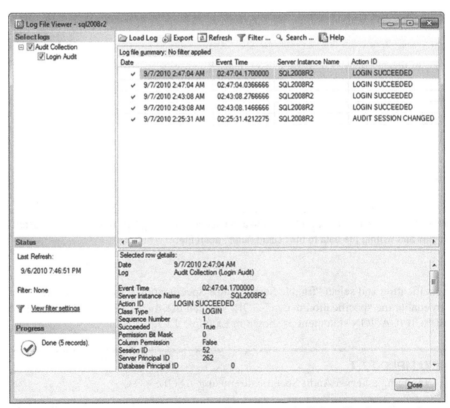

FIGURE 12.4 Showing the audit log for the Audit and Server Audit Specification shown in Figures 12.2 and 12.3.

EXAMPLE 12.8

T-SQL code to view the audit information from the specified audit log.

```
select TOP(1000) *
from fn_get_audit_file('D:\Program Files\Microsoft SQL
Server\MSSQL10_50.MSSQLSERVER\MSSQL\Log\*_3fb9ea26-29c9-408c-a7bb-
eb27371ac3d8*',null,null)
order by event_time desc,sequence_number
```

When looking at the output from the fn_get_audit_file system function, the columns of importance are the succeed column, which tells you if the action (in this case a login attempt) was successful; the server_principal_name, which tells you the login name that was used to connect; and the additional_information column, which contains an XML document that has a variety of information in it including the IP Address from which the user was attempting to connect. If the login was not successful, the server_principal_name may be NULL depending on the cause of the login failure, as the login may not have been transmitted to the server.

In the case of login audit information, there will be two different values in the action_id column. These are LGIS and LGIF, where LGIS is for a successful login attempt and LGIF is for a failed login attempt.

After the Auditing Specifications have been created, they can be modified using either the user interface or the ALTER SERVER AUDIT SPECIFICATION T-SQL statement. In order to make changes to a Server Audit Specification, the Audit Specification must be disabled using the ALTER SERVER AUDIT SPECIFICATION.

NOTE

Ways to Gather Server Audit Data

As the Server Audit data is easily accessed through the fn_get_audit_file system function, the information can be collected into a central repository fairly easily, which would then allow for centralized reporting and management of the audit information. A side benefit of moving the audit information into a central repository is that the information can be more easily secured in this central repository and then it can be on the server's local hard drive. The reason for this is that in order for the SQL Server to write the audit files, it needs to modify access to the files in the folder which stores the files. Now someone who did not want the audit information to be found could use xp_cmdshell to easily delete the files from the folder using code similar to "exec xp_cmdshell 'del c:\My\Path\To\My\Audit\Files /S /Q".

The data can be moved from the audit log through just about any method one would like. Among these methods is moving data through a linked server after a job gets the newest data from the audit log. Another technique could be to use SQL Server Integration Services (SSIS) to query the data from the source server and transfer it to the destination server, pulling out the needed information from the additional_information column. When moving auditing information to a central repository, it is extremely important to be sure to include the original values from the audit without making any modification. This way the extracted information can always be compared to the original information within the repository to verify that the information has not been modified.

Then the changes can be made, and the Server Audit Specification can be enabled, allowing it to begin capturing data again as shown in Example 12.9.

EXAMPLE 12.9

The T-SQL code to disable a Server Audit Specification, changing the specification, then enabling the specification, allowing it to begin capturing data.

```
ALTER SERVER AUDIT SPECIFICATION [ServerAuditSpecification-LoginAudit]
WITH (STATE = OFF)
GO
ALTER SERVER AUDIT SPECIFICATION [ServerAuditSpecification-LoginAudit]
DROP (SUCCESSFUL_LOGIN_GROUP)
GO
ALTER SERVER AUDIT SPECIFICATION [ServerAuditSpecification-LoginAudit]
WITH (STATE = ON)
GO
```

One very important item that needs to be audited is any change to the auditing, in order to ensure that the auditing has not been disabled and to allow unaudited changes to be made to the data within the database. Without auditing the configuration of the Auditing, there is no way to guarantee that the auditing configuration today is the same as it was yesterday.

USING xEVENTS FOR AUDITING LOGINS

One of the features introduced in SQL Server 2008 is the Extended Events features, also called xEvents. Extended Events are system level events which are triggered when specific things happen within the SQL Server database engine. The variety of things which can be monitored by Extended Events is very large, and will not be covered here in its entirety. One of the things which Extended Events can monitor for is for logins to the database engine.

The beauty of the Extended Events system is that the event is logged before it is allowed to be completed. So for example if we wanted to create an Extended Event session which would allow us to capture login information to the SQL Server we

---

NOTE

Auditing the Auditing

When you audit your auditing configuration, the SQL Server will successfully audit the changes to all the auditing specifications on the server, with the exception of the auditing specification that is auditing the auditing. When the Audit Specification is disabled to allow a change, this will be the last line audited by the Audit Specification. When the specification is enabled, this will not be logged, nor will any of the changes made to the Audit Specification that is auditing changes to the Auditing.

> **NOTE**
>
> More about xEvents
>
> You can read more about Extended Events in the great book Mastering SQL Server 2012 Extended Events by Jonathon Kehayias.

would know that all the successful login attempts are being captured as the SQL Server will trigger Extended Events to capture the information before the login is allowed to complete.

Capturing Login Information

Due to the flexibility of extended events we can capture a great deal of information about the person logging into the SQL Server instance. This includes the application which they are using (as specified by the application_name parameter of the connection string) the client machine name, the ANSI settings they are using, the ID number of the database they are connecting to, if they are using the Dedicated Admin Connection (DAC) to connect as well as the time which they connected. The T-SQL used to create the Extended Event is shown in Example 12.10.

> **EXAMPLE 12.10**
>
> Creating an Extended Events session to monitor successful logins to the Microsoft SQL Server Instance.

```
CREATE EVENT SESSION login_event
ON SERVER
ADD EVENT sqlserver.login(SET collect_options_text=(1)
   ACTION(sqlserver.client_app_name,sqlserver.client_connection_id,
sqlserver. client_hostname,
      sqlserver.context_info,sqlserver.server_instance_name,sqlserver.
server_principal_name))

ADD TARGET package0.asynchronous_file_target
   (SET FILENAME = N'c:\xEvents\Logins.xel', METADATAFILE =
N'c:\xEvents\Logins.xem')
WITH (EVENT_RETENTION_MODE = ALLOW_MULTIPLE_EVENT_LOSS)
GO
ALTER EVENT SESSION login_event
ON SERVER
STATE=start
GO
```

In addition to logging successful logins to the system, you may wish to also monitor logoffs as part of the same Extended Events session. This way you would have an audit trail which shows when a user connected and when they disconnected providing proof that they were (or were not) using the system. Adding the logoff auditing to the session would require simply adding a second ADD EVENT section to the T-SQL shown in Example 12.10, as shown in Example 12.11.

EXAMPLE 12.11

Monitoring all logins and logouts via Extended Events.

```
CREATE EVENT SESSION login_event
ON SERVER
ADD EVENT sqlserver.login(SET collect_options_text=(1)
    ACTION(sqlserver.client_app_name,sqlserver.client_connection_id,
sqlserver.client_hostname,
            sqlserver.context_info,sqlserver.server_instance_name,
sqlserver.server_principal_name)),
ADD EVENT sqlserver.logout(
    ACTION(sqlserver.client_app_name,sqlserver.client_connection_id,
sqlserver.client_hostname,
            sqlserver.context_info,sqlserver.server_instance_name,
sqlserver.server_principal_name))
ADD TARGET package0.asynchronous_file_target
    (SET FILENAME = N'c:\xEvents\Logins.xel', METADATAFILE =
N'c:\xEvents\Logins.xem')
WITH (EVENT_RETENTION_MODE = ALLOW_MULTIPLE_EVENT_LOSS)
GO
ALTER EVENT SESSION login_event
ON SERVER
STATE=start
GO
```

In addition to the values included in Example 12.10 and Example 12.11 there are a lot of other values which can be captured depending on the needs of the audit. Some other values which can be captured are shown in Table 12.1. The values shown in Table 12.1 are not an exhaustive list of items which can be captured.

Event Loss Settings

You will notice in Example 12.10 and Example 12.11 that the EVENT_RETEN-TION_MODE is configured for ALLOW_MULTIPLE_EVENT LOSS. It is important to know what this setting means when configuring events for auditing. The EVENT_RETENTION_MODE setting tells the Extended Event session what should happen to the calling command if the event is not able to be written to the Extended Events logs due to system load. If the setting is set for ALLOW_MULTIPLE_EVENT_LOSS like it is in Example 12.10 and Example 12.11 then logins would be allowed to continue even if the event could not be logged. If the setting is configured for the value ALLOW_SINGLE_EVENT_LOSS than only a single event at a time could be dropped while succeeding causing any other events that could not be logged during the same stretch of time when the system was overloaded to fail if they cannot be logged. The third setting of NO_EVENT_LOSS means that the event must

Table 12.1 A List of Some of the Values Which Can be Captured by an Extended Event Which is Monitoring Logins

Name	Description
client_app_name	Name of the client application which is connecting
client_connection_id	ID of the connection by the client
client_hostname	The hostname of the connecting computer
collect_system_time	The system time when the login was attempted with 100 micro-second precision and interrupt tick resolution
database_id	The ID of the database which the user is connecting to
database_name	The name of the database which the user is connection to
is_system	If the connection is a system process or a user process
nt_username	The Windows NT username of the connection user
numa_node_id	The NUMA node which the user connection was processed by
process_id	The Windows process ID
server_instance_name	The name of the SQL Server instance which handled the login
server_principal_name	The name of the Service Principal which handled the login
server_principal_sid	The SID of the Service Principal which handled the login

always be logged. When doing critical auditing the NO_EVENT_LOSS audit might be the one which you select, however doing so may cause system issues if the system becomes overloaded as the users would not be able to log into the database engine if the system became too busy.

Typically it would be recommended to not configure a login audit via Extended Events with NO_EVENT_LOSS unless the Extended Event was configured for a specific user. Starting with SQL Server 2012, the event session supports adding WHERE clauses to the event creation instead of just the viewing of the captured data. This is done by adding WHERE clauses to each of the ACTION sections of the CREATE EVENT SESSION statement as shown in Example 12.12.

EXAMPLE 12.12

Creating an Extended Event session to monitor a single user's logins.

```
CREATE EVENT SESSION login_event
ON SERVER
ADD EVENT sqlserver.login(SET collect_options_text=(1)
   ACTION(sqlserver.client_app_name,sqlserver.client_connection_id,
sqlserver.client_hostname,
               sqlserver.context_info,sqlserver.server_instance_name,
sqlserver.server_principal_name)
      WHERE sqlserver.nt_user = 'CAPT-MAL\dcherry'),
ADD EVENT sqlserver.logout(
   ACTION(sqlserver.client_app_name,sqlserver.client_connection_id,
```

```
sqlserver.client_hostname,
                sqlserver.context_info,sqlserver.server_instance_name,
sqlserver.server_principal_name)
        WHERE sqlserver.nt_user = 'CAPT-MAL\dcherry')
ADD TARGET package0.asynchronous_file_target
    (SET FILENAME = N'c:\xEvents\Logins.xel', METADATAFILE =
N'c:\xEvents\Logins.xem')
WITH (EVENT_RETENTION_MODE = ALLOW_MULTIPLE_EVENT_LOSS)
GO
ALTER EVENT SESSION login_event
ON SERVER
STATE=start
GO
```

When monitoring just a single users as shown in Example 12.12 use of the NO_
EVENT_LOSS setting is much safer as a single user should not be attempting to log
into the database that often and because the other users logins would not be triggering the event to begin with there should be no risk of the login failing due to not being
able to log the event.

Viewing Login Audits

Viewing data which has been captured by extended events is done through T-SQL by
using the fn_xe_file_target_read_file system function as shown in Example 12.13.
This function will return no data until the Extended Event capture listed above has
been configured, started, and data has been captured by it.

EXAMPLE 12.13

Querying the captured login and logoff data using sys.fn_xe_file_target_
read_file.

```
SELECT data.value('(event/@name)[1]', 'varchar(30)') Event,
        data.value('(event/action[1])[1]', 'varchar(max)') [UserName],
        data.value('(event/action[2])[1]', 'varchar(max)') [HostName],
        data.value('(event/action[6])[1]', 'varchar(max)') [ApplicationName],
        data.value('(event/data[6])[1]', 'varchar(max)') [ANSI_Settings],
        data.value('(event/@timestamp)[1]', 'datetime') EventDate
FROM
    (SELECT CONVERT (XML, event_data) AS data FROM sys.fn_xe_file_target_read_file
        ('c:\xEvents\Logins*.xel', 'c:\xEvents\Logins*.xem', NULL, NULL)
    ) entries
order by data.value('(event/@timestamp)[1]', 'datetime') desc
GO
```

There would be no need to use extended events on a SQL Server instance which is
already configured to monitor for logins and logoff by using the Server Audit Specifications discussed earlier in this chapter. This is because Server Audit Specifications

use Extended Events under the covers to handle the monitoring and data collection, so using both Server Audit Specifications and Extended Events on the same system would be rather pointless as the same information would be audited twice. Both options are available to the database administrator so that they can make the decision as to which option is better for their specific situation.

AUDITING SYSADMIN DOMAIN GROUP MEMBERSHIP

Another potential area which can be exploited by people wishing to grant themselves membership to the System Administrators fixed server role is by attacking Active Directory directly. Typically all the people who would need to be members of the System Administrators fixed server role (which would typically be the Database Administrators) have all their domain accounts placed into a single domain group then that domain group is simply added to the System Administrators fixed server role on each of the SQL Server instances.

While this process makes it very easy to give new Database Administrators and Database Consultants admin rights to the SQL Server there is an inherent risk to this as well. Any account who is not a supposed to be a member of that group but is will also be a member of the System Administrators fixed server role on the SQL Server instances. Because the SQL Server does not control the membership of this domain group, SQL Server itself cannot audit the membership of this group. This means that the group membership should be audited manually on a regular basis to ensure that the group membership has not changed.

In addition to this, the domain group which is used to grant membership to the System Administrator fixed server role should be secured so that the only people who can add or remove members from this domain group are the domain admins. Typically, especially in larger companies, groups other than Windows Administration team, such as the internal Help Desk, would handle Active Directory group changes. While this is normally a fine procedure to have in place, there are some domain groups which these other teams do not have access to so that they are unable to give themselves higher level privileges. By default these would include domain groups like the Domain Admins, Enterprise Admins, etc. The domain group which grants sysadmin rights to the SQL Servers should be treated like another high level permissions group along the same lines as the Domain Admins and Enterprise Admins groups. By having support personal other than the Domain Admins granting membership to this group presents an unacceptable risk of someone being put into the sysadmin fixed server role either by accident or on purpose.

The simple fact is that the people in the Help Desk or another group which have permissions to manage the bulk of the Active Directory security groups are probably lower level staff. These lower level staff while a trusted group of employees are typically paid less, have less experience, and are not given the keys to the entire enterprise. They therefore should not have the ability to grant themselves or anyone else, either by accident or on purpose, administrative level rights to the SQL Servers within the enterprise.

DATA MODIFICATION AUDITING

Auditing of Data Modification in versions of Microsoft SQL Server 2008 and older is much harder to do because it all needs to be done manually. Microsoft SQL Server 2008 R2 introduced the Change Data Capture (CDC) feature to the product. Once configured, CDC is used to capture all insert, update, and delete activity that occurs on the tables in question.

Adding any auditing to the database will increase the CPU load by some extent as additional work is being performed by the database engine. To keep this increase to the minimum, only audit the information required so as to reduce the performance impact on the database engine. The amount of additional load that will be added to the database by enabling Change Data Capture will depend on a variety of things, including the number of transactions per second and the number of columns that are being changed within each transaction.

CHANGE DATA CAPTURE CONFIGURATION

Before you can use Change Data Capture, it must be enabled on both the database that is to be monitored and the specific tables within the database that are to be tracked. CDC is enabled on a specific database using the sys.sp_cdc_enable_db system stored procedure as shown in Example 12.14. Change Data Capture is disabled by using the sys.sp_cdc_disable_db system stored procedure.

EXAMPLE 12.14

Enabling Change Data Capture on the MyDatabase database.

```
use MyDatabase
GO
EXEC sp_cdc_enable_db
GO
```

When the sys.sp_cdc_enable_db system stored procedure is run, a new user will be created within the database with the name cdc, as will a new schema named cdc, which will hold the Change Data Capture tables. The tables that are created are as follows.

1. cdc.captured_columns, which contains one row for each column in each table that is being tracked.
2. cdc.change_tables, which contains one row for each table being tracked.
3. cdc.ddl_history, which contains the schema modification changes to the tables that are being tracked.
4. cdc.index_columns, which contains one row for each index column within the tables that are being tracked.

5. cdc.lsn_time_mapping, which contains one row for each transaction that has rows in a table being tracked. This is used to map the time transactions that are logged to the specific log sequence number (LSN) that logged the change. There may be rows in this table when there are no changes, which allows for the completion of LSN processing in time periods of low or no user activity.

After Change Data Capture has been enabled for the database, it can then configure Change Data Capture for the specific tables that need to be tracked. This is done using the sys.sp_cdc_enable_table system stored procedure. The stored procedure sys.sp_cdc_enable_table has nine parameters, but only three of them are required. These required parameters are as follows.

1. @source_schema, which is the schema of the table to be tracked.
2. @source_name, which is the object name (without the schema) of the table to be tracked.
3. @role_name, which is the name of a database security role that will be created if it does not already exist. This role can be ignored, or it can be used to assign permissions to users so that they can access the data that Change Data Capture has captured. Multiple captured tables can use the same role, but any user who is a member of this role will have access to read the captured data for all those tables.

The six optional parameters for the sys.sp_cdc_enable_table system stored procedure are as follows.

1. @capture_instance, which is the name that will be used to capture the change data for this specific table. If not specified, the system will auto generate a name based on the values of the @source_schema and @source_name parameters.
2. @supports_net_changes, which indicates whether the captured data should support querying for net changes in addition to row-level changes. If this parameter is set to 0, then the functions that support this querying are not created. If this parameter is set to 1, which is the default, then the functions that support this querying are created.
3. @index_name, which indicates the name of the unique index that can be used to uniquely identify the rows within the source table. If the @index_name value is included, the specified index takes precedence over the defined primary key columns as the unique identifier that Change Data Capture uses.

> **NOTE**
> CDC Must be Enabled at the Database First
> If you do not enable Change Data Capture at the database level before you attempt to enable it at the table level, SQL Server will throw error message 22901. This message informs you to enable CDC on the database before attempting to enable it on the table.

4. @captured_column_list, which indicates what columns within the specified table should be tracked. If not included, all columns are tracked. The column list is a comma-separated list of columns and can be quoted using double quotes ("") or square brackets ([]) as needed. If a column list is specified, then all columns that are included in the primary key (or the index specified by the @index_name parameter) must be specified.
5. @filegroup_name, which is the filegroup where the Change Data Capture tables should be created. If not specified or if a NULL value is passed in, then the default file group will be used.
6. @allow_partition_switch, which tells the SQL Server if the SWITCH PARTITION command of the ALTER TABLE statement can be executed against the monitored table. If the value is set to 0 (the default is 1) and the table is partitioned, data cannot be moved between partitions. This is done to ensure that CDC data matches the actual data in the table. The SWITCH PARTITION command of the ALTER TABLE statement will move data between partitions, but this change is not logged by Change Data Capture. Thus data captured will not match the source table data if data is moved from one partition to another.

Enabling Change Data Capture to capture all changes on all columns can be easily done using just the first three parameters – @source_schema, @source_name, and @role_name, as shown in Example 12.15.

EXAMPLE 12.15
Enabling Change Data Capture for the table dbo.MyTable with the role name cdc_MyTable.

```
exec sys.sp_cdc_enable_table @source_schema='dbo',
@source_name='MyTable',
@role_name='cdc_MyTable'
```

QUERYING CHANGED DATA

Querying data from the Change Data Capture tables is done through a system of table-valued functions. For each table being tracked by CDC, a function whose name starts with "cdc.fn_cdc_get_all_changes_" and ends with the name of the capture instance as specified by the @capture_instance parameter (or the @source_schema and @source_name parameters if the @capture_instance parameter is not specified) of the sys.sp_cdc_enable_table system stored procedure.

If the @supports_net_changes parameter of the sys.sp_cdc_enable_table system stored procedure was set to 1 (or true), then a table-valued function whose name starts with "cdc.fn_cdc_get_net_changes_" and ends with the name of the capture instance as specified by the @capture_instance parameter (or the @source_schema and @source_name parameters if the @capture_instance parameter is not specified) of the sys.sp_cdc_enable_table system stored procedure will also be created. This "cdc.fn_cdc_get_net_changes_" function allows the user to query for the net changes instead of the individual changes.

Querying these table-valued functions requires use of the cdc.lsn_time_mapping system table. This table will show the transaction log LSN and will map it to the system time that the LSN was logged. These LSNs must be used to pass into the table values functions as the first two parameters. Both table-valued functions require three parameters:

1. from_lsn is the first LSN to process.
2. to_lsn is the last LSN to process.
3. filter_option accepts one of two values "all," which returns all values within the LSNs, or "all update old," which returns both the old and new values for each row. The "all update old" value will return twice as many rows as the "all" option, as the "all update old" returns one row for the old value and one for the new value.

The easiest way to get the needed data from the cdc.lsn_time_mapping table is to use the system functions sys.fn_cdc_get_min_lsn and sys.fn_cdc_get_max_lsn. The min_lsn function accepts a single parameter, which is the name of the capture instance that is specified when creating the capture and the function returns the minimum stored LSN for that table. The max_lsn function does not accept any parameters and returns the most recent LSN for the database. These functions are used in conjunction with the cdc.fn_cdc_get_all_changes and cdc.fn_cdc_get_net_changes functions.

EXAMPLE 12.16

Sample T-SQL code showing the usage of the Change Data Capture functions to return data.

```
DECLARE @from_lsn binary(10), @to_lsn binary(10)
SET @from_lsn =
sys.fn_cdc_get_min_lsn('dbo_MyTable')
SET @to_lsn = sys.fn_cdc_get_max_lsn()
SELECT * FROM cdc.fn_cdc_get_all_changes_dbo_MyTable
(@from_lsn, @to_lsn, N'all');
GO
```

USING XEVENTS FOR DATA MODIFICATION AUDITING

We saw earlier in the chapter how we could use XEvents to monitor for logins to the SQL Server instance. We can also use XEvents to monitor for people who are making data changes directly to the database tables when they should not be. As you can see from the sample code in Example 12.17 we are collecting a good amount of information about the person running the query and the query which was run.

EXAMPLE 12.17

Sample XEvents capture which collects all changes to data tables.

```
CREATE EVENT SESSION [monitor_data_modification] ON SERVER
ADD EVENT sqlserver.rpc_completed(
    ACTION(package0.collect_system_time,sqlserver.client_app_name,
            sqlserver.client_connection_id,sqlserver.client_hostname,
            sqlserver.client_pid,sqlserver.context_info,sqlserver.database_id,
            sqlserver.nt_username,sqlserver.query_hash,sqlserver.session_id,
            sqlserver.session_nt_username,sqlserver.sql_text,sqlserver.transaction_id,
            sqlserver.transaction_sequence)
WHERE ([statement] LIKE N'%UPDATE %'
        OR [statement] LIKE N'%DELETE %'
        OR [statement] LIKE N'%INSERT %'))
,
ADD EVENT sqlserver.sql_batch_completed(
    ACTION(package0.collect_system_time,sqlserver.client_app_name,
            sqlserver.client_connection_id,sqlserver.client_hostname,
            sqlserver.client_pid,sqlserver.context_info,sqlserver.database_id,
            sqlserver.nt_username,sqlserver.query_hash,sqlserver.session_id,
            sqlserver.session_nt_username,sqlserver.sql_text,sqlserver.transaction_id,
            sqlserver.transaction_sequence)
WHERE ([statement] LIKE N'%UPDATE %'
        OR [statement] LIKE N'%DELETE %'
        OR [statement] LIKE N'%INSERT %'))
ADD TARGET package0.asynchronous_file_target
    (SET FILENAME = N'c:\xEvents\DataModification.xel', METADATAFILE =
N'c:\xEvents\DataModification.xem')
WITH (EVENT_RETENTION_MODE = ALLOW_MULTIPLE_EVENT_LOSS)
GO
```

In Example 12.17 we are only monitoring for insert, update and delete statements as in this case are not worried about users reading data (that will be covered later in this chapter).

Once the data has been captured by the xevent code you will need to monitor it to see who has been mucking around with the data. This can be done using the sample code shown in Example 12.18.

EXAMPLE 12.18

Code showing how to query the data captured in Example 12.17.

```
SELECT data.value('(event/@name)[1]', 'varchar(30)') Event,
        data.value('(event/action[3])[1]', 'varchar(max)') [UserName],
        data.value('(event/action[10])[1]', 'varchar(max)') [HostName],
        data.value('(event/action[12])[1]', 'varchar(max)') [ApplicationName],
        data.value('(event/data[8])[1]', 'varchar(max)') [Batch_Operation],
        data.value('(event/@timestamp)[1]', 'datetime') EventDate
FROM
    (SELECT CONVERT (XML, event_data) AS data FROM sys.fn_xe_file_target_read_file
    ('c:\xEvents\DataModification*.xel', 'c:\xEvents\DataModification*.xem', NULL, NULL)
    ) entries
order by data.value('(event/@timestamp)[1]', 'datetime') desc
GO
```

USING SQL SERVER AUDIT FOR DATA MODIFICATION

In order to use SQL Server Auditing to capture rogue data modification you must first create a SQL Server Audit in which to capture the audit data. After the audit has been created a Database Audit Specification can then be created.

When creating a Database Audit Specification connect to the server you wish to audit using object explorer. Navigate to the database in question and then navigate to the Security branch of the tree, then the "Database Audit Specification" branch of the tree. Right click "Database Audit Specification" and select "New Database Audit Specification" from the context menu that opens. In the "Create Database Audit Specification" window which opens you can select the "Audit Action Types" which you wish to monitor. To monitor for data medication select INSERT, UPDATE and DELETE one of each line of the window as shown in Figure 12.5.

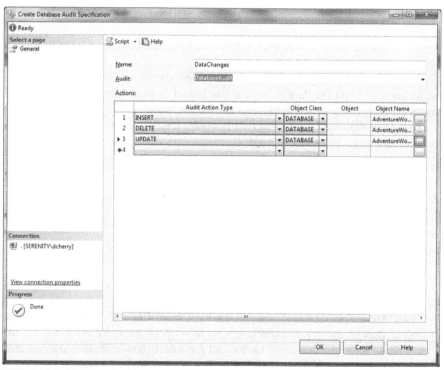

FIGURE 12.5 Showing the Database Audit Specification settings window.

The Database Audit Specification can be created using T-SQL as well as by using SQL Server Management Studio as shown in Example 12.19.

EXAMPLE 12.19

Sample code showing the creation of a Database Audit Specification.

```
CREATE DATABASE AUDIT SPECIFICATION [DataChanges]
FOR SERVER AUDIT [DatabaseAudit]
ADD (INSERT ON DATABASE::[AdventureWorks] BY [public]),
ADD (DELETE ON DATABASE::[AdventureWorks] BY [public]),
ADD (UPDATE ON DATABASE::[AdventureWorks] BY [public])
GO
```

DATA QUERYING AUDITING

Auditing when someone runs a query against database tables has historically been the hardest audit to perform, with the traditional answer being run start an SQL Trace against the engine looking for select statements and logging that information somewhere where it can be easily read. Starting with SQL Server 2008, Microsoft has had a solution for this auditing problem, and that is to use the server-side auditing, which was discussed earlier in this chapter, but instead of creating a Server Audit Specification create a Database Audit Specification.

Before you can configure a Database Audit Specification, however, you must create an audit to write the data to, unless you intend to write to an existing audit, as discussed earlier and shown in Figure 12.3 and Example 12.4.

To create a Database Audit Specification using the SQL Server Management Studio User Interface, follow these steps:

1. Connect to the database instance using the object explorer.
2. Navigate to the "Databases" folder.
3. Navigate to the Database you wish to create the Database Audit Specification in.
4. Navigate to the Security folder.
5. Navigate to the "Database Audit Specification" folder.
6. Right click on the "Database Audit Specification" folder and select "New Database Audit Specification."

A Database Audit Specification, which would be used to capture select statements, should have its "Audit Action Type" set to "SELECT." When you create a Database Audit Specification, you can set the Object Class to Database, Schema, or Object, depending on how wide you want to set your audit. An audit that has the Object Class set to database will capture all the select statements that are executed against the specified database, as shown in Figure 12.6. An audit that has the Object Class set to Schema will capture all select statements that are executed against the

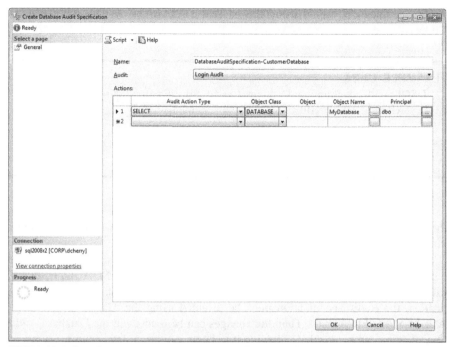

FIGURE 12.6 Creating a Database Audit Specification to monitor all select statements issues against the MyDatabase database.

specified schema. An audit that has the Object Class set to Object will capture all queries that are executed against the specified object.

Database Audit Specifications can also be created using the CREATE DATA-BASE AUDIT SPECIFICATION T-SQL statement as shown in Example 12.20.

EXAMPLE 12.20

Creating a Database Audit Specification using T-SQL to monitor all select statements against the database MyDatabase.

```
CREATE DATABASE AUDIT SPECIFICATION [DatabaseAuditSpecification-
CustomerDatabase]
FOR SERVER AUDIT [Login Audit]
ADD (SELECT ON DATABASE::[MyDatabase] BY [dbo])
GO
```

As with the Server Audit Specifications, the Database Audit Specification must be enabled before it can be used. Enabling can be done by right clicking on the Database Audit Specification in the object explorer and selecting the "Enable Database

Audit Specification" or by using the ALTER DATABASE AUDIT SPECIFICA-
TION statement as shown in Example 12.21.

EXAMPLE 12.21

T-SQL code enabling a Database Audit Specification using the ALTER
DATABASE AUDIT SPECIFICATION statement.

```
ALTER DATABASE AUDIT SPECIFICATION [DatabaseAuditSpecification-
CustomerDatabase]
WITH (STATE=ON)
```

Once the Database Audit Specification has been enabled, data will be captured to
the Audit specified when the Database Audit Specification was created, and it can be
viewed using the log explorer discussed earlier in this chapter.

After the Database Auditing Specifications have been created, they can then be
modified using either the user interface or the ALTER DATABASE AUDIT SPECI-
FICATION T-SQL statement. In order to make changes to a Database Audit Speci-
fication, the Audit Specification must be disabled using the ALTER DATABASE
AUDIT SPECIFICATION. Then the changes can be made, and the Database Audit
Specification can be enabled, allowing it to begin capturing data again as shown in
Example 12.22.

EXAMPLE 12.22

The T-SQL code to disable a Server Audit Specification, changing the
specification, then enabling the specification, allowing it to begin capturing data.

```
ALTER DATABASE AUDIT SPECIFICATION [ServerAuditSpecification-LoginAudit]
WITH (STATE = OFF)
GO
ALTER DATABASE AUDIT SPECIFICATION [ServerAuditSpecification-LoginAudit]
DROP (SUCCESSFUL_LOGIN_GROUP)
GO
ALTER DATABASE AUDIT SPECIFICATION [ServerAuditSpecification-LoginAudit]
WITH (STATE = ON)
GO
```

SCHEMA CHANGE AUDITING

Like auditing select statements, auditing schema changes have traditionally been difficult to make without running a server-side trace. Like auditing select statements,
this problem has been solved starting in SQL Server 2008, as have auditing schema
changes, by using the Database Audit Specifications.

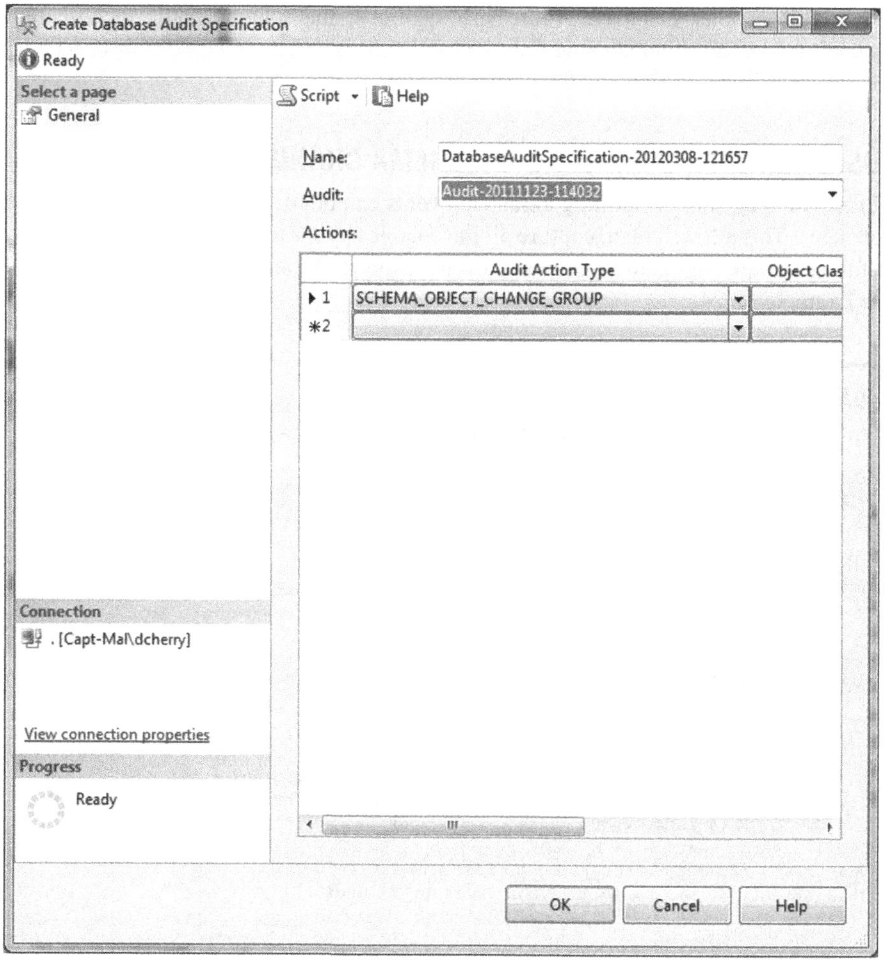

FIGURE 12.7 Creating a Database Audit Specification which will audit all schema changes.

To audit schema changes, there is a specific Audit Action Type that will track all schema changes; this is the SCHEMA_OBJECT_CHANGE_GROUP, as shown in Figure 12.7. This will then log all schema changes to the specified Audit destination.

Like the other Database Audit Specifications, you can also create a schema audit in T-SQL, as shown in Example 12.23.

EXAMPLE 12.23

T-SQL Code to create the schema change audit shown in Figure 12.7.

```
CREATE DATABASE AUDIT SPECIFICATION [Object_Changes]
FOR SERVER AUDIT [Login Audit]
ADD (SCHEMA_OBJECT_CHANGE_GROUP)
```

Like the other Database Audit Specifications, the schema audit specification would need to be enabled using the ALTER DATABASE AUDIT SPECIFICATION T-SQL statement or by using the object explorer.

USING EXTENDED EVENTS FOR SCHEMA CHANGE AUDITING

Like with data change auditing extended events can be used for auditing for schema changes. This allows you to capture all the changes by the extended events subsystem of the database engine to an extended events capture. A sample capture can be found in Example 12.24.

EXAMPLE 12.24

Sample code to collect database object changes via Extended Events.

```
CREATE EVENT SESSION [monitor_schema_change] ON SERVER
ADD EVENT sqlserver.rpc_completed(
    ACTION(package0.collect_system_time,sqlserver.client_app_name,
            sqlserver.client_connection_id,sqlserver.client_hostname,
            sqlserver.client_pid,sqlserver.context_info,sqlserver.database_id,
            sqlserver.nt_username,sqlserver.query_hash,sqlserver.session_id,
            sqlserver.session_nt_username,sqlserver.transaction_id,
            sqlserver.transaction_sequence)
WHERE ([statement] LIKE N'%ALTER%')),
ADD EVENT sqlserver.sql_batch_completed(
    ACTION(package0.collect_system_time,sqlserver.client_app_name,
            sqlserver.client_connection_id,sqlserver.client_hostname,
            sqlserver.client_pid,sqlserver.context_info,sqlserver.database_id,
            sqlserver.nt_username,sqlserver.query_hash,sqlserver.session_id,
            sqlserver.session_nt_username,sqlserver.transaction_id,
            sqlserver.transaction_sequence)
WHERE ([batch_text] LIKE N'%ALTER%'))
ADD TARGET package0.event_file(SET filename=
N'C:\xEvents\SchemaChange.xel',max_rollover_files=(0))
GO
```

USING POLICY-BASED MANAGEMENT TO ENSURE POLICY COMPLIANCE

Policy-based Management, which was introduced in Microsoft SQL Server 2008, can be used to audit the servers automatically on a regular basis either when the server starts or on a regular schedule, such as daily or monthly. Policy-based Management can be used to audit a wide variety of security-related settings to ensure on a regular basis that the settings are set correctly. Once the Policies and Conditions are set (these are defined more fully in Chapter 4 in the section entitled "Using Policies to Secure Your Instance") and the policies are configured to check automatically, the results are easily available for viewing by using the Log viewer by right clicking on the Policy Management folder and selecting "View History."

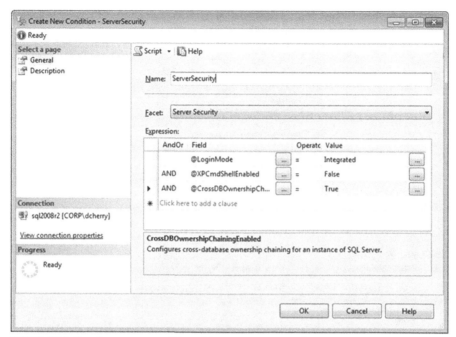

FIGURE 12.8 Creating a new condition which evaluates three instance wide settings.

Policy-based Management can be accessed in the object explorer within SQL Server Management Studio by:

1. Navigating to Management
2. Navigating to Policy Management

Conditions can be created with multiple expressions in them, as long as the expressions are all within the same Facet. In the Facet shown in Figure 12.8, three expressions are being monitored, which all must pass in order for the condition to be successfully evaluated.

After creating the conditions that you wish to evaluate, policies need to be created, such as those in Figure 12.9, to evaluate the condition and run it on a schedule. Additional information about the conditions that are monitored by the policy can be entered on the Description page, including a link to a webpage that can be set up with more information.

If you manually evaluate a policy such as the ones created in Figure 12.9 by right clicking on the Policy and select evaluate on the context menu, a screen will pop up with the results of the evaluation, as shown in Figure 12.10.

Clicking on the "View…" link in the "Target details" section of the "Evaluate Policies" window shown in Figure 12.10 will bring up the window shown in Figure 12.11, which shows exactly which expressions were evaluated and the results of each expression.

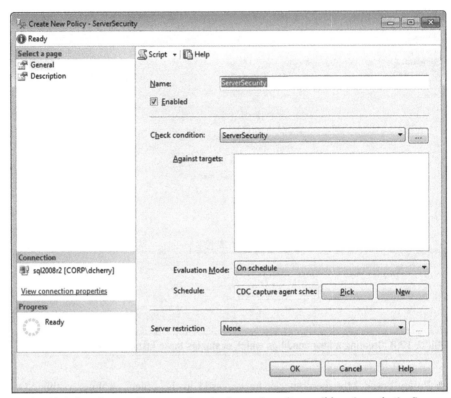

FIGURE 12.9 Creating a policy to monitor the Server Security condition shown in the figure.

When policies are evaluated on a schedule there is a way to see if those policies were evaluated successfully or not. Within the SQL Server Management Studio this evaluation can be done by right clicking on the Policies folder under the "Policy Management" folder and selecting "View History" from the context menu (you can also right click on a Policy and select "View History"). This will bring up the Log File Viewer, which will be configured to view the policy history. When a policy has failed, you can drill down into the entry of the evaluation, which will give you a Details link, shown in Figure 12.12, which, when clicked, will present the same screen shown in Figure 12.11.

Using SQL Server Management Studio is great when you have only a couple of policies on a couple of servers. However, if you have dozens or hundreds of servers, you could easily have thousands or tens of thousands of policies whose results you would have to check. In this case your best bet would be to create a central repository and use either an SQL Agent job or an SQL Server Integration Services (SSIS) package to query for the policy evaluation history from the msdb.dbo.syspolicy_policy_execution_history table and the msdb.dbo.syspolicy_policies table. To get the details of which Expression succeeded or failed, that information is located in msdb.dbo.syspolicy_policy_execution_history_details table, specifically in the result_detail column.

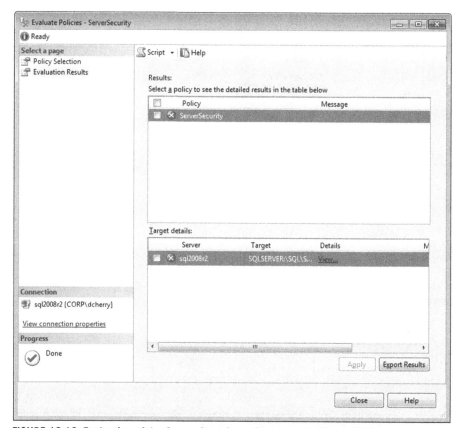

FIGURE 12.10 Evaluation of the Server Security policy shown in Figure 12.9.

C2 AUDITING

C2 auditing is an auditing specification which was designed by the United States government Department of Defense and is probably the oldest form of auditing within Microsoft SQL Server. C2 auditing is an option that will configure the SQL Server instance to record all attempts to access statements and objects within the instance. When C2 auditing is enabled, the information is written to a log file within the default log folder.

The C2 auditing data is written to a file until the file reaches 200 Megs in size, at which point the SQL Server engine will close the file and begin writing to a new file. This will continue until C2 auditing is disabled or until the hard drive fills, at which point the database engine will shut itself down and it will not be able to be restarted until space has been made available.

C2 auditing can be enabled in two ways: by using SQL Server Management Studio as shown in Figure 12.13 (or SQL Enterprise Manager for SQL 2000 and older) or by using the sp_configure system stored procedure.

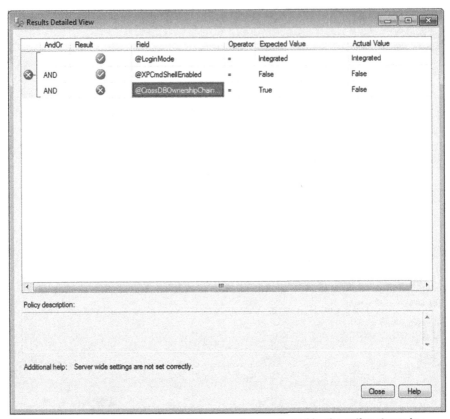

FIGURE 12.11 Showing the results of the expressions evaluated by the policy shown in Figure 12.9 with one expression failing and two expressions succeeding.

In order to enable C2 auditing using T-SQL, the sp_configure procedure is used. Before C2 auditing can be enabled, the advanced options setting must also be enabled using the sp_configure procedure, as shown in Example 12.25.

EXAMPLE 12.25

T-SQL code used to enable C2 auditing.

```
EXEC sys.sp_configure N'show advanced options', N'1' RECONFIGURE WITH OVERRIDE
GO
EXEC sys.sp_configure N'c2 audit mode', N'1'
GO
RECONFIGURE WITH OVERRIDE
GO
EXEC sys.sp_configure N'show advanced options', N'0' RECONFIGURE WITH OVERRIDE
GO
```

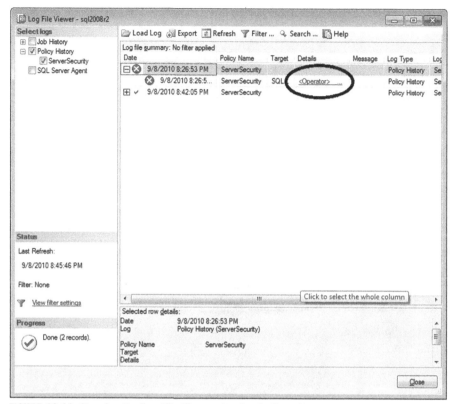

FIGURE 12.12 Showing the Log File Viewer showing Policy History.

In either case using SQL Server Management Studio or sp_configure to change the C2 auditing setting, there is no restart of the database engine to begin the C2 auditing. With either configuration method the auditing change will begin immediately.

When using sp_configure on an SQL 2000 server or older, change the schema from sys to dbo. C2 auditing has been superseded by "Common Criteria Compliance" starting in Microsoft SQL Server 2008. As of the writing of this book, C2 auditing has not yet been deprecated.

COMMON CRITERIA COMPLIANCE

Common Criteria was first ratified in 1999 as an international standard, although it was not introduced into the SQL Server platform until the SQL Server 2005 release of the product. The Common Criteria standard is maintained by more than 20 nations and is recognized by the International Standards Organization as ISO standard

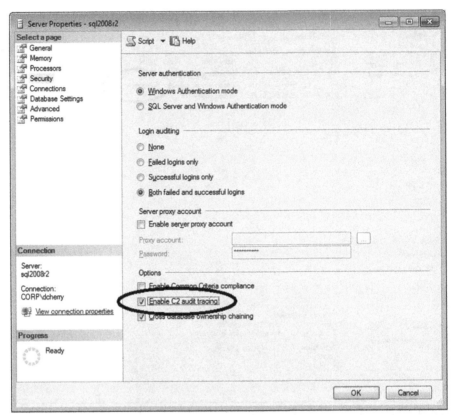

FIGURE 12.13 Showing where to enable C2 auditing on the Security Tab of the instance properties in SQL Server Management Studio.

15408. The specifics behind Common Criteria can be found at http://www.common-criteriaportal.org/.

Three elements are required for Common Criteria within Microsoft SQL Server. The first element is called Residual Information Protection (RIP), which requires that memory be overwritten with a known pattern before the memory can be reallocated to another process. This RIP process, while making the data in memory more secure, can slow down system performance because of the memory rewriting. The second element involves turning on login auditing. This login auditing is exposed within the SQL Server by including the last successful login time, the last unsuccessful login time, and the number of attempts between the last successful and current login times within the sys.dm_exec_sessions dynamic management view. The third element is that column-level GRANTs do not overwrite table-level DENY privileges.

Common Criteria can be enabled via SQL Server Management Studio by viewing the properties of the instance and by viewing the security tab as shown in

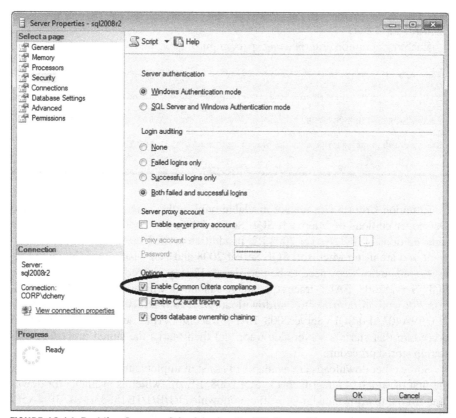

FIGURE 12.14 Enabling Common Criteria using the SQL Server Management Studio.

Figure 12.14 or by using the sp_configure system stored procedure as shown in Example 12.26.

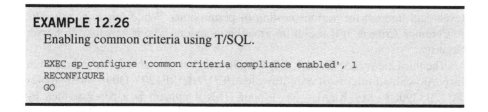

EXAMPLE 12.26

Enabling common criteria using T/SQL.

```
EXEC sp_configure 'common criteria compliance enabled', 1
RECONFIGURE
GO
```

Like enabling C2 auditing, Common Criteria is an advanced option that must be made visible by turning on advanced options using sp_configure as shown in Example 12.27.

EXAMPLE 12.27

Enabling common criteria using sp_configure.

```
EXEC sys.sp_configure N'show advanced options', N'1' RECONFIGURE WITH OVERRIDE
GO
EXEC sys.sp_configure N'common criteria compliance enabled', N'1'
GO
RECONFIGURE WITH OVERRIDE
GO
EXEC sys.sp_configure N'show advanced options', N'0' RECONFIGURE WITH OVERRIDE
GO
```

Common Criteria is a feature available only in the Enterprise, Evaluation, and Developer editions of Microsoft SQL Server 2005, 2008 and 2012, as well as the same editions of SQL Server 2008 R2, in addition to the Data Center edition.

If you are using Microsoft SQL Server 2008 and you wish to use Common Criteria, some extra steps need to be performed. First, you need to run a script called SQL_Server2008_EAL1_trace.sql, which can be downloaded from Microsoft at http://download.microsoft.com/download/9/5/F/95FDD106-4E98-47B4-B676-7FDB9A403AF0/SQL_Server2008_EAL1_trace.sql. This script creates a stored procedure that starts a server-side trace and then marks the stored procedure as a startup stored procedure.

Some other downloads are available to assist in implementing Common Criteria, the first of which is integritycheck_SQL2008_EE.zip, which is available for download from http://download.microsoft.com/download/1/B/1/1B18883E-BDBF-4A58-861B-C6A551A172DA/integritycheck_SQL2008_EE.zip. This zip file contains a batch file and an XML document that will ensure that the files making up the SQL Server 2008 binaries are unchanged. It does this by comparing the files on the server's hard drive against the known MD5 hashes for each of the files.

The second file is permission_hierarchy.zip, which is available for download from http://download.microsoft.com/download/B/F/8/BF81F5DE-8CD5-4531-87A1-F57D9ED09E0D/permission_hierarchy.zip. This zip file contains a set of PDF documents that show how permissions are related to each other at various levels and through the various nesting of permissions. While this is not specific to Common Criteria, it is useful information to anyone who is new to SQL Server Security.

The third file is MS_KEAL1_ST_1.2.pdf, which is available for download from http://download.microsoft.com/download/E/1/2/E12F1277-D096-44FB-8442-EC77B3790C88/MS_KEAL1_ST_1.2.pdf. This document is a paper written by Roger French, and it describes in painstaking detail the goals for the Common Criteria certification of the database engine of Microsoft® SQL Server® 2008. The abstract for this document is "This document is the Security Target (ST) for the Common Criteria certification of the database engine of Microsoft® SQL Server® 2008."

The fourth file is MS_SQL_AGD_ADD_1.3.pdf, which is available for download from http://download.microsoft.com/download/C/7/6/C763829F-6F3C-4A70-9D97-37F8482FF2E1/MS_SQL_AGD_ADD_1.3.pdf. This document is a paper, also written by Roger French, that builds on the information in the MS_KEAL1_ST_1.2.pdf. The abstract for this document is "This document is the Guidance Addendum for the Common Criteria certification of the database engine of Microsoft® SQL Server® 2008."

SUMMARY

A wide variety of auditing options are found within Microsoft SQL Server. As applications are moved from older versions of Microsoft SQL Server to the newer versions, more and more auditing features are made available. As future versions of the product are released, even more auditing options will surely be made available, which we have seen with the introduction of being able to do auditing through extended events in SQL Server 2012.

REFERENCES

French, Roger. "MS_KEAL1_ST_1.2.pdf." *MS_KEAL1_ST_1.2.pdf*. Microsoft, January 23, 2009. Web. September 25, 2010. download.microsoft.com/download/E/1/2/E12F1277-D096-44FB-8442-EC77B3790C88/MS_KEAL1_ST_1.2.pdf. Copied the abstract and referenced the file for download by the user.

French, Roger. "MS_SQL_AGD_ADD_1.3.pdf." *MS_SQL_AGD_ADD_1.3.pdf*. Version 1.3. Microsoft, January 30, 2009. Web. September 25, 2010. download.microsoft.com/download/C/7/6/C763829F-6F3C-4A70-9D97-37F8482FF2E1/MS_SQL_AGD_ADD_1.3.pdf. Copied the abstract and referenced the file for download by the user.

Server Rights

13

INFORMATION IN THIS CHAPTER:

- OS rights needed by the SQL server service
- OS rights needed by the DBA
- OS rights needed to install service packs
- OS rights needed to access SSIS remotely
- Console apps must die
- Default sysadmin rights
- Vendor's and the sysadmin fixed server role

This chapter talks about the permissions that various people should have on the production SQL Servers, and about the risks of running command line services.

When working with Microsoft Azure SQL Database, as of the writing of this book, in summer 2014 the only section of this chapter that applies to you is the last, "Console Apps Must Die." The remaining sections do not apply to Microsoft's Microsoft Azure SQL Database as Microsoft handles the installation of the database engine and the installations of the Microsoft Azure SQL Database service packs and hotfixes. The SSIS pieces do not currently apply as Microsoft Azure SQL Database does not offer SSIS as part of the Microsoft Azure SQL Database product. Now all that being said, if you are using Microsoft Azure SQL Database if a VM role, or on Amazon's EC2 service you have a normal standalone SQL instance so it needs to be secured just like any normal on premise SQL Server instance.

SQL SERVER SERVICE ACCOUNT CONFIGURATION

When you install Microsoft SQL Server one of the screens of the installer asks you to supply the accounts which the various SQL Server services should be running under. On this screen you can select the local system account, the network service account, a domain account, or a windows account for each of the SQL Server services. When installing SQL Server a decision must be made if a local account will be used for the services, if a single Windows account will be used for all the services or if a single separate Windows account will be used for each of the services.

ONE ACCOUNT FOR ALL SERVICES

The easiest approach from an administrative standpoint is to use a single domain account to run all SQL Services on every Microsoft SQL Server within the enterprise. However, from a security standpoint this technique is the weakest of the three techniques. This technique is easy to use because only a single domain account is created and that same account is used for each SQL Server in the enterprise. The downside, from a security perspective, to this technique is that if any SQL Server in the enterprise is compromised the attacker then has access to every other SQL Server in the enterprise. The reason that this is the case is that the account which the SQL Server runs under is typically a member of the sysadmin fixed server role which gives that account rights to everything within the database. The account is a member of the sysadmin fixed server role so that SQL Agent jobs can run and have full access to the database engine for running jobs such as index maintenance, database backups, and other actions which would require access to all the objects within the database engine. An additional maintenance overhead with this technique is that when a database administrator leaves the company and the SQL Server's password must be changed all the SQL Server instances need to be restarted at once. From an ease of maintenance prospective if the SQL Server's within the enterprise use the lock pages in memory setting this setting only needs to be granted to a single domain account and can be easily enough pushed out via GPO to all the SQL Servers in the enterprise, however, there are several options available which are discussed later in this chapter.

SQL Server's AlwaysOn Availability Groups

SQL Server 2012 introduces the feature called "AlwaysOn Availability Groups" which is the new high availability feature, which was further enhanced in SQL Server 2014. When deploying AlwaysOn Availability Groups within a Windows Cluster all the SQL Server core engine services which will be hosting the AlwaysOn database must be running under the same Windows domain account, especially if you intend on using the AlwaysOn Availability Group Listener.

The reason that the accounts that are running all the SQL Server services need to be a domain account is that the Service Principal Name (SPN) needs to match for all the servers in the cluster, which requires that the service account be the same. If they are not the same when the Availability Group is moved to run on another machine users who attempt to connect to the database using Windows Authentication will

> **NOTE**
> AlwaysOn Availability Groups is out of scope
>
> While I would love nothing more than to write up the full details of what AlwaysOn Availability Groups is and how it works that is way outside the scope of this book as this is a security book not a high availability book.
>   Sorry.

receive Kerberos errors as Active Directory would not be able to correctly handle their authentication ticket.

ONE ACCOUNT PER SEVER

The next easiest approach from an administrative standpoint is to use a different domain account for each server which has Microsoft SQL Server installed, but the same account for running each of the installed SQL Server services. This technique requires that a new Active Directory account be created for each SQL Server which is installed in the enterprise. This is a secure technique given that the SQL Servers do not have access to each other's data by default, unless specific rights are granted to one SQL Server to access another SQL Server's data. The additional administrative effort comes from needing to manage all the various usernames and passwords in some sort of repository. With the one account for all servers approach discussed earlier in this chapter there is only a single account to be maintained, which can be easily enough given to new database administrators as needed. With this approach there are dozens if not hundreds of accounts which need to be managed and deleted when SQL Servers are removed from production.

With regard for password changing when using this technique things are both simpler and more complex all at once. The technique makes password changes harder because there are dozens or hundreds of domain account which now need to be changed, potentially all at once when a database administrator leaves the company. However, the process is simpler as not all the SQL Services in the enterprise need to be restarted at once. The passwords can be changed in smaller batches so that only a few servers and applications need to be restarted at a time greatly reducing the impact of the changes and greatly increasing the chance that the password will be changed.

ONE ACCOUNT FOR EACH SERVICE

The approach which has the most administrative overhead yet is the most secure is having a single domain account for each of the services which the SQL Server service installs. This has the administrative overhead of requiring that anywhere from three to ten or so domain accounts be created each time a new SQL Server is installed within the enterprise. However, because each account only has the very minimum rights that are needed for that account to function if any account is compromised the amount of damage which the attacker can do with the compromised credentials is kept to a minimum.

Like with the one account per server this technique has administrative perks and downsides. The downsides become pretty obvious in a large enterprise which has hundreds or thousands of servers running Microsoft SQL Server, there are hundreds, thousands or even tens of thousands of domain accounts that would need to be changed. The upside is exactly like when using one account for each SQL Server in that they can be changed in patches. When you have this may accounts just for running SQL Server it is possible that it may take months or years to changes all

> **NOTE**
>
> Give a Guy a Break Already
>
> Yes, yes. I am aware that the really old versions of SQL Server like SQL Server 6.5 and SQL Server 7 required that the account that was running the SQL instance be a member of the local administrators group. But this is not the 1990s so we should not be setting up our servers like that anymore unless we really need to. And by really need to I mean because some third party application vendor does not know how to properly write an application causing massively elevated permissions to be required.

the account passwords when they are changed as even with hundreds or thousands of SQL Servers at a company there may only be a small team of 10–20 people who manage the SQL Servers who would need to handle the password changes.

USING LOCAL SERVICE ACCOUNTS FOR RUNNING SQL SERVER SERVICES

Another option which is used much more frequently than it should be is to use the local system accounts to run the SQL Server services. While on newer versions of Windows such as Windows 2008 and higher this is less of a problem, on older versions of Windows this is an unacceptable security risk. There are two local system accounts which the SQL Server installer will let you pick during the installation process. One of the Local Service account and the other is the Network Service account. On older versions of Windows Server (Windows Server 2003 and earlier) these accounts were effectively members of the local administrators group on the server which gave the SQL Service more rights than it needed.

This becomes less of an issue on the newer versions of the Microsoft Windows operating system, specifically Windows 2008 and newer, because when services are run under these accounts they are not actually run under these accounts. New pseudo account are created called "NT SERVICE\MSSQLSERVER" or "NT SERVICE\SQLSERVERAGENT," basically the domain name is "NT SERVICE" followed by the name of the service for the account name. This allows each service to function within its own security context and not have access to the resource of another service. It also allows for the granting of Windows security rights at a much more granular level such as the logon as a service right shown in Figure 13.1.

Granting additional rights to these service specific "NT SERVICE" accounts requires knowning the specific account which you want to grant rights to. This is due to the fact that these are special system accounts, which do not technically exist so you cannot search for them in the normal account search dialog boxes in Windows Local Security Policy editor or SQL Server Management Studio. As you cannot search for these accounts you must type the names in manually when granting them rights.

The upside to using these service specific accounts is that there are no passwords to change as you do not have access to these passwords. Another upside to these services is that if the service which the account is running becomes compromised the

FIGURE 13.1 Showing various "NT SERVICE" being granted individual rights under Windows 2008 R2.

STORY TIME

So This One Time While Writing This Book

So when I was writing this book, specifically Chapter 7 titled "Analysis Services," I ran across some of the problems which I have talked about in this section of this chapter (guess where I got the idea for this section for). While working with SQL Server Analysis Services I was trying to get the screenshots for all the objects like those shown in Figure 6.8 and I keep getting errors while processing the cube. This is because in my haste to get the SQL Server services installed on my machine I had set up the services to start up under the local service account instead of under a single domain account like my SQL Server did. Because of this when the SQL Server Analysis Services service attempted to log into the locally installed SQL Server database it could not because I needed to specifically grant the "NT SERVICE\MSOLAP$SSAS" service rights to the SQL Server instance (as I noted in Chapter 6 the SQL Server Analysis Service and Reporting Service services were installed as a named instance called SSAS giving us the stranger than normal account name).

And yes I did almost name this side bar "So this one time at band camp..." but that just led to images of a trumpet going somewhere that trumpets should just never go, and I did not really need that while sitting on an airplane. If you do not catch that reference go check out the American Pie movies and get back to me. You are welcome for that mental image. I now return you to your regularly scheduled book reading.

attacker would not have access outside of that service, unless that service account has been granted specific rights.

Like anything that has an upside there is a downside or two as well. These downsides include not being able to change the password of the account if it was to become compromised, and the inability to easily grant rights across servers. When running the SQL Server services under the network service account, the SQL Server can access rights outside of itself. And this works great, until you understand how the domain authentication process works when accessing these remote resources.

For an example lets say that we have a SQL Server called SQL1.contoso.local and a file server called files.contoso.local. The SQL Server service and the SQL Server Agent service are both configured to run under the local network service on their machine. There is a job which runs a T-SQL batch which includes the BULK INSERT statement which is used to load up a text file from the file server. In order to grant the SQL Server the right to access the network share and read the file on the file server we have to grant the computer account for SQL1.contoso.local rights to the network share. This is done by granting the Active Directory account CONTOSO\SQL1$ rights to the network share. So far so good. But we now find out that any process which is running under the network service account on SQL1.contoso.local now has rights to the network share and can read the file (or write to the file depending on how the rights to the network share are configured). This suddenly becomes a problem as any user who is logged into SQL1.contoso.local now also has the same rights to that network share that the SQL Service has. From a security perspective this is a pretty bad idea.

NOTE

Selecting The Right Approach

Hopefully by the time you have gotten to this part of this chapter you have been thinking about your own company and which of these approaches will fit best into your shop. Obviously changing from one of these approaches to another requires a LOT of work and is not a project that should be taken lightly. In larger shops a project like this could take months or years.

While I would love to be able to tell you which of these approaches would work best in your specific shop, that just is not possible to do in the abstract like this. There are several factors to consider before selecting which of these approaches should be used including the size of your shop, the number of database adminstrators in the shop (in this context anyone who has the passwords that the SQL Server runs under is counted as a database adminsitrator), and how complex the application design is, and how often you plan on changing service account passwords. If after thinking through all these items and thinking about your specific company, if you do decide to change the approach that you are going to use to run your SQL Server databases do not rush the project. For most applications and servers there will be a LOT of discovery which needs to be done to ensure that the account changes do not adversly impact the stability of the enviroment and the uptime of the applications.

After all, while we may not like it, the best security practices have to be tempered against system managability. If they did not we would still be in the stone ages as the only truly secure server is one that is powered off and stored in a concrete room with no doors or windows.

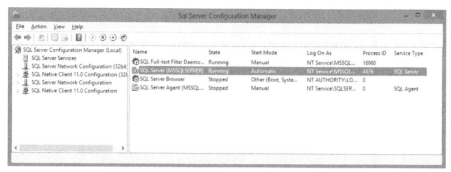

FIGURE 13.2 SQL Server Configuration Manager.

In addition to the NT Service accounts which have been discussed there are also Network Service accounts which are displayed as Network Service\MSSQLSERV-ER. These Network Service accounts work much the NT Service accounts except with the exception that the Network Service accounts have the ability to access network resources while the NT Service accounts only have the ability to access resources on the local server.

Changing the Service Account

Setting the service account can be done during installation or it can be changed after installation by using the SQL Server Configuration Manager. To make the change in the SQL Server Configuration Manager open the SQL Server Configuration Manager from the Windows Start Menu. Open it opens select "SQL Server Services" from the menu on the left then double click on the specific SQL Server service from the menu as shown in Figure 13.2.

From the SQL Server Service properties page which opens select the "Log On" tab. To use the Local System Account, the Local Service Account or the Network Service account select the "Built-in account" radio button and select the needed option from the dropdown menu as shown in Figure 13.3. To use a local or domain account, select the "This account" radio button and specify a Windows account and the password for this account.

When using a local system account, network service account or local service account (a description of these three accounts can be found in Table 13.1) the account will be shown in the Account Name field as shown in the disabled Account Name field in Figure 13.3. This can look incorrect when you first open the service properties, but this is normal as it displays the service specific name instead of displaying a generic option from the dropdown menus. There is no need to change the radio button to "Built In" from "This Account" if a network service, local service or local system account is specified.

After changing the start up service account to and from any of the available options the SQL Service must be restarted in order for the changes to take effect. To

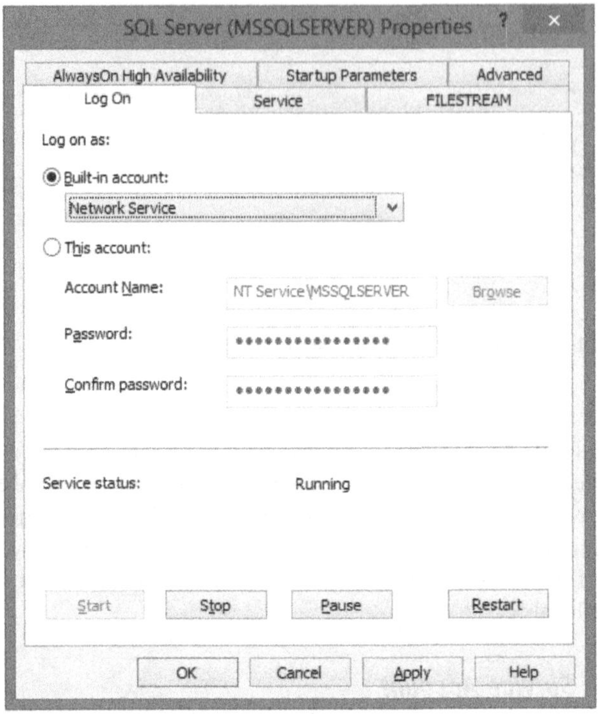

FIGURE 13.3 SQL Server service properties dialog.

make the changes take effect click the Apply button, then "Yes" on the dialog box which appears which informs you that the SQL Service needs to be restarted as shown in Figure 13.4. Clicking "No" on the dialog box shown in Figure 13.4 will prevent the changes to the service configuration from being saved.

Table 13.1   Local Accounts

Account Name	Description
Local system	The SQL Server Service runs under the account of the computer. The SQL Server Service only has access to resources on the local server.
Network service	The SQL Server Service runs under the account of the computer. The SQL Server Service has access to network resources, but under the context of the computer account not under its own account.
Local service	The SQL Server Service runs under the a service specific account called NT Service\MSSQLSERVER.

FIGURE 13.4 **Confirm account change dialog box.**

CREDENTIALS

Credentials are a funky addition to the SQL Server database engine. First introduced in SQL Server 2005 credentials were very misunderstood and infrequently used. Credentials are another special kind of login that can be created. They are used specifically along with SQL Server Agent proxy accounts, discussed later in this chapter. A credential in effect allows the SQL Service to impersonate another domain account when running processes outside of the SQL Agent process. The biggest difference between a traditional Windows account being granted rights to SQL Server via a Windows Login and a credential is that when creating a Windows login only the login is stored within SQL Server. When a credential is created both the Windows accounts username and password must be stored within the SQL Server database so that the SQL Server can use this information to start processes.

Creating a credential is quite easy. Within the object explorer panel connect to the SQL Server which the credential should be created on. Navigate to Security > Credentials then right click on Credentials and select the "New Credential" menu item from the context menu. On the window which opens name the credential and specify the username and password of the account which the SQL Server should use as shown in Figure 13.5.

The creation of credentials can also be done via T-SQL as well as the SQL Server Management Studio User Interface. Credentials are created by using the CREATE CREDENTIAL statement which was introduced in SQL Server 2005 when credentials where first introduced as shown in Example 13.1.

EXAMPLE 13.1

Using the CREATE CREDENTIAL statement to create a new credential with T-SQL.

```
CREATE CREDENTIAL [Sharepoint Account] WITH IDENTITY =
N'BACON\SharePointServiceAccount', SECRET = N'SuperSecretPa$$w0rd!'
GO
```

After a credential has been created it cannot be used for much by itself. You cannot use a credential to log into the SQL Server and you cannot use the EXECUTE AS statement with a credential. If you needed to use an account as a credential as well as give it the ability to log into the SQL Service database engine then a login which

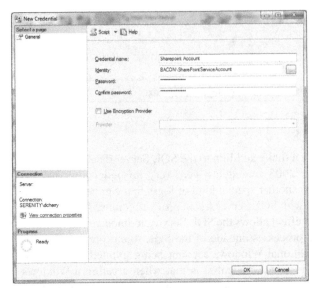

FIGURE 13.5 Showing the filled out new credential screen.

uses the same domain account as the credential would need to be added as a login to the SQL Server instance just as any domain account would be.

There are two system catalog views which are used with credentials. These are the sys.credentials and sys.principal_credentials system catalog views. The sys.credentials system catalog view contains the information about each credential such as its ID number, name, domain account, when it was last created and when it was last modified. The sys.principal_credentials system catalog view shows mappings between principals and credentials. When tradition logins are created (this does not apply to conainted users) they can be mapped to a specific credential. This allows the user to access the Windows OS via T-SQL and have the access at the file system via the credential. This is especially handy if you have staff who log into the SQL Server using a SQL Login and need to bulk insert data, or run other statements which might access the Windows operating system directly. While a credential can be mapped to many logins, a login can only be mapped to a single credential.

To map a credential to a login edit the login in question. Check the box which says "Map to Credential" and select the correct credential from the dropdown to the right of the checkbox as shown in Figure 13.6. After selecting the credential click the Add button to the right of the dropdown, also visable in Figure 13.6. The credential will be moved to the list shown below the dropdown menu, shown blank in Figure 13.6.

Adding a credential using T-SQL is done by using the ALTER LOGIN and specifying the login and the credential to be mapped together as shown in Example 13.2.

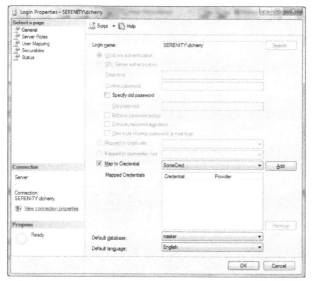

FIGURE 13.6 Adding a credential to a login using SQL Server Mangement Studio.

EXAMPLE 13.2

Adding a credential to a login by using T-SQL.

```
ALTER LOGIN [SERENITY\dcherry] ADD CREDENTIAL [SomeCred]
GO
```

If the password for the Windows account which the credential is using is changed the credential must be updated. If the password for the credential is not updated then any users or SQL Agent jobs (via a proxy account discussed later in this chapter) which attempt to use the credential will receive an error message.

SQL SERVER AGENT PROXY ACCOUNTS

SQL Server Agent proxy accounts are tied directly to SQL Server Credentials, which were talked about earlier in this chapter to the point that SQL Server Agent proxy accounts cannot be used at all without having one or more credentials created on the server.

NOTE

Review Time

So you thought that you would be all smart and skip the credentials section because it was long and boring looking? Time to go back and read it. Without it you will be lost.

It's OK, I will wait.

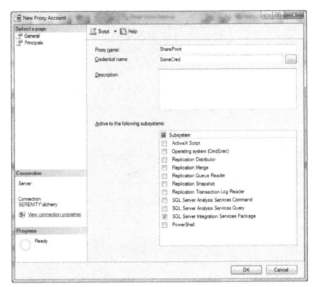

FIGURE 13.7 Showing the creation of a proxy account for SQL Server integration services using SQL Server Management Studio.

Proxy accounts are used to configure specific job steps within SQL Agent jobs to run under different Windows accounts, either local or domain, which are different than the account which the job owner is set to. There are a variety of reasons to do this, the most common is that there are network resources which need to be accessed by the job step which the account which the SQL Server Agent account does not have rights to and those rights cannot or would not be granted for one reason or another.

To create SQL Server Agent Proxy accounts connect to the SQL Instance you wish to add the proxy accounts to in object explorer and navigate to "SQL Server Agent" > "Proxy Accounts," and right click on "Proxy Accounts" and select "New Proxy..." from the context menu which appears. Within the "New Proxy Account" window which opens name the proxy which you are creating and select the credential which will be used. On this screen you must also specify the SQL Server Agent subsystems which the proxy account can be used for. The list of items shown in the subsystem list (shown in Figure 13.7) should look pretty familiar as this is the same list of job step types which are available in SQL Server Agent.

NOTE

Your Results May Vary

Depending on the version of SQL Server that you have installed and the components which you have installed your list of subsystems which is shown in Figure 13.7 may be different than what is shown in Figure 13.7.

Creating a proxy account can be done in T-SQL by using a few different stored procedures from the msdb system database. The first is sp_add_proxy which is used to add the proxy and map it to the credential. The second is the sp_grant_proxy_to_subsystem stored procedure which is used to grant the proxy account rights to a specific SQL Agent subsystem. The use of these procedures is shown in Example 13.3. The code in Example 13.3 references a @subsystem_id parameter which can be found by querying the dbo.syssubsystems system catalog view in the msdb database.

EXAMPLE 13.3

Creating a proxy account using T-SQL.

```
CREATE CREDENTIAL [Sharepoint Account] WITH IDENTITY =
N'BACON\SharePointServiceAccount', SECRET = N'SuperSecretPa$$w0rd!'
GO
```

In the case of the example shown in Figure 13.7 and Example 13.3 the proxy account which is created is only available for use by members of the sysadmin fixed server role. If users who are not members of the sysadmin fixed server role will be creating jobs, or if jobs will be created with their login as the own rights to these credentials needs to be granted to the logins for those users. These rights can be granted in SQL Server Management Studio by clicking on the Principals page when creating a new principal (or by editing the principal). On this page, shown in Figure 13.8 simply click the Add button and select from the shown list of logins the logins which need the rights to use the proxy. Rights to a proxy can also be granted to fixed or user defined server roles or msdb database roles from this screen as well.

Logins can be given access to rights to proxy accounts by using T-SQL as well as SQL Server Management Studio. This is done by using the sp_grant_login_to_proxy system stored procedure found within the msdb database as shown in Example 13.4.

EXAMPLE 13.4

Granting the SQL Login "anotherLogin" rights to the "SharePoint" SQL Server Agent proxy account.

```
EXEC sp_grant_login_to_proxy @proxy_name=N'SharePoint',
@login_name=N'anotherLogin'
```

Anyone who is given rights to the proxy can use the proxy for any of the subsystems which that proxy has access to. If different users should be using the same credential for different subsystems then different proxies should be created against the same credential.

FIGURE 13.8 Granting the SQL Login "anotherLogin" rights to a SQL Server Agent proxy.

OS RIGHTS NEEDED BY THE SQL SERVER SERVICE

The Microsoft SQL Server service needs specific rights in order to function correctly. Older versions of Microsoft SQL Server required extremely high-level permissions at the Windows operating system (OS) to function, usually requiring being a member of the local administrators group. Starting in Microsoft SQL Server 2000, the Windows account that runs the SQL Server no longer needs to be a member of the local administrators group. The SQL Service needs just a few permissions granted to it. When installing Microsoft SQL Server 2000 or newer, the installer will automatically grant the Windows account, which will run the Microsoft SQL Server service, the correct rights, if it does not already have these rights.

WINDOWS SYSTEM RIGHTS

The rights that are required to be granted to run the SQL are as follows.

- Log on as a service
- Replace a process-level token
- Adjust memory quotas for a process

If it becomes necessary to change the Windows account that the SQL Server runs under, then the new account that will be running the service will need to be granted these rights. If the "SQL Server Configuration Manager" is used to change the Windows service account, when using Microsoft SQL Server 2005 or newer these changes are made automatically for you. When using Microsoft SQL Server 2000, the permissions changes need to be made manually. If when using Microsoft SQL Server 2005 or higher the change is made using some method other than the "SQL Server Configuration Manager," then these changes would also need to be made manually. The easiest way to make these changes is to add the new account to the local Windows group, which was created during installation. This group is named "SQLServerMSSQLUser$*ServerName*$*InstanceName*," where the *ServerName* and *InstanceName* values are the name of the server and the SQL Server instance, respectively. When the instance is the default instance, the *InstanceName* value will be MSSQLSERVER instead of default.

When changing the Windows account that the Microsoft SQL Server Agent is running under, similar changes need to be made to the local group "SQLServerSQL AgentUser$*ServerName*$*InstanceName*," again where the *ServerName* and *InstanceName* values are the name of the server and the SQL Server instance, respectively. This local group has the same security rights as the groups starting with SQLServerMSSQLUser. In addition, this group grants the Windows user that will be running the Microsoft SQL Server Agent service the "Replace a process token level" and the "Bypass traverse checking" rights. These additional rights are needed in order for the various impersonations the SQL Server Agent will do to function.

When changing the Windows account that the SQL Server Integration Services (SSIS) runs under, similar changes need to be made to the local group "SQLServerDTSUser$*ServerName*" where the *ServerName* value is the name of the server.

It is highly recommended that the SQL Server not be run under the local system account as the local system account grants the SQL Server more rights to the operating system than are actually needed. By granting the SQL Server more rights than it needs, either by giving the Windows account more rights than it needs or by having the services run under the local service account, an attacker can obtain local Administrator rights on the server.

The SQL Server should never, ever be run under a domain account that is a member of the "Domain Admins" group. The "Domain Admins" group is a domain group that is created in all windows domains, and gives all members of the group administrative rights to all computers within the Windows Domain. There are few, if any, valid reasons to run the SQL Server under a domain admin account. When an SQL Server is run under a domain admin account if attackers were to get into the SQL Server database and get access to the operating system via the SQL Server database, they would then have domain administrator rights and they would have the ability to create or delete accounts for users or computers, as well as make changes to any server within the company.

SQL SERVER'S NTFS PERMISSIONS

When first installing SQL Server, the installer will modify the permissions on the folders where the database files are installed in an attempt to limit access to the database files. When the Microsoft SQL Server service is not running under an account that has local administrator rights, additional NTFS permissions need to be accounted for. As one example, the SQL Server service will not be able to create databases at the root of a hard drive or mount a point when the Windows operating system is running Windows 2008 or higher. This is because the NTFS and UAC permissions do not allow users who do not have administrative access to create files at the root level of the hard drive.

Another feature, which many find to be an annoyance, is as follows: When using Microsoft SQL Server 2005 or higher and a database is detached, the NTFS permissions for all the database files that make up the database are changed, removing the NTFS permissions for all users except for that of the user issued the database detach command. In Microsoft SQL Server 2008 and higher, the Windows account that is running the SQL Server database will also be left as having NTFS permissions on the files that make up the detached database. On SQL Server 2008 and higher, the database can be reattached right away, as needed. On SQL Server 2005, before the database can be attached, the NTFS permissions must be changed to allow the SQL Server engine to have rights to the database files. This must be done for all the database files that make up the Microsoft SQL Server database.

MANAGED SERVICE ACCOUNTS

Managed Service Accounts (MSAs) are a combination between domain accounts and virtual accounts such as the "Network Service\MSSQLSERVER" accounts which are discussed in this chapter. Managed Service Accounts are user accounts created within the Active Directory domain for a specific Windows service on a single Windows server. The benefit to the Managed Service Accounts over a traditional domain user account is that Managed Service Accounts never need to have their passwords changes as the Windows server which runs the service which uses the account will automatically change the password for the account every 30 days. Because the password change is automated and controlled by the Windows operating system itself the passwords are able to be changed without the need to take an outage of the SQL Server service. Managed Service Accounts are available starting in Windows Server 2008 R2 and SQL Server 2008 R2.

Managed Service Accounts are created within Active Directory just like any other user account, with the exception of having a dollar sign ($) placed after the username. While a normal domain user might look like "DOMAIN\UserName" a Managed Service Account will look like "DOMAIN\UserName$." When the account is created the password field should be left blank as the Windows Operating System will set the password manually when you configure the service to use the account.

Due to the fact that the Windows Operating System will be what creates the password and changes the password, Managed Service Accounts are not able to be used on clustered instances of Microsoft SQL Server as of Windows Server 2012 R2 and SQL Server 2014 as there is no way for the Windows servers to exchange the password with other members of the Windows cluster. When using AlwaysOn Availability Groups, Managed Service Accounts should also not be used as you should be using the same domain account for each instance which is working as a database replica within the AlwaysOn Availability Group configuration (more information regarding AlwaysOn Availability Groups and their security requirements is available earlier in this chapter).

Microsoft SQL Server is configured to use a Managed Service Account just like any other account by using the SQL Server configuration manager shown in Figures 13.2 and 13.3. Managed Service Accounts make for a great way to configure domain user accounts for standalone SQL Server instances as the password is changed automatically by the server every time the password expires without any downtime to the SQL Server service.

OS RIGHTS NEEDED BY THE DBA

A database administrator (DBA) does not need many rights to the SQL Servers operating system. This is because the DBA should not be managing the operating system that runs the Microsoft SQL Server Service. The management and patching of the base operating system should be handled by the members of the systems administration team and not by the DBA team.

The DBA may, however, from time to time need rights to the Windows OS, which will allow viewing performance metrics. If the company has a performance monitoring solution such as System Center Operations Manager (SCOM), the DBAs can grant the System Center Operations Manager rights to view the captured performance data. However, at times the DBAs may need the ability to collect real-time performance data directly from the performance monitor. The right to use a performance monitor remotely can be granted by adding the DBAs to the "Profile system performance" local system right. This local system right grants users that have the right the ability to connect to the system remotely and gather performance monitor data.

Some of these performance metrics can be accessed via the "sys.dm_os_performance_counters" dynamic management view from within the SQL Server instance. This allows the DBA to access the performance monitor data and to log it into a table or simply view the record set by querying the needed information from the dynamic management view without having any special operating system level permissions. The only performance monitor counters which are available within the sys.dm_os_performance_counters dynamic management view are the SQL Server specific performance counters. The number of counters which are available within this dynamic management view varies between versions and hardware configurations. For example, the number of buffer pool counters which are returned will depend on the number of NUMA nodes on the server.

USER ACCESS CONTROLS

User Access Controls (UAC) are implemented in Windows to prevent applications from making system changes without permissions of the person running the application. This includes in many cases Microsoft's own software which is running.

A perfect example of this can be found when access is granted to the SQL Server database instance via the local Administrators group on the Windows OS, and when an application is run on the server's console by an administrator which needs access to the SQL Server database instance such as SQL Server Management Studio. If UAC is enabled on the server and SQL Server Management Studio is started normally then SQL Server Management Studio will get an error message stating that the user is not able to connect to the database instance. This is because of how UAC works. The way UAC blocks this access is that by default any user who is logged into the servers console and who is a member of the local administrators group will not have the local administrators group in their security token which is passed to the applications to see what group the user is a member of. Effectively this makes the applications think that the user is not a member of the local administrators group.

In order to bypass UAC the application must be launched with Administrative permissions. This is done by right clicking on the shortcut in the start menu for the application (or the actual application itself) and selecting the "Run as Administrator" option. If the user has administrative rights to the Windows OS then the local administrators group will be left within the security token and the SQL Server Instance will see that the user is a member of administrators group and the user will then have access to the SQL Server Instance.

UAC has a variety of options available which are discussed in more detail in Chapter 6.

DUAL ACCOUNTS

When the DBA needs access to the server's console, it is recommended that a second account be set up and used to access the server's console. This is recommended for a couple of reasons. First, this allows the systems administrators to selectively allow the DBA to have access to the SQL Server's console as needed. Second, it will prevent the DBA's roaming profile from being loaded onto the server's system drive. We want to keep user profiles off of the SQL Server's hard drive so that the amount of extra data sitting on the server's OS drive is minimal, and to keep the risk of any viruses on the server to the minimal. This does add a layer of complexity to the system as the DBA now needs to keep track of two usernames and passwords and the DBA will need to ensure that this admin account has the needed rights to both the database and the server so that the needed operations can be performed.

OS RIGHTS NEEDED TO INSTALL SERVICE PACKS

While DBAs do not typically need rights to the Windows operating system, there are times when they do. Specifically, this is the case when a Microsoft SQL Server Service Pack or Microsoft SQL Server Hotfix needs to be installed on the Microsoft SQL Server Instance. The system administrators should not be installing these service packs and hotfixes against the Microsoft SQL Server instance as the systems

---

STORY TIME

Best Practices Only Work When They Are Actually Followed

One particular company that I worked for, whose name shall be protected to protect the stupid, took security to the extreme. It also took efforts to bypass security to the extreme as the security made getting any work done within the limits of the security next to impossible. Every person within the IT Department had two logins – their normal login, which was first initial followed by last name, and a second login – the same as the first with an "-a" after the username. The employees used the normal account to log into their workstations and the "-a" account to log into the servers. Normal accounts were not allowed to access into servers, and the "-a" account was not allowed to access the workstations. Normal accounts were not permitted to be admins on workstations, and all software had to be done by the help desk. On paper this security looks great, providing total separation between the servers and the workstations.

In practice, however, a few things were done to make it a little easier. The first thing done was, at some point in the past, the domain account that the SQL Server Services was run under was added to the "Domain Admins" group. This was done so that the SQL Server's would also have admin rights on their servers and so that jobs that needed to access remote machines would always have the network access they needed.

When I started working there, after I got my workstation, I was given the username and password for the SQL Server, and I was told that the account had domain admin rights, so I could use it to give myself admin rights on my workstation and install whatever I needed. I could then also give my "-a" account admin rights to my workstation so that I could connect to the admin share on my workstation from the server to get scripts and stuff to and from my workstation, effectively bypassing the security boundary that had been drawn between the workstations and the servers.

Because of this separation in the accounts, the database developers had a hard time getting things done. They liked to use the debugging features of Microsoft SQL Server 2000's Query Analyzer that requires having admin rights on both the workstation and some higher end rights on the server as well. But in order for them to connect to the database engine they had to launch Query Analyzer under their "-a" account which did not have admin rights on the workstation, and because they were database developers they did not have sysadmin rights on the database server either. As they were database developers and not DBAs, they did not have the password for the SQL Service account and so they did not have a way to get the permissions they needed.

Because of the security, getting anything done in any sort of timely manner was basically impossible. Everyone in the DBA group used the SQL Service account to give themselves access to get done what they needed to get done, effectively making the security next to useless.

What made the security at this company the hardest to deal with was the fact that it followed a white paper from Microsoft to the letter on how domain security should be set up. This would normally be fine, except that there was no consideration taken as to how this security would affect the way the company needed to conduct its business. When designing a security policy, a balance needs to be found between a locked down environment and the employees' needs to get their jobs done. Security should protect with as little interference as possible.

---

administrator should not have rights within the Microsoft SQL Server instance in order to complete the service pack or hotfix instance.

When the Microsoft SQL Server service pack or hotfix needs to be installed, the DBA will need to be granted administrative rights to the Microsoft SQL Server's operating system to complete the service pack and hotfix installation. This level of permissions is needed so that the service pack or hotfix can update the Microsoft SQL Server binaries within the "C:\Program Files\Microsoft SQL Server\" folder (or wherever the binaries are installed to).

OS RIGHTS NEEDED TO ACCESS SSIS REMOTELY

By default, only members of the local administrators group have the ability to connect to the SQL Server Integration Services (SSIS). This can prevent developers from accessing the SSIS in the development environment, as well as preventing the SQL Server service from connecting to the SSIS.

Fortunately, correcting these rights is a fairly easy process to complete without granting the users rights to the SSIS without making the user a member of the local administrators group. The needed change involves granting the user or users additional rights to the MsDtsServer DCOM object (or the MsDtsServer object that has a number such as 100 after it) within the Windows operating system. This change is easily done in a few easy steps:

1. Click Start.
2. Click Administrative Tools.
3. Click Component Services.
4. When the Component Services application opens, open the "Component Services" tree menu.
5. Open the Computers tree menu.
6. Open the "My Computer" tree menu.
7. Select the "DCOM Config" tree menu.
8. Locate the MsDtsServer object in the window on the right. When using SQL Server 2005, the object will be called MsDtsServer. When using SQL Server 2008 (either the R1 or R2 release), the object will be called MsDtsServer100. When using SQL Server 2012 the object will be called MsDtsServer110. When using SQL Server 2014 the object is called "Microsoft SQL Server Integration Services 12.0."
9. Right click on the correct object and select properties from the context menu that opens.
10. Select the security tab on the properties page that opens.
11. Under the "Launch and Activations Permissions" section, select the Customize radio button and select the Edit button.
12. Select or add the Windows user or Windows group (using groups is recommended to keep management simple) that needs the rights to connect and grant them the "Remote Launch" and "Remote Activation" rights or the "Local Launch" and "Local Activation" rights (or all four rights), depending on what rights are needed as shown in Figure 13.9.
13. Click OK to close this screen.
14. Under the "Access Permissions" section, select the Customize radio button and select the Edit button.
15. Select or add the Windows user or Windows group (using groups is recommended to keep management simple) that needs the rights to connect and grant them the "Remote Access" and/or "Local Access" permissions as shown in Figure 13.10.
16. Click OK on each screen and close the Component Services.

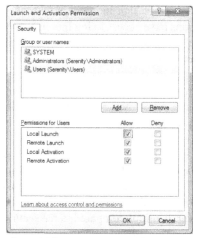

FIGURE 13.9 Showing granting addition launch and activation permissions to all members of the local Users group.

CONSOLE APPS MUST DIE

One of the biggest nightmares from both a security and an operational perspective is to require that the server be logged in either on the console or on a remote session by a user so that console-based applications can be run.

From a security perspective, this is a problem because if a virus or worm were to be installed on the server, then either or both could easily be launched under that

FIGURE 13.10 Granting remote access to the members of the local Users Group for the SSIS service.

user's account. This also requires that the person who needs to be logged into the server to run the applications have access to log into the server. This person is usually the developer who wrote the application, which means that the developer needs to have access to the production server.

From an operational perspective this creates problems because the server cannot be rebooted without the user, who needs to be running the applications and to be available to log into the server and restart the applications. When it comes to patching, this is a major problem since the system cannot be kept up to date with the needed security patches.

This problem can be fixed by ensuring that the application is written to be used as a Windows service. There is little difference between writing a Console application and a Windows service. The biggest difference is that the Windows service does not have a console output to write debugging information like the Console Application does. This change, however, is minor compared to the security and operational issues this solves.

Applications that cannot be converted to a Windows service application can usually be configured to run as a Windows service by using the svrany.exe and instsrv.exe applications, which is provided as part of the Windows Resource Kit. Using these applications any application can be configured to run as a Windows service. The syntax for these applications is shown in Example 13.5.

EXAMPLE 13.5
Syntax used by instsrv.exe and srvany.exe to create a custom service.
instsrv.exe MyServiceName c:\reskit\srvany.exe

After creating a custom Windows service, you can verify that the service was created correctly by looking in the Windows registry under HKEY_LOCAL_MACHINE\SYSTEM\CurrentControlSet\Services\MyServiceName. If the key exists, then the Windows service was created correctly. After verifying that the key was created, a couple of changes will need to be created under the folder. The first key that needs to be created is a key named "Parameters" with the class left blank. If the application requires no parameters, then leave the value blank; otherwise set the value to the parameters that the application needs. The second key which needs to be created is one named "Application," which is of the class of REG_SZ. The value of the Application string should be the full path to the application as well as the application name and extension such as "c:\windows\system32\calc.exe."

Once these changes have been made, the registry editor can be closed and the service can be started. If the service needs to be run under a domain account, it can be set up using the Services application from within the Administrative Tools folder in the Control panel. The service should not be configured to run under the developer's account; it should instead be configured to run under a new domain account that is set up for the sole purpose of running these Windows services.

STORY TIME

Console Apps Are Just Way Too Common

I have worked at a few different companies that for one reason or another have had console applications that were critical to the business. Unfortunately, all too often these mission-critical command line applications would end up being closed or paused.

A critical patch would be installed on the Windows OS, causing the server to reboot, and the person installing the patch would forget to log back into the server's console. Or someone would remote desktop into the server and start up a second copy of the applications, causing all sorts of problems.

When you have command line applications running, something as simple as a mouse click can completely stop the command line application. By clicking within a DOS window that is running an application, the command line application can be stopped in its tracks as the command window has gone from an interactive mode to selecting text to be copied. If these applications were configured to run as a Windows service, then these problems would have been avoided, thereby escaping production outages.

FIXED SERVER ROLES

Fixed Server Roles, which you may have seen mentioned though out the book so far, have been in SQL Server since it was first introduced, they are in fact a holdover from SQL Server's roots as a fork of the Sybase database engine. Fixed Server Roles are pre-configured roles within the database engine that grant privileges, typically high-level privileges. The most famous, and most abused of these fixed server roles, is the sysadmin fixed server role which gives any user whose login is a member of the sysadmin fixed server role complete control of the SQL Server instance without any ability to revoke or deny any rights from members of this role. There are a total of 9 fixed server roles including the sysadmin fixed server role and the public fixed server role which grants a minimum level of permissions so that the user has the ability to log into the database engine.

The bulkadmin fixed server role is the newest of the fixed server roles after being added in SQL Server 2005. This fixed server role grants its members the ability to bulk insert data using BCP, SSIS or the BULK INSERT statement without granting them any additional rights. Prior to SQL Server 2005 in order to bulk insert data into the SQL Server using any method required being a member of the sysadmin fixed server role. The bulkadmin fixed server role is the only fixed server role which Microsoft has added to the SQL Server Database Engine since the database engine was changed from the Sybase code base in SQL Server 4.2.

The dbcreator fixed server role gives its members the rights to create databases and restore database on the database instance.

The diskadmin fixed server role gives its members the rights to manage the disks within SQL Server specifically it allows them to add files to existing databases on the instance.

The processadmin fixed server role gives its members the rights to view processes and kill processes for any users on the SQL Server instance. This fixed server role can be a handy role to give to help desk personal if they need the ability to kill users processes so that nightly batch processing can continue.

The securityadmin fixed server role gives its members the ability to create and drop logins for the instance, create users within databases, change fixed and user defined database role membership and to grant rights within any database within the instance. The securityadmin does not have the permissions to modify the members of the fixed server roles.

The serveradmin fixed server role gives its members the ability to change most system wide settings and to shut down the SQL Server instance by using the SHUT-DOWN command.

The setupadmin fixed server role gives its members the ability to create and drop linked servers.

USER DEFINED SERVER ROLES

User defined server roles, which were introduced with SQL Server 2012, allow for creating custom server wide roles for use when the fixed server roles do not grant the rights needed. User defined server roles can have any server wide right granted or denied to them allowing for a great deal of flexibility when granting server wide roles. As an example, if several development teams share a single SQL Server instance and all of the development teams needed the ability to run SQL Profiler against the SQL Server instance a user defined server role could be granted, then the developers could be placed in the role and the role granted the right to view the system state which grants them the rights to use SQL Server Profiler against the system. Without using user defined server roles the developers would need to be granted the view server state right to each of their domain accounts, or to the various domain groups which need the rights.

Creating a user defined server role can be done either in T-SQL as shown Example 13.6 or via SSMS as shown in Figure 13.11.

EXAMPLE 13.6
Creating a User Defined Server Role using T-SQL.

```
CREATE SERVER ROLE [UseProfile]
GO
GRANT VIEW SERVER STATE TO [UseProfile]
GO
```

There are a huge number of potential use cases for user defined server roles. This inlcudes creating roles for junior level database administrators that need limited but elevated permissions, creating roles for auditors, developers, managers, or end users that need consistent but elivated instance wide permissions on the SQL Server instance. Another great use for user defined server roles is to allow systems admistrators to be able to fail over an always on group.

FIGURE 13.11 Creating a user defined server role using SQL Server Management Studio.

ALWAYSON AVAILABILITY GROUPS

As AlwaysOn is deployed within companies the systems adminstrators may insist that they have the ability to fail the availability group from one replica of the availability group to another without the assistance of the database administraton team just like they would be able to do when using a traditional SQL Server instance which is installed as a clustered instance. The database administrator would want to grant this level of access without making the systems administrator a member of the sysadmin fixed server role. This could easily be done by using a user defined server role. When making user defined server roles for AlwaysOn control the rights need to be deployed on all the replica servers of the availability group.

INSTANCE WIDE PERMISSIONS

There are a lots of server permissions which can be granted to user defined server roles. This includes granting rights to all the various endpoints on the server, logins, availability groups, or other server roles. There are also 31 rights in SQL Server 2012 and below which can be granted against the instance such as VIEW SERVER STATE or ALTER ANY CONNECTION. Some of these rights are rights which anyone who administrates a SQL Server instance should be familiar with, such as the VIEW SERVER STATE right as this right allows any user with the right to view the running processes for other users within the instance. This can be very useful for developers who need to view applications which are running within SQL Server without having administrative rights. These 31 instance wide rights are the same rights which would need to be granted to specific logins on versions of SQL Server which are older than SQL Server 2012.

SQL Server 2014 introduces three new instance level rights. These new instance level rights are "Select All User Securables," "Impersonate Any Login," and "Connect Any Database." These three new permissions are part of the separation of duties framework which has been introduced in SQL Server 2014.

Select All Database Level User Securables

This permission allows users to query data from any object within any database within the SQL Server. Denying this right will deny the user from being able to query any data. When this permission is denied to a login it overrides all other permissions (with the exception of not overwriting permissions granted by the sysadmin fixed server role). As an example a user could be granted the CONTROL SERVER right which would allow them to backup all databases, view all data on the SQL Server and perform many administrative functions. Once the user is denied the SELECT ALL USER SECURABLES right the user will be able to perform all actions, except view user data within the database tables.

Impersonate Any Login

The IMPERSONATE ANY LOGIN right allows the login to use the EXECUTE AS statement to impersonate any login which exists on the SQL Server. This is very useful for having operations teams which need to verify that a user can or cannot perform a specific action without the operations team needing to have systems administration rights on the instance.

Connect Any Database

The CONNECT ANY DATABASE right allows the user to connect to any database without needing to have a user within the database. The user would have no rights within the specific database unless those were specifically granted, however, the user would be able to verify that the database existed and the status of the database (online, offline, in recovery, etc.). If rights had been granted to the guest user the users with the CONNECT ANY RIGHT would have the ability to access those resources. The same would apply to any rights which are granted to the PUBLIC fixed database role.

FIXED DATABASE ROLES

There are 10 fixed database roles which are created within each database. These roles grant a variety of rights within the database in which the fixed database roles exist. The fixed database role which grants the highest level of permissions is the db_owner fixed database role. This role grants the members of the role effectively full permissions to the database. Members of the db_owner fixed database role cannot have access to objects denied or revoked. Any user within the database can be added to the db_owner fixed database role. Whatever user is mapped to the dbo database user will automatically be a member of the db_owner fixed database role as will any members of the sysadmin fixed server role. Logins within the sysadmin fixed server role cannot be removed from the db_owner fixed database role without removing them from the sysadmin fixed server role. Only members of the db_owner fixed database role can add members to the db_owner fixed database role.

The members of the db_accessadmin fixed database role have the ability to add or remove users from being able to access the database. In this role, they can create database users for logins which already exist, as well as remove users from the database.

Members of the db_securityadmin fixed database role can also add users to any of the fixed database roles with the exception of the db_owner fixed database role. The members of the db_securityadmin fixed database role can also manage all permissions within the database.

Members of the db_backupoperator have the ability to backup the database. It is important to remember that members of the db_backupoperator fixed database role do not have the ability to restore the database. Restoring the database requires instance level rights to be granted to the users login.

The members of the db_ddladmin fixed database role can run any DDL statement within the database. This gives the members db_ddladmin fixed database role the ability to create, alter, or drop any object within the database. The members of the db_ddladmin fixed database role do not have the rights to view the data within the objects, only to change the objects.

The members of the db_datareader fixed database role have the ability to read the data in any table or view within the database. The members of the db_datawriter fixed database role have the ability to write to any table or view within the database. The members of the db_denydatareader cannot read any data within the database, no matter what other permissions have been granted to the user. Membership of the db_datareader fixed database role is overridden by the sp_denydatareader fixed database role if the user is a member of both fixed database roles. Access to read data via stored procedures is not effected by the db_denydatareader fixed database role.

The members of the db_denydatawriter cannot write any data within the database, no matter what other permissions have been granted to the user. Membership of the db_datawriter fixed database role is overridden by the sp_denydatawriter fixed database role if the user is a member of both fixed database roles. Access to write data via stored procedures is not effected by the db_denydatawriter fixed database role.

All uses who have access to the database are members of the public database role. This role grants the most basic rights to the database so that user can open the database without issue. While the public fixed database role can have additional rights granted to it, this should not be done as all users are members of the public fixed database which includes the guest account. If the guest account is enabled within

> **NOTE**
>
> The Roles You See May Vary
>
> Depending on the version of Microsoft SQL Server you have installed and the features which are enabled you may see more or fewer roles within the MSDB database.
>
> You may notice that not all of the roles within the MSDB database follow the same naming convention. This is because the different teams within the SQL Server product group all create and name their own fixed database roles and there are not any fixed standards which they need to follow when naming database roles.

the database then all users of the database instance will have all rights granted to the public role.

FIXED DATABASE ROLES IN THE MSDB DATABASE

The msdb database has many more database roles created within it than any other database does by default. In addition to the normal nine database roles the MSDB database will have another 18 database roles created within it.

The members of the DatabaseMailUserRole have the ability to use database mail.

The members of the db_ssisadmin have the ability to create, modify and delete SQL Server Integration Services packages from the SSIS repository within the MSDB database.

The members of the db_ssisltduser, which stands for SQL Server Integration Services Limited User, have the ability to change and run their own SSIS packages but not the ability to change or run other users packages.

The members of the db_ssisoperator fixed database role have the ability to run any users SQL Server Integration Services package, but can only edit their own packages.

The members of the dc_admin fixed database role have administrator rights to the Utility Control Point which the instance is a member of. The members of this role have CREATE, READ, UPDATE and DELETE rights to the data collector configuration.

The members of the dc_operator fixed database role have the ability to manage the system data collector for the Utility Control Point. The members of this role have Read and Update rights to the data collector.

The members of the dc_proxy fixed database role have rights to view the system data collector for the Utility Control Point.

The members of the PolicyAdministratorRole have the ability to deploy and execute policies against the database using Policy Based Management.

The members of the ServerGroupAdministratorRole have the ability to manage the server group membership when using the instance as a central management server.

> **NOTE**
>
> For More Data Collection Security Information
>
> For more Data Collection Security information please refer to http://msdn.microsoft.com/en-us/library/bb630341.aspx.

The members of the ServerGroupReaderRole have the ability to user the instance as a central management server as it grants the users the rights to read the objects which contain the central management server's metadata.

The SQLAgentOperatorRole is the most privileged of the three SQLAgent fixed database roles. This role grants the members of the role the ability to run jobs, enable and disabled jobs and enable and disable job schedules. The members of the SQLAgentOperatorRole do not need to own the job or job schedule in order for the changes to be made. Enabling and disabling jobs and job schedules is only available to the members of the SQLAgentOperatorRole by using the stored procedures. They will not be able to make these changes via SQL Server Management Studio's UI. The members of the SQLAgentOperatorRole are automatically granted all the permissions which are granted to the SQLAgentReaderRole and the SQLAgentUserRole.

The SQLAgentReaderRole is the middle role of the three SQLAgent fixed database roles. Members of the SQLAgentReaderRole can view the jobs on the SQL Server instance, and they can view the job history of any job on the instance. The members of the SQLAgentReaderRole can only modify SQL Agent jobs which they are an owner of. The members of the SQLAgentReaderRole will automatically be granted any rights granted to the SQLAgentUserRole.

The SQLAgentUserRole is the least privileged of the three SQLAgent fixed database roles. This role grants the user the ability to create and modify jobs, but they can only modify jobs which they own. By default they cannot delete job history, changing this right requires granting the user the right to execute the system stored procedure sp_purge_jobhistory. With this right granted the user would only be able to purge the job history for jobs which they own. Attempting to purge the job history for other jobs would return an error message back to the user.

The members of the TargetServersRole have the ability to use the "Multi Server Administration" feature of the SQL Server Agent.

The members of the UtilityCMRReader fixed database role have the ability to view the data captured in the Utility Control Point tables and views. This fixed database role also grants execute on a few of the Utility Control Point functions.

The members of the UtilityIMRReader fixed database role have the ability to view the data internal data capture tables of the Utility Control Point such as the

---

NOTE

Multi Server Administration?

This feature allows a single SQL Agent server to push jobs to multiple servers making job management easier under some situations. This feature is rarely ever used as typically we do not want a single job running against multiple SQL Servers all at the same time.

When I was at Tech Ed 2010 working in the SQL Server booth a customer asked me about the feature in SQL Server 2012 (called "Denali" at the time) and the PM who was working the booth with me thought that it had been removed from the product (it has not been). I actually had to show him on the demo machine that the feature was still there.

dbo.sysutility_mi_configuration_internal and dbo.sysutility_mi_cpu_stage_internal tables among others.

The members of the UtilityIMRWriter fixed database role have the ability to modify the data within the internal data capture tables. The UtilityIMRWriter fixed database role is a member of the UtilityIMRReader fixed database role which is how the members of the UtilityIMRWriter fixed database role are granted access to read these same tables. The UtilityIMRReader and UtilityIMRWriter fixed database roles are used by the Utility Control Point for data processing, not for end user use. The end users who are granted rights to view data in the Utility Control Point will be members of the other groups mentioned in this section.

USER-DEFINED DATABASE ROLES

User defined database roles have been available for many releases now as they date back to the Sybase code base which SQL Server used to be based on. The user defined database roles are the most common and the recommended way to grant permissions to users within the database. User defined database roles are recommended in this way due to the fact that the permissions are guaranteed to be the same for all members of the group, and it keeps the permissions within the database much easier to deal with. If there were 10 users in a database who all needed the same rights, and those 10 users needed a new right granted to them, granting that right to a role is much faster and easier than granting the rights to the 10 specific users. This becomes doubly true as the application gets more users on it and those 10 users become 100 or 1000.

Any right which can be granted to an object within the database can be granted to a user defined database role. This includes granting rights at the object (table, view, procedure, function, certificate, etc.) level, or the schema level. User defined database roles can be nested giving even more flexibility. Not only can user defined database roles be nested by they can also have fixed database roles be made members of the user defined database roles as well as having user defined database roles being members of fixed database roles.

Creating a user defined database role is done quite easily using either the CREATE ROLE statement in T-SQL or by using SQL Server Management Studio. The CREATE ROLE DDL accepts only two parameters which are the name of the role as well as the owner of the role as shown in Example 13.7. The "Authorization dbo" portion of the statement shown in Example 13.7 is optional and only needs to be included when another user should be considered to be the owner of the role.

EXAMPLE 13.7

Showing the syntax for the CREATE ROLE DDL statement.

```
CREATE ROLE MyRole Authorization dbo
GO
```

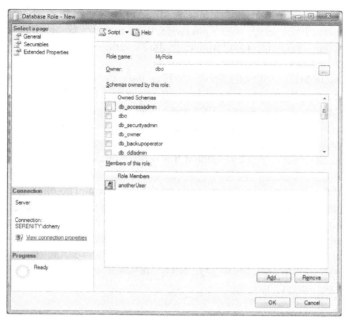

FIGURE 13.12 Creating a new role using SQL Server Management Studio.

Creating a user defined role in SQL Server Management Studio is quite easy. Navigate to the database which the role should be created in within SQL Server Management Studio's object explorer. Within the database navigate to Security > Roles > Database Roles and right click on Database Roles and select "New Database Roles" from the context menu which opens. Enter the name of the role and the owner of the role, optionally setting the permissions and membership of the role then click OK as shown in Figure 13.12.

DEFAULT SYSADMIN RIGHTS

When installing a new SQL Server, special attention needs to be paid to who becomes a member of the sysadmin fixed server role. The sysadmin fixed server role grants all members of the role full rights to the entire database engine. Anyone who is a member of the sysadmin fixed server role can do anything they want, and there is no way to stop them.

When installing Microsoft SQL Server 2000 or older, anyone who is a member of the Administrators group will automatically be made a member of the sysadmin fixed server role. This includes any domain administrators or any other users who are members of the Administrators group. This group is shown within the Microsoft SQL Server engine as the BUILTIN\Administrators login. Best security practices dictate that this group should be removed from the sysadmin fixed server role. Before removing this group from the sysadmin fixed server role, the DBAs should be added to the sysadmin fixed server role. Otherwise, there may not be any members of the sysadmin fixed server role to administrate the system, especially if the instance is running in Windows only authentication mode.

When using Microsoft SQL Server 2005 or later, the local Administrators group is not made a member of the sysadmin fixed server role by default. During installation of the Microsoft SQL Server 2005 and higher database engine, the installer asks for the groups or logins that should be made members of the sysadmin fixed server role. If no one is added to this list, then only the sa account will be a member of the sysadmin fixed server role. This is fine if this is the intended installation. However, if the server is installed using the Windows Authentication only mode, then there are no members of the sysadmin fixed server role on the instance and no one can manage the database instance. For this reason during the installation the DBAs need to be added to the sysadmin fixed server role so that the DBAs can manage the instance. When going through the installer, no error message is displayed if there are no Windows logins or groups that are assigned to the sysadmin fixed server role. This can make it very easy to install the Microsoft SQL Server instance without any members of the sysadmin fixed server role.

VENDOR'S AND THE SYSADMIN FIXED SERVER ROLE

All too often when installing a vendor's application, the vendor says that the login to the SQL Server instance needs to be a member of the sysadmin fixed server role. And all too often, the vendor is lying and does not actually need to be a member of the sysadmin fixed server role. Vendors typically say that they need the greatest permissions possible because it is simply the easiest way to ensure that their application will have the rights needed to run. For the bulk of vendor installation processes, only the login that is used to install the application needs to be a member of the sysadmin fixed server role. The login that runs the vendor application typically only needs to be a member of the dbo fixed database role. However, the login may need additional rights beyond this to function, such as the ability to create jobs or to create databases depending on the application design.

Getting a vendor to say what server wide rights the application actually needs can be difficult at best, especially if the application has already been purchased. If the DBA can get involved in the purchase process early on, the DBA will have a better chance of getting the information needed from the vendor. When possible, applications that require being members of the sysadmin fixed server role should be avoided. When preventing the purchase of the application that needs to be a member of the sysadmin fixed server role is not possible – which is probably 99.9% of the time – the application should be placed on its own instance or its own virtual machine. In that way, the impact of having the application being a member of the sysadmin fixed server role can be mitigated, and the application does not have the ability to impact any other applications or databases within the enterprise environment. This placement of

> **NOTE**
>
> **Some Vendors Actually Know What They Are Talking About**
>
> When installing applications such as the Blackberry server, RIM (Research In Motion) sort of knows what they need. They recommend that the account the Blackberry will connect to the database be a member of the sysadmin fixed-user role. Later in the documentation, however, they actually state that they only need to be a member of the dbcreator fixed server role and the securityadmin fixed server role. While these are still broad permissions, they are a much lower-level set of permissions than that which would be granted by the sysadmin fixed server role.

the application on its own instance or virtual machine may have additional licensing costs and should be explored beforehand and possibly billed back to the business unit purchasing the application.

SUMMARY

Some specific permissions can be easily granted so that people only have the rights that are necessary to get done what they need to get done, without having full rights to the operating system. When security is taken to the extreme, employees will quickly find ways to work around it in order to get things done, bypassing the security that is designed to protect the data and the systems and the company.

SQL Server Agent Security

14

INFORMATION IN THIS CHAPTER:

- Proxies
- SQL agent job steps
- Granting rights to proxies
- Job ownership

This chapter talks about the various permissions which can be used to allow non-privileged users to use some of the more powerful portions of the SQL Server Agent job system.

PROXIES

Proxies are used by the SQL Server Agent to run job steps under specific Windows accounts which are different from the account which runs the SQL Server Agent. Proxies are created based on Credentials. To create a proxy, connect to the SQL Server instance using the object explorer. Within the object explorer navigate to SQL Server Agent then Proxies. Right click on Proxies and select "New Proxies" from the context menu which opens. This opens the "New Proxy Account" screen as shown in Figure 14.1.

In the "New Proxy Account" window enter the name which you with to name the proxy account within the "Proxy name" field. In the "Credential name" field, enter the name of the Credential which you wish to bind the proxy account to. You can use the button with the three dots, shown in the upper right of Figure 14.1, to search for the Credential from the available Credentials on the instance. In the "Description" field you can enter an optional description to save information about what the proxy will be used for or other notes about the proxy.

At the bottom of Figure 14.1 you can see the list of available subsystems which can be used by the proxy. When creating a proxy it is recommended to only make the proxy account active for the specific subsystems which the account needs to be used for. As seen in Figure 14.1 multiple subsystems can be selected, however, this is not required. Additional subsystems can be added after the proxy has been created by editing the proxy and checking additional subsystems.

Proxy accounts can be created via T-SQL as well as via SQL Server Management Studio. Proxies require using two different stored procedures from the msdb database

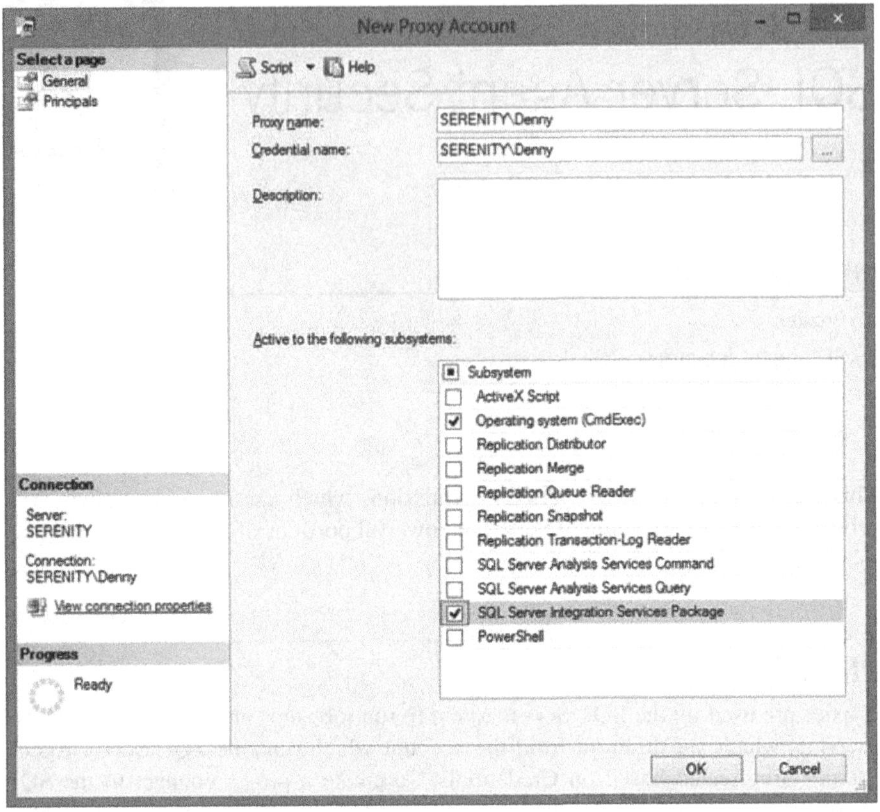

FIGURE 14.1 "New Proxy Account" window.

Table 14.1 Parameters for the sp_add_proxy Stored Procedure

Parameter Name	Description
@proxy_name	The name of the proxy account.
@credential_name	The name of the credential which the proxy account is bound to.
@enabled	If the proxy account is enabled or disabled where 1 is enabled and 0 is disabled.

to create the Proxy. The first is the sp_add_proxy stored procedure which creates the actual proxy. The second is the sp_grant_proxy_to_subsystem stored procedure which is used to grant the proxy account access to the specific subsystems.

The sp_add_proxy stored procedure accepts three input parameters as shown in Table 14.1.

The sp_grant_proxy_to_subsystem stored procedure accepts four input parameters as shown in Table 14.2.

Table 14.2 Parameters for the sp_grant_proxy_to_subsystem

Parameter Name	Description
@proxy_name	The name of the proxy account.
@proxy_id	The ID number of the proxy account.
@subsystem_id	The subsystem which the specified proxy account should be granted access to. The available list of Subsystem IDs are listed in Table 14.3
@subsystem_name	The name of the subsystem which the specified proxy account should be granted access to. The available values are ActiveScripting, CmdExec, Snapshot, LogReader, Distribution, Merge, QueueReader, ANALYSISQUERY, ANALYSISCOMMAND, Dts, and PowerShell.

Table 14.3 Available Proxy Subsystems

Subsystem ID	Subsystem Name	Subsystem Description
2	ActiveScripting	Microsoft ActiveX Script
3	CmdExec	Operating System
4	Snapshot	Replication Snapshot Agent
5	LogReader	Replication Log Reader Agent
6	Distribution	Replication Distribution Agent
7	Merge	Replication Merge Agent
8	QueueReader	Replication Queue Reader Agent
9	ANALYSISQUERY	Analysis Services Query
10	ANALYSISCOMMAND	Analysis Services Command
11	Dts	SSIS package execution
12	PowerShell	PowerShell Script

SQL AGENT JOB STEPS

Job steps within the SQL Server Agent are used to run whatever operation needs to be run by the SQL Server Agent job. Every type of SQL Server Agent job step type available has a proxy option with the exception of the T-SQL Job steps.

To change the account which will be used to run the SQL Server Agent job step, edit the job, then the job step. Change the "Run As" option to the proxy account you wish to use as shown in Figure 14.2, or select "SQL Server Agent Service Account" to use the account which runs the SQL Server Agent, which is the default.

After clicking OK on the job step and OK to save the job, the next time the job runs it will be run under the account which is specified in the drop down menu (Table 14.3).

To run a T-SQL job step a proxy account cannot be used. This is because T-SQL job steps do not need to authenticate against the operating system like all the other job step types do. In order to run a T-SQL Job Step as a different SQL Server user

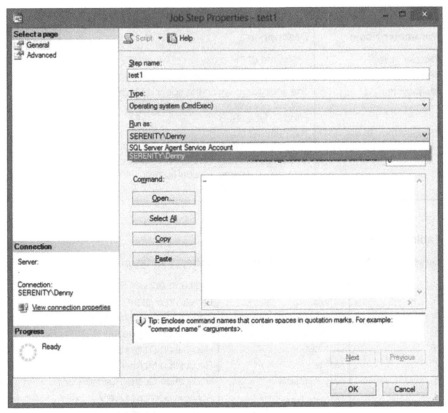

FIGURE 14.2 Job step properties.

ensure that the job step type is set to the job step type to "Transact SQL (T-SQL)" then select the Advanced tab on the left. From the advanced tab at the bottom of the window there is a "Run as user" field as shown in. Select the ellipsis button to select a user. The users which are in the master database are the users which are found within the master database. To have additional users appear in the list add them to the master database (Figure 14.3).

To add a proxy to a job step via T-SQL specify the @proxy_name parameter when using the sp_update_jobstep stored procedure and pass the name of the proxy account as the value of the parameter. This can be done for new jobs when the sp_add_jobstep stored procedure is used as well.

GRANTING RIGHTS TO PROXIES

Permissions can be granted to proxy accounts which allow specific users who are creating jobs to be able to use specific proxy accounts. This allows users who are not members of the sysadmin fixed server role to run SQL Agent job steps under a

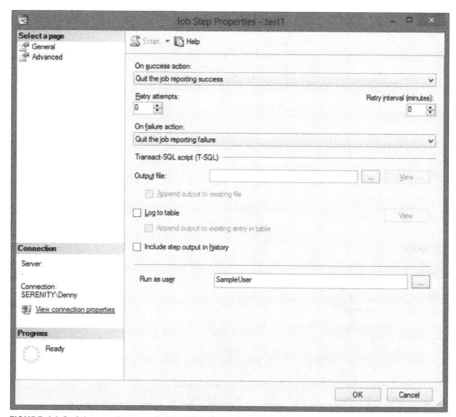

FIGURE 14.3 Advanced page of a T-SQL job step.

different Windows account. Members of the sysadmin fixed server role do not need to have permissions granted. Permissions can be mapped to a login within the SQL Server instance, a role within the MSDB database or a server role.

When viewing the properties of a proxy, either on creation of the proxy or after the fact selecting the permissions page allows you to grant users the ability to use the proxy as shown in Figure 14.4. To remove a permission from a login or role simply select the role and click the "Remove" button shown at the bottom of Figure 14.4.

After navigating to the properties page, simply click the "Add" button, then on the new window which opens select category you wish to grant permissions to, then the specific user or role you wish to grant permissions to as shown in Figure 14.5.

Granting users or roles permissions to a proxy can be done via T-SQL as well as through SQL Server Management Studio's Graphical User Interface. Two separate stored procedures in the msdb database are used for permissions management for proxies, one to grant permissions to a proxy called sp_grant_login_to_proxy and one to revoke permissions to a proxy called sp_recoke_login_from_proxy.

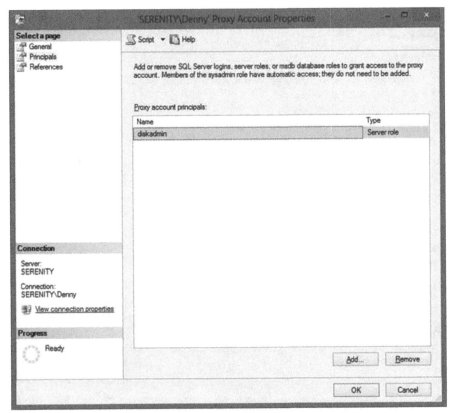

FIGURE 14.4 "Principals" page of the proxy creation and editing window.

The stored procedure sp_grant_login_to_proxy supports five parameters as shown in Table 14.4. Either the parameter @proxy_name or @proxy_id must always be specified as well as one of the other parameters.

The stored procedure sp_revoke_login_from_proxy supports three different parameters as shown in Table 14.5.

NOTE

Fixed Server Role?

You may be asking yourself why is the parameter called @fixed_server_role when it supports both fixed and user defined server roles?

The answer to that is simply because the when proxies were first introduced in SQL Server 2005 Microsoft did not have any idea that there would be user defined server roles introduced in SQL Server 2012 and it would have been much easier for the SQL Server development team to simply change the functionality of the parameter called @fixed_server_role then it would have been to change the parameter to @server_role as that would break the existing scripts that people may have which use this stored procedure.

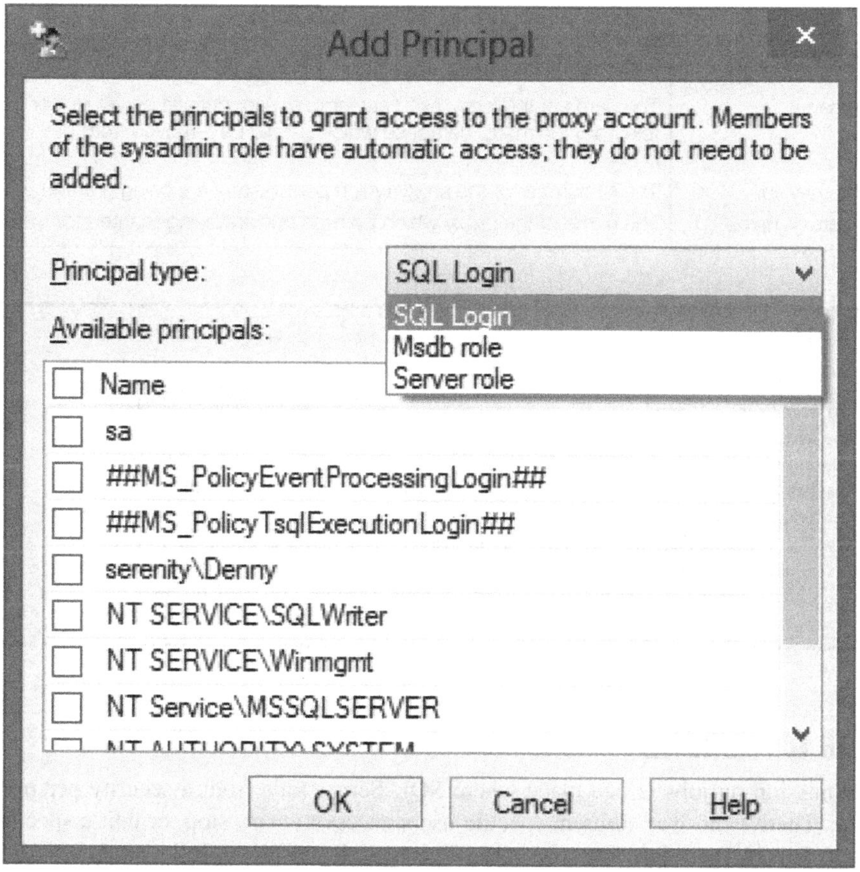

FIGURE 14.5 User or role selection page.

Table 14.4 Parameters for sp_grant_login_to_proxy

Parameter	Description
@proxy_name	The name of the proxy which permissions are being granted to.
@proxy_id	The ID number of the proxy which permissions are being granted to.
@login_name	A specific login which is being granted rights to the specified proxy.
@fixed_server_role	The name of a fixed or user defined server role which is being granted rights to the specified proxy.
@msdb_role	The name of a role from the msdb database which is being granted rights to the specified proxy.

Table 14.5 Parameters for sp_revoke_login_from_proxy

Parameter	Description
@name	The name of the login, fixed server role, user defined server role or role from the msdb database which should be removed from this proxy.
@proxy_id	The ID number of the proxy which permissions are being granted to.
@proxy_name	The name of the proxy which permissions are being granted to.

NOTE

What About Duplicate Names?

So what happens if you have a fixed server role and a role in the msdb database with both having the same name and you want to just remove one of them from having permissions to a proxy? The stored procedure sp_revoke_login_from_proxy will actually remove both of them from the database. Unfortunately there is no way around this by using this stored procedure. The stored procedure is written with the assumption that there would not ever be a user, server role or msdb database role with the same name. Because of that if you are in this situation you will need to delete the needed rows from the msdb.dbo.sysproxylogin database table manually instead of using the stored procedure. If you do use the stored procedure you will need to simply grant the needed permission back after deleting it.

JOB OWNERSHIP

Permission on jobs is one place where SQL Server fails from a security perspective. There is no way to grant specific users access to start, stop, or edit a specific SQL Server Agent job. Users have to be given rights to the SQL Server Agent roles (discussed in Chapter 13) which gives them specific global rights to the SQL Server Agent and either their jobs, or all jobs, but not to just some jobs which are owned by other users.

Members of the sysadmin fixed server role are the only users who can change the ownership of SQL Server Agent jobs.

SUMMARY

In this chapter you have learned how to run SQL Server Agent job steps as different users than the SQL Server Agent service account by using proxies. Proxies are a very powerful tool which can allow you to run jobs which have high level access to systems without the SQL Server Agent having those rights all the time when the job is not running.

Securing Data

15

INFORMATION IN THIS CHAPTER:

- GRANTing rights
- DENYing rights
- REVOKEing rights
- Table permissions
- View permissions
- Stored procedures
- Functions
- Service broker objects
- Separation of duties

In this final chapter we are looking at the securing of the data within the SQL Server instance. As you have probably noticed by now the rest of the chapters in this book are more about securing the network, or the instance, or granting rights through the roles within the database engine. In this chapter we are looking at securing the information within the database at the smallest levels possible such as the row or column level.

By default SQL Server takes a view nothing approach to the data within the databases. In prior versions such as SQL Server 7 and SQL Server 2000 the metadata within the database engine was not secured as well as it could have been. This metadata would have included items such as the objects within the database, the databases within the instance, logins at the instance level, etc. However, starting with SQL Server 2005 even the meta-data has been locked down with a deny by default approach for most if not all of the metadata. When it comes to the metadata the approach now has become that the user can only see information about their own connection and nothing else unless they have been granted special rights to view more data.

As we plan the data security strategy for Microsoft SQL Server we should be keeping the best practice of granting the user the minimum possible permissions to the data within the database that they need to do their job. There are several reasons that we want to secure the data in this way. The biggest reason being that if the user does not need to be able to see the data, then there's no reason that they should be able to see the data. Users who can see data they do not need to see present a potential security risk. While we would love to be able to trust our users and give them access to information beyond what they need to do their job, as Database Administrators we simply cannot trust anyone. Our job is to protect the data, no matter how many people we upset in the process.

GRANTing RIGHTS

When granting rights within a SQL Server database rights can be granted to specific users, to user defined database roles or to fixed database roles. It is recommended that rights should only be granted to user defined database roles instead of to specific users or to fixed database roles. This gives a security schema which is much easier to manage with the least amount of work.

There are four commonly used rights which can be granted to tables and views within the SQL Server database. These rights are to SELECT, INSERT, UPDATE and DELETE. Each of these privileges is pretty self-describing. Granting the SE-LECT right to a user allows them to see the data within the table or view that the right is granted up. Granting the INSERT right allows a user to add new rows to the table or view. Granting the DELETE right allows a user to delete existing rows from the table or view. Granting the UPDATE right allows a user to modify the rows which already exist within the table or view.

Stored procedures and functions have five additional rights which can be granted to them which are EXECUTE, VIEW DEFINITION, ALTER, CONTROL and TAKE OWNERSHIP. The EXECUTE right, which can also be shortened to EXEC, allows the user being granted the right to run the stored procedure. The VIEW DEFINITION right gives the user being granted the right the ability to review, but not modify, the code which makes up the stored procedure. The ALTER right gives the ability to change the code which makes up the stored procedure. The TAKE OWNERSHIP right gives the user who has been granted the right the ability to become the owner of

---

NOTE
There are Actually More Than Four Rights

There are actually more than four rights available for tables and views. The four rights listed above handle basic data access, while the other rights handle more complex operations within the database engine. These rights include ALTER, CONTROL, REFERENCES, TAKE OWNERSHIP, VIEW CHANCE TRACKING and VIEW DEFINITION. While it is important to know about these rights, this chapter is all about securing the data within the objects, not the schema or auditing data. So while I'm not going to be speaking specifically to these rights within this section, you the reader should know of these permissions in the event that you need to use these. Typically these rights are not granted on objects within databases as only highly privileged users such as members of the db_ owner fixed database role or the sysadmin fixed server role need the ability to use the rights which these permissions would grant, and the members of these roles would already have these rights.

As you continue through this chapter you will see these additional permissions in screenshots, so I wanted to be sure to explain at least briefly what these permissions where and more importantly why I was not specifically speaking to them in this chapter.

the object. The CONTROL right grants the user the other four possible rights (EXECUTE, VIEW DEFINITION, ALTER, and TAKE OWNERSHIP) on the object.

Granting rights to tables, views, functions and stored procedures, as well as any other object within the SQL Server instance, is done via the GRANT statement. In Example 15.1 a user named msouza is being granted the SELECT right to the table dbo.Orders.

EXAMPLE 15.1

Granting the SELECT right to the user msouza.

```
GRANT SELECT ON dbo.Orders TO msouza
GO
```

Multiple rights can be granted to a table by simply including them in a comma separated list using the same format as shown in Example 15.2 where the user msouza is granted SELECT, INSERT and UPDATE rights to the dbo.Orders table.

EXAMPLE 15.2

Granting several rights to the user msouza in a single command.

```
GRANT SELECT, INSERT, UPDATE on dbo.Orders TO msouza
GO
```

When granting rights there is no difference in granting the rights in a single statement or in multiple statements. The rights are cumulative so the user will get each of the rights no matter what order they are granted in them.

Granting rights to stored procedures and views is done in the exact same way as with tables and views. The permissions being granted are listed in a comma separated list, if there is more than one right being granted, with the object and the username or role which the right is being granted to as shown in Example 15.3.

EXAMPLE 15.3

Granting multiple rights to a stored procedure.

```
GRANT EXEC, VIEW DEFINITION on dbo.QueryOrders to msouza
GO
```

Not all rights are as easy to grant as tables, view, procedures and functions. Some objects require that the GRANT statement (as well as the REVOKE and DENY statements discussed later) be told what kind of object they are. This includes objects such as Certificates, End Points, Symmetric Keys, Asymmetric Keys, Message Types, Contracts, Services, Routes, Remote Service Bindings, and Broker Priorities. These objects require that you specifically call out the type of object that it is before making the security change. This is done by placing the object type name and two semicolons before the object name as shown in Example 15.4.

EXAMPLE 15.4

Granting control of a certificate to the user msouza.

```
GRANT CONTROL ON Certificate::MyCert to msouza
GO
```

The object names are simply spelled out, including spaces as needed. As shown in Example 15.5 we grant the CONTROL right on a symmetric key to a user.

EXAMPLE 15.5

Granting control of a symmetric key to the user msouza.

```
GRANT CONTROL ON Symmetric Key::MySymmKey TO msouza
GO
```

Granting rights to server wide objects is done using the same technique. In Example 15.6 we see how to grant rights to an Endpoint which has previously be created on the database instance.

EXAMPLE 15.6

Granting a user the connect right to a non-standard T-SQL Endpoint.

```
GRANT CONNECT ON EndPoint::MarksEndPoint to msouza
GO
```

With any objects which rights are being granted to, if the object name contains special characters such as spaces then the object name, and only the object name should be contained within square brackets as shown in Example 15.7.

EXAMPLE 15.7

Granting the login msouza rights to connect to the T-SQL Endpoint named "TSQL Default TCP."

```
GRANT CONNECT ON EndPoint::[TSQL Default TCP] TO msouza
GO
```

When granting rights to objects there is an optional parameter which can be specified when granting any right to any object. This additional parameter is the WITH GRANT option. This allows the user to not only have and user the right being granted, but it also gives them the ability to grant rights to other users within the database. The syntax for this right is quite simple; at the end of the existing GRANT statement simply place the "WITH GRANT" syntax at the end as shown in Example 15.8.

EXAMPLE 15.8

Showing the syntax for the WITH GRANT portion of the GRANT statement.

```
GRANT SELECT, INSERT, UPDATE on dbo.Orders TO msouza WITH GRANT
GO
```

Rights can be granted to objects by using SQL Server Management Studio's Object Explorer as well as with T-SQL for most objects. Most of the objects within the database can have their permissions controlled through the object explorer with the exception of some of the more exotic objects such as Certificates, Symmetric Keys, and Asymmetric Keys.

To change the permissions on an object navigate to the object in the object explorer. Right click on the object and select properties from the context menu. If properties are not listed then the permissions for the object cannot be managed from within object explorer and T-SQL will need to be used instead. Even if there is a properties option on the context menu for the object this does not mean that for sure that you can manage the permissions from within the object explorer. With the properties window open select the Permissions page for the object. This is where the various permissions can be modified as shown in Figure 15.1.

On the permissions screen the user whose permissions are being modified needs to be selected. This is done by clicking the "Search" button and locating the user or role which should be modified. Once the user or role has been selected the available permissions for the object become available in the bottom part of the screen. From this screen simply select the rights which the user should be granted. If you wish to give the user the ability to grant the right to other users, you may also check the WITH GRANT checkbox.

If you check the WITH GRANT checkbox you will notice that the checkbox in the GRANT column is checked automatically. Likewise if after checking the WITH GRANT checkbox if you uncheck the GRANT checkbox the WITH GRANT checkbox will automatically be unchecked as well. This is because there is no way to specify the WITH GRANT right without granting the user that same right. Along these lines if you check the DENY checkbox, which we'll discuss more in the next section, the GRANT and WITH GRANT checkbox are automatically unchecked.

After setting the various permissions for the user click the OK button to save the permissions changes.

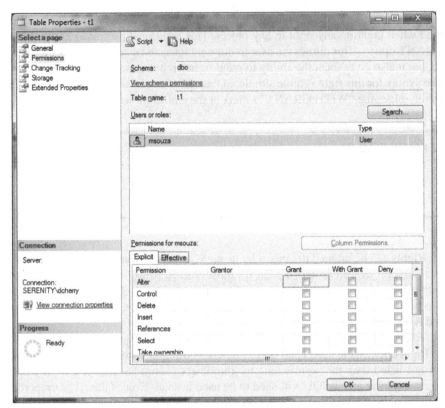

FIGURE 15.1 Showing the granting of rights to a table.

DENYing RIGHTS

Denying users rights to objects takes away any permissions which have been granted to them through any GRANT statements, no matter what. The rule when it comes to permissions is pretty simple, DENY will always win over GRANT. This is an exception to this rule when using column level permissions which is discussed later in this chapter. If for example a user is a member of two roles, and both those roles have been granted select rights to the table dbo.Orders, but the user has been denied the select right on that table the user will not be able to select from the table. Similarly if the user has been granted the select right on the table and one of the roles which the user is a member of have been denied rights on the table the user will not be able to access the table. In Microsoft SQL Server there is no way to override the fact that the user has been denied rights to an object unless that user is a member of a database level or instance level administrative fixed role.

The T-SQL syntax for denying rights to objects is exactly the same as the syntax for granting rights, with the exception of replacing GRANT with DENY. Example 15.9 shows the syntax for denying a right to a user.

EXAMPLE 15.9

Denying the SELECT right to the user msouza on the dbo.Orders table.

```
DENY SELECT ON dbo.Orders TO msouza
GO
```

Like the GRANT statement the DENY statement allows for the denying of multiple rights in a single statement using a comma separated list of the rights to DENY as shown in Example 15.10.

EXAMPLE 15.10

Denying multiple rights to a user on a table in a single T-SQL statement.

```
DENY SELECT, INSERT, UPDATE, DELETE ON dbo.Orders to msouza
GO
```

SQL Server Management Studio can be used to deny rights just like it can be used to grant rights. Navigate to the same screen shown in Figure 15.1. Instead of clicking on the checkboxes in the GRANT or WITH GRANT columns clicking the checkbox in the DENY column and clicking the OK button will deny users the rights to the object.

REVOKEing RIGHTS

Revoking rights is done much is the same way as granting or denying rights to users. The syntax is the same as with the GRANT and DENY statements simply replacing GRANT or DENY with REVOKE. Revoking rights does exactly what it sounds like, it removes the specified right from the user or role. The right which is being removed could be either a GRANT or a DENY. For example if a user had been granted the SELECT right on the table dbo.Orders and had been denied the DELETE right on the same table, both of these rights could be removed using the REVOKE statement shown in Example 15.11.

EXAMPLE 15.11

Revoking multiple rights from a user in a single statement.

```
REVOKE SELECT, DELETE FROM dbo.Orders TO msouza
GO
```

The reason that this can be done in a single statement without specifying that a grant and a deny are being revoked is because you cannot have a grant and a deny for the same object for the same user. If a user is granted the select right, then denied the select right if you were to query the system catalog views for the permissions the user would only have the deny right listed.

Rights can be revoked within SQL Server Management Studio's Object Explorer as well as via T-SQL. Navigate to the properties page shown in Figure 15.1 earlier in this chapter. By unchecking any unwanted permissions and clicking the OK button any un-needed permissions will then be revoked from the object.

TABLE AND VIEW PERMISSIONS

Both tables and views have 10 permissions that can be granted on them, less in older versions of Microsoft SQL Server.

Most of the permissions shown in Table 15.1 are available in all versions of Microsoft SQL Server. The prime exception to this is the View Change Tracking permission which was introduced in SQL Server 2008 when Change Tracking was introduced to Microsoft SQL Server.

Permissions to tables and views can be granted using SQL Server Management Studio or by using T-SQL. When using SQL Server Management Studio permis-

Table 15.1 Permissions Which are Available for Tables

Permission Name	Description
ALTER	This right allows you to change the schema of the table including adding columns, changing column data types, dropping columns, and dropping the table.
CONTROL	This right allows you to make any changes to the table, permissions on the table, the schema of the table, the extended properties of the table, etc. This permission gives the user the same rights as if the user owned the object.
DELETE	This right allows you to delete rows from the table.
INSERT	This right allows you to insert downs into the table. Rows can be inserted as singleton inserts, or bulk inserts provided that the user has the bulkadmin fixed server role.
REFERENCES	This right allows the user to create foreign keys that reference the table.
SEELCT	This right allows the user to query the rows within the table.
TAKE OWNERSHIP	This right allows the user to take ownership of the table.
UPDATE	This right allows the user to make changes to data within the table.
VIEW CHANGE TRACKING	This right allows the user to view the change tracking configuration for the table.
VIEW DEFINITION	This right allows the user to view the schema of the table.

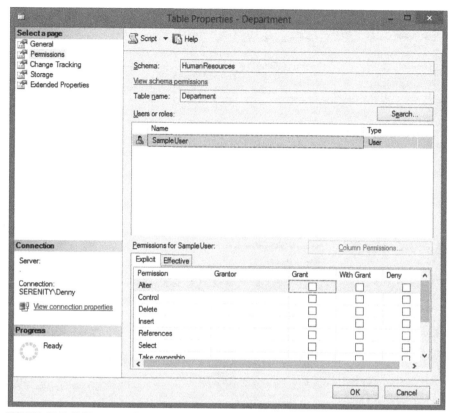

FIGURE 15.2 Table properties window on the Permissions tab.

sions can be granted to objects by editing the user, or the object. If multiple users need to be given rights to an object then editing the table or view is more efficient. If a single user need rights to a multiple objects then editing the user is more efficient.

To edit the permissions for an object, shown in locate the object in object explorer. Right click on the table and select properties. When the table properties opens, select the "Permissions" page. Clicking on the "Search" button allows you to search for the user which needs permissions granted to it.

After selecting the user, the available permissions are shown in the bottom of the window, as shown in Figure 15.2. Check the permissions which need to be GRANTed, granted WITH GRANT, or denied and click the OK button to grant the permissions.

To grant permissions to multiple tables at once locate the user within the object explorer within the database. Right click on the user and select properties from the context menu. When the user properties opens, select the Securables tab where

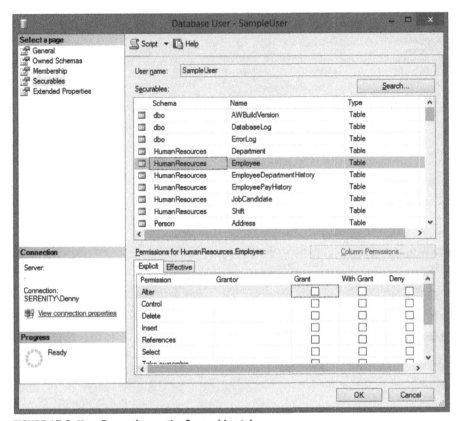

FIGURE 15.3 User Properties on the Securables tab.

permissions can then be modified. Click the "Search" button, shown in Example 15.3, and locate the objects which you want to grant rights to.

Once the tables have been found, select each table and grant the correct set of permissions for that table. After all the permissions have been selected click the OK button to modify the rights on the database.

Permissions can be granted by using T-SQL as well as by using SQL Server management studio. Permissions are granted by using the GRANT or DENY commands, which are discussed earlier in this chapter and as shown in Figure 15.2.

EXAMPLE 15.12

Granting a user select permissions to a table

```
GRANT SELECT ON MyTable TO SampleUser;
```

COLUMN LEVEL PERMISSIONS

With tables and views permissions are not limited to just the entire object. Rights can be granted, denied and revoked at the column level as well as at the object level as well. The ability to grant rights to specific columns within table is very important as this allows the user to use the data which they need within the table without having access to the other data. This can be very handy when dealing with high security data such as medical data, credit card information, passwords or other personally identifiable information. These column level permissions should be in additional to column level encryption which is discussed in Chapter 4 of this book.

Working with column level permissions is done by specifying the list of columns in a comma separated list within the GRANT, DENY or REVOKE statement as shown in Example 15.13.

EXAMPLE 15.13

Granting rights to specific columns within a table.

```
GRANT SELECT ON [dbo].[Orders] ([OrderId], [OrderDate]) TO [msouza]
GO
```

Column level permissions can be managed using SQL Server Management Studio's Object Explorer as well as T-SQL. To manage the column level permissions in SQL Server Management Studio navigate to the same permissions window shown in Figure 15.1 then click on the "Column Permissions" button. This will open another window shown in Figure 15.4 which allows the granting or denying of rights to the specific columns within the table.

When using column level permissions there is an additional step which users will need to take in order to access the table. This additional step is that the user must write the queries to not request the columns which the user does not have rights to. If the end user in the example shown in Figure 15.4 were to write a query using SELECT * FROM dbo.Orders the user would get an error back from the database engine for each column which they do not have access to saying that the SELECT permission was denied on that column, which would look similar to that shown in Figure 15.5.

In order for the sample user in Figure 15.4 to be able to view all the columns which they have rights to each column must be specified as a separate column in the SELECT statement. Unfortunately the user cannot simply query the sys.columns catalog view to see what columns they have rights for as the sys.columns catalog view will return all the columns for all the tables which the user has the rights to view any of the columns on.

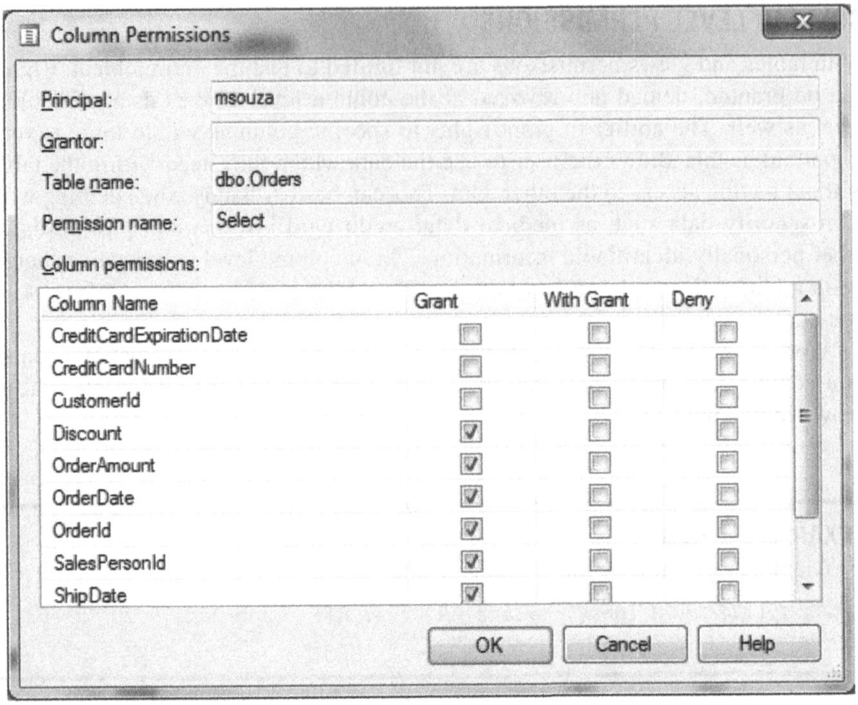

FIGURE 15.4 Showing the screen which grants rights to specific columns within the tables.

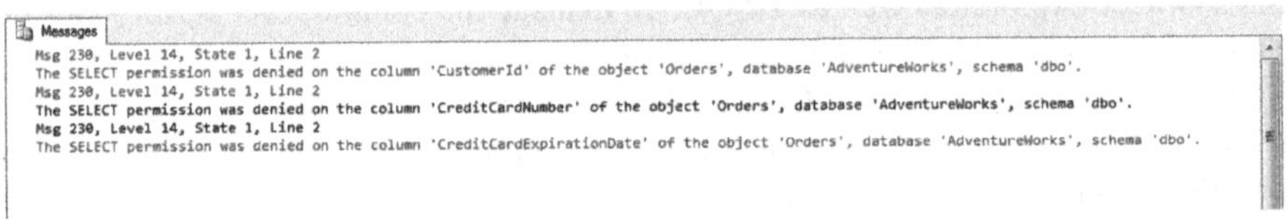

FIGURE 15.5 Showing the error messages if the user msouza were to run a SELECT * FROM dbo.Orders query when column permissions have been applied.

NOTE

Column Level Grant and Table Level Deny

One thing to keep in mind when dealing with column level permissions is that there are two different ways that SQL Server will handle Column Level Grants when the user has been denied access to the table.

By default when a user has been specifically denied access to a table within the database, and then they are granted rights to view specific columns the access to the columns is granted. However, if the "Common Criteria" security policy has been enabled on the SQL Server instance this will be changed in that the table level deny will now overwrite the column level grant. For more information about "Common Criteria" please see Chapter 11: Auditing for Security.

ROW LEVEL PERMISSIONS

Granting rights at the row level is probably one of the hardest security concepts to configure in Microsoft SQL Server. This is because there is no built in way to provide row level security in Microsoft SQL Server. The concept behind row level security is that a user is granted rights to a subset of the rows in the table, and those rows are the only rows which the user is allowed to see. This sort of security would be similar to the concepts used in multi-tenant databases where you have rows for multiple customers stored in a single database and the application always passes in an Account Id or Customer Id or in some other way identifies which account the customer is allowed to see, based on the credentials they used to authenticate to the SQL Server. However, the difference here is that we need to provide this sort of protection while giving the users direct access to query the database directly without using our custom written app.

The exact technique which is used to handle this level of security will depend a lot on the database design and the function of the database application. No matter the database design the one big rule which always applies is that we cannot force the user to specify the account number or any other identifier as we cannot validate that they are passing in their identifier. This means that we need to use something which we know that they have which will be unique across all of the customers who will be accessing the database. The most reliable way of doing this would be to use the username which they will be using to log into the database to figure out which rows of data the end user will have access to.

In general the way that this works is to create a view which the user would have permissions to, and that view then handles the access rights for the user instead of giving them access to the base tables. An example table would be the dbo.Orders table which has been used throughout this chapter so far. Before we can create the view we must create a mapping table which will be used to filter all the other tables which the user attempts to access. The table which would be used to filter the dbo. Orders would look similar to that shown in Example 15.14.

EXAMPLE 15.14

A sample table to use for row level filtering.

```
CREATE TABLE SqlUserMapping
(CustomerId int,
SqlUserName sysname,
Active bit
CONSTRAINT PK_SqlUserMapping PRIMARY KEY(CustomerId, SqlUserName))
```

When the table in Example 15.14 is created we use that table joining it to the Orders table as we create our view as shown in Example 15.15.

EXAMPLE 15.15

A row filtering view against the orders table.

```
CREATE VIEW v_orders
AS
SELECT Orders.*
FROM Orders
JOIN SqlUserMapping ON Orders.CustomerId = SqlUserMapping.CustomerId
     AND SqlUserMapping.SqlUserName = SUSER_SNAME()
GO
```

For each customer is who allowed to log into the database an unique SQL Login, or contained user is created a row must be inserted into the SqlUserMapping table so that the view v_orders will allow them access to the rows which they need access to.

If there are columns that we know for a fact the users who the row filtering is being setup for will never need such as the Credit Card information in the example dbo.Orders table, these columns should be removed from the view instead of then using column level permissions against the view as this will greatly improve the user experience when running queries against the views.

Row Level Permissions and Active Directory Groups

Using Active Directory Groups to do row based filtering is a surprisingly complex task. This is because Microsoft SQL Server does not have direct access to the domain groups that a user is a member of within Active Directory.

STORED PROCEDURE PERMISSIONS

Stored procedures have five permissions which can be assigned to users (Table 15.2).

NOTE

Row Level Permissions and Performance

Once we setup the views to allow the users to only see their specific rows we now need to do some performance tuning. Odds are the users which will be writing the queries against this data would not be using the same queries that the line of business application will be using. If the queries were the same, the users would not need to have direct SQL Access. This can be a bit challenging as you do not know what kinds of queries the users will be running.

One good first step that you can take would be to setup an index on each table using the CustomerId (or other identifying value) with all the other eligible columns as included columns. This will effectively create a second clustered index on the table that is based specifically on the fact that the CustomerId will always be used to filter (which we know that it will). We can assume that the people writing the queries probably would not be SQL Query Writing experts so if it probably a safe assumption that the queries will often have SELECT * in them.

Table 15.2   Permissions for Stored Procedures

Permission	Description
ALTER	Make changes to the stored procedure
CONTROL	This right allows you to make any changes to the stored procedure including the extended properties of the object, etc. This permission gives the user the same rights as if the user owned the object.
EXECUTE	This right gives the user the ability to run the stored procedure.
TAKE OWNERSHIP	This right gives the user the ability to take ownership of the stored procedure
VIEW DEFINITION	This right gives the user the ability to view the code which makes up the stored procedure.

NOTE

Granting Permissions to Objects

Granting permissions for stored procedures can be done through SQL Server Management Studio and T-SQL much like tables and views can. Because the process is exactly the same, with only the permissions themselves being different I'm going to save a lot of paper by not including the same text and very similar screenshots over and over again.

Please review the instructions in the table and view section of this chapter as sell as Figures 15.2 and 15.3 and Example 15.12 on how to grant permissions to objects.

SIGNING STORED PROCEDURES, FUNCTIONS AND TRIGGERS

Signing of stored procedures can be done to allow users to execute stored procedures without needed to explicitly give them the rights to run the stored procedure. This sort of code signing is very useful when permissions chains are broken or cannot be followed for some reason, for example when dynamic SQL is being used to execute the stored procedure. In some cases the EXECUTE AS clause (discussed later in this chapter) can be used to execute the stored procedure under the context of another user. The difference with signed stored procedures is that the signed stored procedure is still executed under the context of the user who is running the stored procedure, where using the EXECUTE AS clause causes the stored procedure to run under the context of the user specified within the EXECUTE AS clause. Stored procedures can be signed with either a certificate or an asymmetric key.

Signing a stored procedure, function or trigger is done by following a four-step process.

1. Create the certificate using the CREATE CERTIFICATE statement
2. Create a database user to bind the certificate to
3. Grant the user created rights to the objects which will be signed
4. Sign the objects using the ADD SIGNATURE statement

The first step to signing objects within SQL Server is to create the certificate. This is done with the same CREATE CERTIFICATE statement which is discussed in Chapter 5. If the object to be signed is a database level object then the certificate should be created within the user database. If the object is a server level object, such as a DDL trigger then the certificate should be created within the master database.

EXAMPLE 15.16

Creating a certificate

```
CREATE CERTIFICATE CodeSigningCert
with subject='My Code Signing Cert'
```

The second step is to create a loginless use within the SQL Server database which will map to the certificate. Once the user is created the permissions will be granted to this user.

EXAMPLE 15.17

Creating a user mapped to a certificate

```
CREATE USER MyCodeUser
FROM CERTIFICATE CodeSigningCert
```

After permissions have been granted to execute the objects which will be signed, the objects can then be signed by using the ADD SIGNATURE statement.

EXAMPLE 15.18

Signing a stored procedure using the certificate which was created

```
ADD SIGNATURE TO [dbo].[uspGetWhereUsedProductID]
BY CERTIFICATE CodeSigningCert
```

EXECUTE AS FOR STORED PROCEDURES

The EXECUTE AS clause within the definition of a stored procedure can be used to change the context of the execution of the stored procedure. The EXECUTE AS clause supports for different values which are CALLER, OWNER, SELF or a specific user. By default stored procedures are executed with the context of the OWNER of the stored procedure unless otherwise specified.

If CALLER is specified then the user running the stored procedure must have permissions on all the objects which are referenced within the stored procedure. If SELF is specified it is the same as if tht specific user had been specified where the specified user is the user who created the stored procedure. When a specific user is specified then the stored procedure executes under the security context of that specific user. This means that this user account must have permissions to the objects which are called by the stored procedure.

More can be read about EXECUTE AS in Chapter 9 of this book.

IN MEMORY OLTP NATIVELY COMPILED STORED PROCEDURES

Permissions for the In Memory OLTP Natively Compiled Stored Procedures are the same when it comes to granting rights to the stored procedures. Inside the code of the stored procedure something is a little different. While normal T-SQL stored procedures can have their EXECUTE AS clause set to be CALLER, OWNER, SELF or a specific user within the database, in SQL Server 2014 the stored procedures must be configured to EXECUTE AS OWNER as permissions chaining of In Memory OLTP objects is not supported in SQL Server 2014.

FUNCTION PERMISSIONS

Functions have seven permissions which can be granted to users which are shown in Table 15.3. Of these six apply to scalar functions and six apply to table functions. The difference is that the select permission is only available to the table function and the execute permission is only available to the scalar function.

SERVICE BROKER OBJECTS

While Microsoft SQL Server includes a wide variety of objects within the SQL Service Broker, many of these objects have permissions which can be managed.

Table 15.3   Permissions Available for Functions

Permission	Description
ALTER	Make change to the object.
CONTROL	This right allows you to make any changes to the function including the extended properties of the object, etc. This permission gives the user the same rights as if the user owned the object.
EXECUTE	This allows the user to execute scalar functions.
REFERENCES	This allows the user to use the function as a foreign key.
SELECT	This allows the user to select from table functions
TAKE OWNERSHIP	This allows the user to take ownership of the function.
VIEW DEFINITION	This allows the user to view the definition of the function.

MESSAGE TYPE

Message types have a single permission which can be granted, which is the REFER-ENCES permission. This permission allows the user who has the permission to create contracts which use the message type.

CONTRACTS

Like the message type the contracts within SQL Service Broker only have a single permission which is the REFERENCES permission. Users with this permission may build services which bind to the contract.

QUEUES

Queues have permissions which users can be granted rights to. Queues have seven permissions which can be granted which are found in Table 15.4.

SERVICES

Services within SQL Service Broker have two permissions which can be granted. The first is the REFERENCES permission which gives the user the right to create routes on the service. The second is the SEND permission which allows users to send messages to the service and the queue underneath it.

ROUTE

There are no permissions which can be granted for SQL Service Broker routes.

REMOTE SERVICE BINDINGS

There are no permissions which can be granted for Remote Service Bindings.

Table 15.4   Permissions Available for Service Broker Queues

Permission	Description
ALTER	Allows the user to change the settings for the queue.
CONTROL	Gives the user the same permissions as the owner of the object.
RECEIVE	Gives the user the ability to receive messages from the queue.
REFERENCES	Gives the user the ability to create services which reference the queue.
SELECT	Gives the user the ability to query from the queue without receiving messages from the queue.
TAKE OWNERSHIP	Allows the user to take ownership of the queue.
VIEW DEFINITION	Allows the user to view the definition of the queue.

BROKER PRIORITIES

There are no permissions which can be granted for Broker Priorities. Creating broker priorities requires having ALTER DATABASE permissions.

SEPARATION OF DUTIES

SQL Server 2014 enhances the concept of separation of duties where users can be given permissions to perform administrative actions such as backing up databases while not being able to query the data within the database tables. More can be read about these new permissions within the section titled "User Defined Server Roles" in Chapter 13.

This separation of duties concept provides for a much more secure database environment due to the fact that administrators no longer need to be able to see data which resides within the systems which they are managing. While this separation of duties concept cannot be applied to members of the sysadmin fixed server role it allows for people who are managing the system without being members of the sysadmin fixed server role to be more limited in what they can see while still doing their day-to-day jobs.

When it comes to what permissions are needed to complete the tasks needed by a database administrator, there are only a few tasks which actually require being members of the sysadmin fixed server role. On a day-to-day basis most database administrators do not need to be members of the sysadmin fixed server role, and can instead logins with lesser permissions most of the time.

IMPLEMENTING SEPARATION OF DUTIES

Some companies are now requiring that the database administration teams perform their day-to-day operations without being members of the sysadmin fixed server role. In order to meet this goal a solid understanding of the fixed server roles and the server wide permissions is required. When it comes to designing a security model with separation of duties in mind the first thing which needs to be done is to identify the actions which the database administrator needs to perform. In many companies the day-to-day work which needs to be performed is reviewing logs, reviewing execution plans for poorly performing queries, and deploying changes to applications as well as SQL Server Agent job monitoring.

Reviewing SQL Server error logs and the Windows Application and System logs within SQL Server Management Studio requires being a member of the securityadmin fixed server role as well as by having EXECUTE rights on the master. dbo.xp_readerrorlog extended stored procedure. SQL Server Agent job monitoring can be done by granting the SQLAgentReaderRole within the msdb database. Monitoring for performance, long running queries, and querying the execution plan cache can be completed by granting the VIEW SERVER STATE right within the instance.

Of the tasks which were identified as needing to be performed only deploying new applications and changes to existing applications truly requires being a member of the sysadmin fixed server role. And even in many cases this still is not the case. Often time software upgrades only require membership within the db_ddladmin fixed database role. The permissions which are required will depend on the application and the changes which are being made. In some cases no data change permissions are needed, in other cases there are, it simply depends on the changes which are being made to the application and the permissions which the developer of the installer, if there is one, expects.

SUMMARY

There are a variety of ways that the actual data within the database can be secured. These include granting rights to tables, allowing users to grant rights to others, denying rights, revoking rights at the table and/or column level, as well as setting up the database schema to specifically allow the filtering or rows at the row level giving the appearance of a separate database for each customer without having to setup and maintain a database for each customer instead using the much simpler to manage multi-tenant database approach.

External Audit Checklists

The information in this appendix is meant to be a guide. Each audit has a different set of criteria that must be met to be passed, and each auditing company and each individual auditor has a different interpretation of the specification that defines each audit. The information provided here should be used as a guideline to give you the best possible chance of passing the audit on the first try.

One thing which makes compliance with the various laws which govern the systems, which we build and manage, is the fact that the majority of these laws are not specific in how things should be configured. The laws which define these various compliance requirements are very broad and very vague when it comes to telling you how to secure the information. Mostly these laws define what the penalties are for not complying with the laws but deciding how to comply with the laws is left to the auditor who audits the company and the IT department staff members who make the decisions on how to secure the systems and the data.

PCI DSS

PCI compliance is designed to ensure that a company is providing a secure platform for the use and transmission of credit card information and customer account information. The PCI DSS (Data Security Standard) was designed by the founding members of the PCI council. These founding members include: American Express, Discover Financial Services, JCB International, MasterCard Worldwide, and Visa, Inc.

The goal of the PCI DSS specification was to lay out standards that cover network security, corporate policies and procedures, network architecture, and application design among other critical measures. The PCI council continues to enhance the

---

> **NOTE**
>
> **Make no assumptions...**
>
> When working with an auditor, always answer the question being asked, and only the question being asked. The auditor will hopefully be answering specific questions, which should require specific answers. If an auditor asks a question that is very broad, there is nothing wrong with asking for clarification of the question. Don't assume that you know what question the auditor is asking because if the auditor is asking one thing, and you assume the opposite, your wrong assumption could cause the company to fail the audit.

requirements of the PCI DSS specification to ensure that the PCI DSS specification remains a relevant specification in today's ever changing technology world.

PCI CHECKLIST

- Install and maintain a firewall designed to protect customer card information.
- Replace all default system passwords with user-defined passwords.
- Encrypt all customer data.
- Encrypt all data being transmitted over the network using IPSec and/or SSL.
- Install antivirus software on all servers that host, transmit, or receive customer information.
- Keep antivirus software on servers up to date.
- Restrict access to view customer information to those that require access.
- Shared logins should be disabled.
- All users should have a unique logins to all systems.
- Restrict physical access to the data center to systems administrators and network administrators only.
- Audit all access and changes to customer information.
- Test security access to network resources on a weekly or monthly basis.
- Your Credit Card Processing company is PCI DSS compliant.
- Electronic copies of customer credit card numbers are not stored.
- Management has approved the removal of all tapes to offsite storage.
- Drives that contain customer data are totally destroyed before being disposed of.
- Have a written policy in place with regard to employee access to customer data.
- Firewalls must prevent direct access from the Internet to systems that contain customer data.
- Default SMNP community strings have been changed.
- Default vendor-supplied passwords are changed before the device or computer is attached to the company network.
- Unneeded vendor-provided accounts have been removed or disabled.
- WiFi access point passwords have been changed.
- No unencrypted WiFi connections are available on the company network.
- All remote access to systems that contain account data is done over an encrypted connection.
- Never store all data from any one track stored on the credit card.
  - Cardholders Name
  - Primary Account Number
  - Expiration Date
  - Service Code
- Card Validation Code or Value are not stored.
- PIN Number is not stored.
- Application shows no more than first 6 digits and last 4 digits of credit card number unless for specific reasons.

- Use SSLTLS or IPSEC when transmitting data over the public Internet.
- Have written policies in place to prevent sending credit card information via e-mail, instant message, chat, etc.
- All systems are patched with all current patches.
- All critical security patches are installed with one month of patch release.
- Is cardholder data only accessible by those requiring such access to complete their job duties.
- Vendor accounts are enabled only when needed by vendors.
- Printouts with cardholder data are stored in secure, locked cabinets.
- Tape backups that hold customer data should be marked as classified and secured from unauthorized personnel.
- All media that leaves the secured facility must be transported by secured courier.
- All hard copies of customer data must be shredded with a crosscut shredder, incinerated, or pulped.
- Wireless Access Points should be tested quarterly to ensure that only authorized devices can gain access.
- Wireless Access Points should audit the devices that connect to them.
- Network scans must be run quarterly against all Internet facing systems. Scan must be run by a PCI SSC Approved Scanner Vendor.
- Network scans should be run any time there is a significant network change. Scan must be run by a PCI SSC Approved Scanner Vendor.
- Written security policy must be established, published, maintained, and disseminated to all IT employees. Policy must be reviewed and updated annually and as needed.
- Acceptable usage policies must be written and cover the use of all technologies such as remote access, VPN, WiFi, PDA, e-mail, and Internet access.
- Ensure that security policies clearly define information security policies for all employees and contractors.
- Ensure that security policies clearly define security incident, response, and escalation procedures to ensure effective handling of all security incidents.
- Create a security awareness program to ensure that all employees are aware of the importance of cardholder security.
- Ensure that all service providers and partners have policies in place to ensure cardholder data security is maintained.
- An up-to-date list of all service providers and partners with which cardholder data is shared is maintained.
- Service Providers PCI DSS compliance is audited annually.
- A change control process is in place for all network changes.
- A network diagram is maintained which documents all partner and service provider connections.
- Firewalls exist between public networks and all company networks.
- Firewalls exist between all DMZ (demilitarized zone) networks and internal networks.

- All network ports and protocols that are allowed through firewalls must have a business justification and must be documented.
- Firewall and router rule sets must be reviewed every 6 months.
- Firewalls to and from networks that contain cardholder information must block all network traffic that is not critical to the business at hand.
- Network access from WiFi networks to networks that hold cardholder data should be blocked.
- Restrict outbound network access from servers holding cardholder data to other networks, including the public Internet.
- The database must be on a server on the internal network, separate from the DMZ.
- NAT or PAT must be used to mask internal IP addresses from the Internet.
- Computers with remote access, including computers personally owned by employees, who have direct account to cardholder data have personal firewalls installed.
- WiFi networks are configured to use strong encryption for all network access.
- Each server fulfills only one function.
- Unnecessary services and protocols are disabled on each server.
- All unnecessary functionally is removed from each server.
- Cardholder data that is retained is only kept for the minimum amount of time as required by business processes and regulatory requirements.
- Primary Account Number is stored using one-way hash, truncated value, index token, or strong encryption technique.
- Encryption keys should be accessible by the minimum number of employees and contractors as possible.
- Encryption keys should be stored in the minimum number of locations as possible.
- Encryption keys must be rekeyed annually.
- Encryption keys that have become compromised must be retired and removed.
- Employees that have access to encryption keys must sign a document stating that they understand the responsibilities that go with this access.
- As of June 30, 2010 no WiFi network uses WEP (Wired Equivalent Privacy) for encryption and authentication.
- All viewing and changing of customer account information must be logged within the application.
- All input from customers must be validated for cross-site scripting, SQL Injection attacks, malicious file execution, etc.
- All error handling must be tested prior to each deployment.
- All secure cryptographic storage must be tested prior to each deployment.
- All secure communication must be tested prior to each deployment.
- Role-based access controls must be used within the application.
- Development, QA (Quality Assurance), and production environments must be separated.
- Separation of personal duties between development, QA, and production environments.

- Production Primary Account Numbers are not used within development and testing (QA) environments.
- All accounts used for development and/or testing must be removed prior to releasing application to production.
- All changes to application code must be reviewed prior to changes being released to production.
- Change control procedures are followed for all changes to all system components, including scope of change, impact of change, management approval, and rollback procedures.
- All web-based applications are coded based on secure guidelines such as the Open Web Application Security Project Guide.
- Public facing web applications must be reviewed annually, as well as after each release, to ensure the application successfully prevents all known threats and vulnerabilities.
- Access to customer data should follow the minimum rights to complete the job specified for all application users.
- If rights are not specifically defined as granting access to information, the default right should be to deny access.
- Management must approve all access changes for a group or single employee.
- All user accounts must have a password or two-factor authentication in place before granting any system access.
- Two-factor authentication must be used for all VPN or remote access.
- All passwords must be transmitted in an encrypted form between end user and application.
- User identity must be verified before password resets are completed.
- First-time passwords must be set to a unique value for each new password, and passwords must be reset after first use.
- Access for terminated users must be terminated immediately.
- Passwords must be changed every 90 days.
- Passwords must be at least 7 characters.
- Passwords must contain both characters and numbers.
- Once a password has been used, it cannot be used again for at least four additional passwords.
- After failing to enter a password correctly six times, the user account must be locked out for at least 30 minutes.
- If the user's terminal (desktop, application, etc) has been idle for 15 minutes, then the user must specify username and password to reactivate the session (unlock the computer).
- No anonymous access to databases that contain customer data.
- Video cameras must monitor data center access, and recordings must be kept for at least 3 months unless prohibited by law.
- Video camera footage must be monitored.
- Physical access to network switches must be restricted.
- Employee badges must be visible in order to more easily identify unauthorized personnel in the data center.

- All data center visitors must be logged and escorted.
- Offsite backup site security must be reviewed at least annually.
- Backup media inventory must be performed annually at least.
- The following information must be audited
  - All user accesses to cardholder data
  - All actions taken by persons with administrative rights
  - All accesses to audit information
  - All login attempts
  - All changes to system auditing
  - Creation and deletion of system objects
- Auditing must include the following
  - User triggering the event
  - Type of event
  - Date and time of event
  - Success or failure
  - Origination of event
  - Identity of affected data, component, or resource
- All system clocks are in sync.
- Auditing information is secured and cannot be altered.
- Audit trail files are protected from unauthorized viewing and modification.
- Audit trail files are backed up to a centralized log server or media, making it difficult or impossible to modify the audit information.
- Changes to existing log data should trigger an alert to security personnel (alert should not be triggered for adding new audit information).
- All logs for intrusion detection systems (IDS), and authentication, authorization, and accounting protocol (AAA) servers must be reviewed daily either manually or via an automated process.
- All auditing information must be kept for at least 1 year, with at least 3 months being available for immediate inspection.
- Network layer penetration testing must be performed annually.
- Application layer penetration testing must be performed annually.
- Intrusion detection systems must monitor all network traffic into cardholder systems and alert security personnel to suspected compromises.
- File integrity solutions must monitor critical system files, configuration files, and notify personnel of unauthorized changes.
- Technology that can compromise security (laptops, WiFi network access, etc) must be approved by company management.
- Copying of cardholder data to local hard drives and removable media is prohibited.
- Employees should review security policies annually.
- All potential employees should be screened prior to hire to minimize risks.
- Policies need to be in place to document personal responses to a security breach. This policy must be tested annually.

SARBANES-OXLEY

The Sarbanes-Oxley Act of 2002 officially known as the Public Company Accounting Reform and Investor Protection Act within the US Senate and the Corporate and Auditing Accountability and Responsibility Act within the US House of Representatives and known as Sarbanes-Oxley, SarBox, or SOX is probably one of the biggest headaches that IT professionals have to deal with today. This legislation was written and passed as a reaction after a number of corporate accounting scandals, including Enron, Tyco International, Adelphia, Peregrine Systems, and WorldCom. The Sarbanes-Oxley Act contains 11 titles that range from various responsibilities for corporate executives to criminal penalties for violations. Implementation of the act falls onto the Securities and Exchange Commission (SEC). The SEC adopted dozens of rules in order to implement the Sarbanes-Oxley Act, including the creation of a new semi-public agency called the Public Company Accounting Oversight Board (PCAOB). The PCAOB is tasked with overseeing, regulating, inspecting, and disciplining the accounting firms that fulfill the role of auditors of the public companies that must follow the Sarbanes-Oxley Act.

The overall usefulness of the Sarbanes-Oxley Act has been a nagging question since the first drafts of the act were written. This debate comes from the overall complexity of the act and the cost of implementing the auditing which is required to be in compliance.

The section of the Sarbanes-Oxley Act that is of greatest importance to IT professionals is Section 404, labeled as Assessment of Internal Control, which basically means that management must produce an internal control report annually that documents "the responsibility of management for establishing and maintaining an adequate internal control structure and procedures for financial reporting" as per Title 15, Section 7262, of the US Code. This report must also "contain an assessment, as of the end of the most recent fiscal year of the Company, of the effectiveness of the internal control structure and procedures of the issuer for financial reporting."

The end result of a Sarbanes-Oxley Audit allows for the Chief Executive Officer (CEO) and Chief Financial Officer (CFO) to be able to report to the financial community that the financial systems that store and report on the company's financial data are accurate. In the IT space, this accuracy is maintained through proper controls and procedures that ensure that modifications to the systems are made only by trained, approved personnel. This includes having proper procedures in place in the event of a systems or location failure so that proper reporting can continue.

SARBANES-OXLEY CHECKLIST

- Is there a Disaster Recovery (DR) plan for each datacenter?
- Is there a Disaster Recovery (DR) plan for each line of business application?
- Are their controls in place preventing users from accessing application data that they shouldn't have access to?

- Ensure that regular audits are in place confirming that physical systems inventory matches purchased inventory.
- All users must have a distinct username that allows them to be identified in all auditing methods. This username must be used to allow any computer system access.
- Ensure that only members of the sysadmin fixed-server role are able to make changes to the accounting or finance databases without using the specified application.
- Ensure that no users are members of the dbo fixed database role on the accounting or finance databases.
- Ensure that no users are members of the sysadmin fixed-server role on the accounting or finance database instances.
- Ensure that all viewing of data is audited within accounting and that finance applications are audited.
- Ensure that all data changes to data within accounting and finance applications are audited.
- Use extended protection between finance and account users and the database servers and application servers to ensure that man-in-the-middle attacks are not successful.
- Ensure that all data change audit information is stored securely and cannot be easily changed.
- Ensure that all data change audit information is reviewed regularly to ensure that only authorized personnel are making changes to the financial systems.
- Ensure that all auditing is fully audited to ensure that changes to auditing specifications are logged with the name of the person who changed the audit and what changes were made.
- Application developers should have no access to production systems using either the line of business application or the database management tools. Any rights granted to developers for troubleshooting purposes should be revoked as soon as the troubleshooting has been completed.
- Development, QA, and Staging databases must not contain customer data, as other employees within the company will have access to these environments. Any customer data that is loaded from production financial or accounting systems must be masked to prevent personnel with access to these systems from gaining access to customer data they should not have access to.
- Database backups of financial and accounting databases must be encrypted before being taken offsite.
- A change control committee must be established with membership of IT management, as well as business stakeholders, to review and approve all changes made to all financial and accounting applications, or any systems solution that affects the financial and accounting applications.
- No changes to any accounting or financial system may be made without management approval as well as approval by a change control committee.

- All changes to financial and accounting systems have been tracked.
- All changes to sysadmin fixed-server role on servers have been approved by management.
- All changes to the Domain Admins domain group have been approved by management.
- All changes to Windows domain groups within sysadmin fixed-server role have been approved by management.
- Members of the Domain Admins domain group should go through background checks prior to employment or promotion.
- Members of the sysadmin fixed-server role or the domain groups that are members of the sysadmin fixed server role should go through background checks prior to employment or promotion.
- Ensure that a high-availability solution has been defined for financial and accounting systems to prevent system outages in the event of system failures.
- Ensure that feeds from line-of-business applications to financial and accounting systems can survive database restores without duplicating data within the financial and accounting systems.
- Personnel who administer development and/or QA systems should not have administrative access to production systems.
- Ensure that changes to the system passwords, including the sa login, are logged via an approved change control processes. The password itself should not be included within the change control; only the fact that the password has been changed should be included.
- All system passwords should be kept in a secure environment so that should all personnel who know the password leave the company at once a member of management can retrieve the passwords if needed. Ideally, they should be written down sealed in a tamperproof envelope that is signed and dated over the seal and placed in a safe or other secure location outside the control of the IT staff. A safe under the control of the Director of Human Resources or the Legal department is a typical location.

NOTE

So what does all this really mean?

The key thing to remember about mechanisms like Sarbanes-Oxley is that the Act isn't so much about dictating specific controls to put into place, but about having plans in place that relate to those controls. The Sarbanes-Oxley Act is about ensuring that the C-level executives (CEO, CIO, COO, etc.) are able to stand up and say that, yes, these numbers are correct, and that the company has policies and procedures established to ensure that these numbers will always be correct.

Those policies and procedures are totally up to the company, as long as the C-level folks feel that they are good enough to keep the company running and keep the financial reports accurate. While these policies and procedures will probably be very long and very complex (they are written by lawyers for lawyers for the most part), the policies and procedures can be very simple. If the official approved company policy is that systems can be changed at will with no documentation, then that's fine, as long as it is the company policy. If the DR policy is that all members of upper management throw their hands into the air and run around like fools singing Ave Maria, then so be it. As long as the executive team feels that they can still say with certainty that the financial reports are accurate, then that is good enough.

Now the odds are that the executive team isn't going to accept upper management throwing their hands into the air and running around like fools singing Ave Maria as an acceptable DR plan. When the executives state that the financial reports are correct, they are doing so under the penalty of federal prison time if it turns out that the reports they certified were incorrect, especially if they knew that the measures that the company took were insufficient to create correct reports. Based on the desire of most, if not all, executives to remain out of federal prison, you probably won't be hearing Ave Maria sung around the office any time soon. If, however, you do, please for the love of god video tape it and post it on YouTube for the rest of us to watch.

HIPAA

The Health Insurance Portability and Accountability Act of 1996, Privacy and Security Rules, also known as HIPAA, was passed in order to ensure that patient medical data is stored in a secure manor and is only accessed by the patient's medical provider for medically relevant reasons. Unlike PCI, which has a clearly defined set of policies, and SOX, which has a loosely defined set of policies, HIPAA is an even looser set of policies. HIPAA provides some very basic guidelines that must be interpreted by the auditor and the administrator of the system in order to determine whether the system meets the privacy requirements of the act.

HIPAA CHECKLIST

- Audit all data reads no matter how data is read, within the application or within the database engine directly.
- Audit all data changes no matter how changes are made.
- All users must have a distinct username that allows them to be identified in all auditing methods. This username must be used to allow any computer system access.
- Ensure that only members of the sysadmin fixed-server role are able to make changes to the patient data without using the specified application.
- Ensure that no users are members of the dbo fixed database role of the patient data databases.
- Ensure that no users are members of the sysadmin fixed-server role of the patient data instances.
- Ensure that employee work areas are set up in such a way as to prevent people from standing behind the employee viewing patient data without authorization.
- All paper records should be secured, preventing unauthorized access to records.
- All paper records that contain patient data set to be discarded must be shredded using a crosscut shredder or pulped allowing for the total destruction of all data.

- Database backup patient data databases must be encrypted before being taken offsite.
- Ensure that all auditing is fully audited to ensure that changes to auditing specifications are logged with the name of the person who changed the audit, and what changes were made.
- Application developers should have no access to production systems using either the line of business application or the database management tools. Any rights granted to developers for troubleshooting purposes should be revoked as soon as the troubleshooting has been completed.
- Development, QA, and Staging databases must not contain customer data, as other employees within the company will have access to these environments. Any customer data that is loaded from production systems must be masked to prevent personnel with access to these systems from gaining access to customer data they should not have access to. This includes randomly masking patient identifiers, names, diagnoses information, etc.
- Any patient data transmitted over an insecure network, such as the Internet, must be encrypted before transmission over the insecure network.
- All changes to sysadmin fixed-server role on servers have been approved by management.
- All changes to Domain Admins domain group have been approved by management.
- All changes to Windows domain groups within sysadmin fixed-server role have been approved by management.
- Members of the Domain Admins domain group should go through background checks prior to employment or promotion.
- Members of the sysadmin fixed-server role or the domain groups which are members of the sysadmin fixed-server role should go through background checks prior to employment or promotion.
- Ensure that changes to the system passwords including the sa login are logged via an approved change control processes. The password itself should not be included within the change control; only the fact that the password has been changed should be included.
- All system passwords should be kept in a secure environment so that should all personnel who know the password leave the company at once a member of management can retrieve the passwords if needed. Ideally, they should be written down sealed in a tamperproof envelope that is signed and dated over the seal and placed in a safe or other secure location outside the control of the IT staff. A safe under the control of the Director of Human Resources or the Legal Department is a typical location.

The Health Insurance Portability and Accountability Act of 1996 Privacy and Security Rules isn't supposed to secure systems, but it is designed to protect patient medical data from people who aren't authorized to view that data. Much of HIPAA is about training personnel to ensure that they follow the procedures so that they don't violate the act, which should be followed up with technical procedures that can be used to audit that the act is being followed.

STORY TIME

HIPAA means business

In March 2008 several medical professionals lost their jobs and probably ended their careers in the process when they took it upon themselves to access the medical records of Britney Spears. In January 2008, Ms Spears was put on a 72-h psychiatric hold at UCLA Medical Center in Los Angeles after she was deemed to be threat to herself or others as defined under Section 5150 of the California Welfare and Institutions Code.

Apparently, at some point after Ms Spears was admitted at least 19 hospital personnel accessed her medical records without a medical need. UCLA reported that 13 of these people had their employment with the facility terminated and six others were suspended. Fortunately for UCLA and unfortunately for the medical professionals, UCLA's IT systems were designed to track this access and report on potential problems. The termination of these employees shows the seriousness with which HIPAA violations should be taken by employees and the people who design these systems.

SUMMARY

Although the checklists in this appendix aren't perfect, they will get you past most auditors. Every auditor has a different checklist when performing a compliance audit; this is one of the reasons that these audits can be so difficult to deal with. In putting together these checklists, a great deal of research was done to give companies the greatest chance of passing these audits the first time instead of having to be re-audited. Typically, these audits are very expensive to conduct, and being able to avoid a re-audit can save much more than it would cost to go through this checklist in advance.

REFERENCE

Carr, J. Breach of Britney Spears patient data reported – SC Magazine US. *IT Security News and Security Product Reviews – SC Magazine US*. N.p., March 19, 2008. Web. October 9, 2010. http://www.scmagazineus.com/breach-of-britney-spears-patient-data-reported/article/108141.

Subject Index

Printed in the United States
By Bookmasters